A Black Army

From 1941 to 1945, 30,000 African-American infantrymen were stationed at Fort Huachuca near the Mexican border. It was the only "black post" in the country. Separated from white troops and civilian communities, these infantrymen were forced to accept the rules and discipline that the US Army, convinced of their racial inferiority, wanted to impose on them. Mistrustful of black soldiers, the Army feared mutiny and organized a harsh segregation that included strict confinement, control of the infantrymen during training and leisure, and the physical separation of white and black officers to diffuse any suggestion that equality of rank translated into social equality. In this book, available for the first time in English, Pauline Peretz uncovers America's tortuous relationship with its black soldiers against the backdrop of a war fought in the name of democracy.

Pauline Peretz teaches American History at the Université Paris 8 and is a senior member of the Institut Universitaire de France. She is the author of several books, including *Une armée noire*, the French edition of this book.

Military, War, and Society in Modern American History

Series Editors

Beth Bailey, University of Kansas
Andrew Preston, University of Cambridge

Military, War, and Society in Modern American History is a new series that showcases original scholarship on the military, war, and society in modern US history. The series builds on recent innovations in the fields of military and diplomatic history and includes historical works on a broad range of topics, including civil–military relations and the militarization of culture and society; the military's influence on policy, power, politics, and political economy; the military as a key institution in managing and shaping social change, both within the military and in broader American society; the effect the military has had on American political and economic development, whether in wartime or peacetime; and the military as a leading edge of American engagement with the wider world, including forms of soft power as well as the use of force.

A Black Army
Segregation and the US Military at Fort Huachuca, Arizona, 1941–1945

Pauline Peretz

Université Paris 8

Originally published by Éditions du Seuil as *Une armée noire: Fort Huachuca, Arizona (1941–1945)*, translated from the French by Arianne Dorval

Shaftesbury Road, Cambridge CB2 8EA, United Kingdom

One Liberty Plaza, 20th Floor, New York, NY 10006, USA

477 Williamstown Road, Port Melbourne, VIC 3207, Australia

314–321, 3rd Floor, Plot 3, Splendor Forum, Jasola District Centre, New Delhi – 110025, India

103 Penang Road, #05–06/07, Visioncrest Commercial, Singapore 238467

Cambridge University Press is part of Cambridge University Press & Assessment, a department of the University of Cambridge.

We share the University's mission to contribute to society through the pursuit of education, learning and research at the highest international levels of excellence.

www.cambridge.org
Information on this title: www.cambridge.org/9781009521499

DOI: 10.1017/9781009521512

Originally published in French as *Une armée noire: Fort Huachuca, Arizona (1941–1945)*, © Éditions du Seuil 2022

First published in English by Cambridge University Press & Assessment 2025

This publication is in copyright. Subject to statutory exception and to the provisions of relevant collective licensing agreements, no reproduction of any part may take place without the written permission of Cambridge University Press & Assessment.

When citing this work, please include a reference to the DOI 10.1017/9781009521512

Printed in the United Kingdom by CPI Group Ltd, Croydon CR0 4YY

A catalogue record for this publication is available from the British Library

A Cataloging-in-Publication data record for this book is available from the Library of Congress

ISBN 978-1-009-52149-9 Hardback

Cambridge University Press & Assessment has no responsibility for the persistence or accuracy of URLs for external or third-party internet websites referred to in this publication and does not guarantee that any content on such websites is, or will remain, accurate or appropriate.

Contents

List of Figures		*page* vi
Acknowledgments		x
List of Abbreviations		xiii
	Introduction: An Experiment in Race Relations	1
1	An All-Black Post in the Middle of the Arizona Desert	15
2	Fourteen Thousand Black Infantrymen	38
3	Separated by the Color Line	64
4	A State-of-the-Art All-Black Hospital	77
5	Fry: City of "Vice"	99
6	A "Plantation"?	122
7	Respectable Women	134
8	An Experiment in Integration	156
9	The First Departure	169
10	A Southern Ambiance	186
11	The Mecca of Entertainment?	208
12	Ready for Combat	232
	Conclusion: The Outcome of an Experiment	252
	Notes	272
	Sources and Select Bibliography	314
	Index	321

Figures

0.1 View of the old post from the water tanks on Huachuca Mountain. © Pauline Peretz. *page* 13

1.1 Aerial view, Fort Huachuca's old post, looking toward Mexico (1950). © Fort Huachuca Museum. 16

1.2 Fort Huachuca and its environment. © Arizona State Archives. 17

1.3 *The Founding of Fort Huachuca*, a mural by Lew Davis, 1943. © Fort Huachuca Museum. 18

1.4 Plan drawn up by the Post Engineer Office in September 1945. © Arizona State Archives. 27

1.5 Troops marching in the new cantonment. © Fort Huachuca Museum. 28

1.6 Main Street of Bisbee, Arizona, May 1940, photographed by Russell Lee. © Library of Congress. 30

1.7 Aerial photo of the new cantonment looking east toward Fry, 1943. © Fort Huachuca Museum. 36

2.1 "Soldiers lined up at a PX to buy cigarettes, hamburgers etc.," May 19, 1942. NARA, Army Signal Corps. 45

2.2 Poster 1 "Stop Rumors." © Arizona Historical Society. 46

2.3 Poster 22 "Gonorrhea the crippler." © Arizona Historical Society. 47

2.4 "Maj. Gen. Hall, 93th [sic] Division Commander, watches his sandwich being prepared at the picnic," May 20, 1942. © NARA, Army Signal Corps. 50

2.5 "Maj. Gen. Hall, 93th [sic] Division Commander, Fort Huachuca, Ariz., is shown shaking hands with a small boy at the picnic grounds," May 19, 1942. © NARA, Army Signal Corps. 51

2.6 Combat training in the abandoned city of Charleston. © NARA, Army Signal Corps. 56

2.7 "2nd Lt. Arthur Bates waits for zero hour to give the command to attack." © NARA, Army Signal Corps. 58

List of Figures vii

2.8 "Soldiers of the 93rd Infantry Division facing a mock gas attack." © NARA, Army Signal Corps. 60
2.9 Training in the use of the M3 anti-tank gun. © NARA, Army Signal Corps. 60
2.10 "The 93rd Infantry Division's commanding general, Major General Fred W. Miller, looks on as soldiers in his command ring up scores on the rifle range." © NARA, Army Signal Corps. 61
3.1 Aerial photo of Mountain View Club (building on the left) and of the 25th Regiment cantonment (on the right) taken in 1956. © Fort Huachuca Museum. 72
3.2 Mountain View Club at the time of its inauguration. © Fort Huachuca Museum. 73
4.1 The black hospital medical team, September 17, 1942. © William Allen Collection, Moorland-Spingarn Research Center, Howard University. 78
4.2 An aerial view of Station Hospital No. 1 (on the left side) and Station Hospital No. 2 (on the right) (1942 or 1943). © Fort Huachuca Museum. 80
4.3 "Lieut.-col. Bousfield climbing the steps to Mountain View Club." © Fort Huachuca Museum. 88
4.4 Station Hospital No. 1's nurses in 1943. © William Allen Collection, Moorland-Spingarn Research Center, Howard University. 95
4.5 "The first day of training at the hospital for Waac Thelma R. Johnson." © NARA, Army Signal Corps. 97
5.1 "Prostitution Area, Fry," May 5, 1943. © Arizona State Archives. 108
5.2 Spectators at the show put on by the Hollywood Victory Committee for the men of Fort Huachuca, September 6, 1942. © NARA, Army Signal Corps. 114
5.3 The Greentop in 1943. © Arizona State University. 118
5.4 Col. Hardy giving his inauguration speech at the Greentop, in front of Scott's mural *Fighting for Uncle Sam*. © Fort Huachuca Museum. 120
7.1 Waacs marching from train to Fort Huachuca, December 7, 1942. © US Army Women's Museum, Army Signal Corps. 135
7.2 "Auxiliaries Ruth Wade and Lucille Mayo further demonstrate their ability to service trucks as taught them during the processing period at Fort Des Moines and put into practice at Fort Huachuca." © NARA, Army Signal Corps. 144

7.3 Waacs working in the HQ Annex at Fort Huachuca. © Fort Huachuca Museum. 146

7.4 "Waac cooks prepare dinner for the first time in new kitchen at Fort Huachuca," December 5, 1942. © NARA, Army Signal Corps. 149

7.5 Members of the 32nd and 33rd Companies of the WAAC playing basketball at Fort Huachuca. © NARA, Army Signal Corps. 151

8.1 "Capt. C. E. Janison, from Chicago, Illinois, shown administering nitrous oxide anesthesia to a patient in surgery, Fort Huachuca." © NARA, Army Signal Corps. 159

8.2 A nurse, photographed in front of an ambulance. © Fort Huachuca Museum. 160

9.1 A soldier holding a 105-mm shell. © Charles E. Steinheimer/The LIFE Picture Collection/Shutterstock. 171

9.2 A group of soldiers identifying positions on their maps. © Charles E. Steinheimer/The LIFE Picture Collection/Shutterstock. 172

9.3 Combat training in front of the Huachuca Mountains. © Charles E. Steinheimer/The LIFE Picture Collection/Shutterstock. 173

9.4 The captain of an infantry company (left) and his first sergeant (right) in a company administration building. © Charles E. Steinheimer/The LIFE Picture Collection/Shutterstock. 174

9.5 Black and white officers relaxing in a mess hall. © Charles E. Steinheimer/The LIFE Picture Collection/Shutterstock. 176

9.6 "The Negro Division Prepares to Go Overseas." © NLIA, *Life Magazine*, 1943. 179

9.7 "In sweltering desert heat, immediately after a 25-mile hike, Negro soldiers of the 93rd Division march on the parade ground at Fort Huachuca, Ariz." © NLIA, *Life Magazine*, 1943. 180

9.8 "With arms folded and steel helmets pulled down over their heads, Negro soldiers roll by in their vehicles during the division parade." © NLIA, *Life Magazine*, 1943. 181

9.9 "Top Sergeant Jackson weighs 236 pounds, has been in Army 24 years." © NLIA, *Life Magazine*, 1943. 182

9.10 Original photograph taken by Charles Steinheimer. © Charles E. Steinheimer/The LIFE Picture Collection/Shutterstock. 183

List of Figures ix

9.11 "Using handie-talkie radios, Negro Lieut. Vasco de Gama Hale works [...] with Major Thomas Simpson in directing live-ammunition practice." © NLIA, *Life Magazine*, 1943. 183
9.12 "In fire direction, Major Allan Carrell supervises the work of Pvt. Leon Smith, in a foxhole, who is computing artillery ranges for the battery and radio operators." © NLIA, *Life Magazine*, 1943. 184
10.1 Inspection of M10 tank destroyers by soldiers and Wacs. © Fort Huachuca Museum. 192
10.2 The barbecue organized by Col. Hardy (center), surrounded by officers of the 92nd Division. © Fort Huachuca Museum. 198
10.3 Inspector General Benjamin Davis standing in front of the post's HQ. © Fort Huachuca Museum. 202
11.1 Singer Lena Horne performing at a show organized by the Hollywood Victory Committee. © Fort Huachuca Museum. 211
11.2 Members of the Bureau of Special Services with boxer Joe Louis. © Fort Huachuca Museum. 214
11.3 *The Apache Sentinel*. © Arizona State Library/Arizona Memory Project. 215
11.4 "Huachuca soldiers reading the first issue of the *Blue Helmet*," September 19, 1942. © Fort Huachuca Museum. 216
11.5 The music section office headed by Captain Joe Jordan. © Fort Huachuca Museum. 218
11.6 A jazz concert in one of the service clubs. © NARA, Army Signal Corps. 219
11.7 Anna Russell and Lew Davis working side by side in the painting workshop. © NARA, Army Signal Corps. 221
11.8 From left to right, Vernon Winslow, Richmond Barthe, Col. E. Hardy, Lieut.-col. Nelson, and Hale Woodruff at the inauguration of the black art exhibition. © Fort Huachuca Museum. 223
11.9 *Progress of the American Negro*, Charles White, oil on canvas. © NGAA, Howard University. 225
11.10 The opening of the Black Art Exhibition at the Mountain View Club. © Fort Huachuca Museum. 226
11.11 Two of the five panels of the mural painted by Davis in 1944. © NGAA, Howard University. 228
12.1 Gen. George C. Marshall inspects a mess hall of the 92nd Division. © Fort Huachuca Museum. 244

Acknowledgments

I am immensely grateful to Beth Bailey and Andrew Preston, whose interest and trust in my research ensured that the story of the segregated African-American soldiers at Fort Huachuca would be known to English-speaking readers. I would also like to express my warmest thanks to Arianne Dorval, who used such beautiful language to make this narrative as vivid in English as it is in French.

Prior to this English version, the book had a French history. I might not have embarked on this research project without the support of Mélanie Traversier and Patrick Boucheron, who encouraged me to pursue the intuition that valuable knowledge could be gained from the Huachuca experiment. Before welcoming the book into the fine collection "L'Univers historique," Patrick Boucheron took a generous interest in this curious research object, as he had done earlier with the secret file of the Dreyfus Affair. I am most grateful to him for showing confidence in me. At Éditions du Seuil, Caroline Pichon endorsed the manuscript and, in a spirit of trust and exchange, helped me give it the finished, illustrated form it has today. Her support did not waver when the decision was made to give it new forms.

This book first took shape as an unpublished manuscript submitted for a French habilitation to supervise research. My warmest thanks go to Romain Huret, supervisor of this academic work, for accompanying me in a constantly stimulating dialogue. The manuscript was revised in response to the questions, perplexities, and recommendations of my very generous jury members: Stéphane Audoin-Rouzeau, Raphaëlle Branche, Mario Del Pero, Karl Jacoby, Taline Ter Minassian, and Claire Zalc. I am deeply grateful to each of them for venturing into unfamiliar territory and pushing me to pursue the highest standards of excellence. Their reading of my manuscript was incredibly inspiring, both for this book and for others to come.

I learned about the Huachuca experiment while conducting research with Thomas Grillot and Yann Philippe on the desegregation of veterans' hospitals in the United States. I therefore owe to them my encounter with this astonishing research topic and much of the knowledge I acquired about the hospital world. Their friendship and expertise are invaluable to me. I also benefited from the groundwork laid by Mathilde Estève, my former graduate student at the Université de Nantes, who wrote a remarkable master's thesis on the black hospital at Fort Huachuca.

Through my exchanges with several American colleagues, I came to realize just how lively and fascinating the racial history of the US Army could be. Tom Guglielmo, Robert Jefferson, and Beth Bailey generously provided me with bibliographical advice and resources, and were kind enough to discuss my preliminary hypotheses with me. Mitchell Duneier and Alondra Nelson raised pointed questions that greatly advanced my understanding and analysis of the type of segregation practiced at the fort. More recently, Jennifer Mittelstadt shared illuminating and fascinating insights during a presentation of the book at the History Department of Rutgers University.

In all of the archive centers I visited in the United States, I met people who were eager to help me move this project forward. At the Fort Huachuca Museum, Stephen Gregory proved to be more dedicated and knowledgeable than I could have hoped for. Despite difficult working conditions, he took the time to guide me through the places and intricacies of World War II military history, the details of which he masters like no other. At the National Archives in College Park, Eric Van Slander was always available to help me locate Huachuca-related files in boxes or record groups that I would not have thought of consulting myself. At the Arizona State Library, Sativa Peterson gave me access to the fort's historical publications that she was in the process of digitizing. At the African American Museum in Philadelphia, Dejay Duckett and Richard Watson infected me with their enthusiasm for the personality of Anna Russel Jones.

The encouragement and support I received in Europe were just as important. First, I would like to thank my father, Henri Peretz, who shared with me the classic sociological works on African Americans, asked me the right questions about the photographs I showed him, and was kind enough to conduct archival research on my behalf at the Chicago Public Library. I am also grateful to Hélène Solot, who gave me access to unpublished archival documents as well as to the first findings of her research project on the work of social scientists in the US Army during World War II. I am indebted to Christine Knauer for providing me with useful archival documents and bibliographical references on racial integration in the US Army. I also owe much to Elie Tenenbaum, my shadow advisor on the purely "military" dimensions of the research topic.

A number of dear friends helped me to take the plunge, and eventually to complete the project. Many thanks go to the team of the online journal *La Vie des idées* (my chosen intellectual family), as Nicolas Delalande's advice and Ivan Jablonka's encouragement to boldness were essential to my reflection. I am also deeply grateful to Endika, who came later in the history of this project, for reading my work and showing such confidence in me; his insights allowed me to make valuable additions and refinements to the manuscript.

My visits to the United States were made possible by the support of the Institut d'Histoire du Temps Présent, the research center with which I was affiliated while conducting my investigation and writing the manuscript. A grant from the Gilder Lehrman Institute in New York funded my fieldwork in Arizona. The renewed hospitality of Maria Coppola and Ruth Horowitz enabled me to carry out my research with much appreciated peace of mind. The Institut Universitaire de France, the Université Paris 8-Vincennes Saint Denis (where I teach), and the Institut d'Histoire du Temps Présent funded a large part of the translation of this book; the rest was funded by the Centre National du Livre.

Finally, I am most grateful to Peter, Ezra, and Armin, who understood my interest in Arizona's African-American soldiers and encouraged me more than anyone else to take this project to completion.

Abbreviations

ACGN	Association of Colored Graduate Nurses
AGCT	Army General Classification Test
AMA	American Medical Association
ANC	Army Nurse Corps
APS	Army Pictorial Service
CCC	Civilian Conservation Corps
FAP	Federal Art Project
FBI	Federal Bureau of Investigation
FSA	Farm Security Administration
FTP	Federal Theater Project
JNMA	Journal of the National Medical Association
LoC	Library of Congress
MP	Military Police
NAACP	National Association for the Advancement of Colored People
NCO	Non-commissioned officer
NMA	National Medical Association
NUL	National Urban League
OCS	Officer Candidate School
OWI	Office of War Information
PD	Phelps Dodge Corp
PHA	Public Housing Administration
PHS	Public Health Service
PX	Post Exchange
PWA	Public Works Administration
ROTC	Reserve Officers' Training Corps
SGO	Surgeon General's Office
USO	United Service Organizations
VMI	Virginia Military Institute
WAAC	Women's Army Auxiliary Corps
WAC	Women's Army Corps
WPA	Work Projects Administration
YMCA	Young Men's Christian Association

Introduction: An Experiment in Race Relations

The year was 1942. The United States had entered World War II on December 8, 1941, following the Japanese attack on its fleet at Pearl Harbor. While the US government claimed to have joined the conflict to defeat the racist regimes of the Axis and to bring about the triumph of democracy in the world, there were places in America where racial hierarchy, whether explicit or not, contradicted this commitment to the founding principle of equality. At two military posts in particular, African Americans were trained in strict segregation under the command of white officers. These two all-black posts were anomalies in comparison to other army bases – all-white bases or segregated bases where whites and blacks trained in distinct spaces under the principle of "separate but equal" upheld by the Supreme Court in the 1896 *Plessy v. Ferguson* decision. The Army had not designed any specific regulations to govern the racial regime that was to be implemented at the two all-black posts.

No minority was as badly affected by army segregation as African Americans during World War II. While some separate units were created for Nisei soldiers, born in the United States to Japanese parents and distrusted by the Army for political reasons, Nisei women were authorized to join integrated units.[1] With the exception of a few dozen scouts who served in separate units in the Army until the early 1940s, Native Americans fought alongside whites and served in all functions by virtue of the exceptional warrior qualities attributed to them.[2] Only blacks were systematically assigned to separate units; only blacks were relegated to buildings specifically reserved for them in training camps. To be black in the US Army during World War II was to have a radically different experience from all other soldiers.

The first of the two all-black posts was located in Tuskegee, Alabama, a segregated city with a majority of black residents, close to the campus of the Tuskegee Institute, which was founded in the late nineteenth century by former slave Booker T. Washington. The institute's mission was to educate African Americans and demonstrate their excellence and exemplary character to white society. In 1923, it fought to host the nation's only Black Veterans Hospital; it then began to offer aviation courses, becoming the first black college in the country to provide such training to African Americans. When black activists finally succeeded, with the support of First Lady Eleanor Roosevelt, in forcing their way into the Air Force, against the resistance of top generals, it was Tuskegee again that delivered pilot training. The nearly 1,000 black airmen who flew in the skies over Alabama, before being deployed in powerful bombers to North Africa and then to Sicily, were celebrated by the African-American community as heroes and as symbols of victory over racial prejudice in the military. As former pilot Omar D. Blair stated in a 2012 interview, "we wanted to prove to people around the world and particularly the people in the United States of America that black people could do something besides unload boxes, that we could fly the most sophisticated aircraft and fix the most sophisticated equipment and [perform] all kinds of activities."[3] The men of Tuskegee finally came out of the shadows in 1995, with a film celebrating the exploits of the "freedom flyers."[4] During the war, however, the creation of this segregated squadron had been strongly condemned by the National Association for the Advancement of Colored People (NAACP), the nation's oldest civil rights organization, which was founded in 1909. The NAACP had dubbed it the "Jim Crow squadron,"[5] in reference to the southern laws that had institutionalized, a decade after the end of the Civil War, the strict separation of whites and blacks in all areas of social life and the exclusion of blacks from civic life.

As African-American airmen were flying in the skies over Alabama, the infantrymen of the 92nd and 93rd Infantry Divisions – the only two black units of divisional size in the US Army – were learning to fight in the Arizona desert near Fort Huachuca, the second of the two all-black posts. This former Indian War camp, created in 1877 and used until World War I as a base for monitoring the border with Mexico, is nowhere near as famous as Tuskegee and has been ignored by historians and documentary filmmakers to this day.

Nevertheless, a new chapter was opened in the history of the fort when the War Department decided, in 1942, to turn it into the largest black training camp in American history. The aim was to accommodate successively the Army's only two African-American divisions, each composed of 15,000 men. Perhaps it is not surprising that Fort Huachuca has received less attention than Tuskeegee. After all, the infantry was a far less prestigious corps than the Air Force – the modern weapon *par excellence*. Moreover, unlike the Tuskegee airmen, the two divisions had clearly not distinguished themselves in combat: They were – unjustly – reproached for their unpreparedness and cowardice, first in the Pacific for the 93rd Division and then in Italy for the 92nd. The fact that the

Huachuca experience continues to be ignored is also explained by its lower visibility. Lying on the margins of the country, isolated by a mountain range, the fort stands in a desert area of the western United States, not in the South where most African-American soldiers were trained during the war. The racial regime in Arizona was segregation as in the South, but blacks were proportionally far fewer in number and segregation was neither as entrenched nor as explicit.

Lying on both sides of the border separating the United States and Mexico, the borderlands – areas traversed by common natural elements, family ties, capital, ideas, and speeding trains – have always constituted a land of experimentation, one long forgotten by the national narrative. It is in the "Indian country" of the American West that the imperialist policy of the United States was imagined before it was applied as a model of colonial relations in the Philippines, Cuba, and Puerto Rico, thanks to the continuity of military strategy and command personnel.[6] In this dynamic space with porous borders, however, the history of the United States has not merely been one of expansion, domination, or appropriation; it has sometimes taken unpredictable, changing, and ambiguous directions. As the historical lens shifts from the center to the peripheries, entanglements, accommodations, and subversions of US and Mexican state power come into view.[7]

At the end of the nineteenth century, racial hierarchies were shifting and uncertain at the US–Mexico border, and power relations between groups were extremely fluid and sometimes contradictory.[8] It was thanks to a back and forth coming and going between Victoria and San Antonio that William Ellis, a millionaire born into slavery in Texas before the end of the Civil War, was able to cross the color line, passing sometimes as Mexican and at other times as American, and managed to cross social boundaries, becoming a successful entrepreneur and then a baron of the Gilded Age – as the post-Civil War period of prosperity is called. And it was in the cotton fields of the Tlahualilo hacienda south of the border that Ellis attempted a colonization experiment involving 800 African-American sharecroppers from Alabama and Georgia.[9] Between El Paso and Juarez, the border also served as a refuge for African Americans fleeing the violence of Jim Crow, Chinese immigrants targeted in anti-coolie campaigns, and Mexicans threatened by poverty and dispossession under the Porfirio Díaz regime. In that zone, these three groups challenged the fixed and divisive ethno-racial and citizenship categories that the US and Mexican governments were trying to implement at the time.[10] The borderlands were also sites of exception with respect to military technology and strategy. It was in this frontier zone that the US Army tested tanks, armored vehicles, and searchlights, before adopting them in its overseas operations in World War I. Even today, the border is a key site for the development of drones. Fort Huachuca has specialized in this type of technology and is now flown over by a helium-filled, white balloon that monitors the border day and night over several hundred miles. Lastly, it is in this land of exception near Mexico that an unprecedented racial experiment involving the concentration and training of an unparalleled number of African-American soldiers was attempted during World War II.

The pre-war racial consensus was both consolidated and challenged at Fort Huachuca. During the New Deal, southern Democrats, a key component of the coalition that brought Roosevelt to power and had de facto veto power over legislation in Congress, successfully filibustered all bills that aimed to prohibit lynching or to dismantle the Jim Crow regime. Key legislation of the New Deal excluded domestic servants and farm workers – two occupational categories in which blacks were overrepresented – from its scope of application. It also gave local authorities free rein to implement social and employment programs and thus preserve white domination. As a result, the racial hierarchies that had structured American society since the 1880s were left unchallenged during the New Deal, despite the shift of black voters to the Democratic Party, the President's willingness to listen to his Black Cabinet, and the development of specific programs for blacks.[11] In 1941, under pressure from African-American activists, the federal government was forced to declare illegal the employment discrimination practiced in the defense sector and in other industries involved in the national war effort.[12] Yet, at the same time, the wartime Army reinforced internal segregation – in unit composition, in training, and in combat – because it saw this as the only acceptable way of incorporating larger numbers of African Americans into its ranks, in order to satisfy one of the pressing demands made by black activists and the black press. On the pretext that it was not a "laboratory," it aligned the racial regime in its training camps with the segregation that existed in the South. At Fort Huachuca, both the post's commandment and civilian authorities in Cochise County beyond the gates set up barriers – legal barriers and physical ones in the form of separation lines – because they feared the allegedly deviant behavior of black troops – drunkenness, hypersexuality – and their physical proximity. Faced with the rights claims of African Americans, especially officers who demanded the equality to which they were entitled by virtue of their rank, they felt the need to secure the white racial order through the spatial and functional reorganization of the old fort.

Within this enclosed camp, the racial consensus and racial prejudice were simultaneously put to the test. As in other military posts, black soldiers challenged white authority through a series of isolated acts and through organized acts of collective resistance. But the nature of this

Introduction: An Experiment in Race Relations 5

challenge was unique at Fort Huachuca because of blacks' considerable numerical advantage, which was not fully neutralized by the asymmetry of authority between whites and African Americans. Moreover, the presence of an eastern black elite confident in its rights and talents allowed for an unprecedented experiment in racial integration in the medical field. When whites asked to be treated by black physicians, the military could no longer argue that physical proximity between the two races might cause trouble and instill fear in patients. While white commanders did resist the loosening of a racial system based on racist prejudice and degrading practices, old certainties fell away, and some of the civilian and military rules that had previously governed interactions between blacks and whites were no longer respected. The history of Fort Huachuca shows that the racial order, the foundations of which were consolidated at the beginning of the war, was fragile and could be challenged without necessarily resorting to violence. Indeed, despite the sometimes very high tensions, no mutiny or riot ever broke out at Huachuca – unlike the situation in many other training camps, including Camp Van Dorn in Mississippi and Fort Stewart in Georgia.[13] This is probably why the unique history of Fort Huachuca has never been written, as if the absence of violence and deaths justified the disinterest of historians. Nevertheless, understanding what caused this unstable – racial, gender, and border – equilibrium to hold under pressure at first, and then to evolve in a direction that was unimaginable at the beginning of the war, can profoundly renew the interpretation of racial segregation within the US government.

This history of Fort Huachuca is not intended to be the final brick in a "total" history of training camps during World War II. In positioning myself at Fort Huachuca, at the level of the soldiers who made up the only two black divisions of the US Army, I want to approach the local "as a scale of observation whose use must produce specific effects of knowledge."[14] A detailed examination of this border fort, at once normal and exceptional, can yield a more accurate account of the complex nature of racial segregation in the military. The limit case of Huachuca allows us to see, as if through a magnifying glass, the difficulties that the Army encountered in articulating military hierarchy and racial hierarchy, its hesitations in the face of local situations that had been neither imagined nor foreseen, and the improvised arrangements that emerged from changing power dynamics, between the resistance of black soldiers and the fears of the surrounding white community. In the Arizona fort, segregation – of units, spaces, activities, and genders – was reinforced by the Army to accommodate three key demands of African-American organizations: to incorporate an unprecedented number of black soldiers, to accept African-American women as auxiliaries and nurses, and to grant new responsibilities to African-American officers. Intolerable for most, and clearly far from the ultimate goal of integration that was shared by all, segregation appeared to some as a second-best solution because it was presented by the Army as the only possible alternative to the exclusion of blacks from its ranks. As training progressed, this functional, spatial, and gender separation revealed itself to be highly ambiguous. On the one hand, it led to numerous abuses by white commanders, who held the ultimate authority. On the other hand, it created in some parts of the fort (the hospital, the Black Officers' Club, the service clubs, etc.) a togetherness that was appreciated because it opened up new opportunities for blacks, who were no longer in competition with whites; it also enabled African Americans to take back control of some aspects of their lives, particularly in the areas of health, sports, and culture. Clearly, at Huachuca, segregation was not simply the opposite of integration. It gave rise to different racial regimes and even allowed for integration experiments – though, of course, this did not make it acceptable. Moreover, blacks were divided over the form that should replace the segregation regime instituted by whites. There was a reenactment of the opposition about the ultimate goal of the struggle that had long structured the African-American community: There were those who favored real integration, in which blacks and whites would live and serve side by side, and those who advocated for the takeover of spaces and institutions previously held in white hands alone.[15]

It is these contradictions and experimentations that warrant the study of Huachuca as an experiment in race relations within the Army. In his study of the Ungemach garden city in Strasbourg, Paul-André Rosental approached the site as an experiment that despite – or because of – its small size could "help to trace the contours of a phenomenon that is extremely difficult to grasp," namely French eugenics in the twentieth century, and he used it as a "springboard" to tell an embarrassing, difficult history.[16] In choosing the Ukrainian town of Buchach (formerly Polish Buczacz) to narrate the carrying out of genocide at the local level, Omer Bartov showed that there were no passive bystanders and that everyone, whether Polish or Ukrainian, was complicit to some degree in the killing of Jews. He thus renewed the historiography of the Holocaust.[17] I would like my study of Huachuca, which draws on the sources closest to the field, to play a similar role for the history of race in the United States. To that end, I show how multiple racial regimes can coexist within a segregated space, and I highlight the paradoxes associated with the confrontation between different conceptions of interracial relations.[18]

Introduction: An Experiment in Race Relations

While this history of Fort Huachuca is set in time of war and in the confines of the Army, it is also traversed by the ties that African Americans retained with the life they left behind: a geographical origin and the racial regime associated with it, a place in society, and friendship and family bonds that were violently broken. Although it focuses primarily on the racial regime in force in the Army, it also addresses all the other facets of black life, from African Americans' insurance policy to their sexuality, health, family, and relationship to art and entertainment. The history of the black soldiers and women auxiliaries of Huachuca covers a relatively short period of time (1941–1945), but it is punctuated by a rapid series of events that took place far away from Arizona, even beyond national territory: the entry of the United States into World War II, the sequence of battles in the different theaters of operation, the evolution of Allied positions, the end of the conflict, and the death of President Roosevelt.

The history of Huachuca's black soldiers is played out on different interconnected scales. The first is the micro scale of daily life at the fort. The second is the macro scale, namely the scale of the country – the War Department in the federal capital, where the rules governing the training of black troops were adopted, and areas with high concentrations of African Americans, mainly large cities and military bases, which saw the frequent eruption of race riots with effects on training conditions at Huachucha – and that of the different theaters of war, where the troops were deployed after their training in Arizona. Between the micro and macro scales lies the regional scale, which covers Huachuca's relations with its direct environment, from the gates of the camp to the capital of Arizona and the border with Mexico. In short, the history of Huachuca will be told in a constant interplay of scales.[19] To use the metaphor proposed by Carlo Ginzburg, the camera will move from close-ups to long shots.[20]

I therefore write this history as I would report on event sequences that succeed one another on a large animated map of the fort – in the manner of those old Paris metro maps on which diode bulbs lit up in turn – to record the activity of the actors who left traces on it. These lights can be external and can shine all the way from Fry, Bisbee, Tucson, Phoenix, or even Washington. When their intensity is sufficiently strong that they manage to illuminate the far south of Arizona, the narrative describes their effects on the troops in training. There are times when no light shines because archival traces are missing; the narrative then echoes the silence, the absences, before speeding up again. On the contrary, when the light signals left by actors, whether civilian or military, multiply, the narrative slows down to recount the events at length. The focus and pace of the narrative vary according to the depth and intensity of the remaining archival, photographic, and oral traces.

The military archives on segregation in the Army are very voluminous. Yet, the military justice and hospital records of Fort Huachuca, which would have been so useful to my work, were destroyed when the camp was closed in 1947. The personal archives and oral histories produced as part of the Veterans History Project, launched in the 1980s by the Library of Congress to preserve the experiences of American veterans, allowed me to compare overarching analyses of the Army with soldiers' accounts of the war. I examined how the major black newspapers fostered racial pride with stories and portraits from Huachuca that acted as smoke screens concealing the segregation and discrimination practiced at the fort. These realities, I found, were barely mentioned or completely omitted as soon as threats were made to suspend free postage. During my research, I collected several photographs taken by soldiers, journalists, or amateurs that revealed situations or personal relationships about which the archives were silent. More than any written document, these photographs testified to the nature of the interactions between blacks and whites, at least as their authors wished to present them to the outside world – gestures of authority or obedience, body language showing complicity or discomfort. Army Signal Corps photographers were tasked with documenting training for educational purposes and with representing the preparation of soldiers as rewarding and effective;[21] however, details that they had not noticed could slip back into the frames without them knowing it.

Microhistory maintains the illusion of being able to get close to the actors. Yet, during my research, I could hear the actors' voices only in the form of surges or outbursts. Colonial history has shown that judiciary archives are often the only remaining traces for hearing the subalterns.[22] Information on their lives, intimacy, and convictions can be found in the minutes of trials. At Huachuca, inspection reports and personal records produced by the martial court did shed light, via accounts of deviant acts, on the lived experiences of soldiers. But, to gain access to the soldiers' voices, I had to pay to consult them one by one. Throughout the narrative, I draw on oral histories to convey the sensory and concrete dimension of the soldiers' training and to recreate the relationships they formed at Huachuca. I also use the albums and scrapbooks of women auxiliaries (Wacs) and nurses as a visual equivalent of African-American women's voices. On the photographs and postcards, one can see them reclaim their military experience and representation as black women within a white institution. A chance discovery of personal archives provided me with information on remarkable personalities and trajectories – the head of the black hospital, Midian Bousfield, some of his medical colleagues, the playwright Shirley Graham and Wac Irma Cayton (both of whom were in contact with numerous intellectuals and journalists), or the Wac artist Anna Russell. Thus, and paradoxically, the history of the fort is told mainly through the "female gaze" on military life, a life that is often considered as exclusively masculine and as productive of virility.

In contrast to the traditional narrative of World War II, the history of Fort Huachuca yields a dissonant, race-centered narrative. Although the narrative of "the good war" – the title given by radio journalist Studs Terkel to his oral history of the conflict, which became a best-seller after its publication in 1984[23] – has been called into question at least since the 1990s, it is still very much alive in popular culture and on the history shelves of bookstores.[24] The war fought by the so-called heroic generation was presented as a crusade to defend democracy against the racist ideologies of the Axis powers, and it was said to have rebuilt the unity of the nation that had been shattered by the Great Depression. Moreover, the federal government was credited with pursuing and defending the general interest, particularly that of women and African Americans.[25] Novels like Leon Uris's *Battle Cry* (1953) and films like *The Longest Day* (1952) popularized the image of white brotherhood and male heroism in battle. Hollywood cultivated the illusion of racial harmony in the military by depicting fictional multicultural platoons in which Protestants, Catholics, Jews, Asians, and blacks fought side by side.[26] However, as the historian Gary Gerstle has shown, World War II was both a "good war" and a "race war." As such, it brought into conflict two American traditions: "civic nationalism" – based on a commitment to the political ideals of nationhood, equality, inalienable rights, and elected democratic government – and "racial nationalism" – grounded in an ethno-racial definition of America whereby the American people share the same blood and skin color. The war was also a time when American democracy was associated with the internment of Japanese Americans, the endorsement of racist beliefs and practices, and the organization of the military around the opposition between blacks and non-blacks.[27] The racial history of the war inevitably troubles consensual and irenic accounts. At Fort Huachuca, where black soldiers trained without being able to demonstrate their heroism, the traditional narrative of the war is transformed. The memory of military segregation, which was repressed by the Army when it became a powerful tool for racial and social integration in the 1960s, returns to consciousness in this isolated place.

Through the lens of Huachuca, the racial segregation practiced in the Army during the war can be examined for its own sake and not just as a focus of resistance or struggle. The first history of black soldiers in World War II was an official history. Written in 1966 by Ulysses Lee, an employee of the Bureau of Military History, *The Employment of Negro Troops* was primarily concerned with the preparation of blacks for combat and the functions they served in a segregated setting.[28] This seminal work did not perpetuate the reputation of African-American soldiers as bad fighters, but neither did it challenge it. The two unfortunate episodes involving the black infantrymen of the 92nd and 93rd Divisions – the first in the Solomon Islands and the second at the Gothic Line in Italy – did play a part in the Army's decision to postpone racial integration, which had been contemplated at the end of the conflict. In reaction to the extremely harsh judgment of black troops, a counter-narrative later developed that emphasized the heroic acts of soldiers and officers who were decorated after the war (for instance, Vernon Baker, who received the Medal of Honor for his actions in Viareggio in April 1945) or of those who had served in elite segregated units: the 761st Tank Battalion, which cleared the way for the 4th Armored Division in Germany after the Battle of the Bulge; the 320th Battalion, which manned armed balloons off the beaches of Normandy on D-Day to counter the German Air Force; and the Tuskegee squadron of aviators. This struggle to rehabilitate the wartime deeds of black soldiers eventually moved from the theaters of operations to books and museums, where it continues to play out to this day – for instance, in the windows of the National Museum of African American History and Culture, which opened in 2016 in Washington, DC. By shifting the focus from the theaters of operation to the racial treatment of soldiers in training, the interactions of these men with civil society, and the place of women among them, my study departs from activist discussions about the manly heroism of soldiers. In this place of waiting and uncertainty, victories were won on the racial terrain, not on the battlefield; they were not the work of isolated heroes but that of organized groups of men and women who came together to challenge an unjust order.

Historians of race have often looked for the roots of the "long civil rights movement" – which, according to Jacquelyn Dowd Hall, began long before the heroic decade of the 1960s[29] – in the conditions experienced by blacks during the war. Was World War II an accelerating moment in the long struggle for equality? Richard Dalfiume, one of the pioneering authors on the role of African Americans in the Army, has argued that "the seeds [of the civil rights movement] were indeed sown in the World War II years."[30] Yet, more than a time of conquest, the African-American military experience was a source of humiliation. Attempts at racial integration could be counted on the fingers of one hand, and the conditions of return to civilian life were also discriminatory because the GI Bill, the law designed to support returning World War II veterans, was applied in a racist manner.[31] Kevin Kruse and Stephen Tuck have noted that, while the war resulted in a momentary decline in black activism, it also led to a renewed repertoire of actions in the struggle for racial equality.[32] According to Thomas Guglielmo, a "martial freedom movement" developed that set up barriers against authoritarian and discriminatory policies within the Army, but it did not have the characteristics typically associated with the civil rights movement – striking actions, charismatic leaders, presence of women. In his view, this movement must be examined and understood "on its own terms – as a crucial period and type of black political struggle."[33] My study of Fort Huachuca, where acts of resistance took place with varying degrees of intensity, does precisely that: It examines segregation and the forms of opposition to it on their own terms, rather than taking sides in the historiographical debate on the origins of the civil rights movement or the memorial debate on the heroism of black troops.

The Arizona fort also offers a composite and therefore unique cross-section of the African-American community during the war. Social mixing, a well-known function of the Army, occurred naturally at the fort among black soldiers who were physically and psychologically very far from the combat zones – of which they knew little. At Huachuca, men from the South and the North of the country were forced to live in close proximity and left behind very different civilian lives. Those from the South were already familiar with legal segregation. Those from the North, who were generally more educated, more politicized, and more disoriented in Arizona, were experiencing segregation for the first time and were shocked by it. Different categories of people were brought together at the fort: northern workers and southern sharecroppers still reeling from the effects of the Great Depression, but also representatives of the "talented tenth" whom W. E. B. Du Bois described at the beginning of the twentieth century – that is, the 10 percent of African Americans prepared to occupy positions of leadership thanks to a good education.[34] The medical officers at the black hospital belonged to the light-skinned "black bourgeoisie" identified by the African-American sociologist E. Franklin Frazier in the late 1950s.[35] Many of the volunteer nurses and members of the Women's Army Corps (WAC) had already had distinguished careers. In short, Fort Huachuca brought together in one place a very diverse group of people who reacted differently to the racism and segregation practiced in the Army. The available sources allow one to hear a great plurality of voices, each reflecting a singular experience of segregation and a unique response to it – resistance, rebellion, but also accommodation or resignation. Any attempt to reconcile the sometimes contradictory narratives of the Huachuca experience would amount to erasing the ambiguity of positions and situations.

In this history of Huachuca, I also pay particular attention to space as I seek to understand how the fort was organized and impacted by segregation – through the isolation of blacks from whites, the creation of partitions in existing buildings, and the allocation of supposedly equivalent places to whites and African Americans.[36] By reading the sources and examining the photographs with careful attention to place, I try to recreate a space, both inside and outside the camp, characterized by a unique form of segregation because of the great imbalance between the few hundred white officers and the 15,000 black men. In the 1950s and 1960s, the traces of segregation disappeared almost everywhere in the United States, thanks to court rulings and civil rights legislation: "Colored" or "white" signs were removed, and places specifically reserved for blacks were closed down or used for other purposes. At Huachuca, the markers of segregation vanished as soon as the fort closed in 1947, before discrimination in the armed forces was officially abolished by Executive Order 9981 in July 1948. When the fort was reactivated in 1954, it was almost entirely white, and the former black-only buildings were either reallocated to soldiers in training or allowed to fall into disuse. Today, wartime segregation is invisible to the eye, except for those who know where to look.

This became obvious to me when I arrived at Huachuca, almost eighty years after the events that I wish to narrate. Indeed, as my research progressed, I realized that relying on congealed knowledge of the camp's operation would prevent me from imagining what life and training had been like at the post. I therefore chose to consider Fort Huachuca as a site of investigation where present traces of the past can be found, thus drawing inspiration from the "archaeological approach" developed by Guillaume Lachenal. I went looking for "those traces that reenact the past via their present."[37] I did not search for witnesses, as the veterans of Huachuca were now very old and had left Arizona long ago. But I physically experienced the place in order to share sensations with those who had been stationed there during the war – the temperature contrasts, the burning sun, the discovery of unknown fauna and flora. At the foot of the Huachuca mountains, which block the passage to Mexico, I felt the isolation. I had imagined that I would wander freely around the fort, walking through it at my own pace to find answers to my questions. But while I was working at the Arizona State Archives in Phoenix in July 2018, I learned that it is difficult for a foreigner to enter the fort, as it has become a site of production of surveillance and intelligence technology. At Fort Huachuca, the US Army is now designing drones to monitor the border and the enemies of

Introduction: An Experiment in Race Relations

America – in Syria, Iraq, and everywhere else. I may have been a citizen of a friendly nation (although, two days before I entered the fort, President Trump declared at a NATO summit that Europe was an enemy entity), but I was seen as suspicious by virtue of being a foreigner. I therefore had to obtain entry clearance after an investigation. I obtained this authorization with great difficulty, but it did come with an escort who guided and accompanied me throughout my research: Stephen Gregory, a technician at the Fort Huachuca Museum. My luck was that Stephen is probably the person who best knows the history of the fort. The son of a military man, he was born at the black hospital and attended school at the fort. He returned to Huachuca as an adult because he could not stay away for long from the vast, cloudy Arizona skies. In his red jeep covered with dog hair and littered with empty Coke bottles, I discovered the hundreds of acres of barren land on which first the 93rd Infantry Division and then the 92nd trained during the war.

By experiencing the place physically, by crossing it end to end, I came to understand its organization. I discovered a real city – the third largest in Arizona during the war, with a population of up to 15,000

0.1: View of the old post from the water tanks on Huachuca Mountain.
© Pauline Peretz.

inhabitants – which functions independently with its offices, residential area, church, cemetery, playgrounds, schools, stores for customers in fatigues, hotels, and SUV fleet. I also learned about what distinguishes a military post from an ordinary city: the training grounds, the firing ranges, the ammunition and weapons stores, and the combat training areas. I observed, at the post and in its immediate vicinity, the interlocking effects of civilian law and military rule, which are key to understanding how the military authorities acted beyond their territorial scope during the war to address the fears and expectations of the surrounding white community. Seeing in real life how the town of Sierra Vista, formerly Fry, is literally glued to the fort and entirely organized around a boulevard that leads to the military enclave gave me a sense of how the two spaces, civilian and military, function in symbiosis today just as they did yesterday. I arrived with my head full of pictures of black units training in a camp at full capacity; I discovered a camp operating at a slow pace in the middle of the summer and saw that the men in fatigues were white. The only remaining trace of the Buffalo soldiers, the black men who fought the Indians and guarded the frontier until World War I, is a bronze statue of dubious proportions that has become the emblem of the fort. There is no trace left of the African-American soldiers who trained at Huachuca during World War II. The fort of today is not the palimpsest that I had hoped to find. This makes it all the more pressing to tell the history of this place which subverts the traditional narrative of conflict and race.

1 An All-Black Post in the Middle of the Arizona Desert

From the middle of May 1942 onwards, soldiers arrived by the hundreds daily at Fort Huachuca. They came from the North, the East, or the rural South. These young African-American men of the 93rd Infantry Division traveled across the country, first through Mississippi and then through Louisiana, in railroad cars filled with conscripts. Those who had never experienced legal segregation encountered it as soon as they got off the train. White commanders made it clear that they had to follow local rules and customs – enter black stores only, stay away from whites – to avoid causing trouble. The train continued its journey to Texas, New Mexico – the first glimpse of the desert – and, finally, Arizona. These men had never penetrated so deeply into the interior of the country. On the third night of the journey, it was so dark that they saw neither the herds of cattle grazing on the plains nor the open copper mines. Past the San Pedro River valley, the vegetation was scarce and the houses few and far between. When the men finally caught sight of a barrier of mountains that forced the train to stop, they knew that they had reached their destination. Before crossing the gates, they saw a few houses, but nothing resembling a city. At last, they got off the Southern Pacific Railroad cars chartered by the Army. There they were at Fort Huachuca, under the already burning sun, twenty-five miles from all human life, at the southern tip of the country. The 25th Regiment Infantry Band escorted them to their quarters while playing "South of the Border," a 1939 hit song about a trip to Mexico.

These transplants experienced a shock on arriving at the fort.[1] They were struck by the silence and beauty of the desert, the sparse vegetation punctuated by mesquite and cactus, and the purple-shaded peaks soaring over 8,000 feet in front of them. Looking to the northeast on the other side, they saw the plains descending to the San Pedro River, and then, on the distant horizon, behind the town of Tombstone, the mountains again. They had never seen anything like it. A town in the middle of the desert, soon to be the third largest in Arizona, unfolded before their eyes. To the left of the tracks lay the complex of two hospitals, one for blacks and a smaller one for whites, and the quarters of the 25th Infantry Regiment;

1.1: Aerial view, Fort Huachuca's old post, looking toward Mexico (1950). © Fort Huachuca Museum.

to the right stood warehouses and barracks reserved for troops that had yet to arrive. The men could barely make out the old post at the mouth of the canyon, more than a mile in front of them, about a half-hour walking distance. This town, with its main roads and secondary streets, its post office, bakeries, theaters, sports fields, and cemetery, but also its barracks, stockade, storage facilities, and arms depots, was built in a few months on a 110-acre former army reserve to accommodate the black soldiers that America, now at war, was compelled to train for combat.

   A few months before it became a bustling military base, Fort Huachuca was a former "black post" that had fallen into a state of lethargy and whose survival was uncertain. It was saved from closure by the expansion of army segregation, which followed the admission of larger numbers of African Americans into the military. The founding of Fort Huachuca is depicted in a mural by Scottsdale artist Lew Davis that was hung in the white officers' club at the old post in the fall of 1943. The man then in charge of the fort, Colonel Edwin Hardy, thought that telling its founding story in pictures would help reinforce adherence to what had been

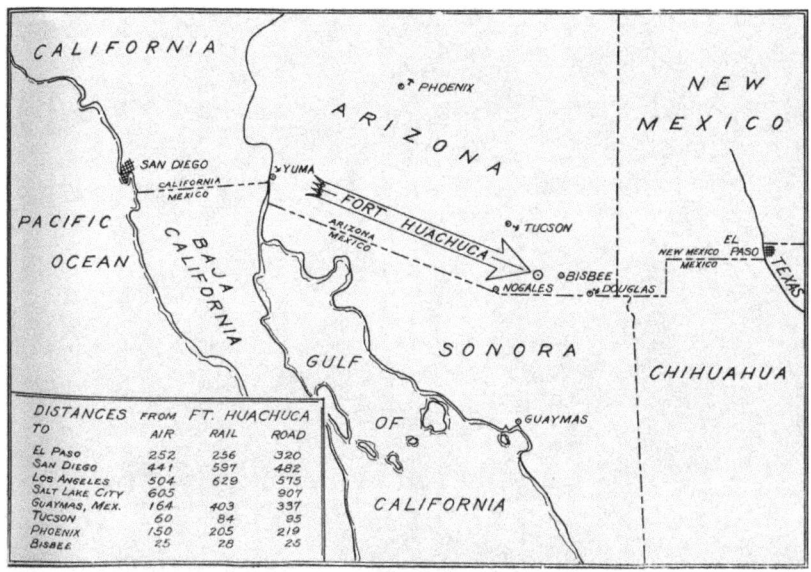

1.2: Fort Huachuca and its environment. © Arizona State Archives.

Huachuca's mission since the late nineteenth century: protecting the nation near the Mexican border. In the center of the three-panel mural, one can see Captain Samuel Whitside, commissioned from Tucson, surrounded by five soldiers of the 6th Cavalry Regiment. Whitside chose the deserted site at the mouth of the Huachuca Canyon that separates two mountain ranges. In the middle of the pine forest, the shady place offered water and grass for the horses, lower temperatures than in the plains, and a natural shelter for protection against attacks by Native Americans. The two side panels depict the armed Apache scouts who helped Whitside control the borderlands against their own; their figures are outlined against a background of blooming yuccas and the silhouette of the Huachuca Mountains, which form a boundary between the United States and Mexico.

Fort Huachuca was built in 1877 as part of a strategy of dispersing the American military presence along the Arizona–Mexico border. One in a string of about fifty camps, this outpost was intended to protect the new settlers of the San Pedro and Santa Cruz River valleys against the uprisings of the Chiricahua Apache. That same year, silver was discovered in Tombstone, twenty miles from the fort in the making; this marked the beginning of a rush of adventurers eager to get rich from the local ore.

1.3: *The Founding of Fort Huachuca*, a mural by Lew Davis, 1943. © Fort Huachuca Museum.

Also in 1877, the Southern Pacific Railroad arrived in the southern part of what would remain, until 1912, the Arizona Territory, connecting the region to the rest of the country. The presence of the fort secured the new settlements, while favoring the development of the mining towns of Tombstone and Bisbee. It also gave birth to a small community of merchants, farmers, and saloon and ballroom owners, right at the entrance of the compound.

From Fort Huachuca, General Nelson Miles organized, in 1886, the surrender of the legendary Apache rebel Geronimo. For several years, Geronimo's raids had terrorized army soldiers, settlers encroaching on Apache lands to dig copper mines, Mexican immigrants, and other rival tribes. The surrender of Geronimo, the second moment of glory in the legend of Huachuca, has since been considered the victory that ended the Indian Wars. It was depicted by Lew Davis in another mural, which was also hung in the fall of 1943 in the white officers' club. *The Surrender of Geronimo*, painted using techniques inspired by Mexican muralists (the use of tempera to enhance colors, the black outlining of figures to give them luminosity through contrast), shows the great Apache chief waving the white handkerchief, followed by Natchez, chief of the Chiricahua Apache. To Geronimo's right is First Lieutenant C. B. Gatewood of the 6th Cavalry Regiment, credited with negotiating the terms of surrender; on either side stand the Apache scouts without whom victory would not have been possible.[2]

The arrival of the black soldiers, the third founding moment in the history of the fort, is not depicted in any painting, even though it had the most lasting effects. Starting in 1892, the fort became one of the main bases for the Buffalo soldiers, the African-American men of the Regular Army who were given this name by the Native Americans they were assigned to fight.[3] In 1866, in the aftermath of the Civil War, Congress authorized the creation of six segregated black regiments: two cavalry and four infantry regiments, which were later merged into the 24th and 25th Regiments. The soldiers who volunteered to join them – mostly freed slaves, uprooted farmers, and young laborers looking for work – were used in a manner quite similar to colonial troops in the European empires: Inside the United States, they were responsible for the pacification of the most recently conquered lands – against Native Americans and against neighbors deemed threatening; outside the United States, they were tasked with conquering new territories, first in the Caribbean and then in the Pacific. In the American Southwest, they were confined to isolated and poorly equipped army posts.[4] When the first Buffalo soldiers arrived at Huachuca in 1892, the Indian Wars had been over for six years. The members of the 24th Infantry Regiment, who had been stationed in the Territories of Texas and New Mexico to secure posts and communities against Native American raids, were assigned to guard the US–Mexico border from Huachuca: This marked the beginning of the black presence and tradition at the fort, which was to last until the end of World War II.

Guarding the border became necessary again when the Mexican Revolution broke out in 1910. The all-black 10th Cavalry Regiment – associated with the wars against Geronimo, Natchez, and the Apache Kid, as well as with the legendary charge of San Juan Hill in the Cuban–American War of 1898 – returned to service. In 1913, it began to patrol the region, which was especially volatile between Nogales and Yuma, while enforcing the neutrality laws and the arms embargo. Following Pancho Villa's raid on the border town of Columbus in 1916, the 10th Cavalry Regiment joined the punitive expedition led by General John Pershing against Mexico and was tasked with deterring banditry and guarding the border.[5] The black troops of Huachuca were not called upon to reinforce Europe after the United States entered World War I, which they interpreted as a sign of distrust. When the Mexican Civil War ended in the early 1920s, calm finally returned to the border. With the exception of Huachuca, all military bases in Arizona were closed by the Army in a period of cutbacks stemming from isolationism. As a result, the fort fell into a half-sleep. It did, however, continue to monitor the border. It was for this very purpose that the 25th Infantry Regiment, which had guarded several military posts, roads, and telegraph lines in various states of the Southwest, was assigned to the fort in 1928.

The remaining black members of the Regular Army – fewer than 4,000 out of 118,000 soldiers and a mere 3 officers in combat units[6] – were stationed at Fort Riley and Fort Leavenworth in Kansas. They had little to do, as they were given only minor tasks because of the poor opinion the Army had of them. In the 1920s, officers who had commanded black units during World War I were asked about their performance. Former 92nd Division Chief of Staff Allan J. Greer responded: "Every infantry and other combat soldier should possess mentality, initiative, and individual courage; all of these are, generally speaking, lacking in the Negro." Likewise, Charles Ballou, former commander of the 92nd Division in Europe, stated that the black soldier "has little capacity for initiative, is easily stampeded or surprised, and is therefore more dependent than the white man on skilled leadership."[7] In emphasizing the unfortunate episodes rather than the glorious moments, the officers succeeded in convincing the general staff that black soldiers were inherently bad fighters. As a result, their white commanders were selected from the worst in the Army, and the bases where they were stationed were either neglected or closed down. In the 1930s, the days of Fort Huachuca appeared to be numbered. The fort remained dormant until its fate was decided.

The community that developed near Huachuca depended entirely on the fort's operation. On the other side of the gates, the town of Fry consisted mainly of vast pastures, in the middle of which stood a few scattered buildings, stores, and drinking places built at the beginning of the century. Fry was home to no more than 200 people, most of them engaged in livestock farming. Three families of Irish origin successively dominated the place while trying to take advantage of the soldiers' presence: the Reillys, who owned a saloon and brothel, the Carmichaels, who were ranchers, and the Frys, who gave their name to the community of Garden Canyon in 1937. When the Southeastern Railroad connecting El Paso (on the Texas–Mexico border) to southern Arizona finally arrived in Hereford near the camp, Erwin and Lilian Fry acquired land east of the Carmichaels, where they opened a school, a post office, and then a liquor store. The fort fueled the economic development of Fry and the neighboring town of Bisbee, drawing its supplies from local merchants and providing administrative and logistics jobs to civilian residents.

Without the fort, Cochise County would have had difficulty recovering from the Great Depression that hit it along with the rest of the country, as its resources were limited to open copper and silver mines and vast desert plains with grazing cattle. Thus, as in many other locations throughout the United States, entrepreneurs welcomed the camp expansion program implemented at Huachuca between 1934 and 1939 by the Works Progress Administration (WPA), one of the main agencies created by the New Deal. What would later be called the "old post" – a triangle pointing toward the mouth of Huachuca Canyon and organized around the parade ground, with the officers' stone quarters on one side and the soldiers' two-story wooden barracks on the other – was renovated and expanded. The red-roofed wooden buildings were repainted, and the plumbing and sewage system was upgraded. A theater was added to the complex that included the old hospital and two schools – one for white children, which was named after Captain Whitside, and another for black children, which was named after Colonel Charles Young, the highest-ranking African-American officer in the Army in 1914, who had distinguished himself while leading operations in Mexico. A multistory building resembling an Italian palazzo and nicknamed the "million-dollar barrack" was built near the string of barracks, without anyone understanding the need for such luxury at the sleepy backwater fort. A new well, a *sine qua non* for any human presence in the desert, was drilled. A Native American adobe village was built to the north of the post to house the last surviving scouts, who were waiting to retire. The eight scouts were transferred with their families to Huachuca from Fort Apache, which had been deactivated in 1922. They now had little to do besides participating in maneuvers and parades or "playing Indian" in traditional dress, a role that was expected of them when distinguished visitors came. Army Signal Corps postcards show the stout, older scouts posing in front of their horses in color-accented white suits, knee-high moccasins, and feathered headdresses. Their presence was a survival from the past.[8] They could have been a metaphor of the fate that the Army was reserving for the fort, but Huachuca escaped uncertainty as soon as the country began preparing for war.

The State of Arizona was indeed one of the main beneficiaries of the expansion of the war effort and the increase in federal government contracts. As early as 1940, Arizona elected officials were advertising the state's advantages in Washington: intense year-round sunshine, mild temperatures, moderate winds – all conditions favorable to aviation; vast stretches of desert for combat training, artillery exercises, and tank maneuvers; and isolation in the interior of the country that guaranteed greater security. With the support of Democratic Senator Carl Hayden, who, as a member of the Appropriations Committee, was one of the most influential elected officials in Congress and had the final say on the allocation of federal funds, Tucson businessmen lobbied in Washington to host an air base. They were granted the Davis-Monthan Air Force Base. Others soon followed: Ryan Field and Marana, also near Tucson; Luke Air Force Base near Glendale, which was to become the largest air base in the world; Douglas Air Field on the southwest border, one of only four air bases in the United States to house black soldiers; and Luke and Williams Air Fields, two other sites where Air Force pilots could train and fly. The Grand Canyon State also offered ground troops the expanse they needed: General George S. Patton's Desert Training Center provided training to soldiers in the Arizona desert at Camp Horn and Camp Hyder. Private contractors accompanied the arrival of the military state in Arizona: The tire producer Goodyear opened a plant in Phoenix to supply parts for combat aircraft; Garrett AiResearch built coolers and turbines for the B-17 bombers at Sky Harbor Airport; and the Aluminum Company of America (Alcoa) produced aluminum parts west of the capital. Together, the "Big Three" turned Arizona's capital city into a major production center for national defense. The ripple effect throughout Arizona was tremendous: Thanks to investments linked to the military effort, the state abandoned cattle raising, mining, and citrus and cotton cultivation and completely reorganized its economy.[9] The impact was felt even in the far south of Arizona, where Fort Huachuca was located.

The "black post" took advantage of the new place that the Army, under pressure from activist organizations, was forced to give to African-American soldiers. In Washington, these organizations vocally challenged the perpetuation of the racial status quo of the interwar period: namely, a segregated Army with a very small black presence. Black former officers of World War I, together with several African-American newspaper editors and leaders of organizations belonging to the Committee on the Participation of Negroes in the National Defense, sensed that the underrepresentation of blacks in the Army would persist in the coming conflict. Therefore, as early as 1938, they advocated for the broader inclusion of African Americans in the military, the creation of a black division and squadron, and the assignment of black soldiers to combat and not just support functions. The NAACP aimed for total integration in the Army. This black mobilization, backed by powerful supporters in Congress, was so strong that the Selective Training and Service Act, the first peacetime conscription law, was passed on September 16, 1940 with two antidiscrimination provisions: The first stated that any man between the ages of eighteen and thirty-six could enlist voluntarily in the naval and land forces regardless of his race or skin color; the second prohibited all forms of discrimination in the selection and training of men. There was no possibility of appeal, however, for those who felt unfairly disqualified by draft boards. Shortly before the presidential election of November 1940, for which President Roosevelt needed the black vote, activist organizations tried to win a major concession with respect to the black presence in the military. Walter White, executive secretary of the NAACP, A. Philip Randolph, president of the National Brotherhood of Sleeping Car Porters, and Arnold Hill, advisor on Negro affairs in the National Youth Administration, demanded the end of segregated units in the Army and the integration of African Americans as individuals. They were painfully unsuccessful on both counts, since the segregation of troops was maintained. But they did make the President commit to a 10 percent quota of black soldiers in the Army, which corresponded to the share of African Americans in the US population. They also had him promise that African Americans would serve in all branches of the Army and not just in support functions. The first of these commitments was fulfilled; the second, however, was not kept.

When the War Department unveiled its race policy on October 8, 1940, black organizations rightfully felt a sense of backsliding. Except for the concession of the black quota, there was a return to the recommendations formulated in the late 1930s for the employment of African-American troops: assign all black soldiers to segregated units; retain a large proportion of blacks in non-combatant units; and abandon the project of integrating small black units into larger white ones.[10] In a statement prepared by Assistant Secretary of War Robert Patterson and endorsed by President Roosevelt, the War Department explained its policy on the employment of African-American troops in these terms:

The policy of the War Department is not to intermingle colored and white enlisted personnel in the same regimental organizations. This policy has been proven satisfactory over a long period of years, and to make changes now would produce situations destructive to morale and detrimental to the preparation for national defense [...]. It is the opinion of the War Department that no experiments should be tried with the organizational set-up of these units at this critical time.[11]

Through the voice of its highest officials, the War Department repeatedly stated that the Army could not be a laboratory for social experimentation and could not force society to accept a racial integration for which it was not ready. This was an implicit reframing of the argument that segregation helps to maintain social order, which had been formulated by the Supreme Court in *Plessy v. Ferguson* in 1896.

To ensure that black organizations would accept this setback, three symbolic Army appointments were announced on the eve of the election. William Hastie, who had been appointed by Roosevelt as the first black federal judge and later served as dean of Howard University Law School in Washington, was named Civilian Aide to the Secretary of War in charge of race relations – he accepted the position on the condition that the War Department would make known his opposition to segregation. Major Campbell C. Johnson was appointed as Special Aide to the Director of the Selective Service System, which was responsible for the selection of conscripts. Colonel Benjamin O. Davis Sr., the highest-ranking black officer, was promoted to the position of brigadier general. Davis had enlisted as a private in the Regular Army after serving as a volunteer in the Spanish–American War. He was named military attaché in Liberia from 1909 to 1912 and served in the Philippines during World War I – typical assignments for an African-American man, who could be entrusted only with command over men of the same color as him or over colonized peoples deemed racially inferior. In 1941, he served in a segregated camp in Kansas as commander of the 4th Cavalry Brigade, whose return to service he had to prepare. This was to be his last assignment before retirement, but the Committee on the Participation of Negroes in the National Defense vocally campaigned for his promotion to the rank of general. The Chief of Staff, General Marshall, offered Davis the position of "inspector and advisor in connection with matters pertaining to the various colored units now in service" under the authority of the Inspector General, Virgil Peterson. His hope was that Davis's appointment would neutralize activist criticism at little cost. The black general had a reputation as a moderate: He accepted segregation in the Army so long as it respected the principle of "separate but equal," and he kept his distance from black newspapers and activist organizations.[12] Of the three appointments, those of Hastie and Davis were to have a major influence on the training of African-American soldiers at Huachuca.

These three appointments were clearly insufficient to satisfy the demands of black organizations, to whose pressure President Roosevelt decided to yield in other areas. In December 1940, A. Philip Randolph issued an ultimatum to Roosevelt: If racial barriers to employment in federal agencies and defense industries were not removed, he would carry out his threat to stage a mass demonstration in Washington on July 1, 1941. Concerned about the potential impact of such a large gathering of blacks on the Mall, the President issued Executive Order 8802 in June 1941, which prohibited discriminatory hiring in federal agencies, labor unions, and industries involved in war-related work – a measure that was rather poorly enforced in Arizona. This order also established the Fair

Employment Practices Committee, an appeals body that ended up being rather ineffective. In return, the President demanded that the March on Washington movement abandon three of its other demands: the abolition of the poll tax (which was applied in certain southern states to prevent blacks from exercising their right to vote), the federal prohibition of lynching, and the end of segregation in the armed forces.[13] As a consequence, the racial status quo remained in force in the military.

The admission of much larger numbers of African-American soldiers into the Army and the continuation of unit segregation were decisive for the future of Fort Huachuca: They guaranteed that the model of the "black post" was not yet a thing of the past. The Cochise County Chamber of Commerce and local elected officials hoped that these decisions would result in an influx of black troops and, consequently, the rebirth of the fort. In their view, this was the perfect time to recall the county's unwavering tradition of welcoming troops since 1877 and to capitalize on the federal government's growing interest in Arizona. With the support of the two state senators, Bisbee businessmen promoted the fort's unparalleled advantages in Washington: extremely large tracts of virgin land; mild temperatures and a dry, healthy climate allowing year-round training; a near-total isolation guaranteeing minimal friction with the local community; and a military tradition waiting to be revived. Yet, the fort, which had expanded little from its original core on the mountainside, was far too small to accommodate an entire division; it was also plagued by a lack of water. Consequently, Huachuca did not appear on the first list of military bases to be expanded or built that was issued by the War Department in the spring of 1940. The state senators realized that new wells were needed. Hayden, assisted by junior senator Ernest McFarland, also a Democrat, convinced the Senate's Committee on Appropriations to fund the drilling of two wells at the east end of the fort. Together with the reservoirs built halfway up the hill above the old post, they would provide water to up to 40,000 men. Following the creation of the second well in the summer of 1940, a first wave of construction was initiated to welcome the African-American soldiers of the 368th Infantry Regiment, who were to join those of the 25th already stationed at the fort. Del Webb, the construction company that had won the vast majority of military contracts in Arizona, put 3,000 men to work 7 days a week to get the new buildings ready for the 5,000 newcomers. According to the *Bisbee Daily Review*, the NCOs' quarters and the 120 barracks were built at a record pace, and new paved roads were laid out.[14] Money began flowing into local businesses. The only people who expressed some concerns were the owners of cattle that grazed near the fort. They were afraid that the state would take over their pastures to create new training and shooting ranges. Overall, however, the prospect of economic benefits eclipsed the fear of an influx of black men into the region.

Thanks to the new wells, lobbying in Washington made sense again. The adoption of the 10 percent quota of African-American soldiers also gave hope to public figures and elected officials in Cochise County. In January 1941, the State Assembly passed a joint resolution signed by Governor Osborn, which mandated the two senators and Representative John Murdock to convince the Army Chief of Staff that an entire division could be trained at the fort.[15] According to the governor, the construction work needed to accommodate so many men would inject millions of dollars into the local economy; it would also give work to thousands of unemployed laborers from Bisbee and Tombstone for a period of several months.[16] On March 21, 1941, the House of Representatives passed a bill appropriating $4 billion to raise and equip an army of 4 million men; the bill included a $3.8 million provision for the fort at the Mexican border. On July 16, the War Department issued a list of fourteen military bases that would be targeted for development if the training of more men became necessary: Fort Huachuca appeared on that list. In total 30,000 men, the equivalent of 2 divisions, were to be stationed at Huachuca[17] – though there were never that many on site at the same time.

No sooner had the War Department confirmed the selection of Huachuca than the Phoenix firm Headman, Ferguson, and Caroll won the lucrative $23 million contract. The new cantonment that was to house an entire division was built in just a few months: It fanned out over the pristine plains east of the old post, stretching toward the San Pedro River Valley. In total 1,200 buildings were hastily constructed of pine boards following standard plans drawn up by the Army: rudimentary, long two-story barracks grouped by unit and laid out in a herringbone pattern, a mess hall, post exchanges (or PXs, stores run by civilians on army bases), two hospital complexes, a fire station, entertainment venues, artificial lakes, shooting ranges, landing fields, and so on.

The extreme isolation of Huachuca was a double-edged sword insofar as the accommodation of several thousand black soldiers was concerned. On the one hand, contact with white civilians was minimized, which limited the potential for altercations. On the other hand, the absence of an adjoining garrison town deprived the soldiers of entertainment and women. There was virtually nothing to do in Fry, and beyond it the desert stretched as far as Bisbee and Tombstone, where African Americans were regarded with the greatest suspicion. Arizona, with a population of barely 15,000 blacks out of almost 500,000 residents in 1940,[18] practiced a very

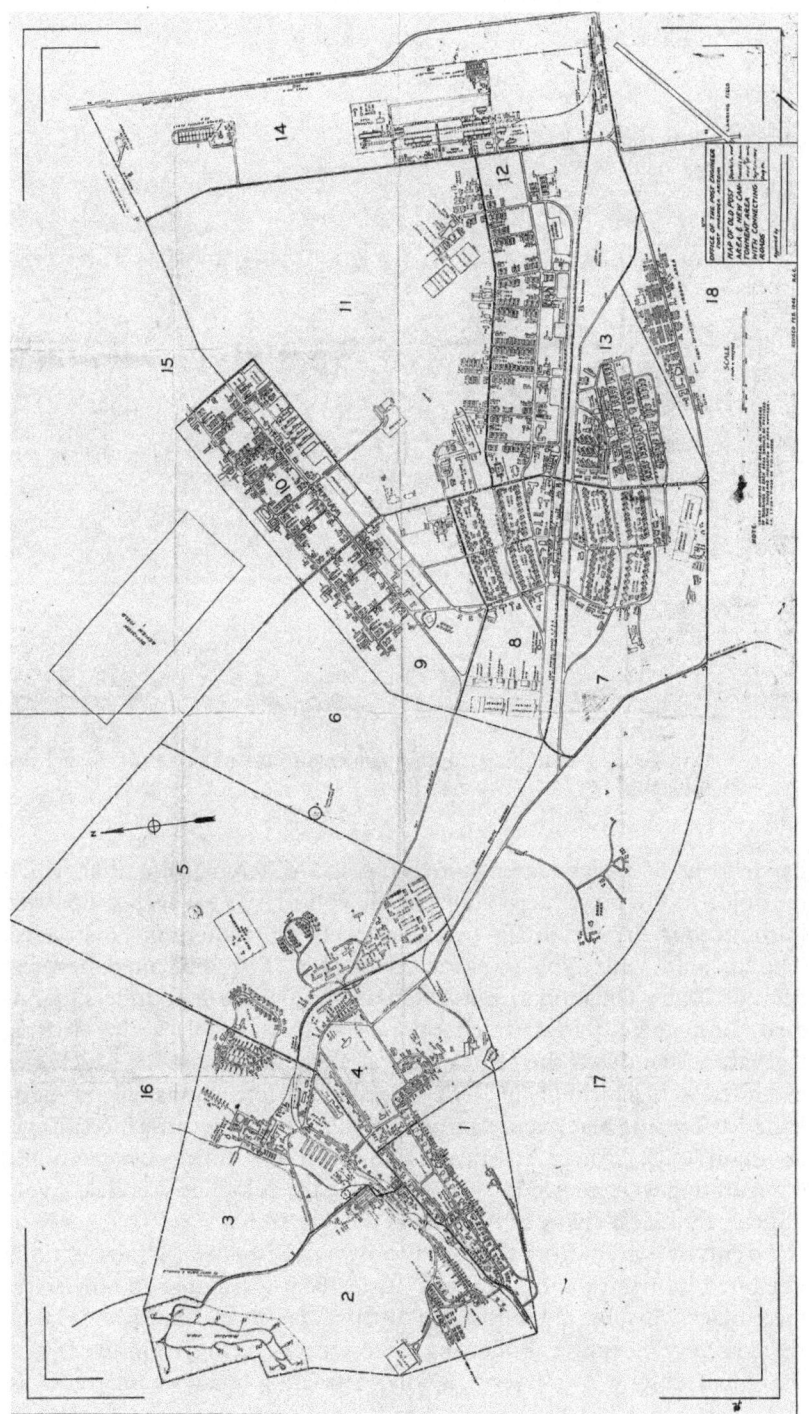

1.4: Plan drawn up by the Post Engineer Office in September 1945. © Arizona State Archives.

1.5: Troops marching in the new cantonment. © Fort Huachuca Museum.

harsh form of racial segregation – not too different from that which prevailed in the most racist states of the country. Legal segregation was introduced in Arizona in 1864 via a law prohibiting interracial marriages. The city of Phoenix, which was incorporated in 1881, replicated the racist rules of Texas, Oklahoma, and Arkansas from where its founders originated. Immediately after statehood was granted in 1912, the Arizona legislature mandated the segregation of elementary schools, which was extended to high schools in 1921. Racially restrictive housing covenants aimed at keeping blacks out of white neighborhoods became increasingly common. Only African Americans who could read entire passages of the Constitution were allowed to vote. Crossing the color line was clearly very difficult for blacks living in Arizona in the late 1930s.[19]

Twenty-five miles from the fort, the town of Bisbee was almost entirely inhabited by whites and Mexicans; in 1940, it was home to only sixty-three blacks. Bisbee had nurtured a distrust of African-American soldiers since its very inception. Following the discovery of copper in the 1880s, the small colony grew very rapidly, attracting many immigrants of

European origin – Poles, Slovenes, Croats, Bosnians, Serbs, Italians, Finns, Swedes, etc. Controlled by the very powerful Phelps Dodge mining company, it became an industrial city in just a few years. Phelps Dodge's policy of providing differentiated employment and remuneration to miners spoiled the initially good relations between whites and Mexicans. The company sent only white workers down the Sacramento Pit, an open quarry dug deep into the earth that formed a veritable pit in red and tawny colors. In other cities, such as Clifton-Morenci, it also had Mexicans work the mine. In 1917, Phelps Dodge, which was now extremely powerful, since it controlled even the municipal police, orchestrated the deportation of striking miners affiliated with the Industrial Workers of the World to New Mexico, with the collaboration of citizen militias and the complicity of the sheriff. Blacks, on the other hand, were never made to work the mines; they were mainly employed as guards. In July 1919, a fight broke out between the men of the 10th Cavalry Regiment and the local police. As a result, the black soldiers of Huachuca, who had frequented the many bars, hotels, and stores of Main Street, stopped going to Bisbee. The small local chapter of the NAACP founded in 1919 quickly disappeared owing to the lack of a sufficient number of members. Now completely deserted by the black soldiers, Bisbee was hit hard by the post-1929 drop in copper production – only a quarter of the miners managed to keep hold of their jobs. Countless workers left the town, and many of those who remained barely survived. Federal funds and programs were a welcome windfall, but they were implemented by county officials in a segregated manner, reinforcing divisions between whites, Mexicans, and blacks.[20]

Copper mining in Bisbee resumed in the early 1940s in response to the defense industry's new need for metal. The Army provided Phelps Dodge with reserve soldiers to work the mine: white soldiers, who were housed in the beautiful building of the Young Men's Christian Association (YMCA), but also black ones, fewer in number and new to the city, who were relegated to a slum on Brewery Gulch that absorbed a good part of their $7 daily income. Mining was segregated, with the two groups working in different pits in an atmosphere of great tension. Thus, on November 9, 1942, Clay H. Moore, a white employee of the mine, stabbed black soldier Willie Diggs, who had come on leave from Huachuca to find lodgings for his grandmother, in front of a Brewery Gulch saloon. When he was arrested and questioned by the police, Moore claimed that he had thought the soldier was a miner because he was not wearing his full uniform. Informed of these events through various letters, Judge William Hastie asked the War Department to conduct an inquiry. The investigation led nowhere, however, and the culprit was rapidly

1.6: Main Street of Bisbee, Arizona, May 1940, photographed by Russell Lee. © Library of Congress.

released.[21] It was clear that there was a form of impunity for racist crimes in Bisbee. Reporters from *Arizona's Negro Journal* had come from Tucson in July to investigate the racial situation in the area; they had experienced segregation for themselves when the Plaza Restaurant in Bisbee had agreed to sell them hamburgers but had refused to let them eat on site.[22] By the beginning of the war, the mining town was no longer a place where black soldiers could go to relax.

The nearest African-American community that could have accommodated Huachuca soldiers was based in Tucson, ninety-five miles away or more than three hours by car. But this community was small, with 1,678 people out of a population of 36,800 that included nearly 6,000 Mexicans.[23] It was therefore of little help. Segregation was still very much alive in Tucson, where it had existed since the city's foundation in 1867 as the capital of the Arizona Territory. Many store owners posted signs in their windows saying "We don't serve Negroes" or "We reserve the right to refuse service to anyone." In 1940, the *Negro Motorist Green Book* listed only one restaurant in Tucson where blacks could go without fear: the Rainbow Grill at 31 West Jackson Street.[24] City police regularly patrolled the area to ensure compliance with segregation rules and practices, sometimes wielding batons or service weapons. Yet, in the fall of 1941, the Federal Security Agency (FSA) and the United Service Organizations (USO) – an ecumenical coalition of six civilian organizations created in January 1941 to provide entertainment for soldiers outside military camps[25] – were planning to open a club in Tucson for the black soldiers of the 25th and 69th Infantry Regiments stationed at Huachuca and for those of the nearby air base. Shirley Graham, who was hired by the USO to organize the soldiers' recreation activities at the fort, recounted the reasons for this decision:

> The USO workers had been instructed to sound out communities surrounding camps, interpret the soldier and work for his acceptance, as far as possible, into healthy, normal community life [...]. We were searching for some Negro community, however small – a church, a club, homes and some girls. Therefore, we were forced to turn to Tucson. After much effort FSA and USO decided to open a club house in Tucson for the soldiers off duty from Fort Huachuca as well as for those Negro soldiers attached to the Air Base just outside of Tucson.[26]

Slated for construction with $50,000 in federal funds, the club would be open to black and white soldiers and to city residents, and it would operate in a non-segregated manner – the USO stood for racial tolerance and openness, unlike the military.[27] Yet, the hostility of the Tucson Chamber of Commerce, which was just as opposed to the coming of blacks as it was to federal intervention, scuttled the project. Attorney Cleon Knapp declared that making Tucson a center for Huachuca soldiers would keep tourists away and would be "injurious to the city." The local notable Monte Mansfield made no secret of his racist sentiments: "I am unalterably opposed to bringing those boys to Tucson. A long time ago we [the Ford Agency] refused to sell Negro boys at Huachuca cars as they wrecked them too fast." The white community simply did not want to be in contact with African Americans; it did not even consider that it might have an economic interest in them.[28] Graham explained white hostility toward the black soldiers in these terms:

> It seems that the USO cannot even operate a small "drop-in" center in the basement of a Negro church there. Only the houses of ill fame in Tucson are opened to the Negro soldiers. Restaurants, movies, parks, swimming pools, are closed to them [...]. Since there is no community for him outside the fort we must bend our efforts towards building something worthwhile for him inside the fort.[29]

Nevertheless, through repeated efforts and by using her influence with the city council, a well-established Tucson resident, Ada McCormick, obtained the creation of a segregated service club for black soldiers living in and around the city.³⁰

Since the communities near Huachuca were decidedly hostile to African Americans, the USO had to devise ways to make their isolation bearable. Graham, who was devoted to the well-being of the black soldiers and had maternal feelings for them, succeeded in convincing the military authorities to offer real entertainment at the fort. Graham's background had not predisposed her to come to Arizona, let alone to work with the military. Previously, she had worked as a playwright for the Federal Theater Project (FTP) in the Works Progress Administration; she had served both as an administrator and as a writer/director for the black troupe that was supported by the FTP in Chicago.³¹ Unable to find work in the theater world, she applied for a position at the USO in 1941 as she needed to feed her children. The organization sent the young African-American woman to the only "all-black post" in the country. Although initially hesitant, given Huachuca's isolation and the workings of the organization that employed her, she eventually became excited about the possibilities in a place where everything had to be created anew. In the October 1941 letter she sent to her mentor W. E. B. Du Bois, the great African-American intellectual and activist who was then teaching at Atlanta University, Graham described the fort in these terms: "This is one of the oldest posts in the United States – divided into a beautiful, rather exclusive little army community and, sprawling out over the desert, the amazing, glaring cantonment where soon there will be fifteen thousand soldiers."³² Graham was able to convince the fort's commander, Colonel McGee, to host the USO's entertainment and instructional programs within the military compound. Huachuca was the only army base in the country to operate like this; the local situation had required pragmatism. This exceptional mode of operation, which stemmed from the racism of the surrounding community, lasted three months. It ended when land was purchased from the Carmichael family in the immediate vicinity of the fort, with the explicit purpose of constructing a cultural center where black soldiers could go without fear of hostility from Fry residents.

Then came the war! Everything in the world changed [...]. I arrived to find an entirely changed Fort Huachuca. I can say no more than that at this time. We are faced with entirely new tasks. The boys have grown to look to us for recreation and amusement. Now, they come in the most important crisis of their life.³³

A keen chronicler of life at the fort, Graham immediately perceived that the entry into the war marked a turning point for the nation, but also for the men who were training at the camp. In late January 1942, she described to W. E. B. Du Bois the panic that gripped Arizona at the thought that the Japanese might threaten the southern border of the country:

> Much that had happened down here on the Mexican border could not be published. We were in no way prepared. When the enemy struck Pearl Harbor, he was also ready to strike other places. You read of troops being rushed down to the west coast of Mexico. There were vital reasons. For years back, Fort Huachuca has been the outpost guarding this lower border. I too, know the terror of waking in the night and hearing planes.
> As a matter of fact, though, these things are not so terrifying as it is to see the faces of men change and harden – to feel the foundations which one has built so carefully cut away; to know the future which I and my sons have planned and worked for so diligently is being blown away by shells which tear men's flesh! And every soldier here becomes my son in uniform.[34]

Although far from the Pacific Ocean, Cochise County was shaken by the surprise bombing of the US naval base in Hawai'i by Japanese aircraft. On December 7, 1941, eight Arizona-born soldiers perished in the sinking of the USS *Arizona*, including a sailor from Bisbee.[35] After Pearl Harbor, Fort Huachuca took up its role as border guard. The War Department indeed feared that Mexico might pose a threat to the United States, as it had during World War I. The 25th and 368th Infantry Regiments then stationed at the fort were sent to the West Coast, Nevada, and Washington State to guard strategic locations. They returned to Huachuca only in April 1942, once the danger had passed. The all-black 93rd Infantry Division was activated at the fort very shortly afterwards.

The decision to reactivate the 93rd Division and to train it at Huachuca was made in the weeks following the attack at Pearl Harbor. The Army had to mobilize ten million men and to prepare them for battle in distant theaters as fast as possible. In this context, the general staff could no longer resist enlisting a large number of African Americans. In many states, however, black applicants were frequently rejected by draft boards on the grounds of ill health or illiteracy (35.6 percent of rejected applicants were African Americans).[36] For this reason, but also because of the exemptions cotton farmers had negotiated to keep their labor force, the enlistment rate of blacks was much lower than that of whites: one out of every two men of service age for the former, three out of four for the latter.[37] When the President ordered the Army to effectively implement the 10 percent quota of black soldiers, the general staff had to find a way to honor this commitment.

On December 8, 1941, the day after Pearl Harbor, a conference was held with the editors of black newspapers and key officials of the War

Department. General Marshall announced the creation of several Reserve Officers' Training Corps (ROTC) units at three black universities, as well as the formation of black units in all branches of the Army, including several infantry divisions.[38] In the 1920s, white officers who had commanded African-American troops during World War I had discouraged, for good and bad reasons, the reactivation of the segregated black 92nd and 93rd Infantry Divisions. In addition, all studies on the use of black troops had advised against the formation of black units larger than a regiment (2,500 men). However, in December 1941, the creation of all-black divisions – made up of black soldiers commanded by white senior officers – seemed like a good solution. It allowed the simultaneous assignment of a good part of the 177,000 black soldiers that needed to be absorbed into the Army in 1942 to meet the 10 percent quota. It made it possible to admit large numbers of African-American soldiers into the Army without derogating from the principle of segregation, which was reaffirmed by the general staff on October 8, 1940. It ensured the representation of African Americans in almost all arms of the military – with all their components and support units. And it had the secondary benefit of neutralizing repeated demands by black intellectuals and activist organizations for the creation of a racially integrated volunteer division.

Three infantry divisions were initially planned. Two were to be created from existing black infantry regiments (the 24th and 25th stationed at Huachuca), newer regiments of the Regular Army (the 366th, 367th, and 368th), and the 372nd Infantry Regiment of the National Guard, which had recently been integrated into the Army. The first black division, the 93rd, was to be formed out of the 24th, 25th, and 368th Regiments already stationed at Huachuca and was to be activated in April 1942; the second, the 92nd, was to be commanded by cadres of the 93rd Division and was to be activated in the fall of 1942.[39] The War Department, however, had to find training grounds for the 15,000 black soldiers who would make up a division. Until then, Army rules had prohibited the stationing of African-American units larger than a brigade on national territory. The Army could have chosen a segregated black–white camp in the South, where three-quarters of the black troops were already training in strict segregation – with their own separate training grounds, barracks, and recreation areas far from the white cantonment.[40] Yet, despite the isolation of the southern camps, interactions between blacks and whites had created tensions as early as 1941. Thus, in August of that year, clashes between black soldiers stationed at Fort Bragg and members of the military police in Fayetteville, North Carolina, resulted in deaths and injuries on both sides.[41] The general staff initially considered housing the 93rd Infantry Division in a camp located near a large black population center in the North, for instance at Fort Dix in New Jersey or at Fort Meade in Maryland,[42] as had been done for the black squadron at Tuskegee in Alabama.[43] Yet, in January 1942, the Operations Division of the General Staff unexpectedly chose to go west: The two black divisions would train in turn at Fort Huachuca, the historic "black post" and the most isolated training ground one could find.[44] The 93rd Division would be the first to move in; the 92nd Division would train in separate regiments at four southern camps until the 93rd left the fort. In 2007, Robert T. Madison, a former architecture student at the historically black Howard University who had served as first lieutenant in the 370th Infantry Regiment of the 92nd Division, humorously commented on that choice: "20,000 African Americans with guns! That's why we were sent in the middle of nowhere in Huachuca, Arizona."[45]

When a reporter for the *Pittsburgh Courier*, the nation's leading African-American newspaper, visited the fort in early 1942, he was amazed at the sheer size of the camp: "the post area is larger than many of our large metropolitan cities and is practically a city within itself, if one can call a military post a city. It cannot be covered on foot within a single day and there is room here for everything a division will ever need."[46] In just a few months, a new cantonment of more than 1,000 buildings had sprung up on the immense, almost deserted area, nibbling away at the plains from the old post. Fort Huachuca was now ready to house the 15,000 men who made up the first black division in American history to train in a single place. This was a stunning rebirth for the old "black post" – the last active fort in Arizona in the late 1930s and one of the last to accommodate black soldiers commanded by white officers – whose survival was still in doubt just a few years earlier.

While the entry into the war was a decisive event, it alone does not explain why Huachuca became the site of a novel racial experiment in the military. What gave the fort a second life was the reinterpretation of army segregation within it – a reinterpretation that was made necessary by the 10 percent quota of black soldiers and that translated into the creation of new segregated units. The fort's isolation was sufficient to restrict contact with white civilians in nearby communities and, consequently, to limit resistance to the presence of so many black soldiers. Huachuca enjoyed exceptional climatic and environmental conditions, in a state that was selected by the federal government to serve both as a rear base for the military effort and as a vast training ground. Lobbying by local businessmen and elected officials had borne fruit. Within months, the Army began to experiment with a new form of training for black troops at the fort.

In the vast borderland of Arizona, the federal government tested the limits of its attachment to democracy, in whose name it had just entered

1.7: Aerial photo of the new cantonment looking east toward Fry, 1943. © Fort Huachuca Museum.

the war against the Axis powers. Arizona was one of the five states selected by the Army for the internment of Japanese Americans who had been deported from California in February 1942. The head of the Western Defense Command, General John J. DeWitt, who coordinated homeland defense in the Pacific, had recommended the systematic incarceration of all Americans of Japanese descent living on the West Coast, on the grounds that it was impossible to ensure their loyalty after the Japanese attack at Pearl Harbor.[47] The principle of equal opportunity, central to American democracy, was also undermined further south, at Fort Huachuca, through the Army's treatment of African-American soldiers. As a result, Arizona became a crucial site for blacks to wage the "double victory" campaign – "victory over our enemies abroad" and "victory over our enemies at home" – launched in February 1942 by the *Pittsburgh Courier*.[48] Since the start of the war, a large section of the African-American population had taken up the cause of defeating the Axis. The "double victory" campaign, however, made a sharp break with the call for truce issued by W. E. B. Du Bois, who in July 1918 had written in *The Crisis* that African Americans should forget their grievances against whites and fight alongside them. At Huachuca, the "double victory" campaign would soon translate into a struggle against the peculiar modalities of racial segregation that prevailed at the fort and against the humiliating prejudices that permeated every aspect of military life.

2   Fourteen Thousand Black Infantrymen

An unprecedented experiment was about to take place at Huachuca. The concentration of so many black infantrymen in a single, isolated location was an anomaly compared with usual practice in the US Army. Everywhere else, the infantry was a predominantly white corps – only one in twenty soldiers was African-American. Considered by white commanders to be of inferior intelligence, black troops were most often assigned to support units, which were increasingly necessary in a war that was no longer static – for every infantryman on the front line, ten soldiers were now needed in the rear. In 1942, 48 percent of black troops served in support units, particularly in the engineer and quartermaster corps.[1] In several other camps, blacks and whites were trained in a segregated pattern that had been tried and tested for many years. Thus, at Camp Claiborne in Louisiana, one of the most important training grounds in the country, the black soldiers of the 761st Tank Battalion were housed in second-rate facilities south of the cantonment and were prevented from moving freely inside the camp.[2] At Fort Huachuca, the white commanders had to imagine a new racial regime for a situation that existed nowhere else.

In February 1942, an anonymous letter by an African-American officer working at the fort's stockade reached Truman Gibson, assistant to William Hastie, the Civilian Aide to the Secretary of War: "Fort Huachuca is a crime against the Negro Race. Remote, dismal, and prejudiced, it is small wonder that many lose their minds out here [...]. Our condition out in Huachuca is vivid proof of how weak, impotent and unwanted we Negroes are."[3] From the perspective of the fort's stockade, the author of the letter could clearly see the dysfunction and manifestations of racial injustice. His testimony confirmed the need to create a new regime of race relations at Huachuca.

The basis of this new racial regime had to be segregation, in accordance with army customs. Segregation was to be instituted through rules and ordinances that had been designed for other places and that mainly covered the non-military aspects of life on training bases. Depending on the beliefs of those who applied them, more or less strict interpretations of segregation were possible. Moreover, in matters of military discipline or justice, general regulations could be implemented in a racially biased manner. Segregation also derived from non-codified practices and habits imported from southern society by white officers, such as the way they addressed black soldiers, the degree of physical proximity they were willing to accept, and the number and type of interactions they had with African Americans during rest periods. This racial regime made up of instituted rules and individual practices evolved as soldiers responded to it and as the general staff became aware of the need to address grievances against the institution. The great social and geographical diversity of the men of the 93rd, however, prevented them from presenting a united front in their response to the emerging racial regime.

Beginning in May, hundreds of recruits arrived daily at Huachuca to join the 369th Infantry Regiment, a new unit that was combined with the 25th and 368th Infantry Regiments to form the new triangular 93rd Division. They were soon joined by three field artillery battalions – the 593rd, 594th, and 596th. In June 1942, a reporter for the *Cleveland Call & Post*, a black weekly newspaper from Ohio, predicted that the men of the 93rd were destined for excellence: "The men assigned to form this 'greatest of them all' will undoubtedly be the 'cream of the crop' and will be the envy of the recruit and the pride of the nation." The journalist was confident that this unit would "confirm its glorious past" and would make itself worthy of the blue helmet, the insignia it had inherited from the former 93rd Infantry Division which had fought valiantly in World War I.[4] In the spring of 1918, the four regiments of the former 93rd had been deployed to France and placed under French command, thus preventing the integration of African-American soldiers into the US Army. After distinguishing themselves in the battles of the Meuse–Argonne Offensive and later in Alsace-Lorraine, the men of the 372nd Regiment had returned to the United States decorated with the Croix de Guerre.[5] This prestigious regiment, however, was not reincorporated into the 93rd Division when the latter was reactivated in 1942. It was the 369th Regiment, formed out of the 15th New York National Guard Regiment, that provided the link between the old unit and the new one, allowing the first black division of the new conflict to boast a glorious past. Nicknamed the Harlem Hellfighters, the men of the 369th had received France's highest military decorations – though they had been excluded from the victory parade on the Champs-Élysées.[6] The most optimistic commentators hoped that the veterans and the new recruits would receive such good training at Huachuca that they would be able to repeat the exploits of 1918.

As a privileged witness to the fort's transformation in the spring, Shirley Graham watched the old-timers of the 25th Regiment "tell their history with pride" to the newcomers, these "young Negroes from Ohio, Indiana, Illinois, Pennsylvania, and New York [with a few] from Texas and Louisiana."[7] Henry Williams, a young recruit, recalled being greeted by the veterans "as if we were family members and they were the appointed heads of family."[8] The veterans of the 25th, who accompanied the new recruits in their initiation into military life, were admired figures. Sergeant A. J. Wells had served in the Army for twenty-five years – twenty of them at Huachuca – first in the cavalry and then in the infantry. Although always highly ranked, he was reassigned in the summer of 1943 to Service Command Unit 1922 in charge of administering the fort after he developed a heart condition. When he died in September of that year, the new football stadium was named after him. Sergeant Percy Roberts had joined the 25th Regiment during the interwar years along with hundreds of other men. Born in the late 1910s in a small Illinois town, he had begun to worry about his future after two years in college. He had initially joined the Civilian Conservation Corps (CCC), one of the flagship programs of the early New Deal designed to put unemployed youth back to work on major projects – this had been his first experience of legal segregation. In 1937, he enlisted in the Army and joined the 25th Regiment, where he remained until the new recruits arrived at Huachuca.[9] Career soldiers – one out of five men in the new division – formed the core of the permanent army, constituted its cadres, and enhanced its cohesion.

The new recruits were younger. Of the 226 veterans of the 93rd Division who responded to a questionnaire sent by historian Robert Jefferson in the early 1990s, 60 percent had been conscripts, 20 percent had been volunteers, and 20 percent had enlisted because of previous military commitments.[10] The black volunteers of Huachuca joined the Army not so much out of political conviction – whether patriotism or opposition to the Axis powers – or because they were attracted to military life, but because they saw it as an alternative to unemployment and as a source of regular income – first-class privates of the 93rd earned $50 a month, with $0.99 deducted for government insurance.[11] This was the case for George Shuffer, born in 1923 in Anderson County, Texas. His family farm had gone bankrupt during the Great Depression because of a series of crop failures. To help his parents, Shuffer had worked odd jobs on nearby farms while still attending high school. He decided to enlist in 1940 along with his two older brothers, even though he had never followed world news and was offered scholarships by several black colleges. He arrived in the 93rd Division in 1942. He and his brothers sent money each month to their family, thus allowing them to get by.¹² Henry Williams, whose parents had recently died for lack of medical care, joined the Army as a volunteer in 1941, just after graduating from Ohio State University. Unsure that he could find a job, he enlisted at age twenty-six to receive training and a guaranteed income. When he was interviewed by the historian Maggi Morehouse in 1997, he recalled being greeted at Huachuca with a kitchen chore that lasted from 3:30 a.m. to 10 p.m. the following evening. He seriously considered deserting, but changed his mind when he was named acting corporal. He was put in charge of Saturday inspections, during which he ensured that the battalion's weapons were shiny. Appreciated by the men of the company, he rarely needed to mention offenders in his report book.¹³

Many conscripts ended up at Huachuca against their will. These men believed that the war was a white man's war and consequently saw no reason to sacrifice several months of their lives to serve in the Army. Some supported the efforts of the black press and black organizations to achieve the goal of equal participation of blacks and whites, but they became ambivalent about service when confronted with military life and segregation at the camp. Thus, Thomas White from Cleveland, Ohio, who was drafted in February 1941 and then selected for Officer Training School before joining the 93rd Division, viewed military service as a form of punishment. Ray Jenkins, a nineteen-year-old grandson of a slave from Memphis, Tennessee, considered asking for a deferment from military duty. The exploitative conditions experienced by his family had made him suspicious of an army led by southern men. He ended up enlisting because of family pressure, and eventually joined the 368th Regiment in Louisiana before the 93rd Division was reactivated at Huachuca.¹⁴

Several of the conscripts had received their political education in the Communist Party during the interwar period and adhered to its interpretation of the war as a conflict between imperialisms. The soldiers who were most critical of the Army's racial policy were, for that matter, clearly identified as communists by the intelligence division of the 93rd Division headquarters.¹⁵ Since the doctrinal shift of 1928, the Communist Party had defended the idea that white supremacy was one of the faces of capitalist domination and had fought alongside black organizations for racial equality and desegregation. It had come to the assistance of African Americans affected by the Great Depression and had created the League of Struggle for Negro Rights, led from 1934 by the writer Langston Hughes. The party had also played a key role in mobilizing support for the Scottsboro boys, who were unjustly accused by the Alabama courts of raping two young white women on a train. Lastly, it had raised the awareness of black party members about the racist ideology of Hitler's regime and had linked Nazism to American white supremacy.[16] After he had joined the Communist Party in 1936, Frederic Jefferson, a New York-born former Pullman porter at Penn Station, had learned about the content of the Nazi program through his regular reading of the *New Masses* and the *Daily Worker*, the party newspaper. He was drafted in October 1941 and attended Officer Training School at Fort Lee before joining the 93rd Division.[17] Nelson Peery, born in 1923 in Junction City, Kansas, had also been politicized via communism. His family had been hard hit by the Great Depression and had moved to Minneapolis in the mid 1930s. There he had looked for work along the railroad tracks connecting Junction City to Los Angeles. Following the Scottsboro trial, he had joined the party and had become aware of the threat posed by Nazism. He enlisted in the Citizens' Military Training Corps in June 1941 and joined the Army soon after at Fort Snelling, in Minnesota. He was later assigned to Huachuca.[18] At the fort, the communists were the most critical of the racial order.

The 14,000 men of the 93rd Division – veterans and new recruits, volunteers and conscripts – had little in common. They came from vastly different worlds and had radically different experiences of race relations – some had endured legal segregation in the South, while others had not. Of the 226 veterans surveyed by Jefferson in the 1990s, 15 percent had come to Huachuca from Ohio, 10 percent from Pennsylvania, 5 percent from Illinois, 10 percent from Texas, 8 percent from Louisiana, 4.5 percent from North Carolina, and 4.5 percent from California.[19] Shirley Graham was surprised to see so few soldiers from the Old South at Huachuca.[20] One reason for the small presence of Southerners was the exemption granted to cotton pickers by local draft boards. In the same sample of veterans, only one in five soldiers had lived in a rural town prior to joining the Army. Moreover, almost half came from cities with more than 100,000 inhabitants – one can imagine their surprise at discovering the desert and its wildlife, their shock at seeing the isolation of the fort. Figures also highlight a great social diversity, with soldiers hailing from the lowest to the highest rungs of the black community. Thus, 20 percent of respondents had previously worked as farm laborers (a figure close to the national average); 32 percent in low-skilled domestic jobs (e.g., doormen, elevator operators, and house servants – this high figure, relative to the approximately 15 percent of working-age black men employed in the domestic sector in 1940, may be explained by the overrepresentation of men from urban areas in Jefferson's sample); and 20 percent in professional occupations (e.g., educators, engineers, doctors, and musicians, compared with 1.8 percent for all African-American men). The high figure for those in professional organizations is surprising, given that the men of the 93rd had obtained very low scores on the tests they had taken upon entering the army. It is likely due to a selection bias in Jefferson's sample of veterans, as respondents were certainly among the 20 percent who had successfully completed high school.[21]

The Army measured soldiers' learning abilities at enlistment using the Army General Classification Test (AGCT). Developed by psychologists in 1939, the AGCT sorted out soldiers into five categories of aptitude for the purpose of assigning them to tasks with varying levels of difficulty. In the Army as a whole, 37 percent of black soldiers from the North and 67 percent from the South had no education beyond elementary school, and the quality of this education was generally lower than that received by white soldiers. As a result, African Americans were at a disadvantage in the AGCT. In early 1942, 73 percent of blacks were classified in the two lowest categories (IV and V), compared with 26 percent of whites.[22] The results were even worse for the men of the 93rd Division: In the spring of 1943, 80 percent of its members were classified in classes IV and V, and less than 1 percent in class I.[23] These results reinforced the prejudice that black soldiers were of lower intelligence and prompted the commanders of the 93rd Division to design a specific training program for them.

The black soldiers were bewildered by the social mixing – the presence of other conscripts whose civilian life and experience of racism were so different from their own. They discovered a total institution that sought to govern every aspect of their lives, both military and non-military, and whose functioning, rules, and codes were completely foreign to them. To get around the anonymity of this new military life, small informal groups were created on the basis of common regional origin. Solidarities were built and attachments were formed around moments of relaxation and shared experiences. Among the soldiers who arrived in March 1941 to form the 368th Infantry Regiment, forty-five young men from the Cleveland area, most of them volunteers, were assigned to Company M – along with others from the neighboring states of Pennsylvania, Indiana, Kentucky, and West Virginia. Indeed, almost all African-American conscripts from Ohio who had enlisted in early 1941 were assigned to Huachuca. These men initially thought that they would return home after a year of service. But when the war broke out, they realized that they would have to stay in the Army until the end of hostilities. Clarence Gaines, a member of the 368th regiment, wrote a column in the *Cleveland Call & Post* in which he detailed the daily life of Ohio soldiers for their families. In particular, he recounted how two soldiers of Company M of the 3rd Battalion, Charlie Rabb and Henry Williams, created an informal support group called the Huachucans to rebuild camaraderie among young men from the Cleveland area. The Huachucans provided entertainment: swing concerts on Sunday afternoons and variety shows at the service clubs – places where ordinary soldiers could go to relax and where evening classes were offered to those seeking to improve their reading and writing skills. Other groups were formed. Thus, the 569th Local Express, made up of fifty-three North Carolina soldiers of the 569th Field Artillery Battalion, organized discussions around the poverty they had fled, the Army's racial policy, or the opportunities they could expect to find after the war.[24] These groups helped to dissipate the anonymity and sense of uprootedness that necessarily accompany incorporation into such a large unit located so far from home.

At the new cantonment, the assignment of each regiment to a specific quarter facilitated identification with the unit and acceptance of collective life. Each quarter was arranged around two rows of barracks, between which stood the collective buildings – the canteen, the service club, and a space for physical exercise and the morning drill – where soldiers could recreate a familiar, human-scaled environment. Sometimes the men escaped to the athletics fields or the outdoor theaters, or they went to buy a hamburger, soda, or beer at the PX.[25]

Inside the barracks, where beds were lined up in two rows facing each other, the space allotted to the men was minimal: a few dozen inches around the bed, the shelf, and the trunk. All soldiers were responsible for order and cleanliness: Beds were made at right angles, uniforms and shoes were put away, and rifles were stored butt down in the center of the room on circular supports placed at regular intervals. For some soldiers, the servile tasks of cleaning and serving – the "Scrub, Sweep, and Mop" evoked in the title of the song by the well-known black vaudeville comedian Timmie Rogers – constituted the entirety of military life. Thus, Robert Galley, a former dishwasher from Palestine, Texas, who dreamed of becoming a radio technician, ended up working in the officers' mess kitchen every second day.[26] Soldiers who scored lowest on the AGCT were assigned to repetitive, low-skilled tasks that were considered humiliating. These tasks were not a big change from what the men had known as civilians in the fully segregated labor market of the South or the still largely segregated one of the North. They also prevented them from seeing the Army as a place for learning and gaining qualifications. Rogers's song further mentioned the risk of going to jail for soldiers on KP ("kitchen patrol") duty who failed to clean the barracks or sweep the mess hall. Yet, far from encouraging submission, Rogers incited desertion – "If you are tired of peeling potatoes and want to go, don't wait for furlough, just go!"[27]

Posters warning of the consequences of insubordination – cancellation of furlough, financial penalties, or military stockade – were displayed everywhere at the camp. Moralizing or threatening instructions in colored capital letters – the voice of the Army – were addressed to black soldiers depicted in stencil form. They encouraged the purchase of war bonds, condemned wasteful practices ("If you waste it ... there is less at home"), stressed the imperative of discipline and courage ("History will judge us by our deeds"), or called for the suppression of rumors ("Stop rumors"). The Office of War Information (OWI) reminded every American, military or civilian, that the slightest piece of information, however trivial, could play into the hands of the enemy ("Loose lips sink ships").[28] The artist Lew Davis created these posters in the silk-screen printing workshop he had opened at the fort. He had noticed that posters depicting only whites were torn down by the soldiers. He made ones that featured African Americans instead of blond, blue-eyed men. Printed in runs of 3,200 copies each month, they covered the walls of Fort Huachuca and those of the 61 other camps where black soldiers were trained. Davis produced simple, direct drawings in bold, contrasting colors, accompanied by short, easily understood slogans. He claimed that he wanted black soldiers to have pride in themselves and in their race.[29]

2.1: "Soldiers lined up at a PX to buy cigarettes, hamburgers etc.," May 19, 1942. NARA, Army Signal Corps.

2.2: Poster 1 "Stop Rumors." © Arizona Historical Society.

Wherever the soldiers turned, they also saw the warnings on the posters exhorting them to maintain sexual hygiene in order to prevent sexually transmitted diseases that were plastered all over the walls of barracks, hospitals, and other places of collective life. Two stencil posters – large swaths of color and thick typography – stood between soldiers and their temptation: "Gonorrhea the crippler" depicted a black soldier moving on crutches with great difficulty; "Syphilis can blind you" showed a man hiding behind dark glasses and begging on a wooden box. At the bottom of each of the two posters was the instruction: "Stop at the pro station" (i.e., the prophylactic station where antibacterial ointments, soap-saturated cloth, and cleaning tissue were distributed). At other camps, posters warned of the loss of masculinity: "Keep your manhood & virility by keeping away from the syph & clap."

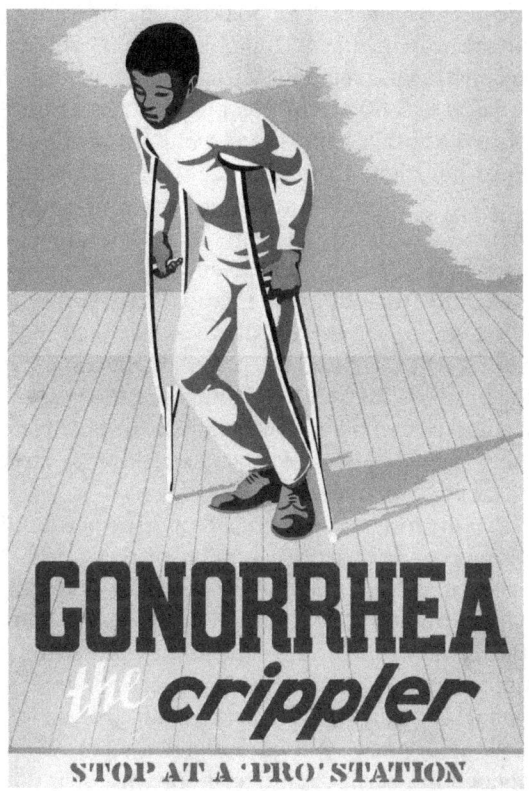

2.3: Poster 22 "Gonorrhea the crippler." © Arizona Historical Society.

These posters were part of the prevention plan initiated by the fort's commander, Colonel Edwin N. Hardy, who had succeeded Colonel McGee shortly before the arrival of the 93rd Division. The plan followed the guidelines of the Surgeon General's Office (SGO), which was very concerned about the high rates of venereal disease among black soldiers. A venereal disease control officer was assigned to the 93rd Division to ensure the implementation of educational programs and the proper functioning of prophylactic stations. The moralization and education of black soldiers went hand in hand. On the one side, camp chaplains, who were seen by the Army as spiritual advisors to the soldiers, encouraged sexual temperance – though without much effect.[30] On the other side, medical services provided prevention advice and care after exposure to risk. At enlistment, each soldier received a sixteen-page booklet devoted to sexual hygiene and venereal diseases. The booklet urged abstinence for medical and patriotic reasons (a soldier with syphilis, it said, would shirk his duty) and warned against sexual relations with infected women. At Huachuca, the infection rate was 85.80 per 1,000 in June 1942 – a figure much higher than that reported at other camps – and one-third of cases were due to recent infections contracted through sex with prostitutes.[31] In view of this, the soldiers were forced to attend an anatomy course on Saturday mornings, where they had to listen to an officer remind them of the risks of unprotected sex with prostitutes, or they were made to watch films on hygiene and sexuality, including the famous "Fight syphilis." Each week a bulletin on the status of venereal diseases was read to the troops and then posted on the walls. It listed the places of infection to be avoided (in Fry and on the border with Mexico), compared the infection rates of the different units, and issued honor rolls and blacklists.[32] However, there is no certainty that the soldiers were paying attention to these warnings or that they even cared about them.

Concerned that the fort he commanded might be penalized for being all-black, Hardy enforced the implementation of the "separate but equal" doctrine to ensure that the soldiers of the 93rd Division received the same treatment as whites trained at other camps. As a conscientious commander, he oversaw the application of army guidelines passed on by the Ninth Service Command, which had authority over the states of California, Oregon, Washington, Idaho, Montana, Utah, Nevada, and Arizona. However, he also designed original initiatives to make sure that black soldiers maintained the best possible relations with their officers and with white civilians outside the fort. This white, blond, blue-eyed officer from Tennessee was a product of West Point Academy, the training school for the military aristocracy, from which he had graduated in 1911. World War I had ended before he could be sent to the front to command troops. Like other officers in command of black soldiers, he had served in the Philippines early in his career, as the general staff felt that leading African-American and Filipino soldiers required the same kind of qualities. He had led one of the segregated Philippine Scout units – since 1922, the United States had retained a full-fledged colonial army of 12,000 men on the islands, presumably to defend them in case of an attack. This horseman with a reputation for a quick temper had also served for several years as a military attaché in Ecuador and Colombia. On his return to the United States, he had modernized Camp Robinson in Nebraska with New Deal funds. When the United States entered World War II, he requested to be assigned to Fort Huachuca as he was too old to be sent overseas. He had the reputation of being tough but fair. He was appreciated by Shirley Graham, who had developed the habit of consulting him when planning the entertainment at the USO. He also received the constant support of black inspector Benjamin O. Davis, who considered him fair and open in his dealings with black officers. General Davis even regretted that some of the initiatives taken by Hardy caused misunderstandings and led some, at the fort and outside, to misjudge him.[33]

Although his office was adorned with a portrait of General Robert Lee,[34] Hardy refused to be dogmatic about racial issues. He was willing to try some fairly bold measures in some situations – including the opening of a military-controlled prostitution compound in front of the fort's gates and a segregated recreation hall funded by black businessmen. However, this cavalry officer, who rode his horse daily, accompanied by his dog Skipper, and never went anywhere without his riding crop, responded as follows when asked about his treatment of officers: "If I have a good horse, be he white, black or pinto, I ride him. That goes for you, officers – if he's no good, I'll get rid of him."[35] One day in September 1942, Hardy summoned the African-American Lieutenant Colonel Midian Bousfield, a physician in civilian life and the director of the fort's black hospital, for a lesson on the Army. He gave Bousfield a long, unsolicited lecture on race relations to convince him that a black man could never be superior to a white man, and reproached him for having advocated the abolition of racial segregation before the students of the white school at the fort.[36] Moreover, when Hardy met with Fry's residents in early 1943 to persuade them to collaborate with the Army in the implementation of prophylactic measures, he stoked their fears of the impact that the alleged hypersexuality of blacks would have on the local community.[37] Except for his pragmatism in the area of race relations and his genuine desire to maintain peace at the fort he commanded, Colonel Hardy remained convinced that whites were superior to blacks, as did other army officers from the South.

Another prominent figure at the fort was Major General O. P. Hall, the commander of the 93rd Infantry Division. This 55-year-old West Point graduate oversaw the military training of the 14,000 black soldiers, a responsibility that few of his classmates envied. Hall, a native of Mississippi, had been appointed to this position by General Marshall, who was convinced that the people of the Old South had a better understanding of the character and habits of black soldiers, because they had been in contact with them in civilian life.[38] In truth, Southerners were the least likely to imagine a different racial order than the one they were used to. In the photographs taken of him by the Army Signal Corps, Hall appears respectful and considerate of blacks, even of those who served him; yet, he also seems to perpetuate a form of authority wherein racial superiority reinforces hierarchical superiority. If he could be

2.4: "Maj. Gen. Hall, 93th [sic] Division Commander, watches his sandwich being prepared at the picnic," May 20, 1942. © NARA, Army Signal Corps.

photographed during recreation time shaking the hand of a black officer's child – who looked at him with a mix of admiration and fear – it was because the inequality between him and the boy was not in doubt.

When the 93rd Division arrived at Huachuca, all the officers under Hall's command were white. The War Department had initially sought to maintain the status quo inherited from World War I, a time when it was held that black officers were poor commanders and that African-American soldiers performed better under white leadership.[39] Yet, these white officers were second-rate, and in some cases, fresh out of school. A significant number of them had graduated from the Reserve Officers' Training Corps Programs at colleges in the South. In contrast to the commanders who had served at Huachuca during the interwar period, they were not West Point graduates. Some were assigned alphabetically to the 93rd Division, without regard to their leadership qualities.[40] Most would certainly have preferred to exercise their authority over other soldiers. In the Army, assignment to black troops was indeed viewed as

2.5: "Maj. Gen. Hall, 93th [sic] Division Commander, Fort Huachuca, Ariz., is shown shaking hands with a small boy at the picnic grounds," May 19, 1942. © NARA, Army Signal Corps.

a mark of punishment or an expression of doubt about one's leadership qualities. The white officers were consequently looking forward to another assignment. Those of higher rank were the first to go; they left behind officers less adept at leading soldiers. According to George Looney, a black First Lieutenant of the 368th Regiment who was stationed at Huachuca in 1941: "The majority of the white officers with the 93rd were people who could not have made it with the 37th or 87th divisions, or any white division of any caliber."[41]

Hall had a reputation for being fair and respectful of soldiers, but the attitude of the officers under his command was brutal, condescending at best. In his memoirs published in 1995, the communist Nelson Peery recalls that morale was very low in his battalion due to the mistreatment:

We griped about the chow, the heat, the dust, the water, and the things that made the army the army. Most of all, we griped about the white supremacist attitude of most of the white officers.... Some of them tried to treat the regiment as if it were their antebellum plantation. They expressed their belief in white supremacy with body language and tone of voice. The worst expression was their slave term, "boy."

After one too many verbal humiliations from their major, Peery and his comrades organized a barracks-wide boycott of the mess hall, demanding a public apology in front of the entire company. The officer resigned himself to this for fear that the anger would degenerate into mutiny.[42] The black soldiers of Huachuca at least had the advantage of numbers.

The first deputy commander of the 93rd division, General Edward Almond, would not listen to the protests. He systematically addressed the men as "Niggers" or "Nigra" in his Virginia accent. On arriving at Huachuca, he summoned the fifteen black officers initially assigned to the 93rd Division and did not hide his contempt or racist prejudice from them. Frank Bolden, the *Pittsburgh Courier* correspondent accredited to Huachuca, recalled the scene years later when he was interviewed for a documentary. Almond, he said, had spoken to them in these terms:

You niggers have no business being officers in the United States Army. You don't have the brains for it. And you don't have the experience for it [...]. I am an officer of the United States Army and I have been assigned here and I will put up with you and I will tolerate you because the Army says so, but I don't believe you'll ever become good soldiers. It's just not in you.

He had added: "You have too much 'monkey blood' in you."[43] According to Bolden, the black officers were dismayed and complained about the insult to General Davis, who had come to Huachuca to inspect the black troops of the 93rd Division one month after it was assembled. However, the black inspector vouched for Almond's leadership qualities and merely asked that he stop addressing the soldiers in derogatory terms.[44]

General Davis was following the recommendations of Judge Hastie, who since late December 1941 had been warning the highest officials in the War Department of the consequences of white officers using abusive language against black soldiers. The Civilian Aide to the Secretary of War had already succeeded in bringing down the general in command of Francis E. Warren Air Force Base, in Wyoming, for using racist words and gestures against his men. In September 1941, the former judge argued: "It is impossible to create a dual personality, which will be on the one hand a fighting man toward the enemy, and on the other hand a craven, who will accept treatment as less than a man at home."[45] Hastie also demanded that an order be sent to commanders prohibiting them from using derogatory language and reminding them of the need to respect the men who served under them. Instructions specifying the manner of addressing black soldiers – preferring the term "colored" to "Negro" and above all to "Nigger" – were also envisaged.[46] Although

General Davis tried to dissuade the Chief of Staff, a memorandum was eventually sent to all generals in command of black troops forbidding them to use insulting epithets against "racial groups."[47] The white commanders at Huachuca must have received the memorandum, but they did not necessarily enforce it. Almond was not reprimanded for his racist and insulting remarks. On the contrary, after three months in Arizona, he was promoted to the position of commander of the 92nd Infantry Division, which was being assembled at Fort McClellan, in Alabama. While his departure provided a sense of relief for the soldiers of the 93rd,[48] individual practices of command remained a source of tension throughout the training of troops at Huachuca.

General Davis was seen by African-American activists and by some soldiers as an Uncle Tom, a token black for the highest white commanders. In Washington, he accepted without protest the segregation he faced in the War Department building – his offices were separated from those of his colleagues at the Office of the Inspector General; he skipped meals to avoid the affront of having to eat alone in the cafeteria. In his correspondence with other high-ranking African-American officers, he described a form of isolation from which he clearly suffered.[49] Yet, he tolerated segregation wherever he saw it – for instance, at Tuskegee, which he inspected in August 1941 without criticizing the racial allocation of buildings, and then again at Camp Lee, in Virginia, and at Fort Bragg, in North Carolina. Every time he recalled that segregation was acceptable so long as the separate buildings and entertainment of blacks were equivalent to those of the white soldiers. Davis was suspicious on principle of the complaints made by black soldiers, whom he considered to be excessively influenced by the press and activist organizations. The reports on black troops he sent to Inspector General Virgil Peterson were generally blind to the suffering caused by humiliation and discrimination; they always sought arrangements to make tense situations bearable and sustainable. Davis was an unconditional supporter of compromise and appeasement. By contrast, Judge Hastie, a civilian in a much more exposed political position, publicly demanded the end of segregation and the elimination of all discrimination against blacks.[50] Two sides of the black response to racism in American society thus opposed each other. They echoed the dispute, which had structured the community since the beginning of the century, between Booker T. Washington, an accommodationist and gradualist, and W. E. B. Du Bois, a radical in favor of obtaining full civil rights immediately.[51]

Before coming to Huachuca, Davis had drawn up a list of issues to be considered that made no mention of race relations. He inspected the fort as if it were a camp like any other, as if he had not been appointed by the

Inspector General to pay special attention to the situation of blacks. What mattered to him was that everything be in order: that the procedures be respected, the registers well kept, the army rules publicized and applied, the men properly equipped to fight. In a terse two-and-a-half-page report he sent to his superiors, Davis sounded very positive. Except for the lack of weapons and ammunition, he did not mention any of the shortages or complaints that were brought to his attention during his five-day stay at the fort. He did not evoke the abnormally high number of desertions (eighteen since the arrival of the division), arrests (seventy-two), and trials; and he wrote nothing about the overcrowded stockade and did not mention the content of his conversations with the prisoners and soldiers who had asked to see him in order to share their grievances.[52]

At first, it was unclear whether the 93rd Division would train under the same conditions as other units. A memorandum prepared by the general staff for General Eisenhower in April 1942 stated that black soldiers should receive more extensive training because of their alleged intellectual, physical, and disciplinary weakness:

The colored soldier requires considerably more training to maintain the tactical efficiency of his unit. However, once he has learned a job well, he performs it satisfactorily and, apparently being less ambitious than the white soldier, is more content. The colored soldier lacks the initiative, imagination, and ingenuity required when routine breaks down. This increases the need for reliable leadership for the colored soldier.

The memorandum added:

The training and equipping of colored units under such circumstances is a dissipation of effort, manpower, and equipment which a nation engaged in a war cannot afford. It is also obvious that a serious internal situation would develop if trained negro troops had to be held immobile in the continental U.S. while only white troops were sent to the firing line.[53]

The decision to be made on the basis of this analysis was not clearly formulated: Should the general staff forgo real training of black soldiers, or should it strive to gain acceptance for the idea of black combat troops so as to prevent tensions or feelings of injustice in the Army and in society? Should it provide black troops with longer and more demanding training to ensure that they would be up to par when assigned to combat zones? After some hesitation, it was decided to subject the soldiers of the 93rd Division to the same training requirements as other infantrymen.

While the decision to send the men into battle had not yet been made, they had to be prepared for war through extremely difficult training – even if, by its very nature, training could never fully approximate the terror of actual combat. The men would be trained in three phases: seventeen weeks of basic training with a focus on individual training; thirteen weeks of unit training, whereby each unit (from the squadron to the regiment) would constitute itself as a combat unit; and, lastly, eleven weeks of combined training with team combat simulation aimed at welding the different units into a division capable of fighting as a cohesive group. Upon completion of the three phases, the division would be evaluated and rated; the men would then move on to maneuvers far away from the camp.[54]

During the first seventeen weeks of training, the soldiers of the 368th and 369th regiments received their instruction from the black NCOs of the 25th Regiment, who had a few years of experience behind them. At first, the new recruits had to get used to army discipline and life in the barracks, internalize the routine of military life, and familiarize themselves with the terminology, the pace, and the places of the camp. After a month, their bodies had to be disciplined. Soldiers began to practice simple exercises: strength training and coordination, marches, and then drills. The aim of this endless repetition, this veritable "dressage" of bodies, was to ensure that the soldiers could execute, without hesitation and without fail, the maneuvers expected of them in situations of extreme stress. Training could easily become a source of humiliation, tipping over into persecution.

Then came the assault courses, the five- to twenty-five-mile marches in the desert, shoulder to shoulder, in a straight line, pack on the back, several times a week, the reconnaissance expeditions, the weapons handling training, the combat simulations. By dint of repetition, soldiers had to acquire basic reflexes; they had to become one with their weapon. Endurance, both physical and psychological, was gained in the desert. This environment was often mysterious and unsettling for the young soldiers, who were sometimes surprised by the presence of tortoises, snakes in cactus thickets, scorpions, coatis, or horned iguanas, or woken up in their bivouacs at night by enigmatic sounds. The semi-desert areas around the fort were suitable for simulated combat, the mesquite trees evoked the jungle, and the surrounding rivers could be used to practice bridge building. But the absence of vegetation and shade made training extremely difficult. In the 1990s, Charles Wesly, a former officer of the 368th Regiment, recalled how difficult it was to keep the soldiers focused in these conditions: "The hardest part of it was there was no real classroom and no shade. You did your instruction out in the desert sun. There were guys sitting on the ground out in the desert sun, and you are doing everything to keep them alert."[55]

The thirteen weeks of unit training mainly focused on tactics and combat simulation, which took the men to the outskirts of the camp.

South of the fort, there was no shortage of empty lots to practice all kinds of shooting exercises. For the first few weeks, howitzers and mortars were dragged on foot to the training grounds in order to save gasoline. The troops had to prepare for whatever conditions might arise on the front. They learned to fight in all types of weather and with increasingly powerful weapons.[56] Street fighting was practiced in the abandoned mining town of Charleston, which was rebuilt by the soldiers for training purposes. Located fourteen miles from Huachuca near the San Pedro River, Charleston did not enjoy the glory of Tombstone despite its share of clashes and murders. The buildings deserted by saloonkeepers, gamblers, and dancers some sixty years earlier were now in ruins and were used to simulate close combat. To prepare the men for the terrifying sounds that would ring out on the battlefield, firing was performed with live .30-caliber rounds – once they were finally delivered.[57]

Indeed, the shortage and obsolescence of military equipment, especially ammunition and rifles, was a major concern when the 93rd Division arrived at Huachuca. The defense industry had not produced enough material to equip the US Army while also supplying the Allies.

2.6: Combat training in the abandoned city of Charleston. © NARA, Army Signal Corps.

Consequently, the general staff gave priority to equipping white units that were deployed in theaters of operation; training camps came afterwards, especially those where African-American soldiers were stationed. It took a while for the industry to produce weapons and tanks at a rate sufficient to ensure that all troops were equally equipped.[58] Right after Pearl Harbor, an editorial writer for the *Baltimore Afro-American* predicted that African-American soldiers would not be properly equipped. He denounced this derisively: They obviously could not defend the country with "a dust brush, a mop, and white apron ... armed only with a whiskbroom and a wide grin," referring to the tools used by black domestics in the South to do their work.[59] When General Davis came to Huachuca in July 1942 to carry out his first inspection, the officer in charge of military equipment informed him of the extent of the shortage. For the soldiers to be able to train properly, the following was needed: 60 AT 60 mm pistols, 96 .50-caliber machine guns (MGs), 35 .30-caliber light MGs, 291 Browning automatic rifles, 6 81-mm mortars, and 9 half-tracks, not to mention accessories for the artillery, spare parts for small arms, tear gas, and orientation maps. Some exercises could not be performed, and others had to be adapted so that weapons could be shared among soldiers.[60] For many weeks, the military police lacked the ammunition to load their pistols.[61] A First Lieutenant of the 25th Regiment, George Looney, later testified: "In those days, the white soldiers got all of the new equipment and the blacks got the cast-offs, this was true of everything, including bullets."[62] The tanks arrived at Huachuca only in 1943, along with the 92nd Division.

Several photographs taken by the Army Signal Corps in the spring of 1942 show the dilapidated equipment and the obsolete strategy that was being taught to the soldiers.

Placed under the authority of unit commanders, army photographers were torn between public relations objectives (praising the quality of the training and weaponry, emphasizing the successes of units), the requirement not to divulge confidential information, and the need to produce images for educational purposes.[63] In a photograph from May 1942, the men can be seen training in a trench dug in the grounds of the camp. The soldiers are still equipped with Brodie helmets, a legacy of World War I that was retained by the US Army until the beginning of the year, and are training for a type of war that was no longer being waged – World War II was not fought in trenches, but in jungles, deserts, and mountains. In another photograph, we see them on maneuvers, perfectly lined up, bayonets in hand, as in 1918.

Frank Bolden, the *Pittsburgh Courier* reporter to whom the Army Public Relations Office had granted correspondent status, the rank of honorary

58   A Black Army

2.7: "2nd Lt. Arthur Bates waits for zero hour to give the command to attack." © NARA, Army Signal Corps.

Major, and privileged access to the fort, stayed at Huachuca for several weeks to cover the training of the 93rd Division.[64] He never mentioned the shortages or delays; on the contrary, he wrote articles that were full of praise. He probably feared censorship and the loss of his accreditation after he was summoned by the FBI in the summer of 1942.[65] On July 4, he published a long article describing the holiday parade, in which 1,500 men and 50 officers from the 93rd Division marched to the sound of the 25th Regiment Infantry Band before General Hall and Bisbee's top elected officials. Modern combat training had not resulted in the disappearance of the parade as a cohesive group practice and modality for controlling bodies through close order. Bolden celebrated the unwavering patriotism put to the service of exemplary precision and discipline, and he extolled the quality and speed of the maneuvers carried out by the four infantry companies who had been in training for only ten weeks. He sought to convey the power of the weapons that had been entrusted to the Tan Yanks – short for Tanned Yankee, the nickname given to black soldiers: mobile vehicles, firearms, anti-tank weapons, mortars for the infantry, and so on. Together, these weapons presented "a far different spectacle from that of World War I." Bolden concluded: "They are going to make things tough for our sworn enemy. They deserve everything that America can give them, because they will repay it a thousand-fold. Their skill and ability will someday become a legend in the land of the free and the home of the brave."[66] Readers could not suspect that this parade performed under the vigilant gaze of the white authorities might have been a source of humiliation for African-American infantrymen. Sensitive to the need to foster, for political reasons, a martial and virile image of black soldiers to counter white prejudices about their laziness and unfitness for combat, the journalist was quick to praise the recruits' speed of learning, their ability to swallow the desert dust and resist the scorching temperatures without slowing down. The following October, when the 93rd was in the unit training phase, he wrote: "Today, the average Tan Yank is beginning to look more like a combat soldier than ever. He is hard and sinewy, more agile than when he first reported as a raw 'cruit.'"[67] In January 1943, he estimated that the division was ready to go to combat and posed a threat to the enemy.[68] Within a year, however, a quarter of the soldiers of the 93rd were sent back to civilian life because of disabilities or poor physical condition.[69]

Of the two objectives of the "double victory" campaign identified by the *Pittsburgh Courier* in February, Bolden's articles emphasized patriotism and loyalty – the fight against racism in the United States became secondary. From the summer of 1942 onwards, Bolden wrote numerous reports on the training of the 93rd Division that went along with the Army's public relations strategy toward blacks, which consisted in changing the representation of all-black units as ill-equipped and trained for a war of the past. His articles were largely illustrated with Signal Corps photographs provided by the military authorities.[70] These images depict a division trained like the others, subject to the same requirements, and enjoying the same esteem from its superiors. The men pose, alone or in platoons, performing the actions they have been taught: An ordinary soldier, kneeling, is about to ignite a stick of dynamite; several men crouch down as they wait for charges to detonate around a tree. The soldiers are also caught in action: A group of ten men climb a stone wall with rifles hoisted over their shoulders; others emerge from trenches behind smoke screens with heavy loads on their backs; soldiers of the 593rd Field Artillery Battalion unload 105-mm howitzers from trucks and fire them; a handful of men advance into the desert with rifles pointed forward while resisting a gas attack.

In all of these Signal Corps photographs, the exercises appear to be going well; the men seem proud of their new skills and show no resistance to the

2.8: "Soldiers of the 93rd Infantry Division facing a mock gas attack." © NARA, Army Signal Corps.

2.9: Training in the use of the M3 anti-tank gun. © NARA, Army Signal Corps.

authority of the white officers. Thus, Major General Fred W. Miller, cigarette in hand, standing above his men lying on the ground for target practice, appears as a benevolent and just authority, concerned with the success of his soldiers.

With these photographs, the Army wanted the outside world to know that the 93rd Division was training in the best possible conditions and was ready to fight the enemy. It showed that bodies were toughening and taking a liking to adversity and that physical fatigue facilitated the acceptance of discipline and authority. It suggested that the men performed the actions expected of them, obeyed the orders that were addressed to them, and merged into the group with which they would soon become one.

Nevertheless, training remained a site where officers exercised their power over soldiers, a place where black bodies were disciplined by white men. The humiliating character of training was sometimes mentioned in the correspondence of infantrymen or the later testimonies of veterans. Below the veneer of patriotism and harmony, resistance was brewing. At

2.10: "The 93rd Infantry Division's commanding general, Major General Fred W. Miller, looks on as soldiers in his command ring up scores on the rifle range." © NARA, Army Signal Corps.

the end of 1942, nearly a third of patients hospitalized in the fort's black hospital showed symptoms of mental and physical illness. A medical officer of the Ninth Service Command, which had authority over the hospital, diagnosed one out of three patients with psychogenic symptoms born of a desire to leave the Army:

> A few patients had neurocirculatory asthenia. The majority complained of sticking pains at the left nipple, pain in the chest, shortness of breath on exertions, and pains in the legs. A few complained of nervousness and would begin to shake for the examiner's benefit. The remainder complained of back pain, pains in the extremities, or of pains in old surgical wounds or in scars of injuries or in old injuries all of which had been dormant for years before induction. Thus, the heart, the back and the extremities, or old scars and injuries were the loci to which the primitive minds projected the symptoms born of a desire to escape.[71]

More and more soldiers feigned illness or developed psychosomatic symptoms, and the black hospital became a refuge from military life. The commander of the hospital, Midian Bousfield, was well aware of this. In particular, he noted that several men of the 25th Regiment had mutilated their bodies to get out of training and stay safe in his facility.[72] Yet, doctors did not bring the cases of malingerers to the attention of the military justice system. The cost of direct resistance to orders was high – a stay in the stockade, a court-martial – and many weeks of training remained before leaving the camp. Passive resistance and faking illness were therefore preferred to open confrontation.

Not surprisingly, the racial regime that was effectively applied to the Huachuca soldiers strayed considerably from the official principle of "separate but equal." The infrastructure made available to the men of the 93rd was not substandard, but the training and equipment they received were not, at least initially, equivalent to those of white soldiers elsewhere. White officers' practices of command were sometimes tainted by racial prejudice that the Army itself condemned – including behaviors such as addressing the soldiers in derogatory terms. In the absence of military justice records, it is difficult to know how the articles of war were applied in cases of insubordination or indiscipline. The number of hospitalizations is a first indication of an emerging sense of injustice, though it is difficult to say whether it was related to race or to the soldier's condition. This latent uneasiness, if it existed, did not yet translate into a concerted and collective response to a racial regime that was still in the making. The social and geographical diversity was too great, and there was too much variation in the levels of tolerance toward racism depending on the men's experiences of civilian life and expectations of army service – expectations that were sometimes projected into the post-war future. As it were, white commanders were not so much concerned about the resistance of black soldiers as they were about that of black officers. It is in relation to the latter that they sought to maintain, through vexation and physical separation, the privileges of rank and office associated with their skin color and status.

3   Separated by the Color Line

In February 1942, three black officers entered the USO service club at the gates of Fry. They were the first to do so – if one excludes Captain John A. DeVeaux, one of the fort's chaplains and a veteran of the 368th Regiment, who until then had been the only African-American officer to serve at the camp. The soldiers who had been enjoying themselves in the lounge stopped what they were doing and applauded the three officers at length. They were full of pride and admiration for these men who were to become their superiors. In their eyes, the officers' presence represented a victory over prejudice: It meant that blacks could finally be accepted as equals to whites in the military institution.[1] This was indeed a breakthrough in the racial history of the Army.

In 1940, only ten black officers from World War I, including a few chaplains, were still active in the Army. At the end of the conflict, the general staff had discouraged black officers from joining the permanent army on the grounds that they had not lived up to expectations in combat.[2] In 1939, black newspapers and organizations began to press for the resumption of officer training for African Americans. Such training was intended to open a path of upward mobility for blacks within the armed forces and to satisfy African-American soldiers' demands to be commanded by their own. The Army granted the request – the only breach in the racial consensus that had governed the military since World War I. The number of black officers would be increased and officer training integrated. This decision, which benefited only the African-American elite, was taken for reasons of cost and efficiency – the segregated training provided until then was deemed inadequate. In July 1941, the Officer Candidate School (OCS) at Fort Benning opened its doors to blacks.[3] Several members of the first class were selected from among the most qualified soldiers of the 369th Regiment who were present at Huachuca in 1941.[4] Two hundred black officers graduated each month from the OCS. In response to activist protests, the Secretary of War, Henry Stimson, agreed in February 1942 to have them assigned to regular units.[5] Yet, the white commanders were reluctant to entrust the command of troops to black officers, whose leadership abilities they doubted. Prejudice was still very strong within the general staff, as evidenced by the memorandum prepared for General Eisenhower in April 1942: "The most important consideration that confronts the War Department in the employment of colored officers is that of leadership qualifications. Although, in certain instances colored officers have been excellent leaders, enlisted men function generally more efficiently under white officers."[6] Such prejudice meant that the number of black officers soon exceeded that of available assignments.[7] Fort Huachuca was an ideal outlet for the growing surplus: The size of the 93rd Division and the magnitude of the camp created significant needs, and Fry already had a long tradition of welcoming blacks.[8]

When the 93rd Division was reactivated at Huachuca in May 1942, only twenty-five black officers were attached to it. The new OCS graduates, however, began arriving in droves: A total of 640 entered the fort in the spring of 1942 alone. Most incoming officers were freshly trained second lieutenants assigned to support units, in particular the newly formed Special Service Companies in charge of entertainment.[9] Reuben Fraser, a native of St. Louis and a graduate of Lincoln University (Missouri), an institution established in the aftermath of the Civil War to educate freed slaves, was commissioned as second lieutenant in the Special Services Battalion of the 369th Regiment. He was tasked with preparing educational and entertainment programs for the illiterate or semi-illiterate soldiers of the division.[10] With the exception of the medical corps, which was largely composed of more senior officers from civilian life, the only officers above the rank of first lieutenant at Huachuca were a captain and a major: The former served as chaplain and the latter was in charge of entertainment.[11] The two men were very isolated and torn between their need to integrate into their Corps and the soldiers' expectations that they would advocate for their rights.[12]

Many of the first black officers at Huachuca had enlisted voluntarily for economic reasons. First Lieutenant George Looney, born in Douglas in the far south of Arizona, had grown up on the fort, where his father had patrolled the frontier with the 9th and 10th Cavalry Regiments. After graduating from Tombstone's integrated high school – an exception in Arizona at the time – he had been forced to abandon college to support his parents. He enlisted as an infantryman at Fort Huachuca, where he initially served as a bugler. In 1941, he was selected as one of the cadres of the incoming 368th Regiment and was made a platoon sergeant. In 1943, as high casualties were causing a shortage of officers in the military, he took the AGCT test like other men of the permanent army. Ranked in the first class, he was sent to the OCS at Fort Benning and then to Camp

Swift, before being reassigned to Huachuca as an officer of the 25th Regiment.[13] Durward P. Griffey, a native of Kentucky, had found only low-paying and difficult jobs after graduating from high school in 1939. To improve his financial situation, he joined the military in February 1941. In view of his excellent results on the AGCT, he was selected for officer training at Fort Benning, where he graduated among the first in his class. He then joined the 369th Regiment at Huachuca.

Other officers at the fort had studied at top black universities – by comparison, less than 2 percent of African Americans had a bachelor's degree.[14] George N. Leighton, born in 1912 in New Bedford, Massachusetts, had worked for several years as a janitor before being accepted at the prestigious historically black Howard University, which was established in the federal capital in the aftermath of the Civil War. He entered the Army Reserve in June 1940. He was then admitted to Harvard, where he hoped to earn a law degree. Yet, in March 1942, he was called to attend the OCS at Fort Benning. He was later assigned to Huachuca. William McKinley Thomas's trajectory was also one of excellence – this time in the medical field, where black officers were accepted from the very outset of the war. A little older than Leighton, McKinley Thomas came from the South, specifically from Leavenworth, Kansas. After graduating from Wiley Black University in Texas, he had studied at Meharry (Nashville, Tennessee), one of the best African-American medical schools in the country. Upon graduation, he had worked as a physician in his hometown at Saint John Hospital and Cushing Memorial Hospital. He was the first black physician to graduate from Carlisle Barracks Medical Field Service School, and he was assigned as deputy commander to the 318th Medical Battalion of the 93rd Division in May 1942.[15]

For blacks, officer status was a racial and social victory won through persistent struggle. This status achieved after integrated training brought many privileges: the command of men, the power to make decisions instead of merely executing orders, a place in the military meritocracy, and housing and social life in distinct locations. As such, it created distinctions within a group that was hastily considered homogeneous by white society. In addition to prestige, the title of officer brought a higher income: $150 per month for a second lieutenant (three times the income of a private) – out of which a little more than $6 was deducted each month for insurance – and about $150 more for those with dependents. In practice, however, black officers did not enjoy the racial equality promised by integrated training and the attribution of rank. While the title of officer may have earned blacks some form of consideration beyond the gates of the fort, it did not protect them from racial prejudice in the larger white society. Most importantly, the military experience was profoundly different for African Americans because white officers refused to consider them as peers and because segregation was imposed on them as soon as training activities were finished at the end of the day.

The most glaring manifestation of inequality in the military was the application of distinct promotion policies on the basis of race. For African Americans, promotion was much slower and arbitrary; in some combat units, it was completely blocked. An army directive in force until March 1, 1943 stated that black lieutenants could command only companies or batteries. There was also an unwritten rule that no black officer should have a white man under his command – as in southern society, whites were to remain in a position of superiority under all circumstances. Thus, for an African American to obtain a promotion, all whites of equal or higher rank in the same unit had to have been promoted beforehand. This rule amounted to endorsing racial hierarchy: Since black and white officers had been trained together in the same schools, such differences in rank could not be explained by differences in qualification. General Davis himself recognized that this practice validated "a different status for colored officers, [who feel] that, since they are called upon to make the same preparation and sacrifices, the promotion and assignment policy should be the same for all officers."[16] The question of advancement was particularly sensitive at Huachuca because black officers were rapidly overrepresented at the fort, the 93rd Division being one of the few units to which they could be assigned. In late 1942, more than 150 out of 500 junior officers (second and first lieutenants) did not yet have an assignment. Those who did were stuck at the rank of first lieutenant, or "frozen in grade" as the officers put it.[17] Between January and August 1943, only 126 black officers (i.e., 26 percent) of the 93rd Division received a promotion. The average time to move up a rank went from 5.7 to 10 months. The wait was sometimes very long: It took Roscoe Tyson Spann one year to be promoted from second to first lieutenant.[18] Furthermore, only 15 percent of promotions were from first lieutenant to captain. To move beyond the latter rank, black officers had to leave Huachuca – though it often took a while before a position became available at another base. Shortly after the directive blocking the advancement of black lieutenants was rescinded in March 1943, Davis personally intervened with Major General Fred W. Miller to ensure that the black officers of the 93rd received the promotions they deserved.[19] However, these promotions never came, because the men were already on their way to the front.

At Fort Benning, training was integrated: Black and white officers attended the same courses and were treated as equals. At Huachuca, however, blacks found themselves under the orders of whites and were sometimes humiliated and despised by those who wanted to reassert their power over them. When John Howard arrived at the camp in April 1942, he introduced himself to the commander of his company, Captain Paul Bowen, a native of Alabama: "After I saluted, gave my name and rank, and indicated I was reporting for duty, Captain Bowen didn't look up from his desk. He only said 'I hate niggers.'" As for Leo Logan, a native of Kansas and a lieutenant in the 25th Regiment, he recalled in the early 1990s how he had been humiliated by Major General Raymond Lehman: "The Commanding General visited our company area one day and chewed me out in front of my men for not reporting properly. He ordered my company commander to court-martial men and he held up the company commander's promotion when he wouldn't do it. I was later accused of shooting at the general which I did not."[20] Logan's authority had been undermined in front of his own men, which had definitely compromised his ability to elicit the expected behavior from them. In some cases, the humiliation experienced by black officers led them to turn against their white counterparts and to act in solidarity with their black soldiers.[21]

Black officers of the 93rd Division were never left to command men on their own; they were supervised at all times by higher-ranking white officers. A unique experiment in all-black leadership – a first in the Army – was nevertheless attempted at Huachuca. The commander of the 369th Regiment, Thomas Fenton Taylor, a native of Tennessee who had graduated from the military academy in 1915 and was one of the few white officers with a reputation for fairness and justice among his men, suggested placing a battalion under the command of a black officer, Major Charles Blackwood. A former World War I First Lieutenant, Blackwood had fought with the 365th Infantry Regiment in St. Dié, France, in 1918. Having returned to civilian life at the end of the conflict, he had become one of the first African Americans to graduate from the Diesel School of Engineering in Chicago and had worked as an engineer for the Burlington railroad. In March 1942, he was recalled by the Army and sent to the OCS at Fort Benning. He was then assigned to Huachuca in June. Impressed by the respect Blackwood garnered from his men, Taylor recommended him to the commander of the 93rd Division. The black major was first tasked with training the illiterate men of the 369th Regiment and then placed in command of its First Battalion.[22] He was involved in selecting the best black officers to assist him, and white officers were transferred to make room for these men.[23] After three months, the experiment was considered a failure by Major

General Raymond G. Lehman, commander of the 93rd Division since May 1943:

I personally watched the battalion closely and gave it quite a bit of time. [...] It was by far the poorest battalion of the nine infantry battalions in the division. It fell down in every respect – administration, housekeeping and training. My colored striker told me that the Negroes did not respect their colored officers, and that they often said to him that they did not want to go into combat as members of the 1st Battalion, 369th Infantry Regiment. Major [...] was incapable of getting compliance with division and regimental orders from the elements of his battalion, of making these orders effective on down through the compagnies and platoons.[24]

General Lehman's analysis of this failure rested on the prejudice, inherited from slavery, that blacks were not effective when commanded by their own: Superiors were said to lack leadership experience and inferiors were deemed unwilling to let other blacks exercise authority over them.[25] Yet, three months was a short amount of time for such a groundbreaking experiment. The difficulty Blackwood experienced in enforcing his authority was never attributed to inadequate training or to a personality unsuited to the position. It was the supposed failings of blacks as members of the same race that were seen as the source of the problem. The diagnosis of failure doomed any other similar experiment and reinforced the prejudice against black officers in matters of authority.

What really inflamed the anger of black officers at Huachuca was their separation from whites during leisure time, as this inscribed the breach of equality within the space of the camp. For the Army, the fact that black and white officers enjoyed the same rank did not entail their social equality outside of training. Yet, while the military hierarchy naturally functioned as a racial filter by mechanically separating black soldiers from white officers, this filter function did not operate at the officer level. In order to reestablish physical separation and inequality between blacks and whites, the Army allocated officers' living and recreation spaces on the basis of race. In some cases, segregation was also implemented in eating spaces. In the southern society that had shaped Colonel Hardy and Major General Hall, blacks and whites eating in the same room was an absolute taboo because it left open the possibility of social intimacy between them.[26]

The most senior black medical officers lived alongside whites on officers' row, an alley of stone houses and trees located along the parade ground at the old post – though with each of the double houses shared by two families of the same skin color. These black officers entertained their friends or colleagues at home on their days off. They also had access to the swimming pool behind the alley, but only on the last day before draining. Indeed, as in the rest of the country since the 1920s, swimming was segregated at Huachuca; whites feared contact with the naked bodies of blacks, whom they saw as carrying contagious diseases or as posing a threat to women.[27]

The rest of the black officers did not live at the old post, whose sturdy and comfortable houses were primarily reserved for their white counterparts. The most senior were lodged in the much more rudimentary wooden buildings of the new cantonment. At Huachuca, the architecture itself was discriminatory. Construction plans for the new cantonment had provided housing for only 636 officers.[28] The arrival of many more men made the housing problem worse. When General Davis came to inspect the camp in July 1942, twenty officers of the 368th Regiment complained that they had to sleep and eat in the buildings of the 25th; as for the officers of the 318th Medical Battalion, they brought up the problem of overcrowding – in some cases, three men had to share a small room.[29] The previous month, a War Department order had mandated black officers and soldiers to evacuate their homes to make room for civilians working on military bases across the country. The order became effective at Huachuca in September 1942: Black officers and soldiers had to leave their lodgings in favor of civilians who happened to be all white – a replacement that the officers interpreted as racial discrimination.[30] Thus, many of the black officers were housed with their families outside the fort, in places where their presence was not welcome and in conditions incompatible with their status and income. Fry offered the advantage of proximity, but the only available housing for them was Quonset huts of dubious comfort and hygiene, which they often had to share with prostitutes.[31] Some of the officers' wives were housed in Benson – a white town located about thirty miles north of the camp, more than an hour's drive away, where no entertainment was available for blacks – first in huts built in the 1930s to house Mexican workers, then in tourist bungalows that had been abandoned during the war.[32] And yet, Benson was notoriously racist: Many cafes and ice cream parlors refused to serve African Americans, even officers.[33]

In some units, black officers were also segregated from their white counterparts during meals. The forty officers of the 368th Regiment who had arrived in July 1942 ate with the white officers of the 25th at first. Soon, however, they were directed to tables reserved for African Americans in a corner of the building. A mess hall was then built for the black officers of the 25th and 368th Regiments, where they were forced to eat their meals. First Lieutenant Vincent Browne of Company D of the 368th, a political science teacher at Howard University in civilian life, refused to obey and boycotted the segregated mess hall by having lunch with his men despite the threat of a court-martial.[34] He wrote several letters to Professor Ralph Bunche – who had collaborated with the Swedish economist Gunnar Myrdal on a famous study of the black condition commissioned by the Carnegie Foundation and published in 1944 under the title *An American Dilemma* – asking for help in obtaining the transfer that would save him from Huachuca's racism. Gradually, these living conditions created strong resentment among black officers. Several of them asked to meet with Inspector Benjamin Davis when he visited the fort; they complained that their quarters were overcrowded, that supplies were insufficient, that the officers' barber would not cut their hair, and so on. As in the other military bases he had inspected, Davis equivocated and considered that the situation of blacks was not so bad.[35]

There was one especially offensive peculiarity at Huachuca that the African-American inspector seemed unable to grasp: a black-only officers' club created on the initiative of the War Department, which had provided funds for its construction and operation.[36] Until then, there had been only one club at the fort: the Lakeside Club, attended both by white officers and by the few black officers present at the fort. However, the number of black officers increased significantly with the arrival of the 93rd Division. In reaction to this, Colonel Edwin Hardy sent a memorandum on June 4, 1942 announcing to all officers that the clubs would now be racially allocated:

Effective as soon as clubs can be put into operation, Officers clubs at Fort Huachuca will be as follows:
 – Lakeside Club (club near pond, 0.5 mile east of Old post), membership: all white officers on duty at Fort Huachuca
 – Mountain View Club, 200 yards southwest of guest house, 25th area cantonment, membership: all colored officers on duty.[37]

The clubs were places where officers, their families, and their friends could relax after training, where they could meet and mingle regardless of rank for a game of cards, a drink, or a show. Thus, in separating black and white officers, the War Department prevented any possibility of informal closeness and understanding between the two groups. It placed a further obstacle to the building of esprit de corps and unified leadership, and made it clear that it did not believe in equality of rank between officers.

The two clubs were supposed to be equally pleasant and friendly, following the classic logic of "separate but equal." Yet, they were located in areas of the fort with very different levels of prestige. The Lakeside Club had been built before the war at the old post, where the command headquarters was based and the white officers lived. It had a man-made lake where one could go boating or fish for trout and bass, as well as a swimming pool exclusively reserved for white officers.

Located less than a mile east of Lakeside toward Fry gate, the more recent Mountain View Club had been constructed in haste. It stood at the southwest end of the new cantonment reserved for black troops, right next to the 25th Regiment's quarters, at the end of a dirt road, across from the athletic field.

Mountain View was oriented toward the mountains and offered breathtaking views. The grounds of the club were bounded by a low stone wall that protected it from the desert and included a garden shaded by arbors and planted with oleanders. Designed to last a short time, the building was relatively simple. There was only one improvement over standard officers' clubs at other camps: the windows with their panoramic views. In the center of the two-story building was a large foyer organized, on the one side, around an imposing brick fireplace and, on the other, around two staircases leading to a long balcony overlooked by Charles White's large painting *Progress of the American Negro*. The first floor was used as a lounge or a dining room furnished with simple armchairs and tables or

3.1: Aerial photo of Mountain View Club (building on the left) and of the 25th Regiment cantonment (on the right) taken in 1956. © Fort Huachuca Museum.

3.2: Mountain View Club at the time of its inauguration. © Fort Huachuca Museum.

else as a ballroom or a conference room. Mountain View, in short, provided only basic comfort. Moreover, unlike Lakeside, it did not have rooms to accommodate guests.[38]

Yet, what was being contested was not so much the architecture of the place as its very existence. Black officers, who had been trained alongside whites at the OCS and performed the same command functions as them during the day, felt insulted by the black officer's club because it consecrated their inferior status in the military. Almost 200 of them returned their Mountain View membership card and demanded to be readmitted to Lakeside. They wrote in large numbers to the black press to denounce the introduction of segregation against them.[39] When Lieutenant Colonel Bousfield arrived on June 14, 1942 to head the black hospital, he was appointed ex officio governor of the club as the highest-ranking black officer at the fort. Convinced that challenging white authority would give arguments to the general staff in support of the thesis that blacks were undisciplined and placed their group interests ahead of the nation's victory, Bousfield demanded that all medical officers working under him resume their membership. But they continued to boycott Mountain View and tried to prevent their colleagues from entering the club. They also sent letters to black newspapers in which they referred to the place as an "uncle Tom's cabin."[40]

The black officers at Huachuca did receive the support of Judge William Hastie, who, on July 1, 1942, sent a letter to the general staff criticizing the creation of the black officers' club: "It is strongly urged that a formal policy be established and announced that wherever colored and white officers are serving with the same organization, no separation of accommodations and facilities shall be made on a racial basis."[41] On this point, as on so many others, Hastie was not heard. In response, the general staff justified the creation of separate clubs by invoking the need to respect local customs:

> As a practical matter, regulation of this problem must be handled in coordination with social customs. For the War Department to attempt the solution by regulation or fiat of a complicated social problem which has perplexed this country for a number of years is bound to produce diversions that may go as far as to affect the full effectiveness of our effort. The intermingling of the races in messing and housing would not only be a variation from well-established policies of the Department, but it does not accord with the existing customs of the country as a whole.[42]

Customs are invoked here in general terms, without reference to the rules that governed racial interactions in Cochise County or in Arizona at the time. For the Army, Huachuca's unique equilibrium between blacks and whites did not call for a departure from the general principles of racial separation, even for men of equal rank in the military hierarchy.

As for General Davis, he was not the ally that the protesting black officers had hoped for; lacking institutional support, their boycott failed. Yet, the African-American inspector did bring the discontent about Mountain View to the attention of his superiors. With General Marshall's approval, he recommended that the War Department cease to reserve facilities for the exclusive use of blacks or whites at camps with a large black garrison: "[T]he disposition and the use of these facilities [should] be left to the decision of the local commanders who are most familiar with the racial problem involved."[43] One can read between the lines that the War Department had made a mistake in instituting racial segregation, and that an arrangement could have been reached at Huachuca without recourse to an explicit racial designation of the two clubs.

By delegating the decision on the use of facilities to local commanders, whose pronouncements were often arbitrary, the Army effectively avoided ruling on a question that was proving highly embarrassing. In the years that followed the opening of Mountain View, the presence of two officers' clubs at Huachuca had to be justified over and over again. When asked about the reasons for this situation during a series of course given to African-American officers in March 1945, Major Hardy repeated that the decision to create a club for black officers lay with the War Department. And he added a new element of justification: the alleged desire of white and black officers to stay among their own during leisure time.[44] Yet, no trace of a demand for segregation on the part of black officers or their families can be found in the archives. Undeniably hampered by the lack of clear policy on the segregation of recreation areas, Hardy devoted much effort to making black social life pleasant. He found an ally in Lieutenant Colonel Midian Bousfield, who also wanted to encourage black officers to reclaim the club and find pride in black social life. As of October 1942, Bousfield wrote to a large number of black personalities – including W. E. B. Du Bois, who at age seventy-five had just published his second autobiography, *Dusk of Dawn*, and was still teaching history and economics at Atlanta University – asking them for signed portraits, which were to be hung at the club as inspiration for black officers.[45] Photographs taken by the Army Signal Corps depict Mountain View as a place where black officers happily went and willingly celebrated important events with friends and family, such as birthdays, wedding receptions complete with cream cakes, and national holidays. Some of the women's testimonies emphasized the possibility of meeting with visiting black artists who, after their performance for the troops was over, would come to relax and have a drink at the Mountain View Club.[46] Less directly affected by segregation, the officers' wives saw the club as a haven from the degrading conditions under which they lived outside the fort. Yet, on every one of General Davis's missions at Huachuca, the segregation of the officers' clubs was denounced as a racial humiliation that had to be ended.

It was only a year later, on August 14, 1943, that the general staff, faced with protests at several camps and the threat of riots, adopted an important directive on recreation areas at military bases hosting black and white troops. From then on, these areas would no longer be explicitly allocated on the basis of race.[47]

In the first period of the Huachuca experiment, the main challenge to the racial status quo was initiated by the highest-ranking African-American officers, who launched collective protests from the very outset. Indeed, black officers were the direct victims of the breach of equality: Although they had undergone the same training as whites in the same integrated schools, they were subject to a discriminatory promotion policy and were segregated from their white counterparts during leisure time.

The racial prejudice of white commanders was revealed by differences in treatment – the rejection of physical proximity with blacks, the refusal to socialize with them, the impossibility of imagining a configuration in which blacks would exercise some form of authority over whites, and the inability to recognize the equality established by training and the attribution of rank. In refusing to build esprit de corps with African-American officers, whites drove black officers to fraternize with black soldiers beyond differences in rank, thereby prompting the development of a closed racial group. As a result, the solidarity of race took precedence over the solidarity of rank. At Fort Huachuca as at other camps, the Army disconnected military hierarchy from racial hierarchy, in accordance with the racial practices prevailing in southern society. White superiority was artificially reestablished to prevent the occurrence of social equality across the color line.

4   A State-of-the-Art All-Black Hospital

Standing shoulder to shoulder, lined up in several dense rows, all black in light-colored clothing – khaki for the men, white for the women; there are perhaps 300 figures in this panoramic view. They form a human barrier in the desert. An expression – the excitement of a new experience, a collective confidence – captured by the lens of a photographer from a neighboring town. An opportunity to show professional and racial pride, and perhaps even patriotism. These men and women left their duties, their patients, and their examination tools to pose on the rocky ground that separates the hospital complex from the gates of the fort. In the distance one can make out Fry and, behind it, the San Pedro Valley. The alignment of bodies reenacts the hierarchy of ranks, functions, and genders. At the top of the flattened pyramid is the highest-ranking African-American officer at the fort, Lieutenant Colonel Midian Bousfield, head of Station Hospital No. 1 – white hair, round glasses, arms joined behind the back.

It is September 1942. The fort's medical staff has just been assembled and the black hospital has recently opened its doors. In June, Bousfield accepted the task entrusted to him by the Surgeon General's Office (SGO): establishing a military hospital for blacks, run by blacks. This decision meant sacrificing the goal of color-blind military medicine that the war might otherwise have helped to realize. For the lieutenant colonel, who comes from the philanthropic circles of Chicago, the demonstration of African-American excellence is worth postponing the fulfillment of that ideal. He has therefore brought together at Huachuca the country's top specialists. They can be seen standing behind him in the second row: DeHaven Hinkson, William Allen, Roscoe Giles, and so on. Leaving behind them a wealthy clientele and a comfortable, middle-class civilian life, these men put aside their hopes of integration to don the uniform and stripes of medical officers. Assisting them are black nurses, who also gave up a status and an unusually high salary in the African-American community. On the photograph, two of them – one smiling, perhaps Captain Mary L. Petty, the other visibly bothered by the sun, Second Lieutenant Olive Bishop – flank Midian Bousfield. They are the female foil to male

4.1: The black hospital medical team, September 17, 1942. © William Allen Collection, Moorland-Spingarn Research Center, Howard University.

authority. The impeccability of the uniforms, the immobility of the poses, and the determination in their eyes convey the seriousness with which the team is preparing itself for the experiment. Together, they will show that white mistrust of black medicine is unfounded.

When construction of the new cantonment began at Huachuca in 1941, a 195-bed hospital made up of 26 buildings was erected southwest of the fort. The twenty-four-bed hospital built in 1885 at the edge of the parade ground had become too small; the buildings, where white doctors had treated white and black patients indiscriminately during the interwar years, were dilapidated and the medical equipment obsolete.[1] After the General Staff decided to assign an all-black division to the fort in December 1941, the construction of a second hospital – reserved for African Americans – was rapidly undertaken. The black hospital was erected on a vast swath of land directly south of the first hospital, which was reserved for whites and renamed Station Hospital No. 2. The two hospitals were connected by a bridge over Avenue B.

At the beginning of 1942, there were 200 station (or post) hospitals in the United States; by June 1943, their number had increased to 425.[2] Placed under the authority of the Service Command, these hospitals were designed to treat members of the local community and limited to relatively easy and banal procedures. In cases of complications, physicians referred patients to the nearest general hospital, which was administered by the SGO. Station Hospital No. 1, with its 670 beds and all-black medical staff, was ready to open at Huachuca in September 1942. Although the black and white hospitals were to operate as independent units, they were both placed under the command of the fort's Surgeon General, Colonel E. B. Maynard, who was already head of the white hospital. Maynard, a white career medical officer born in the South,

A State-of-the-Art All-Black Hospital

4.1: (cont.)

had graduated from the University of Virginia Medical School and joined the Army in 1910. He had served during World War I as surgeon with the First Division – the famous Big Red One – and had since worn the Croix de Guerre with Palm, the Silver Star awarded for gallantry in action, and the Purple Heart adorned with the likeness of General George Washington – decorations earned after twenty-six months of service on the front lines and later in the Army of Occupation in Germany. When he arrived at Huachuca on the eve of the attack on Pearl Harbor, Maynard was tasked with overseeing the construction of the two hospitals.[3] As the fort's Surgeon General, he was responsible for allocating funds and supplies, administering the mess hall, and writing reports. He was also in charge of deciding on the distribution of surgical operations between the two hospitals. According to the order that created Station Hospital No. 1, the facility would treat the soldiers of the 93rd Division and Service Unit 1922 (the unit in charge of administering the post) and the members of the Women's Army Auxiliary Corps, as well as black officers and nurses; the dependents of these groups would be seen in the outpatient clinic. Although skin color was not explicitly mentioned in the order, the designated patients were clearly African-American. All other people at the fort – white people – would be treated at Station Hospital No. 2. The transfer of patients from Station Hospital No. 1 to Station Hospital No. 2 would nevertheless be allowed. In other words, it would be possible for black patients to be treated by white doctors, following a practice that dated back to World War I and was still in force in military hospitals without a black ward.[4] Since the only civilian hospital in the region was located in Bisbee, twenty-five miles away, white civilians working at the fort and in its immediate vicinity would receive care in the outpatient clinic of Hospital No. 2.

The opening of the black hospital was the response of the SGO to African-American physicians' pressing demands to be given the same

4.2: An aerial view of Station Hospital No. 1 (on the left side) and Station Hospital No. 2 (on the right) (1942 or 1943). © Fort Huachuca Museum.

responsibilities as whites in the military. The SGO did not go so far as to integrate black professionals into the Medical and Nurse Corps, as was being requested. But it did entrust them with the care of black patients at an unprecedented level of responsibility and in institutions that they would themselves run.

During their first meeting with the Army Surgeon General, Major General James Magee, on October 14, 1940, the representatives of the National Medical Association (NMA) – an organization representing 5,000 black physicians nationwide that had been created in 1895 in response to the exclusion of African-American physicians from the American Medical Association (AMA) – demanded that African-American professionals have the same access as whites to medical officer positions. They pointed out that during World War I, black doctors had suffered the humiliation of being limited to serving as "regiment medical officers, in other words first aid attendants" and of being barred from working in military hospitals. Magee replied that he was opposed in principle to integrating the Medical Department so long as the Army's racial policy remained in place. About ten days after this meeting, the SGO released a plan for "the utilization of Negro officers, nurses and enlisted men in the Medical Department": "No colored personnel would be called into service until separate black wards would be designated [...] and only where the number of black troops warranted separate facilities." Black wards would be created in the country's two military hospitals where the number of African-American patients was expected to exceed 100: the 25th Station Hospital at Fort Bragg, North Carolina, and the hospital at Camp Livingstone, Louisiana. The two black wards would be run from the outset by African-American doctors, who would care for African-American officers and soldiers in application of the doctrine of "separate but equal." In hospitals without a black ward, African-American soldiers would be treated alongside white soldiers by white doctors.[5] The October 1940 plan thus instituted segregated care in places with high concentrations of black troops in order to reconcile two objectives: offering more positions to black doctors, on the one hand, and preventing them from treating white patients, on the other. The idea was to make room for black physicians without giving in to demands for integration.

Disappointed by the response of the SGO, the NMA, supported by Judge William Hastie, asked for a second meeting with Major Magee. On March 7, 1941, Dr. Vaughn, President of the NMA, Mabel Staupers, Executive Secretary of the National Association of Colored Graduate Nurses (NACGN), and Midian Bousfield, present as Director of the Negro Health Division of the Julius Rosenwald Fund, insisted that black doctors could now treat white patients in civilian life, even in the South, as was the case in Nashville, Tennessee.[6] Moreover, and although this was not brought up at the meeting, black and white doctors worked together in several hospitals of the Old South – for instance, at the John Andrew Clinic of the Tuskegee Institute – and collaborated seamlessly in large city hospitals and teaching hospitals in the North and Midwest; in some cases, black professors even taught medicine to white students.[7] Magee, however, invariably responded:

These lines [between whites and blacks] have been drawn a long time ago – before you and I were born – the problem exists and I don't consider it at all practicable to try to change it. I am quite sure it would be a bad move to so intermingle races that we would have negro doctors treating white patients. The same is true of nurses. [...] A patient voluntarily placing himself under treatment by a doctor is one thing, to establish compulsion is another.[8]

Soon after this second meeting, the Army Surgeon General, who was under constant criticism from the African-American press, proposed to build a black hospital at Huachuca, despite the fact that the NMA had been opposed to this. The General Staff initially rejected the proposal. Yet, when the United States entered the war in December 1941 and it became clear that an entire black division would be coming to train at the fort, the War Department reversed its decision and provided funds for the hospital's construction.[9] In January 1942, the SGO released its "Plan for the Utilization of Colored Medical Department Officers," according to which the "Surgeon General proposes to set up a complete colored medical service with doctors, dentists, nurses and EM [enlisted men]." This service would care for the sick and wounded of the 93rd Division when it would be stationed at Huachuca.[10] A month later, Bousfield was asked to suggest candidates for the future black hospital on the basis of a list of ranks and duties. Then, on the recommendation of Judge William Hastie's office, he was invited by the SGO to head the hospital with the rank of Lieutenant Colonel.[11] Bousfield, who had been one of the strongest advocates of the black hospital movement, accepted the offer without hesitation.

For a long time, medical separatism had been seen as the only possible way of offering work opportunities to black students and providing care to African Americans in a segregated system.[12] Since the 1890s, black professional organizations had been viewed as places where practitioners could demonstrate their expertise, develop strategies of resistance against segregation and racism, assert their dignity, and display a positive group image.[13] Black hospitals – though the racial identity of owners, managers, staff, and patients could in fact vary widely – were established by white municipalities together with black physicians who regarded them as professional opportunities. When, in 1923, the Treasury Department announced the creation of a hospital for black veterans in the South, Robert Moton, Principal of the Tuskegee Institute (which had been created in 1881 by Booker T. Washington and was imbued with the ideals of self-discipline and hard work), and Dr. Plummer, then President of the NMA, made every effort to gain administrative and medical control of the new hospital. They even withstood opposition from local white communities and an uprising organized by the Ku Klux Klan. Their success in the battle for control of the Tuskegee Veterans Hospital was seen as a true victory.[14] In the 1920s and 1930s, the NMA and the National Hospital Association championed black hospitals as the best way to serve the interests of African-American professionals. For the two organizations, it was in this setting that black physicians could demonstrate their abilities and acquire the skills needed in order for them to be accepted in other hospitals. They solicited foundations – chief among them the Julius Rosenwald Fund, created in 1917 by the president of the Sears, Roebuck, and Co. department store chain[15] – for funds to modernize black hospitals. Midian Bousfield, who then headed the Negro Health Division of the Julius Rosenwald Fund, and Peter Marshall Murray, President of the NMA, believed that the support of white institutions was crucial to maintaining high-quality black hospitals. The two men argued that integration was a slow process and that until it was achieved, emphasis should be put on improving the quality of black hospitals and the training of those who practiced in them.[16]

However, not all African-American physicians shared this view. Many of them saw black hospitals as ill-equipped, underfunded, and lagging behind the latest medical developments. They also considered that aid from white philanthropic institutions resulted in excessive white control over black hospitals.[17] According to integrationists, white philanthropy supported some Jim Crow institutions and thus delayed racial equality. As early as the 1930s, the separatist strategy was rejected by some physicians, especially those closest to the NAACP. Dr. Louis T. Wright, a leading advocate of integration, was the most ardent critic of black hospitals and separate medical organizations. Wright was the first African-American physician appointed to Harlem Hospital (where he became chief of surgery) and served as Chairman of the Board of Directors of the NAACP from 1935 to 1952. From these medical and activist positions, he repeatedly condemned black medical institutions as understaffed, underfunded, and ill-equipped.[18] The Manhattan Central Medical Society, which represented black doctors in New York, also championed integration. In 1931, it opposed a proposal by the Julius Rosenwald Fund to build a black hospital in New York in an open letter to its President entitled "Equal Opportunity – No More no Less." It also condemned the Fund for creating "a national hospital program for blacks." And, in August 1932, it attacked the plan to create a second black veterans' hospital in the north of the country in a pamphlet entitled "Identical Care and Treatment by the Federal Government."[19] At the end of the 1930s, the most progressive section of the black medical community rejected separatism.

Yet, in 1942, getting the Army to open a black hospital was still interpreted as a success by some, especially Dr. Bousfield. Born in 1885 in Missouri into a family of barbers, Bousfield had graduated from Northwestern Medical School in Evanston, Illinois, and later from Freedmen's Hospital at Howard University in Washington, DC.[20] He had initially worked at the municipal hospital in Kansas City (Missouri), where he had been one of the first black physicians. Then, in 1912, he had opened his private practice and joined the staff of Provident Hospital in Chicago – the city's first interracial hospital, which later became a black hospital.[21] By the 1930s, he was a physician of national repute and belonged to Chicago's African American elite. He lived in a large house in Hyde Park with his wife Maudelle, the first black woman to graduate from the University of Chicago and the first to become principal of a public high school in the city. The couple entertained their black doctor friends at their home and developed close ties with the city's black businessmen. Thanks to his relations, Bousfield was appointed Medical Director of the black Supreme Life Insurance Company and Chairman of the Public Health Committee of the National Negro Insurance Association. During his two years as President of the NMA (1933–1934), he was considered one of the most active advocates for the interests of African-American patients and physicians. As the Director of the Negro Health Division of the Julius Rosenwald Fund, he devoted much effort to reducing the glaring imbalance in care between blacks and whites – across the country, the number of hospital beds per capita was ten times greater for whites than for African Americans. In addition, Bousfield supported the creation of high-standard specialized medical units in a number of black hospitals, promoted research projects on black health, created training scholarships for African American nurses and doctors, and facilitated the hiring of black nurses in public hospitals of the South by having the Julius Rosenwald Fund pay part of their salaries. Quite naturally, he was one of the personalities in the black medical world who most strongly supported collaboration with white philanthropy.[22] When he addressed white medical associations in the 1930s, he insisted that their support was crucial for the improvement of medical care for blacks, while also reminding them of the need to consult black patients before undertaking any health project that concerned them.[23] In short, in 1942, Bousfield was a moderate. It is understandable why Judge Hastie recommended him to the SGO to head the black hospital at Huachuca: He was experienced and reliable, he had comprehensive knowledge of black medicine in the country, and he was not hostile to separate medicine.

For Bousfield, Station Hospital No. 1 was a professional opportunity that African-American physicians could not afford to miss. In March 1942, he wrote to the member organizations of the NMA:

Except for being a completely segregated unit, it is a victory for the protest against the exclusion of Negro doctors. Much more important, it gives protection to our best physicians in 2 ways: It prevents them from being drafted into the ranks, and gives them great protection by being assigned to a station hospital, which will not be disturbed unless the country is bombed or successfully invaded. The men will likely not see active service with the fighting forces.

The SGO, however, had never given such guarantees.[24] Bousfield was willing to pay the price of segregation to avoid underutilization of black physicians and further frustration over demeaning assignments in the military. As he wrote to W. E. B. Du Bois in October, "there are more highly commissioned Negro officers in this hospital than we have ever had in the Army before."[25]

Some African-American newspapers shared this sense of pride. Although they condemned segregation, they praised the successes of black troops and sought to transform their negative image by emphasizing their patriotism and quality of service.[26] Following the same logic, they presented Station Hospital No. 1 as a major contribution to racial uplift. Thus, the *Chicago Defender* echoed Bousfield's optimism: "For the first time in the history of the United States army, Negro medical professionals will be admitted on the basis of their ability, given adequate rank and the opportunity to do full work in keeping with their training."[27] The *Pittsburgh Courier* praised "the cream of the colored medical profession," which placed the hospital at the level of the best in the country.[28] Dr. John A. Kenney, treasurer of the John A. Andrew Clinical Society (one of the few places where black and white doctors worked together), surgeon at the Tuskegee Institute, and editor of the NMA newspaper since 1916, also saw the hospital at Huachuca as "a stepping stone to that higher prize to which we aspire," an opportunity to demonstrate black physicians' patriotism and ability to run major institutions.[29]

In contrast, Dr. Arthur Vaughn, former president of the NMA, saw the hospital as a betrayal of the goal of racial integration that blacks had pursued since the 1930s.[30] He also considered that the very principle of a black hospital constituted a violation of the compromise reached by the NMA and the SGO at the March 1941 meeting: "At no time during the discussion was the matter of segregated hospitals for Negroes ever brought up. [...] Our organization was the first to insist on integration, not segregation."[31] For its part, the NMA refused to sacrifice the cause of medical integration to satisfy the professional ambitions of a few dozen African-American physicians stationed at Huachuca. At its annual conference in August 1942, it rejected the doctrine of accommodation championed by Bousfield. Likewise, the Manhattan Central Medical Society, which had already opposed the creation of black hospitals in the 1930s, condemned the opening of the "Jim Crow hospital" in Arizona in a telegram addressed to James Magee: "We insist on full integration in all institutions. Only through the abolition of discriminatory practices can the effective force of 14 million American citizens be utilized in the common fight. Especially do we protest the establishment of any jim crow hospital units by the War Department."[32] Bousfield received no applications from New York. The hospital was boycotted by its critics.

The NAACP did not publicly speak out against the black hospital at Huachuca. It was nevertheless opposed to separatism; only a year later it condemned the creation of a new hospital in New York to replace the old Sydenham Hospital – those who supported the project argued that the new hospital would be integrated, but the NAACP feared that it would soon be entirely black.[33] It could be that the association was too busy with the campaign denouncing blood segregation at the American Red Cross.[34] Blood was indeed the focus of civil rights activism in medicine at the time. After a period of exclusion, African Americans had finally been included in the donor program, but in a segregated fashion whereby the collected blood was labeled by race and transfused to a wounded person of the same color as the donor. Until the end of the war, Red Cross leaders and the SGO justified blood segregation by the alleged racial prejudice and preferences of whites; in reality, it was a reflection of their own prejudice.[35] For the NMA and its allies, the black hospital at Huachuca was a bone thrown to black doctors to make them forget their demands for professional integration.

For a hospital built in the middle of the Arizona desert, Station Hospital No. 1 did look good with its eighty-one identical buildings (compared with twenty-six for Station Hospital No. 2) which formed a rhizome-shaped assemblage of one-story pine structures topped with red roofs, aligned in three parallel rows, and joined through exterior corridors. Shortly after the inauguration, Bolden wrote in the *Pittsburgh Courier*,

> I am convinced that there is an opportunity for colored medical officers to make both scientific and military history, because nowhere in this country is there so much concentrated equipment for treatment and research. [...] So do not be surprised if at some future date, this hospital in the Arizona desert becomes known as the "Mayor or Rockefeller Research Center of the War West."[36]

The emphasis was clearly excessive, but the pride was understandable: This was the first time in military history that African-American physicians had been entrusted with the management of a hospital as well equipped as white medical facilities. All distinguished visitors were invited to come and see for themselves the hospital where black soldiers were treated in optimal conditions: the care areas, of course, but also the patients' mess hall, the two-story recreation building, the cinema, the gyms, the library, the solariums, the laundry, the fire station, the morgue, the garages, and so on. A visit to a treatment unit – each organized around a private room and a large thirty-two-bed ward – was a must. The boxer Joe Louis, sporting hero of African Americans and emblematic figure of black patriotism, was photographed by the Army Signal Corps walking through one of the covered corridors connecting the buildings in the company of Bousfield and a group of soldiers. On the photograph, the Lieutenant Colonel can be seen pointing with pride to an extremely large hospital fitted with the latest equipment, where the best African-American specialists in the country have come to practice medicine.

Although hastily built, the black hospital at Huachuca was larger than the largest black civilian hospital at the time, both in number of patients and in surface area. The War Department had allocated $1.6 million for its construction; by comparison, an expenditure of $3 million was needed to build the 1,500-bed Bushnell General Military Hospital (Utah), one of the most modern in the country.[37] The layout of the complex was very similar to that of station hospitals erected at other camps during the same period. The hospital's expansion continued well after its inauguration; in early 1944, it was made up of about 100 buildings and could accommodate 944 patients.

Several services were offered at Station Hospital No. 1: dermatology, urogynecology, surgery, radiology, dentistry, pharmacy, and laboratory analysis. As Bolden wrote in the *Pittsburgh Courier*, "this hospital has the latest in everything. [...] I doubt if it has many rivals in civilian communities." Station Hospital No. 1 had four operating rooms, each fitted with the latest anesthesia equipment (Station Hospital No. 2 had no such equipment), four X-ray units, a plaster room, and a massage room. In the eyes of Bolden and many other visitors, the provision of such high-quality equipment was proof that the Army trusted black doctors and was willing to invest considerable resources to ensure that African-American soldiers were properly treated, even though this was done in a segregated manner.[38] Very few black physicians enjoyed such good working conditions in their civilian practice. In many ways, the Army's decision to equip the black hospital was consistent with the logic that prevailed in the southern states at the time: a dramatic improvement in medical care for blacks in a segregated environment.[39] African-American soldiers benefited both from the construction of the new hospital and from the absence of competition from white soldiers, who would have been the first beneficiaries of the resources invested had they trained at the fort.

The professionalism of the medical team, which was highlighted in numerous articles and photographs in black newspapers, also contributed to the quality of the hospital.[40] The best black doctors in the country had agreed to leave their civilian lives and medical practice to serve at Station Hospital No. 1 and gain recognition from the military. They had been selected by Bousfield with the help of the NMA member organizations, which had circulated the call for applications. The future commander of the black hospital had received 300 applications for 32 medical officer positions and had submitted 65 names to the SGO for the final selection. Excellence, professional recognition, and respectability seem to have been the criteria for what the black press celebrated as a perfect casting. The *Chicago Defender* reporter Enoch Waters praised the team in these terms in his article "*Who's Who* of Negro Medicine Makes Fort Huachuca Hospital 'Best Anywhere.'"[41] With his imposing stature, gray goatee, small round glasses, and fair skin that turned red in the Arizona sun, Lieutenant Colonel Bousfield projected the image of a man who "believes in his job," as Langston Hughes wrote in the *Chicago Defender* in May 1944.[42] On Army Signal Corps photographs, Bousfield never lost his natural authority, such as when he was pictured taking the military salute while climbing the few steps to the Mountain View Club.

4.3: "Lieut.-col. Bousfield climbing the steps to Mountain View Club." © Fort Huachuca Museum.

Almost all of the medical officers at Huachuca came from civilian backgrounds and were acquaintances of Bousfield. Most had lived in large cities of the North – ten in Chicago, nine in Washington, DC – or the South – seven in St. Louis – where professional training and internship for blacks were the best in the country. A good half of them had graduated from Howard Medical School (Washington, DC), Meharry Medical College (Nashville), or the University of Illinois Medical School; since the vast majority of medical schools were closed to blacks at the time, students typically received their training at historically black universities. In the 1930s, there were twice as many applicants as there were internship positions for African-American students each year (approximately 200 applicants for 103 internship positions in 1932); by contrast, the number of internship positions open to whites outnumbered that of applicants.[43] In this context, blacks who did manage to complete their training had to overcome many obstacles – all of them tests of their resilience and determination.

The doctors recruited at Huachuca had previously worked as colleagues in a small number of medical institutions. Twenty of them had practiced at the four best black hospitals in the country – Provident Hospital in Chicago, Freedmen's Hospital at Howard University, Homer G. Philipps Hospital (a nationally renowned institution established in St. Louis in 1937), and Mercy Hospital (founded in 1905 and one of two black hospitals in Philadelphia) – at a time when only 14 of the 129 black medical institutions in the United States met the quality-of-care requirements set by the American College of Surgeons. Five had previously served as director or assistant director in a medical department: Harold Thatcher had been head of dermatology at Provident – he was also considered to be one of the top dermatologists in the country and had a large white patient base in his private practice; Phillip T. Johnson had headed the orthopedics department at Freedmen. Several had held teaching positions at medical schools reserved for black students: Roscoe Giles had been a teacher at Provident, and another four had taught at Freedmen.

These men had trained in the same schools, practiced in the same hospitals, and overcome the same obstacles on their way to excellence. The bonds they formed and their sense of a shared destiny were reinforced by the fact that they all belonged to the black aristocracy of the Northeast. Many of them were of mixed race and probably descended from free men of color who had lived in the large cities of the slave-owning South.[44] Looking at the Army Signal Corps photographs, one can see that many of the medical officers were light-skinned. Midian Bousfield had very pale skin; Hardy reportedly told him that he thought he was seven-eighths white.⁴⁵ Colonel Hugh J. Morgan of the SGO, who visited the hospital in September 1942, wrote in his report to his superiors: "The officer personnel of station hospital 1 were well educated, professionally competent negroes, all of whom represent 'up breeding' by white crossings. I did not see one pure-bred negro officer."⁴⁶

For all these uprooted Northeasterners from privileged backgrounds, adapting to military life in Arizona was difficult. Intermingling made it somewhat easier, and so efforts were made to maintain ties at Huachuca. Bousfield and Julian Blache shared a twin house on officers' row. The specialists from Chicago – Bousfield, Giles, Thatcher, the dentist Renfroe, etc. – socialized outside of work hours along with their wives. Bousfield ensured that the higher-ups stayed connected: He hosted large dinner parties at the officers' club, and on Sundays he invited one of his collaborators to come and listen to classical music at his house. A photograph shows him in the company of a lower-ranking officer, trying to kill boredom, a cigar in his mouth, his dog Nitzi at his feet.

Most of these men had no previous military experience. Like the nurses, they were spared the full military training with physical exercises and weapons handling drills. But they did have to learn military rules and procedures – army protocol, administrative structure, chain of command, health care regulations, and so on. This was insufficient for Inspector Benjamin Davis, who, after his visit to the fort in July 1942, complained to Lieutenant Colonel Bousfield that the civilian doctors had not mastered the fundamental rules and principles of the Army.⁴⁷ At enlistment, these men had been assigned ranks that reflected their civilian experience and training. Bousfield was the highest-ranking officer. His collaborators included majors, captains, and first and second lieutenants – Huachuca's highest-ranking African Americans served in the black hospital. Among the recruited medical officers, only three came from other military hospitals: Lieutenants Everett W. Campbell and Ronald F. Jefferson, previously stationed at Camp Livingston, and Major DeHaven Hinkson, formerly assigned to Fort Bragg and then to Tuskegee, where he had headed the Army's other black hospital (with its twenty-five beds reserved for the black pilots of the 99th Pursuit Squadron and a staff of seven black medical officers and five black nurses).⁴⁸ Captain William E. Allen, who had served as First Lieutenant in the Permanent Army Medical Corps from 1931 on and as surgeon with the 366th Battalion at Fort Devens (Massachusetts), was later assigned to head the X-ray department at Station Hospital No. 1 with the rank of Major.⁴⁹

Major DeHaven Hinkson stood out because of his age, his long military experience, and the central place he occupied in the black bourgeoisie of his hometown, Philadelphia. During World War I, Hinkson had served with the 365th Field Hospital of the 92nd Black Infantry Division before being sent to the Vosges Mountains to accompany the expeditionary force of the 2nd Army. On returning to the United States, he had opened a medical practice on North 40th Street in Philadelphia. There he had treated Charles Barnes, the famous chemist and businessman who had made a fortune from his invention of the antiseptic drug Argyrol. As a reward for curing the millionaire's mysterious pain in the spine, Hinkson had been granted a Barnes Foundation scholarship to study endocrinology and gynecology in Paris and Vienna. This training, which he could not have received in his home country, landed him a position as the first African-American physician at the Philadelphia General Hospital – one of the nation's best – where he was put in charge of surgery and gynecology. In the 1930s, Hinkson had been very active in lobbying the Pennsylvania Assembly for the creation of a black infantry battalion in the state's national guard – Hinkson belonged to a generation that still believed in separatism; yet, his efforts had been unsuccessful. His World War I experience had made him an excellent candidate to head the Tuskegee Army Hospital for black airmen, where he began to serve in April 1941. Hinkson was not only a renowned physician, but also a prominent figure in Philadelphia's high society. As such, he was the first African American to be profiled in the "How America Lives" series of the *Ladies' Home Journal*, the nation's leading women's magazine. An August 1942 article, "Meet the Hinksons," showed him in his beautiful eleven-room house, adorned with a bronze plaque that signaled his practice, along with his wife, two daughters, and singer friends Marian Anderson and Paul Robeson. The newspaper's readers could clearly see who they were dealing with: "Prosperous, educated, well rooted in a community, out of reach of the special pressures south of Mason and Dixon's line, the Hinksons are better off than ninety-nine out of a hundred American colored people." With a nice patient base, a prominent role at the hospital, and two daughters who studied at the nation's top universities, Hinkson could compete with Philly's white elite. He earned $5,000 a year from his private practice, owned a country home in Charlestown (Rhode Island), and went to the theater regularly. With the ongoing war, the major's prior military experience and unabashed patriotism completed this ideal portrait, which was illustrated by a photograph of Hinkson in uniform receiving a visit from his family at Tuskegee.[50] And yet, the major and his family were subject to insidious forms of racism. When he wrote to the Philadelphia Red Cross to ask how his wife could help her country, he received no response. On being transferred from Tuskegee to Huachuca (without a promotion and before Bousfield's arrival), Hinkson realized that he was probably paying the price for his exposure in the press.[51] He had been promised the position of inspector at the black hospital, but his superiors ultimately decided that his work at Tuskegee was not satisfactory enough for them to make good on that promise. Instead, he was offered a position at the outpatient clinic, which in principle should have gone to a young officer. This was a humiliation for this veteran doctor, who had just been celebrated in the press; he complained about it to General Davis, who once again refused to challenge the decision of his superiors and did nothing to correct this injustice.[52] But Hinkson was a true patriot, respectful of the hierarchy; he resigned himself to the position that had been assigned to him.

The patriotic motive was less obvious in the decision of the other physicians to apply for a medical officer position at Huachuca.[53] Their reasons for agreeing to give up a successful career and substantial income from their private practice were often more mundane. The United States' entry into the war meant that they could be drafted at any time, and working in a stateside hospital was a much more engaging prospect than serving as a regiment medical officer overseas. A position at Station Hospital No. 1 also offered the possibility of learning about new cases and acquiring expertise in advanced medical techniques – no small advantage to black physicians who had difficulty updating their skills owing to a lack of positions commensurate with their qualifications. Certainly, the Army's recognition of their professional qualities would add to their credentials once the war was over.

In September 1942, Colonel Hugh J. Morgan suggested that the medical officers at Huachuca "are more interested in furthering their personal and racial aims than they are in the US Army and the war."[54] Bousfield and some of his colleagues made no secret of the fact that they had joined the Army to integrate it from within. Many of the doctors at Huachuca had been very active in the movement for medical integration before the war. The best-known among them was Roscoe Giles, son of a New York reverend, who had served as surgeon at Provident Hospital in Chicago prior to being appointed as head of surgery at Fort Huachuca. Giles had received his medical degree from Cornell University and had landed an internship at Provident after being turned down by Lincoln Hospital in New York. Despite excellent results, he had been unable to find work afterwards. It had taken the intervention of the black alderman Oscar De Priest for him to be appointed as supervisor of the Chicago Health Department and to receive an honorary physician position at Cook County Hospital. Thanks to a grant from the Julius Rosenwald Fund, he had completed his training in Europe and studied trauma surgery in Vienna. In 1915, he had fought for blacks to be accepted as interns at

Bellevue Hospital in New York. Then, in the 1930s, he had campaigned for the AMA, the national organization representing white doctors, to drop the mention "col." (for colored) from its directory. The mention was removed in 1940 as a result of his efforts, and a committee was created in his name to maintain the liaison between the NMA and the AMA.[55] Giles was the first black physician certified by the American Board of Surgery. He also had the reputation of being very popular with his patients, for whom he was available day and night. Another Huachuca doctor who was very involved in the fight for the integration of black staff and patients was Julian O. Blache. A native of Trinidad, Blache had graduated from New York University and then from Howard Medical School, where he had later headed the pathology department. By 1940, he had published several articles on medical integration in the *Journal of the National Medical Association*.[56] He was recruited by Bousfield to head the laboratory department at Huachuca.

Black nurses, who were completely barred from the military during the interwar years, had very different motivations for joining the Army. In her autobiography written in the third person under the pseudonym Hathaway, Prudence Burns Burrel, one of the first nurses to join Station Hospital No. 1, explained her decision to enlist in these terms: "She decided to join the [Army Nurse] Corps to see the world. [...] She had dreams of going to Paris." Burrel did not get to see Paris, but experienced Huachuca instead. She arrived at the fort in late 1942, and "[s]he learned a lot more about segregation than she had ever witnessed in Illinois. She had grown up in an atmosphere of segregated schools, theaters, restaurants, but had never seen signs 'colored only – white only.'"[57] Yet, Burrel did enjoy life at the fort, where she reunited with her brother and her old high school friends while also building new friendships. A native of Mounds (Illinois), she had graduated from the nursing school at General Hospital No. 2 in Kansas City in 1939. She had also studied at the University of Minnesota School of Public Health, paying for her education with a loan from the National Urban League, the organization for the defense of the economic and social rights of African Americans created at the beginning of the century. She had worked as a recruiter for the Red Cross before applying to join the Army. At the very end of World War I, an acute shortage of medical personnel had prompted the Army to accept a small number of black nurses to care for white patients. During the interwar period, however, all applications from black nurses were rejected on the grounds that they lacked proper qualifications. More generally, black nursing graduates had difficulty finding work, and those who did were poorly paid, as African-American nursing schools were considered to offer an inferior level of training. The very strong activism of the NACGN and its Executive Secretary, Mabel Staupers, for whom the fight against discrimination was a priority, was largely unsuccessful in this regard. In June 1942, however, the War Department, under pressure from Staupers, supported by Eleanor Roosevelt, finally agreed to accept a small number of black nurses into the Army Nurse Corps "to care solely for black soldiers in locations dominated by segregated troops." Applications were reviewed by Staupers, who submitted names for approval by the SGO. In total, forty-eight black nurses were recruited, and Burrel was one of them. Behind the romanticism of Burrel's imagined journey, there was indeed a quest for equality.

The recruited nurses, who had worked in the best hospitals in the country, were assigned to the same segregated medical units as black medical officers – at Fort Bragg, Camp Livingston, and Fort Huachuca.[58] Those who came to Station Hospital No. 1 served under Lieutenant Susan Freeman – a graduate of Howard and nurse at Freedmen for twenty years – and then under Lieutenant Mary Petty – a Chicago native and graduate of Freedmen who had served at the Hampton Institute in Virginia, the Seaview Sanatorium in New York, and the black ward at Fort Bragg Hospital. For African-American nurses, being accepted into the military was already a big step forward. Some of them were also happy to be working alongside black doctors rather than under the authority of white men as they had done in civilian life. In 1998, Madine Davis Lane, a 1941 graduate of the Atlanta School of Nursing who had applied twice before being accepted into the Army, recalled her experience as a nurse at Station Hospital No. 1 during the war: "They were all black doctors, and that was my first time working with black doctors (in Atlanta, all our doctors were white, patients black, teachers were white and supervisors were mixed, a white school for white students, a black school for colored across the street – the only classes white and black students had together was public health)."[59] The hospital at Huachuca was a much better professional environment in her eyes. More generally, for African-American nurses, segregation seemed a lesser evil than total exclusion.

Huachuca's black doctors and nurses were assisted by non-commissioned officers (NCOs) and privates, who worked as lab technicians or in the dental and X-ray departments.[60] These men performed routine examinations – blood sampling, blood pressure tests, reflex tests, X-ray examinations, etc. They also distributed medicines to convalescing soldiers in the dispensaries near the barracks, made the first diagnoses, provided light care, and referred patients to the hospital whenever necessary. Half of them had no secondary education, but the other half were overqualified for the duties they were expected to perform. Some of these

4.4: Station Hospital No. 1's nurses in 1943. © William Allen Collection, Moorland-Spingarn Research Center, Howard University.

NCOs were doctoral candidates in medicine, biology, or chemistry who had been assigned to subaltern functions because the Medical Department had not opened enough officer positions for blacks. The *Chicago Defender* reported the case of Private Ernest Anderson, born in Hampton, Virginia, a doctor from Harvard Dental School who had practiced as a dentist in New York for twelve years before returning to Hampton. When he was mobilized in August 1942, he requested a position in a dental department, but was given a job as a dental technician at Station Hospital No. 1. The *Defender* reporter summed up this loss of status in these terms "from PhD to private!" Troye Davis of Rock Hill, South Carolina, suffered a similar downgrading: In civilian life, he had headed the biology department at West Virginia State College; at Huachuca, he worked as a lab technician.[61] With such highly qualified personnel, the quality of care at the black hospital was guaranteed.

In view of their impressive qualifications, the medical staff at Station Hospital No. 1 were given research functions in addition to care functions. Some very innovative experiments were conducted at the black hospital; yet, for each of these, Bousfield had to request approval from his superior, Colonel Maynard. Black Major Roy Brown, an administrative officer in the Medical Department since 1932 and a Huachuca veteran in charge of the office of the fort's Surgeon General (under Maynard's authority), later wrote in his memoirs, "all outside administration, all reports, statistics, and/or requests for funds and that type of thing were made by the commander of the medical division who was the post surgeon."[62] Whenever a dispute arose, Bousfield had no chance of prevailing against this multiply decorated career officer. He did, however, manage to advance many projects by convincing his superior that they would contribute to the fort's reputation. From the very opening of the black hospital, he had wanted the laboratory – where all medical analyses and all chemistry, bacteriology, and clinical biology experiments were performed – to achieve a level of excellence that no other could "ever match."[63] In 1943, Major Hildrus A. Poindexter, an eminent tropical disease specialist and graduate of Harvard and Columbia, spent a few weeks at Station Hospital No. 1 to study malaria's mode of transmission and sensitivity to quinine. The following year, Major Harold Thatcher was selected by the SGO to receive a large number of batches of penicillin, to be used for the treatment of venereal diseases at the fort. Previously, patients had been given Salvarsan, an arsenic derivative, in accordance with the magic-bullet theory developed by the German Paul Ehrlich in 1909. Yet, this drug had serious drawbacks: It was toxic, difficult to administer, and required prolonged treatment. Penicillin production began in 1941 in the United States, and the drug was rapidly introduced in the Army.[64] Bushnell General Hospital was selected by the Army to be the first center to experiment with penicillin on humans. Once the efficacy of the drug had been confirmed, the SGO designated sixteen other hospitals to continue the experiments. Station Hospital No. 1 was placed on the list for two main reasons: Harold Thatcher and the black hospital already had an excellent reputation,[65] and the very high rate of venereal disease at Huachuca (up to one in seven soldiers was infected at some point) would make it possible to test the "wonder drug" on a large scale. In January 1944, Major Thatcher went to Bushnell to study the properties of penicillin and see the first results of the experiments conducted there.[66] On returning to Huachuca, he prescribed the drug to soldiers with gonorrhea, almost all of whom responded favorably.[67] The rate of venereal disease at the fort was gradually reduced.

With his experience as a reformer at the head of the Negro Health Division of the Julius Rosenwald Fund, Bousfield showed great ambition. In the spring of 1943, he fought to establish a teaching and training center at Huachuca, which would be open to all black medical personnel in the

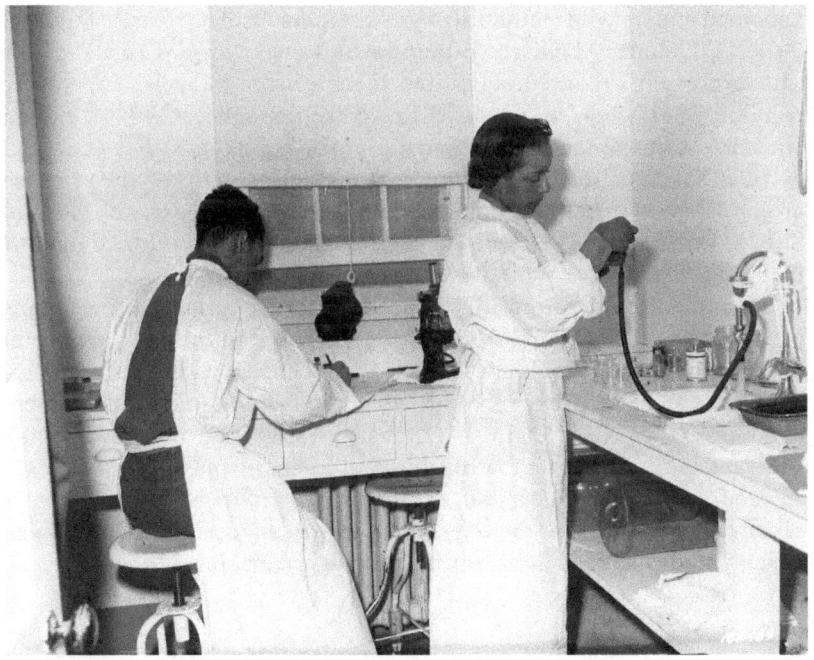

4.5: "The first day of training at the hospital for Waac Thelma R. Johnson." © NARA, Army Signal Corps.

Army and would turn the camp into a center of black excellence in military medicine.[68] Bousfield convinced Hardy that this would be in the fort's best interest; Hardy supported the project and won SGO approval in the fall of 1943. In November, a school of physiotherapy – a very innovative technique in the Army at the time – was opened at the black hospital, where swimming pools and gyms with all kinds of weight-training equipment were already available. Students were trained in hydrotherapy, balneotherapy, and Swedish massage therapy before being sent to field hospitals to treat the wounded. In December, the hospital also instituted a co-ed program for the training of black civilian and military personnel in medical and laboratory techniques. Radiology assistants and then biology and biochemistry technicians were trained with a view to being sent to combat zones. The first class graduated in June 1944 and was assigned to Service Command hospitals.

The two hospitals at Huachuca followed the logic of "separate but equal," with black and white doctors treating patients of their own race in separate facilities. Yet, the separation worked exceptionally in favor of blacks, whose hospital was far superior in terms of size and equipment to the white hospital across the street. Station Hospital No. 1 nevertheless remained under white authority – in the person of the fort's Surgeon General, Colonel Maynard. Bitterness and anger toward this superior who expressed a contempt grounded in feelings of racial superiority regularly surfaced in Bousfield's correspondence with Truman Gibson.[69] On the few Army Signal Corps photographs that show the two men together, the unease born of physical proximity and the pretense of cordiality is palpable – for instance, when Major General William Shedd, Commanding General of the Ninth Service Command at Fort Douglas, visited the fort in 1944.

To gain autonomy from Maynard and Fort Douglas, Bousfield campaigned to have Station Hospital No. 1 upgraded to the rank of general hospital as early as March 1943 – his staff was indeed capable of performing almost all of the procedures available in general hospitals, which were only subject to SGO control.[70] Bousfield also tried to convince the Veterans' Administration that the hospital he commanded could become an excellent veterans' hospital.[71] But neither of these attempts was successful. The Lieutenant Colonel had to devise another, more ambitious strategy to divert the black hospital from its original mission.

5 Fry: City of "Vice"

Concerned about the soldiers' mental equilibrium and general well-being after training, Shirley Graham complained about the insufficient number of women at the camp in a November 1941 letter to Paul McNutt, the director of the Federal Security Agency: "Nothing would so lift the morale of the soldiers of Fort Huachuca, would so quickly stamp out the high percentage of disease, would as quickly find its way into the letters which he writes home as the sight of black girls whom he can aspire to know working in these places. [...] The negro soldier would like to meet girls, clean, independent, intelligent, who share in this work to which he has been called."[1] With these words, Graham painted a picture of the women auxiliaries whose corps would be created by the Army in May 1942. The first Wacs would not arrive at Huachuca until the following December, but in the meantime, there was a singular lack of black women at the fort and in the surrounding areas. Apart from prostitutes and officers' wives, only white women lived on the other side of the gates, some of whom worked on the post. However, according to the unwritten rules of race relations in matters of sexuality – the smaller the distance between blacks and whites, the stricter the segregation – black soldiers were not to approach white women under any circumstances.[2] Thus, to prevent interactions between African-American men and white women outside the fort, the Army kept the soldiers as close as possible to the camp and controlled their leisure time and sexuality. Segregation in the immediate vicinity of the fort seemed to be the only form of spatial organization able to ensure the good health of the men and the non-violation of racial sexual taboos.

The number of places where soldiers could go to relax while on furlough decreased rapidly. Bisbee was declared off-limits to the troops by the fort authorities early on. It was followed by Tucson, in the wake of the "small riot" of June 14, 1942, described by reporter Frank Bolden as a "free-for-all" in the *Pittsburgh Courier*. Around 11 p.m. on a Sunday night, seventy-three Huachuca soldiers had been drinking with civilians on South Meyer Street at the Negro American Legion Hall, known by its patrons as the Dug-out. Two white military police officers (MPs) entered the Hall for a routine inspection and reminded the soldiers that they had to be out of town by midnight because of the curfew in place. The men of Huachuca protested, saying they were in possession of weekend passes. One of the two MPs noticed a soldier slumped at the bar with his shirt unbuttoned and asked him to dress properly. The soldier responded with a blow and a fight broke out. The two MPs left the Dug-out to call for backup from the military police at Davis-Monthan Air Force Base, just outside of Tucson. When Lieutenant McCoy and his men, who had come from the base, tried to enter the Legion Hall, a group of soldiers interfered. One of them, William Curry, hit the lieutenant with a beer bottle and dealt a blow to his companion who had stepped in to help. Meanwhile, the other MPs held the angry crowd back to prevent it from joining the fight. Another call for help was made to the air base and the city police department. Military and civilian police arrived at the scene with sawed-off shotguns and tear gas; they managed to bring under control a situation that could have degenerated and resulted in deaths. Four men were arrested, including two soldiers from Fort Huachuca: Curry was court-martialed for striking Lt. McCoy, and Russell House was tried in a civil court for assault with a weapon.[3] A trivial incident had aggravated the sense of injustice caused by the obligation to cut a furlough short, which was interpreted as the exercise of arbitrary white authority at the expense of the soldiers' freedom. This altercation between the men of Huachuca and the white MPs of the nearby air base was enough to have the former banned from going to Tucson during furlough.

Phoenix, the capital of Arizona, located 185 miles to the north of Huachuca, was then declared off-limits for reasons that did not directly involve the soldiers of Huachuca. In November 1942, the town was the scene of a riot-turned-mutiny, with consequences for all the black troops training in the state. The white population of Phoenix was suspicious of the newly arrived soldiers, as they were not used to living with African Americans. At the time there were only 4,263 blacks in Phoenix out of a population of 65,000[4] – although between 1920 and 1940 the number of blacks had tripled with the arrival of laborers from southern states. Segregation had been enforced since the beginning of the century in restaurants, hotels, swimming pools, buses, public facilities, clubs, schools, hospitals, and even cemeteries; it was later extended to neighborhoods with the gradual introduction of racially restrictive housing covenants. The Great Depression led to a deterioration in the living standards of the African-American community, whose men worked in unskilled jobs and women in domestic service. In addition, the lack of municipal intervention resulted in the degradation of black neighborhoods in the south of the city. These "Nigger towns," as the whites called them, became places of drug use, gambling, and prostitution. The only three restaurants open to blacks listed in the 1940 *Negro Motorist Green Book* were all located in these neighborhoods. Excluded from white society, black Phoenicians had to create their own places of sociability, political organizations, businesses, clinics, and churches. They also opened local branches of the NAACP and the National Urban League to fight their relegation to second-class citizenship.[5]

The numerical balance between blacks and whites shifted when a large number of black troops arrived in Arizona, including the 93rd Division at Huachuca and the 364th Infantry Regiment at Papago Park nine miles from the capital. Phoenix had large training camps in its immediate vicinity, which placed it in the "combat zone." On weekends, the soldiers stationed in the surrounding bases flocked to the capital in search of pleasure or sex. The tension was palpable, and it did not take much for altercations to escalate into violence. Thus, in September 1942, seven black soldiers were killed in an exchange of bullets after a coffee shop owner refused to serve drinks to African-American soldiers.

The riot-turned-mutiny broke out in November during Thanksgiving, which the soldiers were celebrating in the Army that year. As was often the case, the events were triggered by an isolated incident aggravated by a rumor. In the early evening, a black soldier of the 364th Infantry Regiment got into an argument with a young African-American woman he was courting at Mae's Cafe on East Washington Street. Things turned ugly: He hit her on the head with a bottle. An MP from the all-black 733rd Military Police Battalion intervened to calm him down. Drunk and armed with a knife, the soldier resisted. The MP fired a warning shot into the ground, but the bullet ricocheted off the concrete and hit the soldier in the leg. A group of soldiers who had witnessed the scene protested, and a first altercation broke out between them and black MPs. An actual gunfight erupted three-quarters of an hour later at the intersection of Washington Street and 13th Street in the East End Section, one of Phoenix's two black neighborhoods. Soldiers from the 364th Regiment (150 men in total), who had finished the evening in Phoenix and were waiting for the bus to return to Papago Park, saw a jeep filled with armed officers from the 733rd Military Police Battalion stop in front of them. The MPs got out of their vehicle and the men of the 364th broke ranks. A first shot was fired, and the gathering turned into a gunfight with automatic weapons and rifles from the training camp. Three hours of incessant firing ensued.

Between the first shot and the actual gunfight, rumors spread throughout Papago Park. On the bus back to the camp, Pvt. John Sipp reportedly claimed that MPs of the 733rd Battalion had been "shooting on our men." Once at the camp, he encouraged his comrades to return to

Phoenix. According to Private Ollie North's testimony, 200 to 300 soldiers then gathered near the camp to "discuss how 733rd MPs are killing our men." Meanwhile, a man who had been shot in Phoenix was brought back to the camp. This was the event that sparked things off. On the initiative of Captain Joseph Celestine, the men grabbed weapons and ammunition in the company barracks. Shots were fired. Several soldiers took military vehicles and drove to Phoenix with their weapons.[6] The big city was a much better outlet for the frustration and anger that had been building at the camp.

In the city, on-duty MPs from the 777th (white) and 733rd Battalions backed by city police – 100 men in all, including 75 African Americans – stepped in to try to stop the shooting that went off in all directions over a 28-block area. They eventually managed to bring the situation under control. In total 180 people were arrested for questioning, the vast majority of them soldiers. An investigation was conducted by the Ninth Service Command to identify the culprits as well as the source of the weapons that had been used in the city and then hidden after the riots in cars, shacks, or abandoned buildings in the East End Section. A few days later, the victim count was three dead (two black soldiers and one black civilian) and twelve wounded (one white first lieutenant, two white MPs, two black MPs, one white city police officer, one black city police officer, four black soldiers, and one black girl). Brigadier General Benjamin Davis was dispatched to investigate the events, but he said nothing to the press.[7] The judgment of the Phoenix court-martial came down on March 15, 1943. In total fifteen soldiers, including Ollie North, Joseph Sipp, and Joseph Celestine, were convicted of violating Article of War 66, that is, of "mutiny" and incitement to violence. Most were sentenced to fifty years of hard labor. Sipp was sentenced to death. These verdicts were upheld on appeal in California in the spring of 1943. The sentences were extremely harsh: Military justice acted as a disciplinary instrument. An anonymous correspondent from Fort Huachuca wrote a letter to Walter White, the executive secretary of the NAACP, saying that there was nothing surprising about this decision: No black officer had ever sat on a court-martial in the Ninth Service Command, not even at Huachuca, where circumstances had always prevented the participation of blacks who had been considered for the role.[8]

The events of Thanksgiving were described by military justice as a mutiny. To be sure, there had been exchanges of fire at Papago Park, and the men of the 364th Regiment had resisted their commanders' prohibition against taking their companies' weapons and returning to Phoenix. Yet, the violence had occurred mainly in the city, and it had initially involved soldiers before gradually expanding to civilians and city police. The proximity of Papago Park had significantly contributed to the combination of mutiny and gunfight, as the rioters had been able to supply themselves with weapons and ammunition extremely rapidly. The press referred to these events as "the Phoenix riots," using a term that had served to describe many other incidents that had occurred that year. Thus, in January 1942, the Lee Street clashes in the small town of Alexandria, Louisiana, had ended with the death of 12 black soldiers from nearby Camp Claiborne, where 300 men had been training. The violence had been sparked by the arrest, apparently without cause, of a black soldier by a member of a white MP company. The "Little Harlem" neighborhood had exploded. City and state police who had arrived as backup had wielded tear gas, clubs, and weapons to subdue more than 1,000 soldiers and civilians. The War Department later admitted that the police had used violence disproportionately.[9] In March, in Little Rock, Arkansas, a civilian police officer had assisted MPs in striking a black soldier on the head, and the situation had degenerated into a riot. In April, at Fort Dix, New Jersey, an altercation had resulted in the death of two black soldiers and one white MP and in the injury of five African-American soldiers. In most of these cases, tensions stemming from everyday interactions had turned into race riots because of the intervention of the police.

In the "Phoenix riots," however, the racial motive was secondary, if not absent. The shooting had begun with an altercation between a soldier and an MP, both of whom were black, and had turned into a large-scale riot following the spread of a rumor about MPs' harshness – and later abuse – toward the soldiers. Moreover, both blacks and whites were counted among the victims. It was the military justice system that introduced racial inequality in repressing only African Americans. On November 31, 1942, Phoenix's control officer, Colonel Ross Hoyt, decided to follow the example of southwestern cities like Las Vegas in Nevada and Fort Worth in Texas: He declared Arizona's capital city off-limits to Huachuca and Papago Park soldiers, and threatened to make the ban permanent. The mayor of Phoenix raised concerns about the ban because the troops had become a major source of revenue, but to no avail.[10] From December 1942 onwards, the men of the 93rd Division could no longer spend furlough in the state capital.

With Bisbee, Tucson, and Phoenix now off-limits to the Huachuca soldiers, it was in Mexico, a few dozen miles from the fort, that the men could go to relax without the risk of causing a riot.[11] Since the late nineteenth century, the racial order in Mexico had been tolerant and fluid compared with the Jim Crow regime in the North. Thus, for former slaves and their descendants, the country had constituted a refuge or escape, and the border zone had represented a land of opportunity.[12] In 1915, with Prohibition in force in Arizona, "Zonas de Tolerancia" were created in Mexico for Americans in search of alcohol, prostitutes, gambling, or exotic attractions such as cockfights or bullfights. The "districts" of border towns thrived on the regular visits of military personnel stationed at US posts near Mexico.[13] In July 1942, the US consul in Nogales wrote that blacks were welcome in all but two restaurants and dance halls in Sonora; African-American soldiers had become the main source of income for the canteens and brothels.[14] Concerned that the Huachuca soldiers might contract venereal diseases, the Ninth Service Command set up prophylactic stations in Nogales and Naco.[15] The Mexican authorities also implemented preventive measures. Mexican doctors trained in Washington, DC, opened prophylactic stations near brothels and inspected them regularly. Midian Bousfield, who had visited the area, found that the Mexican authorities were much more vigilant than the civilian authorities on the US side of the border.[16] Even so, Nogales and Naco were declared off-limits during infection peaks.

The area to which the soldiers had access in the vicinity of Fort Huachuca was therefore considerably reduced, which instilled in the men a nagging feeling of confinement. Colonel Hardy tried to make this feeling bearable by setting up a prostitution compound and a recreation center at the gates of the fort, which is to say, in civilian territory. Since the opening of the camp, prostitutes had been working in Fry without any regulation. Except during Prohibition, there had always been a brothel in the town. At $3.50 a trick, prostitution became big business for brothel keepers and pimps.[17] In the 1930s, the presence of laborers employed at the fort brought in new women, some of whom probably came from Mexico. These women received clients in trailers and shacks. Many of them married black soldiers or NCOs; as a result, they could not be forced to leave when the commanding general of the 8th Army Corps ordered their deportation. At the beginning of 1942, 200 prostitutes received clients in about 60 shacks or huts lined up next to each other along the road from Fry to Bisbee; the women later worked in trailers and tents. On paydays, soldiers flocked to the sector of Fry adjacent to the fort's gates. There was no running water, no toilets, no garbage collection in this vast slum given over to lawlessness and the pursuit of petty profit, which Colonel McGee referred to as a "racket town." The town had no administration and no elected officials to bring order to the prevailing chaos. McGee became alarmed at the rising rate of venereal diseases among the soldiers. Before the arrival of the 93rd Division, he tried to get the governor to intervene to ensure that Arizona's health and criminal regulations were enforced in Fry and that infected prostitutes were treated in state hospitals.[18] However, neither Cochise County nor Governor Osborn wanted to intervene.

After a visit to Fort Huachuca in September 1942, Colonel Hugh Morgan of the Medical Corps wrote in his report: "The Negro is sexually promiscuous and always will be and if thwarted will become dangerous; therefore one does not make it difficult for negro soldiers to find prostitutes."[19] Morgan thus perpetuated the myth, still prevalent in the military, that black sexuality was debauched, excessive, even dangerous – a myth that fostered a degrading vision of black manhood. When Colonel Hardy met with the residents of Fry in January 1943 to ask for their cooperation in stopping the spread of venereal diseases, he claimed to know blacks well because of his southern background. He said, in a knowing tone, "Sexually a negro is on the same level as an animal. It is his belief that the negro is not responsive to measures designed for physical control and well-being."[20] These stereotypes of the black man as a beastly brute whose uncontrollable sexual appetite could lead him to rape dated back to the Reconstruction period – a time when the South was desperate to keep black men away from white women.[21] As for Colonel E. B. Maynard, the fort's Surgeon General, he wrote in his annual report to the War Department that "the Negro race is more highly sexed than the white race, thus resulting in a greater number of exposures in a given period of time."[22] Maynard had probably read the many surveys conducted in the interwar years that described black neighborhoods as "vice districts."[23] Thus, the three white colonels established a direct link between the so-called hypersexuality of black soldiers and the prevalence of venereal diseases. While the sexual activity of white soldiers was accepted as normal and even desirable for their morale, that of black troops was seen as a threat both to white women and to the men's own health.[24]

Since the turn of the century, medical services had known that African Americans were disproportionately affected by syphilis and gonorrhea, especially in the South. They had blamed this situation on blacks' lifestyle and presumed lack of morality. However, the high infection rates had a lot to do with the fact that black patients were treated in public hospitals, where diagnoses were more difficult to conceal.[25] At the beginning of the New Deal, the fight against venereal diseases had become the federal government's medical priority, and it mainly targeted African Americans. With financial support from the Julius Rosenwald Fund, the Public Health Service (PHS) launched the first campaign against syphilis among black men in the South, which involved the opening of mobile testing and treatment centers in eight southern states.[26] However, the partnership between the PHS and the Rosenwald Fund also resulted in the greatest medical scandal ever to hit African Americans: the Tuskegee experiment launched in 1932, in which 424 black men infected with syphilis were used as unknowing guinea pigs to observe the effects of the disease in the absence of treatment.[27] The Social Security Act of 1935 required southern states to spend 10 percent of their federal funds on syphilis treatments. And, in 1936, the newly appointed Surgeon General of the PHS, Thomas Parran, launched a national campaign to combat the disease, which continued during the war with funding for southern institutions that catered to blacks and whites separately. Special attention was paid to blacks in an ambivalent combination of efforts directed at the most at-risk populations and racist stereotypes.[28]

Despite the mobilization of resources on a new scale, black men were still much more likely to carry venereal diseases at the beginning of the war, as noted by Army doctors during pre-enlistment medical screening. Yet, infected African Americans were far less likely than infected whites to be rejected from the Army. In August 1942, nearly one in three Huachuca soldiers diagnosed with a venereal disease had been ill before being assigned to the fort. The prevalence of venereal diseases later increased owing to unsafe sex. During the first two years of training, the rate of infection was much higher at Huachuca (85‰ per year in June 1942) than in the rest of the Army – although it was lower than the average rate for other black soldiers, which was eight to twelve times higher than that of whites and was rising sharply among troops based in the United States (from 136‰ per year in 1943 to 309‰ in August 1945).[29] This was a constant concern for the fort's commander and doctors. Treatment was considered excessively costly, both in financial terms and in terms of absence from training – between the arrival of the 93rd and late June 1942, 2,643 days were lost and 1,112 prophylactic treatments were given at stations in Douglas, Naco, Nogales, and Fry.[30] The men were forced to attend courses on prevention and were surrounded by posters reminding them of basic preventive measures.

In the first months of training, prostitution at Fort Huachuca was practiced in conditions so degraded and so dangerous to the health of the soldiers that the application of the May Act might have seemed reasonable. This law, passed by Congress in 1941, made it a federal crime to engage in prostitution in areas near military or naval establishments. It also authorized the Secretary of State to prohibit commercial sex work in the vicinity of training facilities when local authorities refused to crack down on it. In practice, commanders tended to allow prostitution because they were convinced that a "real" man needed regular sexual activity. Since they much preferred soldiers to have sex with prostitutes rather than with civilian women – let alone men[31] – they sometimes organized the practice unofficially in the proximity of military bases.[32]

This is what happened at Huachuca, where the prohibition of prostitution carried the additional risk of pushing black soldiers to seek white sexual partners. The forts' commander decided to create right next to the camp a prostitution compound placed under the sanitary and disciplinary control of the Army.[33] Through the control of prostitutes and the provision of immediate care after risky sexual encounters, the Army expanded its reach beyond the limits of the fort.[34] This was a questionable decision given that a March 1941 Army directive had very clearly reaffirmed that "under no circumstances will military personnel or civilian personnel under military control be permitted to make inspections of any character of houses of prostitution."[35] Yet, Colonel Hardy felt that he had to prevent Fry from becoming a "vice town" or a "Negro town" (the two adjectives being used interchangeably), a prospect against which the local press warned local residents.[36] The continued presence of black troops in Cochise County was at stake, as was the soldiers' acceptance of their relegation in an environment that was hostile to them.

Over a period of several days in August 1942, the Army displaced by force all the prostitutes who had been working freely in Fry, along with their shacks and tents. The women had all been examined for possible infections beforehand. Those who were sick were removed by the civilian authorities at the request of the military. The Army then moved the women deemed healthy into a barbed-wire compound in the immediate vicinity of the fort – a triangular piece of land owned by Oliver Fry and located next to North Gate, about a mile south of Fry Gate, the fort's main entrance.

The Hook, as the place came to be called, consisted of a line of small, more or less orderly shacks in which up to 200 women (some of whom were black) sold their sexual services. Two hotels and a betting place belonging to Oliver Fry, where a suspicious crowd gathered after curfew, stood at the tip of the triangle. A water hole was dug in the compound for the women to wash themselves. Military police patrolled the area twenty-four hours a day; they were also put in charge of cleaning up in the absence of intervention by the civilian authorities. Soldiers were allowed to enter the compound only at certain times: from 6:00 p.m. to 9:30 p.m. on weekdays, and from 1:00 p.m. to 10:30 p.m. on Saturdays and Sundays and on the eve of holidays. Entrance to and exit from the area were closely monitored. On the side of the camp, the soldiers had to go through a military police station and then a prophylactic station; they had to go through them again on leaving the compound under threat of court-martial – this being considered necessary because the soldiers saw prophylaxis as complicated and painful. On the other side of the fence, in Fry, the men underwent a medical check-up in an army tent. Those

5.1: "Prostitution Area, Fry," May 5, 1943. 1, Prophylactic station inside the camp; 2, entrance and inspection tent; 3, prostitution area, locally known as "the hook"; 4, Fry Gate; 5, clinic; 6, USO Center; 7, Fry Amusement Center, locally known as the "Greentop"; 10, old prostitution area existing prior to April 1943. © Arizona State Archives.

without symptoms of venereal disease were given four sulfathiazole tablets and an identification card. They had to return the card when they left the zone, after receiving prophylactic treatment.[37] They could then go back to the fort to finish the evening.

From the beginning of 1943 onwards, all prostitutes were registered. In order to be able to work, they had to agree to be fingerprinted and to have their portraits taken. They also had to be able to present identity cards – an extension of a military practice that did not apply to the civilian population. Once the women were registered, the Army could force them to undergo regular medical check-ups. The fort's command took on the functions of moral police; it created a model for regulating prostitution that combined quarantine – a common practice during World War I – and compulsory screening – a method used by the PHS since the 1930s. Hardy was able to convince the residents of Fry that the presence of the Hook on the outskirts of their community was a good thing: This military compound in civilian territory made it possible to confine vice – those who indulged in it and the diseases associated with it – and was therefore acceptable so long as prostitution did not spill over into the rest of the town.

In February 1943, however, an SGO investigation was launched after the Federal Security Agency and representatives of the American Social Hygiene Association filed a complaint to the War Department about the unsanitary conditions prevailing at the fort. The Army could no longer ignore the fact that the May Act was being violated at Huachuca.[38] The Ninth Service Command demanded the end of sanitary and police control of the Hook. In April, an SGO officer in charge of venereal diseases came to Huachuca for an inspection visit, which led him to denounce "vice and corruption at its front door."[39] The infection rate was 63.65‰ in February and rose sharply in the following weeks;[40] Hardy lacked arguments to defend the initiative he had taken against Army directives. Adjutant General Colonel Quigley stated that the fort's commander had committed an "error" by "creating an impression that he was giving official sanction to the existence of prostitution." Hardy, however, was not punished; his misconduct was considered an error of judgment, not a deliberate violation of orders.[41] He also benefited from Benjamin Davis's repeated interventions on his behalf, both in Washington and with the Ninth Service Command; Davis argued in particular that Hardy should be treated leniently, given the specifics of the local situation.[42]

Thus, in the spring of 1943, the fences around the Hook were dismantled, and Hardy was forced to end military control of the zone. The fort's commander then pushed for civilian authorities to exercise this control themselves: He argued that the zone should continue to be monitored so that no pimps, traffickers, or gamblers could enter it and no infected woman could remain within it. Once again, the authorities of Cochise County refused to intervene, citing the lack of funds needed for the crackdown and the difficulty in coordinating civilian and military efforts.[43] In the absence of solutions, the Hook was declared off-limits to the soldiers in August 1943.

The lack of support from county and state authorities remained a persistent problem at Huachuca. The argument that resources were limited likely concealed a fear of intervening on an issue deemed racially sensitive in the extreme. Cochise County and the State of Arizona did accept the presence of the black troops and of the prostitutes who followed in their wake – it is even likely that some residents of Fry benefited economically from it. Yet, the civilian authorities refused to regulate their activities, as this would have required exercising control over them and providing care to them. In December 1943, with the infection rate at 58.7‰,[44] the Army proposed to host a PHS-run treatment station at the Huachuca hospital where infected women would be quarantined and treated – a project conceived by Colonel Thomas Turner, the head of the SGO's Division of Venereal Disease Control. However, the state's Superintendent for Public Health did not follow through with the plan on the grounds that he did not have sufficient staff to provide care, even though Turner was willing to make the medical teams of Fort Huachuca available to the PHS by having the state pay a flat fee for each treated woman.[45]

Once the Hook was declared off-limits, efforts to eradicate venereal diseases were concentrated on the camp. This reorientation followed the decision that the SGO had taken in the spring of 1943 to prioritize education and prevention over repression, after a spike in infection had been observed among black troops. The Army had come to understand that the reason blacks were more affected than whites was not so much because of their hypersexuality but because of their lack of knowledge about hygiene measures and conditions of contamination. In October, the SGO held a conference on "Venereal Disease Control Problems among Colored Troops" in Washington, DC. It then launched a prevention program for blacks that came with reinforced means, including the recruitment of black venereal disease control officers and the building or improvement of equipment at prophylactic stations.[46] The national plan had an impact on the fort, as the soldiers could no longer slip through the cracks of surveillance. The penalties for infected men – deductions from their pay – were lifted to discourage soldiers from evading testing, which they now had to undergo on a monthly basis. Before going on furlough, the soldiers had to repeat the same routine: get a medical check-up, watch a film, and attend a conference reminding them about the risks of contracting diseases during sexual relations with "dubious" women and about the methods of care. James Rucker, who served in a medical battalion of the 92nd Division, saw these classes as a kind of pummeling that reduced soldiers' sexual relations to the mere satisfaction of physiological needs. He regularly confided to his wife that he felt disgusted by the mandatory classes: "Those Saturday morning sex orientation classes which always invariably assume sex relations of soldiers be only relations with diseased, evil prostitutes and as all women being humped together as such ... These haranguing every Saturday only seems a form of advertisement for these brothels, anyway."[47] Before furlough, the soldiers were also reminded of the location of prophylactic stations and were given a kit to use immediately after a sexual encounter.

When they returned to the camp, they had to get another check-up. Elvyn Davidson later recalled that every time he had returned from Mexico, he had received a "shore-arm inspection" and a prophylactic treatment had been injected into his urethra whether or not he had had sex.[48]

In November 1942, Colonel Hardy told the *Pittsburgh Courier* correspondent: "I believe in good, clean, wholesome recreation for soldiers in training."[49] For the fort's commander, the sexual activity of soldiers outside the camp was a major concern because it posed a threat to their health and touched on the taboo of interracial relationships. More broadly, Hardy and the Ninth Service Command worried about the presence of black soldiers outside the fort and about the way they used their free time in a white environment that lay beyond the reach of military rules. They knew that the people of Fry distrusted the Huachuca soldiers. In January 1942, before the arrival of the 93rd Division, three deserters had killed a thirty-year-old cab driver and resident of the town. A civilian court sentenced these men to death by gassing, and they were later executed in Florence prison.[50] These events reinforced Fry residents' prejudice toward the black soldiers.

In this context, Colonel Hardy supported the USO's efforts to open a center for black troops on a piece of land purchased from the Carmichael family near Fry Gate. He believed that the provision of uplifting entertainment by this ecumenical coalition of civilian organizations would help to divert the soldiers' attention from so-called immoral temptations. Shirley Graham, who was in charge of implementing the project, thought that the entertainment would also have a calming function: Benevolent attention and exposure to culture and the arts would make the Huachuca experience more bearable for the soldiers, who doubted the Army's commitment to treating them as equals. With $80,000 from the Federal Security Agency, an imposing building was constructed at the gates of the camp. This "home away from home" – a haven and replica of everyday civilian life guarded day and night by MPs – opened in February 1942. Although the center was located outside the military compound, it was run by the USO in close collaboration with the fort's commander.

Several activities were offered in the large USO building to keep the soldiers from thinking about the war and the frustrations of military life and, incidentally, to turn them away from prostitutes. Shirley Graham feared that the men, who were new to this martial and exclusively masculine world, would be overtaken by idleness or doubt about their virility and place in the Army.[51] This artist and activist for the black cause believed that military service should also be a time for learning and gaining skills that had not been acquired in civilian life. The center therefore offered more or less the same activities as a YMCA: reading in the library, writing letters or listening to the radio in the large room downstairs, sports tournaments, film screenings, etc. Graham designed a genuine cultural program for this remote place in Arizona: exhibitions, conferences, a magazine that issued numerous articles on the edifying lives of key black leaders, plays and musicals in the 1,000-seat auditorium, etc. She hoped that these activities would "inspire these men as to their possibilities," help them "lift up their eyes" and look away from daily humiliations.[52] Indeed, she shared the goal of "racial uplift" with many black intellectuals.[53]

To entertain the soldiers, Graham also invited artists who had agreed to work for Camp Shows Inc. (an independent branch of the USO) for the duration of the conflict. She wanted to introduce the men of the 93rd to forms of entertainment with which they were not familiar. For the most part, the shows presented at the fort were the great all-black hits of the 1930s:[54] Gershwin's opera *Porgy and Bess*; a revival of *Shuffle Along*, the 1921 musical by Noble Sissle that broke from the caricatured imagery of blackface minstrelsy; and *Harlem on Parade*, which was very well received at Huachuca – despite being boycotted at Fort Jackson in South Carolina by 1,000 African-American soldiers on the grounds that it was performed in a segregated setting. Few soldiers of the 93rd had previously had the opportunity to see or hear these great black entertainment stars, who generally performed in large US cities, often in white theaters or clubs where blacks were not welcome. However, the programmers of Camp Shows Inc. took no formal or political risks; they shied away from all forms of artistic radicalism. The shows projected a good image of the United States and of the soldiers who fought in its name. They never questioned the racial status quo; instead, they were meant to appease grievances about segregation.[55]

By highlighting the USO's unique situation in Fry – the isolation, the hostility of the white community – Graham also managed to convince the black entertainment stars who were touring with the Hollywood Victory Committee (an organization composed of patriotic artists from the film industry) to come and perform at Huachuca. These stars were federated into a section called "Negro Talent" and led by actress Hattie McDaniel, the famous Mammy who had won an Oscar in 1940 for playing the faithful maid in *Gone with the Wind*.[56] The men of the 93rd knew these black singers and actors from seeing their photographs in the press; they appreciated their songs, which they had heard on *Jubilee* – an Army radio show that broadcast only black music – while relaxing in the service clubs or the USO center.[57] The Committee's black entertainment stars gave their concerts and shows inside the fort. They met with the soldiers to convince them to purchase war bonds, give them a sense of the importance of their sacrifice for the country, and make them forget the fatigue and frustration of training. In spite of the segregation, black artists enjoyed coming to Fort Huachuca. There they could perform for African-American soldiers the same shows as they did for white troops, but in a form of proximity with their own. They were also certain that they would not suffer the kinds of humiliation – cancellation, lack of housing, etc. – that they experienced elsewhere.

The artists who came to the fort at the invitation of the USO were celebrities who showed impeccable patriotism. Etta Moten, one of the few African-American singers to have performed at the White House and a Broadway great for whom Gershwin had written the role of Bess, gave a concert in January 1942 in the old post theater. Lena Horne, the best-known black artist at the time, visited the camp several times. Horne had begun her career at the age of sixteen as a singer at the Cotton Club in Harlem; she had later been invited by white managers to perform on Broadway and had rapidly moved to Hollywood. She owed much of her success to her light skin, an essential quality in those days for a black actress who wanted to make it in the movies.[58] She first visited Huachuca in September 1942, during a tour organized by the Hollywood Victory Committee for the black cast of the film *Cabin in the Sky*, which was then being shot in Hollywood under the direction of Vincente Minnelli. The adaptation of the 1940 Broadway musical offered new roles to black women – far from the mammies and maids they had played in the past – even as black men were still cast as criminals and buffoons.[59] In total 22,000 people gathered around the open-air stage to watch Lena Horne, Ethel Waters, Louis Armstrong, Eddie "Rochester" Anderson, and the other cast members.[60] The soldiers gave them a standing ovation. The visit left its mark on Army Signal Corps film rolls: On a picture that is unlikely to have been staged, the medical officers sitting next to Colonel Hardy not far from the stage can be seen laughing uncontrollably at what one imagines to be the gags of the performers; behind them, the mass of soldiers seem equally delighted in what looks like a moment of interracial understanding.

Like the USO, the Army wanted to believe that quality entertainment free of political or even reflective content could durably stifle the incipient sense of injustice. The men of the 93rd certainly did enjoy a good show followed by a festive gathering: This was a great diversion from the monotony and frustrations of military life. After the cast of *Cabin in the Sky* left the fort, the picture of the young, light-skinned woman singing behind her microphone was pinned above the beds of many soldiers of the 93rd Division. However, unlike at other military bases, the soldiers lacked

5.2: Spectators at the show put on by the Hollywood Victory Committee for the men of Fort Huachuca, September 6, 1942. © NARA, Army Signal Corps.

a place near the fort where they could relax together, escape the control of the Army, and flee the maternal presence of the USO hostesses, who acted like a form of moral police in their center. Colonel Hardy became aware of this problem early on. In the immediate vicinity of Huachuca, no private recreation or leisure area was open to African Americans. Even before the arrival of the 93rd Infantry Division, drinking establishments had been closed to blacks: The State of Arizona had reinforced segregation in bars near the camp, and Commander McGee had declared all saloons and bars between Fry and Bisbee off-limits to the soldiers.[61] Colonel Hardy had extended the ban to liquor stores, although he had made an exception for the Blue Moon in the Hook.[62] By mutual agreement, the Army and the State of Arizona had reinforced the color line to limit the risk of soldiers getting drunk around white people and to avoid interactions between blacks and whites in recreational spaces, where hostility was generally more intense than elsewhere.

With the cooperation of the superintendent of the Arizona Liquor Licenses and Control department, the Army sought to regulate the illegal market generated by the near-total ban on the sale of alcohol to soldiers. This, however, was a failure. Once again, Hardy opted for a bold solution instead of repression. He decided to open a private recreation center for blacks that would be located outside the fort near the prostitution compound and that would also be under military control.[63] He justified the project by the need to curb vice, lust, and the uncontrolled consumption of alcohol, all of which were regularly highlighted in the local press. Under the guise of moralization and racial pacification, the Army created segregation beyond its territory, with the collaboration of members of a black business bourgeoisie who had benefited economically for decades from the maintenance of the color line. To make the project more palatable, the Army presented the racial assignment of places of recreation and prostitution as a key modality of the cleansing and modernization of Fry. With the support of the Federal Security Agency, the Army would dismantle the slums and shacks to make way for a modern, well-equipped residential town with real streets and an effective sewage system. It would give a more dignified image of what it had generated on its doorstep and therefore of itself. The *Afro-American* faithfully echoed these goals in a November 14, 1942, article entitled "Ft. Huachuca Says Goodbye to Bad Fry." The article, however, overlooked the fact that the centerpiece of this cleansing operation was the *ex nihilo* creation of a form of segregation that no one seemed to be demanding.

In his memoirs, Truman Gibson took credit for the creation of the segregated recreation center, which he defended in retrospect as a means to pacify race relations in the vicinity of the fort.[64] During the implementation of the project, Gibson was assistant to the Civilian Aide to the Secretary of War. A lawyer with degrees in political science and law from the University of Chicago, he had previously served as executive director of the American Negro Exposition, which had been held in the capital of the Midwest in 1940 to commemorate the seventy-fifth anniversary of the emancipation of US slaves and to establish Chicago as the center of the Black Renaissance.[65] He had also worked alongside Judge William Hastie on the 1940 case *Hansberry v. Lee*, in which the Supreme Court had ruled that racially restrictive housing covenants violated the Constitution. In 1941, Hastie took Gibson to the War Department and made him his assistant. When he resigned in January 1943 to protest the Army's racial policy, Gibson took over his position. Yet, rather than challenge the racial status quo within the military, Gibson preferred to make some adjustments to it.

While the real credit for the creation of a recreation center for black troops outside the fort actually goes to Colonel Hardy, the intervention of Judge Hastie's assistant was decisive: In the absence of a black bourgeoisie in Arizona, Gibson convinced African-American businessmen in Chicago to support the project. He was not afraid of being accused of a conflict of interest, since he asked his father Truman Gibson Sr. and his father's partners to invest $75,000 in the construction of the site. These members of Chicago's black bourgeoisie owed their fortunes to the segregation of businesses and services:[66] Gibson Sr. was president of Supreme Liberty Life Insurance Co., a company that had been extremely successful during the interwar period – the total value of its insurance policies was $60 million at the time;[67] Spurgeon J. Morris was a Chicago dentist and probably an acquaintance of Midian Bousfield; R. Black and Earl B. White had made a fortune in the black gambling industry and had a dubious reputation. For the men whom Hardy referred to as "Negro capital," financing the creation of a segregated venue was not problematic, since it could be presented as a patriotic gesture that would allow the Army to continue training African-American soldiers in acceptable conditions.[68]

However, in October 1944, suspicions arose as to the real motives of the businessmen. Had they not taken an interest in the Greentop, as the recreation center came to be called, because the proximity of the fort represented an opportunity to sell insurance to the Huachuca soldiers? Until then, the only life insurance the men had been able buy was that offered by the Army. Yet, the investment decision of the Chicago entrepreneurs coincided with a request by Supreme Life to Colonel Hardy for its sales representatives to be allowed to present their offers to soldiers at the camp. The fort's commander initially refused on the grounds that such solicitation would be a violation of Army rules. Probably fearing that the businessmen would disengage from the project, he suggested opening a company office in Fry where insurance could be offered to soldiers on furlough. A few weeks after the inauguration of the Greentop, Hardy reversed his initial decision and allowed Supreme Life representatives to enter the camp and to present their offers to African-American officers in their mess halls. For two months, starting in August 1943, he even allowed them to sell contracts directly to soldiers inside the camp. Yet, in October 1943, the Army released a circular prohibiting the entry of sales representatives from insurance companies that were not registered in the state where the military base was established – the sale of insurance to soldiers had become an issue at other bases. Supreme Life was therefore banned from Fort Huachuca until it obtained a license from the State of Arizona in April 1944. Hardy then allowed the company's sales representatives to return to the fort, while at the same time denying entry to two other insurance companies. He likely gave preferential treatment to Supreme Life in order to secure its continued participation in the Greentop project.[69]

At the end of 1942, the sincerity of the black businessmen's intentions was not in doubt. The group came from Chicago to visit the camp and its surroundings; it selected a piece of land in Fry that was located behind the USO center on the street starting from Fry Gate. It hired the great architect Paul Revere Williams, who agreed to work without a fee in exchange for a share of future profits. Williams was the best known African-American architect at the time.[70] Based in California, he had benefited greatly from the Los Angeles real estate boom of the 1920s, during which he had built several houses for first-time buyers and then luxurious homes for wealthy clients and Hollywood celebrities. In 1938, *Life* magazine had referred to him as "one of America's most Distinguished Negroes." Shortly before Pearl Harbor, he closed his practice owing to a lack of orders and began to work for the military – he was part of the team that designed the Roosevelt Naval Base in Long Beach, California. The following year, he won the contract for the construction of 125 housing units at Fort Huachuca. The Army felt that it could trust him: He knew the fort and he was black. It was only natural that he would be asked to build the recreation center for African-American soldiers.

In Fry, Williams built a large star-shaped building topped with a flattened green dome – hence the nickname "Greentop." There was hardly anything around, and the nightclub was an attractive place, and not only because of the beer and the dancing waitresses. Drinks were sold at the 120-foot-long bar, which was praised by the black press as one of the longest in the country; around 2,000 soldiers would have to be served there each night. Opposite the bar stood a very large dance hall. There was also a stage where the promoters hoped to attract the great jazz bands of the country. They promised to invite Cab Calloway and Duke Ellington.

To ensure that the soldiers never forgot, despite the beer and the music, that they were in the Army, the African-American investors commissioned William E. Scott to paint a series of eight edifying and patriotic murals. The centerpiece, *New Peace with Victory*, showed a white woman holding up a torch and the olive branch of peace after having set fire to a swastika in the background. On another panel was a huge Uncle Sam who, like an ancient god, overlooked three American soldiers facing the viewer while firing on the enemy. Gibson Sr. and his partners had likely discovered Scott at the 1940 American Negro Exposition in Chicago. Scott had painted twenty-four murals depicting the glory days of African-

5.3: The Greentop in 1943. © Arizona State University.

American history since the abolition of slavery; for instance, the Jubilee Singers performing before Queen Victoria at Fisk University or Marian Anderson singing the national anthem at the Lincoln Memorial. Scott was one of the greatest African-American painters at the time. He had been influenced as much by the impressionist tradition (he had studied in Paris) as by the Harlem Renaissance and the folklore he had discovered in Haiti thanks to a grant from the Julius Rosenwald Fund. He refused to paint only black models and resisted putting his art at the sole service of racial uplift. Although at Huachuca he was working for African-American patrons and producing murals that would be viewed only by African-American soldiers, the black motif was not dominant in his work: there was one black nurse in uniform among the six figures of *New Peace with Victory*; one black man out of three soldiers fighting in the foreground under Uncle Sam's command; a presumably African woman in a scene that seemed to depict the arrival of the US Army in Africa; and no figure at all on the two sections of the globe representing the Euro-African and Asian theaters of operations.

The theme of racial pride was absent from these paintings. Yet, during the same period, Scott did include black themes in a mural he painted for a federal building in Washington, DC. At the time, African-American artists employed by the Works Progress Administration (WPA) were able to use paintings commissioned by the federal government as visual supports to inspire pride in black history, which had been excluded from the official narrative. These paintings were displayed first in places frequented only by African Americans and then gradually in places of federal authority. In 1943, Scott won, ahead of 123 other artists, a national competition launched by the WPA to depict the "contribution of the Negro to the American Nation" inside the Recorder of Deeds building in Washington, DC. His mural showed Frederick Douglass asking Abraham Lincoln to enlist black soldiers in the Union Army, an obvious echo of what was a major goal for African Americans during World War II: demonstrating that they could be as patriotic and as effective as white soldiers.[71]

It was in front of Scott's painting of Uncle Sam rolling up his sleeves that Colonel Hardy, surrounded by Bisbee and Fry's public figures and the fort's highest-ranking white and black officers, gave his speech inaugurating the Greentop in March 1943. There was no longer any doubt about the educational function of these murals which the federal government had been commissioning in large numbers since the beginning of the New Deal. The *Chicago Bee* predicted that the "recreation center" would become the "best ... in the country [...] a pleasure palace."[72] In the presence of Governor Osborn, who had finally responded to the many invitations extended to him by the camp authorities, Hardy gave the blessing of the Army to this black private initiative. The fort's commander had just evaded punishment by his superiors. Indeed, a certain Mr. Lieb from the Office of Defense Health and Welfare, which had been created in September 1941 to meet the needs of national defense, had complained directly to the War Department about the methods of command used by Hardy at the fort. The Inspector General had sent an investigator in early March to examine the conditions under which the Greentop operation had been set up. Although the investigator concluded that Hardy should not have become involved in this commercial project, the Ninth Service Command offered him renewed support.[73] As a result, Hardy was able to inaugurate the Greentop with his head held high and without having to worry about the immediate fate of the recreation center.

At Fort Huachuca, African-American soldiers enjoyed the attention of the most accomplished black bourgeoisie of the time: the capital of some of the wealthiest entrepreneurs, the talent of one of the country's greatest architects, and the art of a man who had been commissioned by the federal government to decorate an official building. The fort's commander also made sure to remove any doubt about the morality of the

5.4: Col. Hardy giving his inauguration speech at the Greentop, in front of Scott's mural *Fighting for Uncle Sam*. © Fort Huachuca Museum.

place. The waitresses working at the bar would have to undergo a medical check-up (the possibility that they might become prostitutes had thus been considered), no alcohol would be served other than beer, and gambling would be prohibited. As the *Pittsburgh Courier* insisted: "Despite the many criticisms and rumors by the inadequately informed, there is no doubt that this recreation center will be an excellent morale builder and NOT a brothel which will prove a great disappointment to those 'gossip mongers' who way say so much and do nothing for the race or for the country."[74]

Military police patrols were organized to prevent prostitution, gambling, and trafficking at the Greentop. However, as in many other cities located near military bases, illicit activities – gambling, prostitution, pimping, hard liquor drinking, drug use, etc. – infiltrated the building and tried to gain a foothold after the closing of the Hook. The presence of an adjoining dormitory for the bar employees and the families of black officers who could not be accommodated at the camp facilitated the development of commercial sex. High-class prostitutes offered their services to officers in the rooms adjoining the Greentop. Some of these activities really did take place, whereas others were mere rumors aimed at discrediting the establishment. In September 1944, after receiving numerous letters denouncing the illegal sale of whiskey and drugs at the fort and inside the Greentop, the FBI referred the matter to the SGO and demanded an investigation. According to the investigator sent to Huachuca by the Inspector General, there were indeed drug and alcohol dealers, pimps, and prostitutes hanging out in the vicinity of the recreation center, but not inside it.[75] The reputation of the Greentop, and therefore that of the Army in charge of running it, were not called into question. The Inspector General protected Colonel Hardy, giving him credit for preventing tensions between the fort and the surrounding white community. In any case, not many people were willing to take over the management of the camp, which from a distance looked like a powder keg.

Faced with the refusal of the civilian authorities to play their role in controlling prostitution and alcohol consumption on the periphery of the camp, the Army took on the functions of moral, judicial, and sanitary police. It devised a new solution that would allow the soldiers to get away from the camp for a few hours without the risk of causing a riot. To neutralize the hostility of the white community and to limit the risk of interracial sex, Colonel Hardy gradually reduced the area to which the men had access outside the fort until they were fixed in its immediate proximity. Taking advantage of the leeway that the Army had given to camp commanders, he projected military authority beyond the limits of the fort, creating segregation *ex nihilo* for the purpose of hosting a prostitution compound and a private recreation center run by the military. The Hook and the Greentop were enclaves for black soldiers located in direct contact with the fort; as such, they resembled military outposts in civilian territory. At the same time as expanding its authority to these enclaves, the Army reinforced the color line beyond its own jurisdiction. The southern commander was unable to devise a regime other than segregation to manage race relations in a civilian context. In his efforts to regulate the men's activities outside the fort, Hardy presented two faces: the first, reserved for the public figures of Fry and Bisbee, was frankly racist; the second was opportunistic and open to dialogue and collaboration with African Americans from the Chicago business community. Insofar as the white community in Fry was concerned, it was willing to tolerate and even benefit from the presence of blacks so long as it did not come into direct contact with them. From the perspective of white order and society, this racial assignment of space worked quite well. Unfortunately, the black soldiers' perspective on the matter is inaudible because of a lack of sources.

6   A "Plantation"?

> Fort Huachuca [...] should be the focal point of every Negro's attention. Here, we shall rise or go down in ignominious defeat. Now is the time – to act! I want to see you and other race leaders; I'd like to lay some facts before Paul McNutt, Walter White, Judge Hastie. Letters won't do. I have a story to tell our audiences wherever they may be gathered [...] I have a story to tell that is vital and important.[1]

So wrote Shirley Graham, shortly after the 93rd Division arrived at Huachuca, in an alarming letter to Percival Prattis, executive editor of the *Pittsburgh Courier*, which had launched the "double victory" campaign four months earlier. At the Fry USO center, where speech was freer than in the military compound, Graham occupied the privileged position of observer and confidante. She listened and shared with her contacts in the black press and the African-American intellectual community what she learned about the camp's racial situation. In her letters, Graham repeatedly stated that she was deeply shocked by the vexations inflicted on the men.[2] Week after week, she recounted that "vital" story of constant humiliation, discrimination, and injustice that recalled the narratives of plantation slavery which some of the men had heard from their parents or grandparents.

Graham believed that she was free to speak out because she was employed by the Young Women's Christian Association – one of the member organizations of the USO coalition – and not by the military. But she was wrong. To silence her, her superiors sought to transfer her to Muskogee, Oklahoma, where the racial situation was far less sensitive. Although Graham resisted by producing letters of support from General Hall, Colonel Hardy, and the commanders of all the companies that formed the 93rd Division, she had to leave the fort on September 18, 1942. She paid a high price for her denunciation of racial injustices. She explained her forced departure to W. E. B. Du Bois in these terms:

I did not leave Fort Huachuca of my own free will. I was literally torn away dispite [sic] the requests, pleas, and even threats of Generals, Commanding Colonels,

USO Citizen Committees throughout the state and finally a petition signed by soldiers representing every company in the 93rd Division! [...] They [the YWCA-USA] ordered me to come into New York for conference. When I got here they coolly informed me that the USO was not interested in some of my activities which were outside the recreational program of USO. They could not consider race problems, etc., etc. It seems that the F.S.A. man out there had written in that I was "using my position as a USO director to influence military and civic affairs" throughout the state. Which was perfectly true [...] not so much as to the "USO position" but as to the influence. [...] No, I didn't want to leave Fort Huachuca. You knew I was getting worthwhile things done out there.[3]

Graham refused to go to Muskogee to work for the organization, which she felt was compromised by its acceptance of segregation. Instead, she took a job at the New York office of the then growing NAACP, where she was entrusted with the task of setting up new branches. She also became an anti-racist activist. In February 1943, she questioned, surely with Huachuca in mind, the Army's racial policy in *Common Sense* magazine: "Is it the intention so to encircle and encompass the Negro by segregation and discrimination that finally we will have a separate and distinct 'nation within a nation'? Even if this were possible, is it desirable – in a Democracy?"[4]

Frank Bolden, the *Pittsburgh Courier* correspondent at Huachuca, was also reduced to silence after saying too much about the fort's racial situation. In early July 1942, he had published the only article about the Tucson riots which had resulted in the arrest of two Huachuca soldiers.[5] In another article published a week later, he had described an episode of violence that had occurred at the fort in late June between soldiers of the 364th Infantry Regiment and black MPs. The article recounted how, on a Sunday evening outside a musical recital attended by 1,500 people, a minor dispute caused by an MP's remark about a soldier's clothing degenerated as a result of the excessive use of force by the military police. Blood was spilled. The court-martial launched an investigation whose conclusions Bolden did not know at the time of writing.[6] The Army criticized the journalist for informing people outside the fort about the violent episode – a sign of dysfunction in the military police – which tainted the image of racial harmony it sought to convey about its training camps. Like all black journalists, Bolden tried to walk a fine line: He wanted to report accurately on what he saw and heard, and in particular on the mistreatment of soldiers, but he also realized that he had to show patriotism in order for his stories and his newspaper to continue being published.

African-American newspapers knew that they were being investigated and monitored by the FBI, and that the Post Office could terminate their mailing privileges at any time. In May 1942, President Roosevelt asked both the Attorney General, Francis Biddle, and the US Postmaster to warn the publishers of major black newspapers that the government might enforce sedition laws against them if they did not moderate their criticism. John Sengstacke, publisher of the *Chicago Defender* since 1940 and founder of the National Newspapers Publishing Association (the umbrella organization of black newspapers), refused to stop publishing articles denouncing discrimination, but he continued to call on African Americans to support the war effort.[7] The two articles Bolden had written from Huachuca were censored in July. Shortly afterwards, the journalist was summoned by the FBI. As a result, he stopped publishing articles on incidents that involved Huachuca soldiers or revealed their unease. He even stopped conveying their complaints for fear that he would be denied access to the fort. However, he did try to evade censorship by getting the black laundresses employed at the fort to take reports typed on bible paper out of the camp.[8] Thus, Graham and Bolden, the two main spokespersons for the Huachuca soldiers, were forced to remain silent, the former by the USO, the latter by the Army. Graham turned to activism to continue denouncing segregation, but she lost contact with the field and the men; Bolden managed to stay in place, but he had to keep quiet. As a result, neither of them was able to report on the cotton-picking project that the Army devised in late 1942 for the black soldiers of Arizona.

Just as the fort's commander was trying to keep the soldiers as close as possible to the camp, the State of Arizona and the War Department considered removing them momentarily by sending them away to pick cotton. For a few weeks, the pursuit of local racial harmony gave way to the search for a solution to a national emergency. Cotton was a crucial raw material for the war effort: It was used to produce uniforms, parachutes, and aircraft tires – the latter being manufactured in Arizona by Goodyear and Rubber & Co. The Secretaries of War and the Navy therefore insisted on cotton being harvested everywhere in the country. However, from the summer of 1942 onwards, Arizona was faced with a severe shortage of labor for the cotton harvest. Since cotton picking was the most difficult job of all, it was typically carried out by poor day laborers; yet, once the war had broken out, these either enlisted in the Army or joined the defense industry, which paid them better and offered them the prospect of social advancement. In view of this, cotton farmers appealed to the governor of Arizona, Sidney Osborn, to help them recruit a workforce that was as cheap as the one they had employed before the war. The recruitment of Mexican workers was initially considered, but the unions objected and recommended paying higher wages to attract American

A "Plantation"?

laborers who had not been drafted.[9] Osborn then consulted with the Farm Security Administration (FSA), the agency set up in 1937 to fight rural poverty. The FSA also advised increasing wages, but its recommendation to pay workers by the hour was rejected by cotton farmers, who preferred to maintain the more advantageous piecework payment.[10] Shortly before the start of the harvest in September 1942, the governor turned to the California War Manpower Commission, which was in charge of allocating manpower among the various sectors of agriculture, industry, and the armed forces; he asked it to set up a volunteer program in Phoenix until workers could be brought in from Mexico or other states.[11] As part of the Victory Farm Volunteers program, all Arizonans – university students, high school students, school children, housewives, soldiers, etc. – were enjoined to show their patriotism by picking cotton. In October alone, 10,000 people volunteered for the cotton harvest, including 120 black soldiers stationed near Phoenix who agreed to devote their day off to the national effort.[12] At the end of October, the US Employment Service, the federal agency created by the New Deal to help the unemployed find work, set up a recruitment program in three states – Oklahoma, Arkansas, and Texas – to find additional cotton pickers for the plantations of Arizona. However, the state's farmers refused to pay the wage of thirty cents an hour required by the US Employment Service. In Texas, where farm labor was also in short supply, cotton farmers resigned themselves to accepting Mexican workers, who had come to the United States in application of the Bracero Program signed with the Mexican government in 1942.[13]

After requisitioning the prisoners incarcerated in Florence prison, Governor Osborn considered recruiting the state's black soldiers for the cotton harvest. Despite their initial reluctance to use troops for civilian duties, the Secretary of War, Henry Stimson, and the Deputy Chief of Staff, Lieutenant General Joseph T. McNarney, agreed in October 1942 to set up a program that would release the men of the 93rd Division from their military duties so that they could take part in the cotton harvest in Pima County, west of Fort Huachuca, and Maricopa County, south of Phoenix. Governor Osborn and Senator Hayden actively supported the program. For the first time, the NAACP reacted violently to a measure that concerned the 93rd Division. The symbolic weight of this decision, which revived old racial stereotypes about African Americans, seemed unbearable. The black organization was also aware that many soldiers resisted the measure. The men of the 93rd Division were outraged that the federal government was considering a replay of traditional southern race relations, with the state in the role of master and the members of the 93rd in the role of slaves. In protest, some of the men of the 369th Infantry

Regiment refused to report for roll call,[14] and several soldiers from the 368th and 25th Infantry Regiments feigned illness or mutilated themselves. They were punished for their insubordination with a few days in the fort's stockade, which came to the attention of Gibson and the NAACP.[15]

Walter White, the NAACP's Executive Secretary, denounced in a letter to Osborn

> the gratuitous insult which is implicit in your request. It is characteristic of uninformed white people to think that the mentality of the majority of Negroes is such that prior to enlistment in the Army they could do nothing but pick cotton [...]. You conspicuously neglected to include in your request that white soldiers stationed in Arizona be assigned as cotton pickers.[16]

The NAACP finally asked the hard questions bluntly: In wartime, were black men really only useful to their country as cotton pickers, that is, in a subordinate and thankless task that reinscribed them in the nation's slave-owning past? Was this difficult job spontaneously assigned to black soldiers because of the alleged experience of their slave ancestors or a knowledge that their commonly southern origins were presumed to give them? Such a measure amounted to reintegrating blacks into the plantation system which their grandparents thought they had managed to escape for good. The insult to African Americans seemed so violent symbolically that the NAACP had to condemn the Army this time.

On February 24, 1943, McNarney presented the program for emergency use of troops on farms in Arizona to the Senate Agriculture Subcommittee.[17] Yet, in a dramatic reversal, the program was cancelled two days later under pressure from African-American organizations and newspapers. The justification offered by Secretary of War Stimson for this reversal was unconvincing: "Further investigation has tended to show that it may not be necessary to call upon the army for help in harvesting the long-staple cotton crop in Arizona [...]. It may be found that what looked like an emergency may not be a sufficient emergency."[18] The Army probably feared that cotton farmers would refuse to pay the required minimum wage of thirty cents an hour. More importantly, it wanted to avoid a racial scandal. Faced with public protests, the federal government backed down. A major crisis was narrowly averted thanks to the decision taken by the FSA at the end of February to send 2,000 cotton pickers to Arizona. The War Department later announced that German and Italian prisoners of war would be mobilized for the next harvest despite the fact that they knew nothing about cotton picking. More global

A "Plantation"?

solutions to the farm labor shortage were considered at the federal level. Thus, a bill providing for a Voluntary War Farm Corps of Youths and Women was introduced in the House of Representatives, and the Commissioner of Education in Washington announced that 500,000 to 600,000 high school students could volunteer for farm work in the spring and summer.

Although a solution to the crisis was found, the War Department's racial prejudice was denounced by those who had been waiting for the slightest mistake to expose it. Thus, in New York, a reporter for the *Amsterdam Star-News* wrote with the frankness of someone who did not need press accreditation:

> That the War Department even considered such a proposition, coming as it does we are inclined to believe, from Southern Negro-haters who want to see black soldiers humiliated, is a stigma that will long remain [...]. Like watermelon eating, bandanna handkerchiefs, banjos, razors jig-dancing, cotton picking is definitely odious to the modern Negro, despite the fact that that form of labor supports to some extent most of the black population of the United States located in the South.

Then, in an openly threatening tone, the reporter recalled that "the principle of slave labor based on black manpower in the cotton fields of the South brought about the Civil War," the most deeply divisive moment in the history of the American nation.[19]

After this affair, which proved challenging for the state, some of the men of the 93rd Division – the exact number is impossible to determine – began to compare the racial regime at Huachuca to the southern plantation of the slavery era. Black soldiers from the South were familiar with slavery, as abolition had occurred only eighty years earlier. Their grandparents had described to them all that they had endured as adults or children on the plantations: complete loss of autonomy, destruction of families, toiling in the cotton fields, abuse, corporal punishment, and deprivation of freedom. Soldiers from the North, with the exception of those whose families had joined the Great Migration of the interwar period (the mass movement of blacks who had left the South to find work in large northern and western cities) probably had a more distant and sketchy knowledge of slavery. For all the soldiers, however, the plantation was the analogy that best accounted for the situation in which they found themselves: The unbearable experience shared by all of their ancestors was still fresh in their memory. The factory, which was sometimes mentioned by soldiers close to the Communist Party, was not familiar to all and was not charged with the same level of racial resentment.

The numerical and power balance between blacks and whites at Fort Huachuca was reminiscent of a plantation. Unlike at other camps, where black and white soldiers lived and trained side by side, only African Americans underwent training at the fort. Thus, although black soldiers represented an overwhelming majority, they were subject to rules that were set and enforced exclusively by whites. As in the southern plantations where slavery had been instituted,[20] a small and dwindling number of whites resided in the noblest and oldest part of the fort and exerted their authority over a mass of blacks who lived in peripheral quarters and performed military and daily tasks following the rules of the Army. This authority was exercised during training and rest periods in forms that ranged from benevolent paternalism to humiliation and from infantilization to subordination.

Like cotton picking, the chores assigned to Huachuca soldiers were routine and grueling and were carried out under a scorching sun in physically demanding conditions. Bismarck Williams, a native of North Carolina who had considered deserting before ending up in the 569th Field Artillery Battalion, recalled in the 1990s that the missions he had been given at the fort – for instance, unloading 450-pound gas cylinders from a truck in the midday sun – and the conditions under which he had been forced to perform them had felt like "plantation work" under the orders of "a typical redneck from Alabama who treated us like we were his slaves." Williams and his comrades responded as they would have done on a plantation or in a factory by slowing down, malingering, or taking unauthorized breaks – strategies of resistance aimed not at overthrowing the system but at self-preservation. On one occasion, they even staged a sit-in, refusing to do overtime when relief failed to arrive.[21] White soldiers also endured their share of drudgery and vexation, and they could also be victims of military arbitrariness. Yet, in the absence of white troops whose fate they could compare with their own, the members of the black divisions interpreted the humiliation primarily through a racial lens.

The plantation motif permeated the entire correspondence of James Rucker, who was transferred from Fort Bragg to Huachuca in the fall of 1943, more than a year after he had been drafted into the Army with five of his brothers. Rucker already had combat experience, but not in a segregated Army. Born into a Christian socialist family, he initially worked for the Civilian Conservation Corps, a relief program that supplied unemployed young men with construction jobs in California from 1933 to 1942. He then volunteered to join the multiracial Abraham Lincoln Brigade in the Spanish Civil War, during which he drove trucks loaded with weapons behind enemy lines. After the defeat of the

A "Plantation"? 129

Republican camp, he returned to Columbus, Ohio, where he became a founding member of the Vanguard League that fought for the integration of public and recreational spaces. He joined the Communist Party and helped one of his brothers get elected as lieutenant governor of the State of Ohio on the party's ticket. He shared his faith in Soviet messianism with Helen Mulnik, a white woman of German origin, to whom he was married by Harlem representative Adam Clayton Powell Jr. during a leave in New York in May 1943. As soon as he arrived at Huachuca, he began writing regularly to Helen, describing to her all that reminded him of the plantation regime:

> November 13, 1943
> Nowadays training has become of second or third place consideration. First place is an emphasis on what is called "control." Like "personnel management" in the Ford Motor co or the plantation overseer system of "control" with a little chain gang. Tradition thrown in slyly. It's very effective how they do it. It's planned "control" and the bond-buyers take it because it's sugar coated over, the nastiest spots. [...] The truth about Jim Crow is that there will be no democratic victory for a Jim Crow army. [...] JC is a relic of slavery existing in the army of a nation that talks democratic thinking to Spain, Argentine and other countries. [...] Why surrender to fascists here, baby them along, and talk tough to fascists elsewhere? That's bullshit!

> November 18, 1943
> This army I am in is Jim Crow from top to bottom. [...] The restrictions, rules, regulations and orders, cease to be military items concerning military discipline. They amount to chain gang concentration camp measures of oppression, carried to a high degree and the JC army has nothing whatsoever in common with a democratic army of national liberation.[22]

Drill or maneuver exercises conducted under the orders of a white commander, which sometimes lasted beyond scheduled hours until late at night and could create a sense of racial humiliation, reminded Rucker of the gang system in which slaves were forced to work at the pace of an assembly line. Unlike forced labor, however, service in the Army was remunerated and came with rest periods. In principle, the Army also prohibited corporal punishment. Yet, at Huachuca, several commanders made no secret of the fact that they sometimes beat their men or had their second-in-command do so: They believed that indiscipline had to be immediately punished in front of the group to deter any further attempts at insubordination. Blows were dealt and jaws were sometimes broken, but commanders were careful not to damage their men too much. Some officers also sent undisciplined soldiers to the desert in the middle of the night and forced them to return to the fort alone.[23] In cases of minor infraction, Article of War 104 authorized company commanders to impose disciplinary sanctions themselves. However, the Army prohibited degrading punishment, and Article 104 permitted only light sanctions – warning, reprimand, temporary suspension of privileges, or imposition of chores such as KP (kitchen patrol) duty.[24] At camps like Huachuca where black troops underwent training, this evidently did not prevent somewhat personal interpretations of Article 104.

Severe sanctions – jail, fines, exclusion, or the death penalty – could be imposed only by a court-martial convened at the request of the division commander. Since there were usually no black officers among the eight to eleven judges who sat at Huachuca,[25] military justice at the fort tended to be harsh on African Americans. Those responsible for the June 1942 riots, which pitted ordinary soldiers against the fort's MPs, experienced this firsthand. On the last Sunday night of the month, twenty-three-year-old Leonard Holmes, with one year of service in Company I of the 368th Infantry Regiment, refused to remove his cap and to fix his tie before entering his regiment's service club when asked to by Curtis Williams, the MP on duty. After a second warning went unheeded, Williams forcibly led Holmes outside. The exchange degenerated into a fight: Williams swung his baton at Holmes, who managed to grab the MP's service weapon, which had fallen out of its holster. The weapon should have been unloaded, as the company's MPs had not received ammunition for several months. Yet, Williams became worried and returned to the club to ask for backup. A second MP, Lazarus Jones, intervened and asked a guard of the 368th Regiment to lend him his loaded weapon. Jones then went out to the large square between the service club and the bowling alley where the two men were standing. He asked Holmes to hand over his weapon. When Holmes refused, Jones fired a warning shot into the ground in his direction. Holmes then drew Williams's gun. To everyone's surprise, the gun was loaded: A shot went off and wounded Jones. Other guards of the 368th stepped in to try to restrain the soldier and protect Jones. Eight rounds were exchanged. Holmes was hit three times: He was wounded in both legs and under the shoulder blades. Two other soldiers sitting in the barracks across Avenue D were hit by stray bullets that pierced the thin wooden walls. The fight only stopped when the ambulance arrived.

An investigation led by Major Frank Davis of the 368th Infantry Regiment was launched three weeks later. It was unable to determine the source of the bullets in the gun used by Holmes. Nor did it validate Jones's claim that he had shot Holmes in self-defense: If Jones had been certain that Williams's gun was unloaded, he would not have felt threatened in the first place. At the court-martial held on August 3, Holmes pleaded self-defense, stating that he had thought the weapon was

A "Plantation"?   131

unloaded; he seemed to be telling the truth since none of the witnesses had seen him load bullets into the gun. The court-martial nevertheless convicted Holmes of shooting Private Jones with "intent to do bodily harm" in violation of Article of War 93. Mitigating circumstances – the injuries he had suffered or the unpremeditated nature of the crime – were not taken into consideration. Holmes was discharged from the Army, lost all his benefits, and was sentenced to two years of forced labor. He was confined in the disciplinary barracks at Fort Leavenworth, Kansas. The punishment was severe. The court-martial had not investigated the source of the bullets. Had it done so, MP Williams might have been punished as well, and a dysfunction might have been identified in the military police of the 368th Regiment.[26]

The first capital punishment to be inflicted by the Army during the war was imposed on a black soldier of Huachuca. In June 1942, James Rowe, a member of Company A of the 318th Engineer Battalion, was tried for stabbing to death a man of the same company, Joseph Shields of New York State. The fight had started with a dispute over a stolen pack of cigarettes. The court-martial convened at the fort unanimously sentenced the young Florida soldier to hanging, a verdict that was upheld by all appellate authorities up to and including President Roosevelt. The hanging, a symbol of the ignominy of the act and the disgrace of the culprit, was carried out on the night of October 17, 1942, in an isolated building of the old post called Hangman's Warehouse.[27] Three months later, Huachuca was the scene of the Army's third hanging of the war. Once again, the accused was a black soldier: Sergeant Jerry Sykes of the 369th Regiment was sentenced to death for stabbing Hazel Craigh, the young wife of a sergeant with whom he had apparently had an affair, at the fort's entrance.[28] Of the first three executions imposed by American court-martials during the war, two concerned black soldiers of Huachuca and the third concerned a white soldier stationed in Melbourne, Australia, who had strangled at least three women in cold blood. As regards capital punishment, the severity of military justice against African Americans at Huachuca was evident.[29] The military authorities' attempt to set an example was probably successful, since no other cases of disputes escalating to homicide occurred at the fort during the war.

Despite the severity of military justice, acts of resistance to segregation and humiliating orders occurred at Huachuca as early as late 1942. As we have seen, these acts recalled some of the mechanisms at work on plantations. In the antebellum period, slaves expressed their opposition – if they had the courage to do so – mainly through indirect individual actions (silent sabotage, malingering, fleeing) rather than through attempts to overthrow the system.[30] The same type of response to military segregation was observed at Huachuca, as the date approached for the soldiers of the 93rd Division to leave for maneuvers.[31] The local press reported two acts of passive resistance: In February 1943, James Bryant was stopped in Tucson as he was looking for work to feed himself; in March, Floyd Jenkins, who had been AWOL for several weeks, was arrested in Tucson for parking a stolen car on the wrong side of the street while wearing a civilian outfit he had borrowed from a friend. At around the same time, a confidential memo between high-level officials expressed concern about the spread of indiscipline and the number of desertion cases, most of which were punished by court-martial.[32] As on a plantation, however, rebellion was limited in both form and intensity.

At Huachuca, it was mainly African-American officers who resisted orders or decisions perceived as unjust or discriminatory: These men viewed racial humiliation as a challenge to their military status. As officers, they were also relatively protected by the Articles of War in case of misconduct, even though the protective clauses were not always applied. It was therefore the best educated and the most secure in civilian life who organized boycotts of eating and recreation places and who challenged unjust judicial decisions. It was also officers who wrote letters asking for outside help – from influential allies in the War Department (Judge Hastie and, to a lesser extent, Truman Gibson, Lieutenant Colonel Bousfield's regular correspondent), academia (W. E. B. Du Bois, Horace Cayton, and Ralph Bunch), African-American organizations (Walter White and Louis Wright of the NAACP, Mary McLeod Bethune, and Mabel Staupers), or the black press (*The Pittsburgh Courier*, *The Chicago Defender*, and *The Afro-American*).[33] In their letters to these allies – all of whom were black and none of whom was in the military (Brigadier General Davis was never considered a potential supporter) – second lieutenants and above described the abuses they had witnessed, hoping that the Army would intervene or that public outrage would be so strong that the local situation would have to be corrected. They did not always obtain the support they sought, because intellectuals and activist organizations had an agenda that did not necessarily overlap with the more concrete concerns of the soldiers; thus, in medical matters, the NAACP was more concerned with fighting the segregation of blood plasma than combating segregated care. Yet, the soldiers and officers of Huachuca were not alone. Some realized this whenever a letter from a concerned mother or father resulted in the provision of legal assistance by the NAACP or the payment of legal fees for the defense of an unjustly punished son – for instance, Private Ollie North, who was convicted after the Phoenix riots of December 1942[34] – or prompted a transfer to another unit. Even though the fort was in a remote location, it was not as politically isolated as a plantation. Far

A "Plantation"?

more powerful forms of support and control existed outside the fort, such that the black experience in a segregated military context was not exclusively one of humiliation and repression.

Despite differences between the economic and racial system of slavery in the antebellum South and segregated military training in Arizona, Fort Huachuca was characterized from late 1942 onwards by confinement, arbitrary discipline, and racial injustice, which many soldiers and officers associated with the plantation that had existed more than eighty years earlier. The loss of autonomy, the separation from family, the outdoor work typical of military training, the perpetuation of violence, and the persistent indignities and inequities of segregation – even as enlistment was supposed to bring full recognition of black citizenship – were all manifestations of what can be called the "afterlife of slavery."[35] The postwar literature took up and popularized this analysis. In 1944, Chaplain Grant Reynolds, a former reverend of Mount Zion Congregational Temple in Cleveland and an ex-activist of the NAACP whose local branch he had directed before volunteering for the Army and landing at Fort Huachuca in 1943, argued in one of the four articles he published in the NAACP magazine *The Crisis* to denounce the Army's racial policy that the comparison made by the men between the military experience and the plantation was relevant.[36] Likewise, Irma Cayton, a second officer in the 32nd Company of the Women's Army Auxiliary Corps, emphasized the power of the nickname "the plantation" in the ten or so unpublished pages in which she described her experience at the fort; she considered that the nickname given to Fort Huachuca by the soldiers was justified given the racial prejudice that informed the way Hardy commanded the camp.[37] Nelson Peery, a soldier of the 1st Battalion of the 369th Infantry Regiment, also took up the analogy in his rather successful autobiography, *Black Fire: The Making of an American Revolutionary*, published in 1995. These men and women were not so much interested in the accuracy of the comparison as in its evocative and mobilizing power, its capacity to arouse indignation and public condemnation of a racial situation that was clearly unjust, though not yet explosive. In 1942–1943, anger and opposition were still expressed in words at Fort Huachuca. If we are to believe the outbursts transmitted to us via letters, testimonies, and the few Huachuca military justice files that can be consulted today, acts of rebellion were limited in number and intensity, as there was not yet a collective movement of resistance at the camp.[38]

7   Respectable Women

On December 7, 1942, five photographers from the Signal Corps and one from the *Pittsburgh Courier* were present at Fort Huachuca. They had come to record the ceremony organized by the fort's commander to welcome the first two companies of black Waacs. Their photographs revealed a tightly choreographed ceremony. The women soldiers got off the train that had brought them to Huachuca from the southwest of the country. Despite the long journey and the heat, they emerged from the cars in crisp, starched uniforms: fitted jacket, knee-length skirt, white stockings, cap with Pallas Athena insignia, bag slung over the left shoulder. Under the authority of their commander, Frances Alexander, they carried suitcases containing their army uniforms and the personal effects they had been encouraged to bring with them as a trousseau – brushes, make-up, curling iron, powder, hairnets, manicure set, etc. They smiled, happy to arrive at the first training camp to welcome black Waacs. They were proud to be pioneers.

As soon as the women were off the train, the companies assembled. The Waacs crossed the camp in review order, walking confidently in rows of three behind their commanders Corrie Sherard and Vera Harrison. The soldiers of the 93rd Division had gathered closely to watch them: Apart from the nurses and the few female civilians who worked at the fort, this was the first time they saw women in the military. Exceptionally, they had been granted a day off to witness the spectacle. Intrigued, they wondered whether these women had come to relieve them of non-combat duties, as the Women's Army Auxiliary Corps (WAAC) assured them, or whether they would become their friends or sexual partners, as they might secretly have hoped. Off camera, several men had climbed on the roofs of the barracks to get a better view; they whistled, booed, and shouted. Fear may have lurked behind this harassment. Would the Waacs strip them of the duties that had so far enabled them to avoid the most arduous tasks? Would the traditional division of gender roles be challenged at the camp? In a poem she wrote while stationed at Huachuca, Lucia Pitts, a Waac employed in the Military Police Office, imagined the thoughts of a soldier who feared the arrival of women in the military:

> You did not really want us here.
> "Women have no place in the Army," you said,
> "Women should stay at home and keep the home-fires burning.
> We want to think of you as sitting and waiting
> For us to come back,
> Dressed in the flimsy gowns which were yours alone
> And which we remember sentimentally;
> Not in uniforms like thousands and thousands of others
> And much like our own.
> We want to dream of you
> As lying down to your rest at night,
> Looking up at the stars and the moon above us all
> And saying a prayer for us."
> Others said, "You were cruel to come in
> And push us out to the firing line . . .
> Do you know that you are sending us to our death?"[1]

7.1: Waacs marching from train to Fort Huachuca, December 7, 1942.
© US Army Women's Museum, Army Signal Corps.

After a while, the 300 women in formation turned back toward the camp entrance, to the right of Fry Gate, where their barracks awaited. Their martial pace echoed their poise and self-mastery, the discipline they had agreed to impose on their bodies during training. One soldier who had witnessed the scene told the *Pittsburgh Courier* reporter: "Huachuca is really on some time; how these women can soldier! Look at 'em march and they don't crack a smile in ranks."[2] Yet, the black Waacs had not renounced their femininity – their hair was pulled back under their hats, their faces were made up, and their olive-green uniforms decorated with gold braid were tight-fitting. They did not look like viragos or transvestites, as the WAAC's opponents claimed. Nothing about them seemed to subvert the image of femininity held by the Army and society at the time.

Lastly, Colonel Hardy delivered a long speech of welcome in front of the new women's quarters, at the edge of the low stone wall marking the boundary between male and female spaces. After the present arms and the salute, the two companies separated into columns and then crossed the low wall so as to stand symbolically on the female side. The commander addressed the Waacs and the men through his microphone, his voice amplified by loudspeakers:

> It is not usual in military activities to give such ceremony, but in your case I feel justified in doing something out of the ordinary. First because you are women and it seems to be in the nature of things that we just naturally pay more attention to women than we do to men. And secondly you are making history. You represent the venture of our government in putting the women of American into uniform as a part of our armed forces. [...] I have the highest confidence in the high standards you will set here for the WAACs. [...] I would say to you: "Consider yourselves brothers and sisters in arms."[3]

The events at Huachuca were unprecedented: For the first time in its history, the Army welcomed at the fort a company of women, black women at that, just as it had welcomed the first black division a few months earlier. Yet, Colonel Hardy was adamant: This break in the Army's racial history did not herald a break in its perception of women. His paternalistic courtliness was evidence that women should remain in their place. On discovering the interior of the barracks, the members of the 32nd and 33rd Companies realized that special treatment had been reserved for them. They found several bathtubs instead of showers, a beauty salon in place of a barber shop. The decoration of the lounges reminded them of the interiors of middle-class houses. There was little to distinguish their new, military life from the civilian life that they had left behind – the only exception being the exclusion of men, which made the barracks look like a female boarding school. Instead of fathers, husbands, and brothers, the person in charge was light-skinned Captain Frances Alexander. She was tasked with enforcing WAAC and Army rules.

In staging the women's arrival at Huachuca, Colonel Hardy sought to dispel the fears of those sections of the Army and society that had opposed the creation of the WAAC in May 1942. The female volunteers, who had been recruited in order to enable soldiers to devote themselves fully to training or combat, were assigned non-combat duties and were expected to facilitate the bureaucratization of the Army. They were not allowed to bear arms. Until July 1943, the Waacs did not have access to the same ranks as men, they were not subject to the same authority, and they did not enjoy the same benefits. When the WAAC was transformed into the Women's Army Corps (WAC), the women were finally considered to be full-fledged soldiers. In the meantime, however, the Army had to reassure skeptics, who felt that placing women in a masculine combat environment posed a threat to the "natural order" of the family and the traditional division of gender roles in American society. To gain acceptance for their enlistment in the Army, the WAAC administration built the image of the irreproachable "woman soldier" who embodied patriotism and courage and did not challenge military rules or contemporary definitions of the "masculine" and the "feminine."[4]

To further reassure public opinion, the WAAC was segregated. This was quite a setback for African Americans, especially since there was no tradition of employing women in the military and the WAAC recruited only volunteers, which should have facilitated the integration of this female army. Having lost this battle, African-American activists redirected their efforts to monitoring the conditions of military training. In the WAAC, as in other army corps, African-American recruits were supposed to represent 10 percent of the soldiers. Yet, activist organizations immediately cast doubt on the willingness of Colonel Oveta Culp Hobby, the WAAC commander and southern wife of the governor of Texas, to apply the quota. They asked Secretary of War Henry L. Stimson to have Hobby assisted by Mary McLeod Bethune, founder and president of Bethune-Cookman College in Daytona Beach, Florida. Bethune was a former member of the President's black cabinet, a close friend of Eleanor Roosevelt, and the current director of the Black Affairs Division of the National Youth Administration, the agency in charge of helping young people back into employment. Colonel Hobby resisted having Bethune as her permanent assistant, but consulted with her informally on several occasions. A great female figure and advocate of "accomodationism," Bethune cooperated every single time. Despite the presence of segregation in the WAAC, she saw the corps as an opportunity for the advancement of black women.[5]

Like the rest of the Army, the WAAC effectively ignored the 10 percent quota. In early 1943, black women represented only 5 percent of the corps.[6] For officers, the proportion was even lower: 2.5 percent in February 1943.[7] Colonel Hobby cited recruitment difficulties that persisted despite the recruitment campaigns aimed at black women.[8] In reality, many obstacles discouraged these women from enlisting. And these barriers were racial, not professional – black women's participation in the workforce was very common (according to the 1940 census, 37.8 percent of African-American women over the age of fourteen were employed, compared with 24.1 percent of white women) and was not seen as tarnishing their reputation by the black community. Dovey Roundtree, a protégée of Mary McLeod Bethune, recalled that in southern cities (e.g., Atlanta, Augusta, or Greenboro), black women were dissuaded, more or less insidiously, from filling out an application form.[9] Sometimes, they preferred not to apply, as they anticipated rejection by the local recruitment board, which was made up of one army officer and two well-established women from the community, all of them white.[10] Numerous discrimination complaints were sent to Bethune; these were strikingly similar to those sent to Mabel Staupers by black nurses who had been turned down by the Army Nurse Corps. In view of this, Bethune recommended that black female recruiters tour African-American campuses and that the first black female officers be given recruitment duties. The Army listened to her. Judy McKinnon, who began to serve at Huachuca in 1943, described the strong impression left on her at the post office by "these Waacs all dressed in those glamorous uniforms, and I went over and talked to them. [...] Oh, they painted a beautiful picture for you of everything. They didn't tell you about the days you had to do KP [kitchen patrol], mop floors, clean latrines. No, they didn't tell you about those days."[11]

A total of 36 black women out of 4,000 applicants were recruited, alongside 790 white women, for the first WAAC officer training class at Fort Des Moines Army Officer Training School. The selection process was drastic. In a statement to the African-American press, Hobby congratulated the recruits on their outstanding achievements:

As I studied their applications, I was impressed by their integrity and their devotion to their country, and I was moved by the intensity of their desire to serve the country. [...] Though a high school education is the minimum requirement for officer training, 75% of the successful applicants have college backgrounds, and the majority of them received degrees from Tuskegee, Wilberforce Ohio, Prairie View, Fisk university.[12]

The selected applications gave a very flattering image of the black Waac. Her education, integration into the community, and embrace of bourgeois norms of sociability made her an irreproachable woman in the eyes of the Army. This was the case of Lieutenant Geneva Ferguson, a former elementary school teacher from Loveland, Ohio, who, at the age of twenty-two, was the first black woman to become a WAAC officer. Many of these women were from the North and, therefore, had never faced segregation before. They were shocked to experience it at Fort Des Moines, in Iowa, a state where it was officially illegal. At the school, black women were assigned to separate companies. They ate, relaxed, and slept in separate buildings.[13] Classes were held on the same premises, but the Waacs were divided in the classrooms on the basis of their skin color, a separation justified by the Army on the grounds that the women were studying in platoons that were themselves organized by skin color. As early as the summer of 1942, the black press denounced the discrimination and humiliation at Fort Des Moines, according to information supplied by the candidates.[14] One of their main sources was Irma Cayton, a member of the first class, who would later be stationed at Huachuca. In her memoirs, Cayton describes how she engaged in an act of insubordination:

During our training course, I busied myself to let the outside know the ridiculous and humiliating experience we face despite the fact that we had volunteered to serve our country. We were assigned to a separate barrack, same my father had been assigned to in World War I. Dining hall entrances were marked colored and white. Tables marked "reserved" making sure whites and colored did not mix. Exposure of this treatment was easy for me as my husband [Horace Cayton] was on the staff of the *Pittsburgh Courier* and had many connections. [Walter] White soon began to visit the camp and articles appeared in various papers regarding this situation. Washington HQ (WAC) soon became disturbed and sent Mrs Mary McLeod Bethune to visit us. [...] I was the only one who spoke up against our treatment only to be advised by Mrs Bethune that she found our treatment to be separate but equal and we should be pleased.

Following this denunciation, Cayton was sidelined at the WAAC headquarters in Washington:

When I arrived it was obvious that some considered me an enemy even before I even arrived. There was no work for us to do. [...] Days went by and I asked the Lt-Colonel in charge if we were ever going to have to work. In his opinion I had been declared a traitor because stories regarding WAAC segregation had been traced to me.[15]

The black press had never been so critical of the discriminatory treatment of African Americans in the military. The NAACP, to which many

WAAC officer-candidates were close, was also heavily involved in this denunciation campaign. Their sources were reliable and could not be suspected of exaggeration: These women from the black intelligentsia were highly educated and were often members of the association. They also had numerous contacts among those Horace Cayton referred to as "race men," those loyal members of the community who devoted their lives to improving the African-American condition and to fostering black pride, consciousness, and solidarity.[16] Above all, it seemed shocking that hand-picked, respectable women who had volunteered for the Army should be segregated when black men benefited from integrated officer training. The WAAC command, which was very disturbed by these denunciations, dispatched Mary McLeod Bethune to see the reality on the ground. The black educator tried to moderate the criticism expressed by the black press. She did not object to the principle of separate training so long as standards were the same for blacks and whites; she was willing to tolerate segregation if it allowed social distinction for the most qualified women in the group. When asked to justify the racial regulations in place, the commander of Fort Des Moines, Colonel Don Faith, vouched that the same opportunities and conditions were rigorously offered to black and white women. The "separate but equal" doctrine he defended in front of his superiors still seemed acceptable to him, even though Iowa state law explicitly prohibited segregation.[17] The racist military order was thus superimposed on civil law. Numerous complaints about segregation at Fort des Moines continued to make their way to the NAACP and to African-American newspapers, mainly through Waacs on furlough in Washington or with contacts in the black press.[18]

Once the black Waacs had completed training, the Army had to find them positions. With the exception of Colonel Hardy, who welcomed them to Huachuca with great fanfare, white commanders were reluctant to accept them in the camps under their authority, even when African-American soldiers were already serving there. At the beginning of 1943, several white commanders reported hostile reactions in their command zones, where white communities demanded that the WAAC stop accepting black candidates. Indeed, across the country, there were signs of growing resistance to the physical proximity that had begun to develop between whites and blacks – men and women alike – in workshops, factories, and public spaces following the application of Executive Order 8802, signed by the President on April 25, 1941, which abolished discrimination in all industries involved in armaments and national defense.[19] The Army also feared that the presence of black women in the corps would dissuade white women from enlisting. However, it was too late to back down and to ban African-American women from the

WAAC. Discouraging applications therefore became part of the Army's unofficial racial policy.[20]

At Fort Huachuca, the absence of white soldiers or Waacs dispelled all fears that the women of the 32nd and 33rd Companies would take the jobs of whites, and the isolation of the camp neutralized the risk of subversion of the local racial order. The first black Waacs who arrived at the fort numbered about 150, a negligible figure compared with the 13,000 male soldiers. Yet, they were very visible on the pictures taken by Signal Corps photographers, who were eager to set up the new experiment as a model for other camps, despite the fact that it could not be reproduced elsewhere, since Fort Huachuca's racial configuration was unique in the United States.

Of all the women stationed at Huachuca, one stood out for the responsibilities she took on and the memoirs she wrote: Officer 2nd Class Irma Cayton. After serving for a while at the WAAC headquarters in Washington, Cayton was able to join the first two black companies at Huachuca. She was initially put in charge of supplies, messes, and quarters, and was later promoted to command the 32nd Company, along with her friend from Chicago, Lieutenant Violet Askins. According to the black press, she was the perfect embodiment of the patriotic African-American Waac who reconciled the two goals of the "double victory" campaign – victory over the Axis powers and victory over racism in the United States. On January 2, 1943, the *Pittsburgh Courier* devoted an entire article to Cayton. The article, entitled "Officer Cayton, typical patriot type, loves army life," quoted her at length:

> If we, of the colored race, hope for a place in the world picture of the democracies, when the peace is established, we must by our untiring efforts, sacrifice, and toil, do all that we can to help win that peace, so that we shall have the right to demand and enjoy those privileges granted to all liberty loving peoples. I joined because I felt it my duty as a citizen, and have never regretted it.

Irma Cayton was convinced that challenging the Army's racial and gendered order from within would lead to its reform. However, the Pittsburgh journalist ignored her denunciation of the discrepancy between the Army's commitments and what was practiced at the camp. Rather, he tried to convince his readers of her respectability and dedication to the group:

> She feels that [colored women] cannot do enough to help this country win the peace. It is as much their patriotic duty to go all out as any other citizen in this country to keep democracy alive. She left a good job, home, and also her husband, Horace Cayton, *Pittsburg Courier* Labor Editor in what could well be called a sacrifice to enlist in the WAAC.[21]

Irma, née Jackson, was a young woman from the black bourgeoisie of Brunswick, Georgia, the daughter of a wealthy doctor who had served in World War I. When the sociologist Horace Cayton met her at Fisk University (a historically black institution) in 1935, he was struck by the light skin of this master's student in social sciences, the attention she devoted to her dress and appearance, and her bourgeois ethos. They soon married and settled in the neighborhood of Bronzeville, in Chicago, in the building financed by the Julius Rosenwald Fund to house middle- and upper-class black families, the Michigan Boulevard Garden Apartments. Horace Cayton obtained a position at the University of Chicago, where he met W. Lloyd Warner. The two men, who were later joined by St. Clair Drake, applied together for funds from the Works Progress Administration to conduct a study of juvenile delinquency in the black community. Four years and 10,000 interviews later, they published *Black Metropolis*, which later became a classic of American sociology. Meanwhile, Irma worked as a social worker and then as a volunteer at the Good Shepherd Community Center, the largest black settlement house in the country, which was run by her husband on the South Side of Chicago. Horace Cayton recounted in his autobiography that they had become members of Chicago's "Negro society," their names appearing regularly in the *Defender*. They were also well introduced to white intellectual circles through Cayton's colleagues. The couple had the writers Langston Hughes and Richard Wright among their close friends, and they socialized with many intellectuals and artists – for instance, the Robesons, with whom they had traveled in Europe before the outbreak of the war. When the United States entered the conflict, Horace publicly condemned army segregation, notably by publishing an incisive article in *The Nation* entitled "Fighting for White Folks." Since he considered himself a race leader, he felt that it was his duty to oppose all forms of injustice and exclusion of blacks in American society, and especially in the Army. He was therefore greatly relieved when the conscription age was lowered, as this meant that he would not have to choose between enlistment and conscientious objection. The Cayton couple, however, was divided over how to respond to segregation in American society, echoing the division in the African-American community and its organizations between those who favored denunciation and those who embraced patriotically motivated compromise. Irma chose patriotism and criticism of the Army from within, as she seemed to believe that reform was possible. She first volunteered with the Red Cross to teach first aid and then joined the Women's Defense Corps of America, before applying for WAAC officer training in July 1942.[22] In choosing to enlist, Irma Cayton openly expressed her political disagreement with her husband, but also sought to regain a measure of freedom as their relationship became more and more strained. The estrangement precipitated their divorce.

Using the rank of lieutenant to which she had been promoted, Irma Cayton, along with her friend Violet Askins, voiced the rights of the members of the companies they commanded. Askins had renounced a job as chief stenographer in the Division of Unemployment Compensation of the Department of Labor in Chicago on the grounds that she had "felt stuck." The two women wanted to make their companies exemplary to ensure that their members would be granted the same rights and privileges as white Waacs. Once the excellence of the black Waacs had been recognized by the fort's commander, Cayton and Askins lobbied for the women to obtain ranks that were comparable to those of the men they had replaced. However, the promotions for which they had fought so hard were granted only after they requested an inspection at the Washington headquarters. Cayton and Askins believed that racial conquests in the Army were possible so long as they were relentlessly pursued; they tried to persuade the women under their command that this was indeed the case.[23]

The other Huachuca Waacs were more concerned with professional advancement and personal emancipation than with racial conquest. They wanted to take advantage of their experience in the Army to live a new life, free from material concerns, social control, and male authority. The break with their previous existence was materialized by the wearing of uniforms and the drill exercises to which they had to submit, just like the men. One photograph shows them in formation behind their captain, Frances Alexander, marching in rows in front of the mountains, with one of them carrying the flag. As Judy McKinnon recalled:

> The hardest thing? Well, I think maybe the drilling. It would be hot, and you would be out there in that sun, parade thing. You'd stand out there maybe on that parade field for thirty minutes in that hot sun at attention. While the commander's flag passed in review, you were standing there at attention. I've seen girls fall out, and the medics would come and get them off the field. Maybe that was the most difficult time. Now, the working I did not mind. Latrine duty, I didn't mind that. KP duty, I didn't mind that. I didn't mind those things. But that was maybe my most difficult thing adjusting to.[24]

Marching on the parade ground was the only aspect of the Waacs' experience that resembled that of the soldiers. Apart from that, they were kept away from the training grounds. A small number of Waacs ended up driving or repairing jeeps and off-road trucks. These women had been interviewed on arrival about their qualifications and wishes and had then been assigned to the job. As some of them told the *Pittsburgh*

7.2: "Auxiliaries Ruth Wade and Lucille Mayo further demonstrate their ability to service trucks as taught them during the processing period at Fort Des Moines and put into practice at Fort Huachuca." © NARA, Army Signal Corps.

Courier reporter, they appreciated being able to carry out these masculine functions they had learned at the camp, as this gave them a sense of pride and autonomy.[25] The staged photographs suggest an unprecedented combination of femininity and technical mastery generally associated with men in the Army: The female mechanics wear pants and plunge their hands into the engine, but they also wear heels and they are employed in larger numbers than men would be for the same job.

Wilnet C. Grayson became Lieutenant Colonel Bousfield's chauffeur in May 1943, and said that she was proud to drive the highest-ranking black man at the camp. On enlisting in the WAAC, she had left behind a chain of beauty salons in Richmond, the capital of Virginia, and the high incomes associated with that. She had interrupted a successful career as an entrepreneur in the beauty industry to serve her country, renouncing a typically female job to occupy a function reserved for men. She explained this decision as follows: "I feel it is the duty of every American woman to lend her strength and talent to help win this war."[26]

As there were no white Wacs to take the best jobs at Huachuca, the members of the 32nd and 33rd Companies had access to administrative positions with major responsibilities. Segregation at the fort meant that blacks did not have to compete against whites. Lucia Pitts was one of the Waacs who maintained the gigantic bureaucracy – a reporting and filing machine – that the Army had become. After giving up a high-level position in the federal administration at the age of forty, she worked at the Post Provost Marshal's office at Huachuca, assisting a white Sergeant Major whom she later replaced. Born in Tennessee at the turn of the century, the Great Migration had taken her to Chicago, where she was the first black woman to work as a stenographer at United Charities, the city's largest charitable organization. She was then employed as a secretary by Anne Wilmarth Ickes, who had been elected to the Illinois House of Representatives. When Anne Wilmarth Ickes's husband, Harold Ickes, became Secretary of the Interior and director of the Public Works Administration (PWA) during the New Deal, Pitts obtained the position of personal secretary to Clark Foreman, the Secretary's Advisor on the Economic Status of Negro, who pushed for the inclusion of African Americans in New Deal programs. She followed him to his post as director of the Division of Public Power at the PWA, and was then promoted to the role of assistant to the Director of Race Relations at the Public Housing Administration (PHA), one of the federal government's most discriminatory agencies. In her curriculum vitae, she noted that she had often been the "first or only Negro in some offices." In 1943, she decided to leave the federal government: She had grown tired of being one of the only blacks in these federal administrations and she no longer wanted to be a token black person, as she wrote in 1968 in an unpublished autobiography. She was hoping to take advantage of the opportunities opened in the defense industry to get a job in the private sector in Chicago, thinking that she would be able to dispense with the protection that federal employment afforded to African Americans. However, Pitts looked for work for several months without finding any. Her application to the WAC meant a return to the federal state and therefore came as a last resort, even though her selection for officer training school at Fort Des Moines guaranteed her an interesting position at Huachuca.[27] At the Post Provost Marshal's office, she put her administrative experience to good use, updating correspondence, carrying out major filing operations, and designing a new system for recording infractions of the law and identifying prisoners. However, she grew bored and applied for deployment to Europe in December 1944.[28]

After her departure, Lucia Pitts made it clear that office work was no sinecure, and that the women who had been employed there had devoted much effort in service of the country. In the rest of her poem dedicated to the soldiers of Huachuca, she wrote:

> We have come in to share as much as we can
> Of your discomfort and your sacrifice.
> We, too, march, and soil ourselves with dirty jobs,
> And rise with the dawn to put in a good day's work
> At the jobs you did before.
> When we seek our bunks at night,
> Our bodies, too, are weary and sore.[29]

Other Wacs were assigned to Fort Huachuca's offices, in particular to the command headquarters, where they held classic female white-collar jobs. They worked as assistants, secretaries, or stenographers, and they reported to white officers. Some Waacs were employed at the switchboard, where they took on a role they had already performed in civilian

7.3: Waacs working in the HQ Annex at Fort Huachuca. © Fort Huachuca Museum.

life. They mastered the complex communication system after just a few days of training.³⁰ They ensured that the isolated post remained connected to the outside world, to neighboring communities, to the Ninth Service Command, and to the Waacs' families and fiancés. A Signal Corps photograph shows the newly arrived switchboard operators masterfully managing the flow of communications under the watchful eyes of the black soldiers who are training them.

The Waacs also worked in large numbers in the two hospitals as medical secretaries or laboratory assistants. Those trained as laboratory technicians got to work alongside the country's leading medical specialists, acquiring skills they were later able to use in civilian life. Ruth Gaddy was a stenographer at Hospital No. 1, where she assisted the country's top specialists. Born in 1918 in Charlotte, North Carolina, she had completed high school and had wanted to pursue her education. However, she could not afford college, as she came from a very modest background – her father was a church janitor, her mother was a housewife, and she had seven brothers and sisters. She joined the Army because she hoped to put money aside to finance her studies, but also because she had been moved by the patriotic appeal of the recruitment posters plastered on the walls of Charlotte's first skyscraper, the Independence Building, where she had worked as an elevator operator. Like the others, she was tested at enlistment. She realized that she was "well above average and was not the stupid child that [she] was led to believe that [she] was." She enlisted at Fort Bragg in October 1942, and was later assigned to Huachuca hospital.³¹ After her day's work, she volunteered at the USO, where she offered literacy classes to soldiers and sang vespers with Phyllis Branch, a professional singer who had long performed in New York nightclubs.

A few Wacs managed to pursue their artistic activities in the Special Services Office in charge of the camp's entertainment programs. Anna Russell, an artist who had come from Philadelphia in December 1942, put her graphic design talents to work on all Special Services publications. She had been the first black woman to graduate from the Philadelphia School of Design for Women, where she had trained as a textile designer. Her realistic style tinged with humor and patriotism served the needs of the fort. She created Huachuca's graphic identity, producing panels, silkscreens, theatrical sets, and illustrations for the newspaper of the post's command office. Her vignettes featured stylized characters in black ink – sympathetic figures who often smiled and were in no way contentious or rebellious. She portrayed the Army as a place of upward mobility, never as a place of repression or humiliation. Anna Russell contributed to the propaganda of the fort's command without any ulterior motive. In her drawing "Dawn of New Opportunity," a Waac is shown being welcomed at the Recruiting Office by Uncle Sam, who points to a "sea of Waac's accomplishments" illuminated by a beautiful rising sun. Russell also depicted the promise of promotion for the black soldiers of the 92nd Division in the form of an elevator that one could take to go from Private First Class to Sergeant – and this even as many soldiers at the fort were denouncing the freezing of promotions.

Discreet and never critical, Anna Russell performed other services for the fort's command. She drew the official plan of the old post, which was approved by Hardy. She also created Christmas postcards that were sold to raise funds for solidarity actions. The coats of arms she designed for the various units were hung in the officers' messes, barracks, and service clubs. The fort's authorities thanked her several times for mobilizing her art on behalf of the Army. She received letters of thanks as well as gifts – in October 1943, Brigadier General Colbern gave her a gold watch on behalf of the 92nd for her painting depicting the insignia of its units. Although not as famous, her work was similar to that of the painter Charles H. Alston, who had joined the Army in 1943 and had served for one year at Huachuca. From 1942 onwards, Alston had worked for the Office of War Information, producing over 100 drawings for the military that celebrated great figures of the African-American community and gave visibility to the black presence.[32]

The press said little about the women who occupied less qualified and less rewarding positions, which were in fact the common lot of the Waacs. At Huachuca as at other camps, the Army resisted allocating functions that might contribute to women's emancipation, even as Colonel Hobby sought to ensure that the military experience was a chance for all the Waacs to break through the glass ceiling. The Waacs therefore found it difficult to escape traditional job assignments.[33] Although traces of this are hard to find on Signal Corps photographs, the vast majority of Waacs worked in domestic jobs (cooking, cleaning, and laundry) that were not very different from those they had held in civilian life – almost 60 percent of black women were still confined to service and domestic jobs in the United States at the time.[34] Yet, there were exceptions. On arriving at the fort, the very young Judy McKinnon asked to attend the pastry training course: "I didn't want to go for the motor pool. I didn't want to get my hands dirty anymore. [...] I did not have any desire to work in the medical field, so I went to cooks and bakers school." As she was aged twenty-one, she had to cheat by pretending she was one year older in order to get in. Judy had joined the WAAC because she needed a steady income and because she wanted to distance herself from family authority. She had been running around in circles in her sharecropping family in Richmond County, North Carolina. She had completed high school, but

7.4: "Waac cooks prepare dinner for the first time in new kitchen at Fort Huachuca," December 5, 1942. © NARA, Army Signal Corps.

could not afford college. The WAAC seemed just right for her. She would be able to send her family $38 each month – the $50 pay minus the $12 insurance.[35]

The pay helped the Wacs forget the disappointment of not being able to gain new qualifications. Although the black press and the Signal Corps photographs portrayed these women in a heroic light, glossing over the vexations they had to contend with, the patriotism they expressed at enlistment could cover up other motives: the need for stable, well-paid employment at a time when only 16 percent of black women obtained jobs in the defense industry and when discrimination in hiring persisted despite the executive order of April 1941,[36] the desire to acquire skills for the post-war period, the fight for racial equality inside the Army, the questioning of traditional gender relations, and the quest for a form of emancipation, even if only temporary.

However, for the WAC's defenders, emphasizing the patriotism that had driven the women to enlist was essential. The writer Langston Hughes, who came to meet the Wacs of Huachuca in June 1944, felt it necessary to reassure readers of the *Chicago Defender* about the motivations and activities of the women soldiers. He therefore paid a generous tribute to their devotion and professionalism:

> I was told in no uncertain terms that WORK it is. The Wacs feel that there is an impression abroad among the public that they are at army posts to entertain soldiers. Such, I was assured, was far from being the case. They are in the army to soldier, to relieve men of various duties, and they are kept busy.[37]

Hughes wanted to remove all suspicion that the Wacs had been assigned to Fort Huachuca to boost the morale of the black soldiers or, more crudely put, to be their sexual partners. Likewise, the photographers of the Ninth Service Command set out to produce soothing images of their daily lives, depicting these as an extension of a type of civilian life that conformed to middle-class moral norms and to the traditional model of femininity. On the Signal Corps photographs, the Waacs can be seen buying cooking utensils from the post exchange, planting flowers next to their barracks, decorating their rooms with pictures of those they left behind, meeting in the lounge to chat, read, or write letters with a cigarette in hand. They can also be seen engaging in reassuring collective activities: photographed from above in swarms as they receive letters that connect them with the outside world; in the gym on roller skates; at Sunday service, receiving their prayer book from the chaplain under the gaze of Colonel Hardy; or singing "We're the WAAC," a song composed by auxiliary Mercedes Jordan. These images evoke an ideal female boarding school in which there is no room for rivalries or protests.

The Army was particularly keen to give the female military experience an image of irreproachable respectability; the future of the WAC depended on it. This was all the more necessary at Huachuca given the pioneering nature of the 32nd and 33rd Companies. The African-American press shared this concern and remained, for different reasons, very attached to the notion of respectability. Respect for the norms of white society – moderation, hard work, good manners, and refinement – and for Victorian morality and sexuality was seen as essential to the production of a virtuous image of black women, as the best way of thwarting racist stereotypes. This imperative of respectability, seen until the interwar period as one of the conditions for access to equality for the community as a whole, was partly challenged and reinterpreted by the working-class women who had come to the North as part of the Great Migration. Yet, the community's political and intellectual elites remained attached to this imperative, especially in situations where the behavior of black women could be cast into doubt.[38] This was the case at Huachuca, where military service was also a time of emancipation and experimentation far from male, family, or marital authority.

Respectable Women

Service at the fort was also an experience of freedom, a time of female complicity. There was a loosening of the family, social, and religious controls and of the professional and financial constraints that weighed on civilian life. The Wacs had free time for leisure, friendship, and flirting, despite the control of peers and superiors. Many Wacs at Huachuca discovered what it was like to have time for oneself, a little money to spend, and cultural and sporting facilities at one's fingertips. On photographs found in private collections intended for family use or as souvenirs, the Wacs pose in pairs or in groups of four, in bunches of bunkmates, still wearing their uniforms after the day's work. Bodies are liberated and revealed in skimpy outfits during sporting events designed to occupy free time – leaning on the starting blocks, making passes on the basketball court reserved for them, or getting out of the pool in dripping bathing suits.

Strong friendships were built. The trio of Chicago officers – Atkins, Cayton, and Woods – was inseparable; the women helped each other out

7.5: Members of the 32nd and 33rd Companies of the WAAC playing basketball at Fort Huachuca. © NARA, Army Signal Corps.

and covered for each other whenever their commander accused one of them of misbehaving. The Wacs of Huachuca went hiking in small groups along the San Pedro River, an oasis in that parched region where one could observe rare species of birds; they attended horse races in Fry; they visited Sonora on the other side of the Mexican border; they stared in amazement into the depths of the Bisbee mining pit and had their photograph taken in front of it. Together these women, who had never had the leisure or the means to travel, experienced nature and a way of life that were completely unknown to them. They borrowed army cars and traveled across the desert to the Mexican border. Anna Russell, Anne Jones, and Corporal Hulda Defreeze – who held a master of arts from New York University and produced maps in the Office of the Post Engineer – set off together on a long furlough that took them as far as California and Disney Studios in Los Angeles. Anna Russel recounted their journey in an album entitled "3 Musketeers of WAC Go West on 'Holiday' Furlough" and illustrated with watercolors, photographs, and autographs acquired in Hollywood. On her return, she filled her scrapbooks with colorized postcards bought along the way, which depicted blooming desert plants – saguaro cacti, yuccas, Spanish bayonets – and modern cities that had sprung up in the desert – such as Tucson's main street illuminated by the neon lights of shops and cinemas.

The thirty-nine-year-old Anna had left a son behind and was very devout. She and her friends were among the older Wacs; they did not have the casualness of the younger, single Wacs, who had no family responsibilities and no preconceptions about sexual activity. Nevertheless, Captain Alexander treated these volunteers like young virgins at a boarding school. She ensured compliance with the rule of chastity imposed on Wacs by Colonel Hobby and with the rules laid down at the camp to keep men away from women: Men were admitted to the Wacs' quarters only at certain times; they could meet women only in the day rooms or lounges; at night, the low wall separating the male and female sections of the camp was guarded by a sentinel. Irma Cayton wrote in her memoirs: "We were kept under constant supervision."[39] She also recalled that the soldiers often tried to infiltrate their barracks at night; the Wacs would arm themselves with brooms to get them out and would shout to alert the military police. However, not all Wacs were hostile to nocturnal visits. Thus, Judy McKinnon regularly sat on the edge of the women's quarters to talk to the soldiers, even though she knew she might be locked up.[40]

On the other side of the wall, the fort's commander and the black officers encouraged soldiers to flirt with the women, whom they described as choice partners, desirable because of their race, patriotism, and excellence. Thus, every issue of the Special Services newsletter included an advice column entitled "How to Date." The column was illustrated with a drawing by Anna Russell: A soldier pretending to consult a book in the library in order to take a look at an attractive Wac. Many other drawings featured an officer and a Wac in civilian clothes who were engaged in flirting. Like the nurses and civilians who worked at the camp, the Wacs were highly coveted because they were few in number compared with the men.

The fort's commanders would probably have liked to apply the same sexual regime to women as they did to men. The WAC command, however, insisted on differential treatment, while also demanding that men and women be given equal responsibilities.[41] To establish the WAC's reputation and to counter accusations that it was a corps of prostitutes, Hobby demanded morality pledges from the women: no sex outside marriage, fidelity to a single partner, and rejection of lesbianism. Until the WAC achieved full military status, the behavior of its members was governed by a "Code of Conduct"; in the event of violation, and especially in cases of extramarital sex or public drunkenness, offending women could be court-martialed and expelled for unbecoming behavior. The Code was abolished in 1943, but Hobby continued to ensure that stricter rules were applied to women than to men in sexual matters. There was indeed a double standard regarding male–female relations at Huachuca: tolerance for men, as long as their health was not at risk, but tight control and sanctions for women.[42]

In the photo albums of the Huachuca Wacs, scenes of flirtation abound: couples sitting in jeeps before a desert trip; a Wac and an officer walking in the Huachuca mountains; couples embracing at impromptu outdoor dances; nurse Nadine Davis Lane posing in the arms of a handsome soldier in front of the cacti around the officers' club. Flirtations were sometimes regularized by marriage, whenever a couple obtained permission from the Army. For the military authority, this was an ideal configuration: The soldier would be able to satisfy his sexual needs with a respectable, uninfected person in a union sanctioned by the Army in the fort's chapel.

However, many of the female soldiers at Huachuca engaged in extramarital sex and thus transgressed the heterosexual norms of the time. Since the WAC denied the possibility of this happening, the women were never given condoms; nor were they taught courses in venereal disease prevention as the Surgeon General's Office demanded. All they received at enlistment was a small booklet insisting on hygiene and abstinence and warning of the dangers of sexual relations with potentially infected men. To avoid exclusion should they be discovered, the Wacs remained as discreet as possible about their sexual activities. As a result, few traces remain of these activities – deviant forms of sexuality being the only exception. Irma Cayton was shocked when she discovered that some of the women in her company engaged in prostitution at the fort's gates on pay and furlough days. An inspector general from the Ninth Service Command came to Huachuca to investigate after he received anonymous letters denouncing Wacs for soliciting. Cayton accompanied him to Fry, where she saw with her own eyes that some of the Wacs sold sex to soldiers. The offending women got off relatively lightly, since they were simply transferred to another camp.[43]

The Wacs also had sexual relations with each other, whether they discovered lesbianism at Huachuca or pursued a practice they had engaged in previously. The WAC rejected applications from women who were suspected of homosexuality by recruiters, fearing that lesbianism would give it the image of an amoral corps. The Commander of the 32nd Company, Violet Askins, found herself at a loss on several occasions, whenever she witnessed intimate relations between women in the barracks. Since she was given no clear guidelines on how to respond, she relied on a manual she had received that encouraged officers to be tolerant of lesbianism:

> You, as officers, will find it necessary to keep the problem in the back of your mind, not indulging in witch-hunting or speculating, and yet not overlooking the problem because it is a difficult one to handle. Above all, you must approach the problem with an attitude of fairness and tolerance to assure that no one is accused unjustly. If there is any likelihood of doubt, it is better to be generous in your outlook, and to assume that everyone is innocent until definitely proved otherwise.

The WAC wanted to avoid public scandals. Moreover, like the criminal justice system, it did not punish lesbianism as severely as the Army punished male homosexuality (i.e., with dishonorable discharge). As elsewhere in society, intimacy between women was tolerated in the corps, which was not sure how to define lesbian acts.[44] Askins was content to move women from one barrack to another without sanction or blame.[45]

Some of the Wacs were sexually assaulted by soldiers and officers. Henrietta Stevenson Ingram, a Wac stationed sixty miles away, at Fort Douglas, recounted cases of abuse. She worked in the laboratory of the fort's clinic, where she performed albumin and glucose assays on the pregnant wives of black officers. She was also involved in testing spinal anesthetics on African-American patients, at a time when epidurals were still in the experimental stage. "Who else would you think they would practice on, but black people?" she wondered fifty years later. She regularly visited Huachuca, where she witnessed several cases of rape of female soldiers.[46] One court-martial file mentions a rape accusation made not by a Wac but by a black civilian employee, Rosalyn Westray, who worked in the fort's laundry. Westray claimed to have been raped in a car near the camp by a second lieutenant of the 371st Infantry Regiment in February 1944. The accused soldier, Ballie Wall, was initially sentenced to life imprisonment for rape under Article 92 of the Code of War – had the alleged victim been white, he would probably have received the death penalty. However, he was finally cleared by the appeals court, where he was defended by a good lawyer: The plaintiff's testimony was riddled with inconsistencies, the medical examinations carried out by Major Thatcher at the hospital did not attest to rape, and the accusation seemed to have been made in revenge against Wall, who had refused to pay for a sexual encounter that had likely been consensual.[47] The sources are extremely allusive on the subject of sexual relations – whether consensual or not – among the Wacs of Huachuca. Nevertheless, the very general remarks made in interviews and the innuendo in certain army documents suggest that transgression and abuse did indeed take place.

Some of the Huachuca Wacs – for instance, Irma Cayton and Violet Askins – actively fought segregation from within the Army, believing that they would be able to achieve substantial reforms and adjustments. Unlike the men, most of whom were not volunteers, the Wacs could have decided to leave the Army and to renounce playing a role in the nation's patriotic project. Yet, in the end, segregation seemed to them a lesser evil than outright exclusion – an option that the Army had considered for some time. Enlistment in the WAC, even under a "separate but equal" regime, was indeed associated with material and symbolic advantages that made this racial regime acceptable for a female elite torn between its desire to benefit from new opportunities and its opposition to segregation. The Wacs ultimately derived sufficient benefits and reasons for pride from this experience to accept black isolation, which they sometimes tried to deflect from within. At Huachuca, the absence of competition from white women allowed the Wacs to obtain positions that gave them some autonomy from male authority and WAC control. Thanks to the friendships they built, the Wacs of Huachuca partly succeeded in circumventing authority, carving out spaces and times of freedom for themselves, though without radically challenging gender roles or the hierarchies of sex and class.

8 An Experiment in Integration

Ever since the opening of the black hospital, Lieutenant Colonel Midian Bousfield had the ambition of subverting the medical segregation imposed by the Army in favor of the integration ardently desired by medical activists. In June 1942, he confided in a letter to Truman Gibson:

> It would soon be possible to run this hospital on an integrated basis – a non-Jim Crow unit if we are permitted. [...] We can at least gradually break down this segregation – if they will let us & just have one big hospital. Perhaps this could happen with me in command – perhaps not – perhaps it could be done without references to command. Fact is it is partially being done now as we are lending professional assistance to the other side. [...] Permit us with Col. Hardy's & Col. Maynard's consent to break down this segregation where & when we can.[1]

The integration Bousfield had in mind was not a clear-cut, definitive abolition of the medical segregation established by Army regulations. Nor did it consist in assigning black doctors and patients to hospitals in proportion to their numbers at the camp. Though never explicitly formulated, Bousfield's aim was to subvert segregation by allowing health personnel to practice medicine in a color-blind manner and by ensuring that patients could freely choose their caregivers as opposed to being mechanically assigned a doctor of the same race as them. Bousfield did not hide the fact that he was favorable to this form of medical integration, not even in his dealings with the Surgeon General's Office (SGO). When, in September 1942, he was asked by Lieutenant Colonel Durward Hall of the SGO where the surplus of black doctors should be assigned in the Army, he suggested opening another black hospital; yet, he also recommended the dispatch of African-American doctors to the front and, above all, the creation of mixed units in which black and white doctors would work together.[2] For Bousfield, the main challenge was to alter the SGO's perception of the quality of care offered by African-American professionals and to demonstrate with facts that the alleged reluctance of whites to be examined by blacks was nothing but a myth.

To this end, Bousfield first had to demonstrate the excellence of the black doctors serving at Station Hospital No. 1. According to the hospital's statutes, treatment priority was to be given to sick or wounded black soldiers and officers. On appearing before draft boards, all applicants for enlistment were subjected to a medical examination: Men who showed signs of weakness were rejected, while those in good health were deemed fit for service. Yet, some of the recruits had an undiagnosed benign or old disease that worsened at the fort and developed into chronic illness. Indeed, blacks' access to health care was still highly problematic at the time. At the end of the 1930s, there was only 1 African-American physician for every 3,000 black patients in the United States – though some African Americans were seen by white practitioners. Moreover, the number of black hospitals across the country fell from 202 to 124 between 1923 and 1944. In the South, where medical segregation was almost complete and where there were no specific public health programs for blacks (with the exception of campaigns against syphilis), the quality of care for African-American patients was very poor, particularly in the countryside. In 1938, Surgeon General Thomas Parran identified the South as "the no. 1 health problem of the nation." During the war, southern blacks had the lowest life expectancy, the highest rates of morbidity, and the highest rates of rejection by draft boards in the country.[3] Unsurprisingly, many Huachuca soldiers were in poor health, despite having been vaccinated against smallpox, typhoid, and tetanus by the division's medical battalions.[4]

Although the hospital was a military facility, most patients presented with classic physical and psychological disorders, not wounds sustained in combat. The daily routine resembled that of a civilian hospital, for it mainly consisted in treating benign illnesses, symptoms of venereal disease, and dental problems. Very few patients suffered from lung disease, because the dry air of the Huachuca mountains prevented the onset of respiratory infections. In the early days, the hospital's doctors mostly treated cases of jaundice or venereal disease – infection rates increased until the implementation of prophylactic measures at the camp, as some African Americans were enlisted despite receiving a positive diagnosis. Dental problems, which were very costly to treat in civilian life, were also common. According to the head of the dental department, Major Earl W. Renfroe, most of the patients seen in the department's three clinics had received only basic dental care prior to enrolling.[5] A monthly checkup was thus instituted to prevent the worsening of dental infections. As Nurse Madine Davis Lane later recalled, the hospital also had to respond to epidemics. Thus, several African-American soldiers in training at Douglas Army Airfield came to Station Hospital No. 1 to be treated for meningitis (with sulfonamide), which they had likely developed as a result of dust storms coming from Mexico. Others showed symptoms of silicosis, their lungs having been irritated by the dust they had inhaled at the base.[6] Cases of Waterhouse–Friderichsen syndrome caused by bacterial infections were also treated. Here again, the black doctors demonstrated their excellence: With the exception of the first two or three cases, all patients with Waterhouse–Friderichsen syndrome were brought out of coma, whereas no other hospital in the Ninth Service Command managed to keep such patients alive.[7]

Under the direction of Major Roscoe Giles, the surgery department performed 300 to 400 operations per month, ranging from the most routine (342 appendicitis surgeries between July 1942 and May 1945) to the most complex (surgeries to treat heart conditions or spinal cord problems caused by training accidents).[8] Giles sometimes had to rectify surgeries performed at other bases by much less talented doctors. Thus, Second Lieutenant Andrew L. Farris of the 559th Artillery Battalion, 92nd Infantry Division, whose testicles had accidentally moved up into his pubic region during inguinal hernia surgery at Camp Custer, was reoperated by Captain Wormley in the Huachuca officer surgery building. Wormley managed to bring down one of Farris's testicles and considered performing surgery on the other testicle one month later.[9]

Soon enough, the successes of the black doctors at Station Hospital No. 1 became known in the area. It was no secret that the black hospital's equipment was far superior to that of the white one because it treated a greater number of patients. All visitors and black journalists agreed that care was provided in the best possible environment. In terms of comfort, hygiene, and the talent and availability of the health professionals, the medical care on offer was irreproachable. In this time of war, press articles marveled at the range of leisure activities that Red Cross employees and volunteers (known as the Gray Ladies) offered to patients and convalescents – films, books, games, etc. The quality of convalescent care was also highlighted. In the spring of 1943, Charles Steinheimer published a photographic essay in *Life* that highlighted the team's professionalism and the trust that the black doctors inspired in patients. Although he had come to Huachuca to photograph the 93rd Division as it left for the front, he had also taken a series of pictures in the hospital that were never published in the magazine. He had entered the operating room, where he had captured the impeccable hygiene, the precision and mastery of gesture, the state-of-the-art equipment, and the attention given to patients.

As early as September 1942, a number of white officers asked to be treated along with their families at the outpatient clinic of the black facility. They wanted to be cared for by the African-American medical

An Experiment in Integration

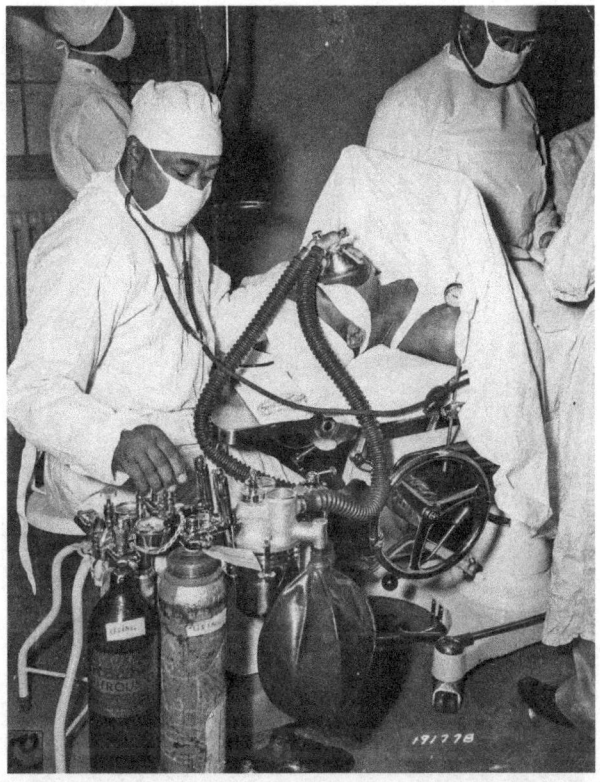

8.1: "Capt. C. E. Janison, from Chicago, Illinois, shown administering nitrous oxide anesthesia to a patient in surgery, Fort Huachuca." © NARA, Army Signal Corps.

officers at Station Hospital No. 1, whose superiority over their white counterparts at Station Hospital No. 2 was well known. Bousfield and his doctors accepted these patients without hesitation. To ensure that influential external contacts were informed of the fact that whites recognized the professional qualities of African Americans, he wrote to W. E. B. Du Bois in October: "We have treated in this hospital high ranking officers – from the Major General in command of the 93rd Division right down the line."[10] In a letter to Truman Gibson written shortly afterwards, he expressed his delight that Major General O. P. Hall regularly came to see Major Thatcher for treatment, as did other white officers and civilians attracted by the dermatologist's excellent reputation. As Bousfield mentioned in a letter to Colonel Durward Hall of the

8.2: A nurse, photographed in front of an ambulance. © Fort Huachuca Museum.

SGO,[11] Thatcher's reputation reached as far as Beaumont General Hospital (over 220 miles away in El Paso, Texas), which sent one of its patients, a white lieutenant, to see the dermatologist.[12]

The African-American press also took great pride in publicizing the fact that white officers serving in nearby posts and then white civilians came for treatment at Station Hospital No. 1 rather than at white military or civilian hospitals, whose doctors had a less favorable reputation. According to journalist Enoc Waters of the *Chicago Defender*, "the work the doctors are doing here in breaking down racial taboos by making sheer ability and performance outweigh prejudice cannot be discounted."[13]

Waters cited three cases of white soldiers and civilians who preferred to be treated at the black hospital: an employee of the tax administration working on the border with Mexico who was ready to travel several dozen miles across the desert to receive treatment at Huachuca; the wife of a white doctor from Philadelphia who preferred to undergo surgery at Station Hospital No. 1 instead of being repatriated to the East – a particularly remarkable decision, given that it came from someone familiar with the medical environment; and two white soldiers who had been injured in a road accident ninety-five miles from the fort and refused to be treated at a nearby hospital.

This integrated care was entirely provided at the outpatient clinic of Station Hospital No. 1. Medical fees were very advantageous in this section of the hospital: The cost of consultation was one dollar and surgical procedures were free.[14] However, whites also came because they could receive treatment without staying overnight.[15] They were therefore able to stay among their own, as the vast majority of civilians living in the Huachuca area were white. They were sure they would not be made to sleep next to black patients, whose lack of hygiene and poor health were greatly stigmatized at the time – fear of venereal diseases often led to mistrust and physical rejection of African Americans. Contact between white and black patients – which was absolutely taboo, as sociologist Charles C. Johnson pointed out in 1943 – was thus avoided.[16] Under these conditions, whites saw no reason to deprive themselves of diagnoses and procedures performed on their bodies by African-American doctors, all of whom belonged to the black intelligentsia and shared many of their social codes.

In the rest of the hospital, however, Army rules were assumed to prevent black doctors from treating white patients. Chicago-born surgeon Roscoe Giles and physician Robert Wilkinson wrote in separate letters to Louis T. Wright, a well-known integrationist in the black community who served as Chief of Surgery at Harlem Hospital and as Chairman of the Board of Directors at the NAACP, that they had been reminded of an SGO directive issued in 1942 or 1943 that prohibited black physicians from operating on white patients, male or female, or from working alongside whites. Yet, the two men, who had been working as civilian doctors a few months earlier and who were used to treating white patients, were not worried about possible sanctions.[17] As far as they were concerned, no one knew the texts on which these rules were based or whether they even really existed. The ban, whose exact purpose remained unclear, did not stand up to the facts. It was circumvented first by patients, then by doctors who wanted to provide the best possible care in a situation where the asymmetry between the excellence of black doctors and the mediocrity of their white colleagues was patently obvious. After a black patient died following a poorly performed hemorrhoidectomy in (white) Station Hospital No. 2, the surgical consultant for the Ninth Army Corps Area recommended, in the second half of 1943, that Station Hospital No. 1 "be given General Hospital privileges, that is [...] be permitted to do any type of operation except Neurosurgery or Elective chest surgery."[18] Thus, despite the rules in place, the surgical consultant decided to transfer virtually all surgical operations to Station Hospital No. 1 in order to avoid any further accidents. Patients were to be transported from one building to the other via the covered footbridge that spanned the road separating the two hospitals. Medical concerns and consideration of the local situation took precedence over the rule of racial separation.

This measure, however, did not apply to obstetrics and gynecology. The provision of gynecological care to white women by African-American doctors remained an absolute taboo for military authorities and white medical organizations alike. Major Harry Kamer, the Chief of Surgery at Station Hospital No. 2 and a specialist in gynecology and obstetrics, alerted the American Board of Gynecology and Obstetrics, which got Colonel Maynard to expressly forbid black doctors from examining white women. Kamer thus became the only doctor to be officially authorized to perform gynecological examinations and surgeries. Yet, a letter from Bousfield to Gibson revealed that many white women sought treatment in the women's building of the black hospital, at the risk of being called "nigger lovers" by white officers.[19]

Shortly after white patients started to visit the outpatient clinic for treatment, the two medical teams began to work together – a collaboration that was imposed on black doctors – and black staff were gradually transferred to Station Hospital No. 2. Indeed, at the hospital across the road, white medical officers were soon in short supply, and the chronic shortage of staff was crippling operations by July 1942.[20] The most qualified white doctors were reassigned to the Pacific or African theaters of operations, where their presence was required owing to the high number of wounded men. Those who remained at Station Hospital No. 2 had neither the knowledge nor the experience of their colleagues at Station Hospital No. 1, whose help they desperately needed to handle complicated cases. Just as Station Hospital No. 2 was losing staff, the surplus of personnel was increasing at the black facility – the SGO had not yet opened up other positions for African-American medical officers and nurses. The promotions that had been promised at the opening of the hospital could not be granted because of the bottleneck of new arrivals.[21] In March 1943, Bousfield finally obtained from the SGO the creation, at Station Hospital No. 1, of a replacement pool of medical officers awaiting a permanent assignment (up to 100 in number), which helped to absorb this surplus. However, this pool was put under the authority of Colonel Maynard, and the imbalance between black and white doctors in terms of number and quality remained glaringly obvious, making the transfer of personnel necessary.

As early as September 1942, three African-American doctors were assigned by order of Colonel Maynard to the white hospital, where they treated both black and white patients. Moreover, the heads of the radiology and laboratory departments at Station Hospital No. 1 were required to work at Station Hospital No. 2, which did not offer these specialties. When, in the second half of 1943, white surgeons were prevented from performing surgeries (with the exception of obstetrical operations), they asked their black colleagues to let them work alongside them as assistants so that they could learn new skills and gain experience.[22]

Yet, just as the project of racial integration of the two hospitals was making progress, with the discreet encouragement of the Ninth Service Command and the tacit agreement of the SGO, the War Department was pushing for the resegregation of medical training. In July 1944, the War Department announced that it had chosen Station Hospital No. 1 to host a training program reserved for African-American nurses. According to Under Secretary of War Robert Patterson, the hospital was the ideal location to familiarize apprentice nurses with the type of – segregated – environment in which they would be required to work after training.[23] Mabel Staupers denounced this "new type of segregation" as a regression, but also highlighted the contradiction between, on the one hand, the assurances given by Patterson a few days earlier that the Army Nurse Corps (ANC) would be integrated and, on the other hand, the creation of a segregated training facility for black candidates at Huachuca.[24] This segregation seemed unacceptable both because it was introduced after the integration of black nurses into the ANC and because it created an asymmetry with the integrated training of black officers which had been instituted after the start of the conflict. For his part, Bousfield saw the opening of the training center for black nurses as an opportunity and as a sign that the quality of the hospital he ran was being recognized – a position for which he was much criticized by his team of doctors.

Yet, the training school, which was run by Captain Mary L. Petty, operated for only three months, from July to the end of September 1944. The school graduated just over 100 nurses, all of whom were assigned to the different military hospitals of the Ninth Service Command.[25] Elinor Powell was one of them. Born and raised in Milton, near Boston, Powell had grown up in an integrated community with mixed schools, but her professional life had confined her to a black environment: She had trained as a nurse at Lincoln School in the Bronx (from which she had graduated in 1943), worked for a few months in Harlem, and then applied for membership in the ANC in 1944. After she was accepted on July 21, she was sent to the segregated training school at Huachuca for basic training.[26] However, the school closed at the end of September as a result of the strong protestations of Mabel Staupers and the opposition expressed by the Personnel Division of the War Department and the Advisory Committee on Negro Troop Policy headed by Assistant Secretary of War John McCloy.[27] Thus, the attempt to introduce a new form of segregation inside the hospital ended in failure.

As the end of the war approached, the departure of part of the 92nd Infantry Division in July 1944 automatically reduced the number of black patients at the fort. At the same time, the imbalance between the staffs of the two hospitals became more pronounced. Under these conditions, the two hospitals were merged under Maynard's direction, and another 12 African-American doctors were transferred along with the head nurse from the black to the white hospital. In protest, Bousfield asked to be demobilized: He felt that he was losing control over the hospital and over his best men, and he feared that the experiment in integration he had initiated at Station Hospital No. 1 would slip away from him.[28] Bousfield was also the subject of an investigation linked to the opening of the Greentop that was most certainly aimed at destabilizing him and undermining his medical integration project. In October 1944, he was accused of helping his friend Gibson Sr. sell Supreme Life insurance policies at the camp. As Supreme Life's Medical Director, Bousfield received dividends from the company. Had he encouraged soldiers to take out insurance policies by highlighting his connection with Supreme Life? According to the investigation, Bousfield was unaware that his name was mentioned in the brochures presenting the policies to the soldiers. Had the black doctor from Chicago pressured Hardy into allowing Supreme Life to canvas the fort and had he profited from the company's presence at the camp? Once again, investigators found no evidence of wrongdoing. Finally, had Bousfield organized a narcotics racket outside the fort using hospital supplies? The accusation proved unfounded once more. Nevertheless, doubt was cast on Bousfield's integrity. Who could have been trying to discredit him for trafficking and venality? The source of the rumors is not identified in the archives. However, given the level of tension between the two hospitals, it is quite possible that they were spread by his white colleagues at Station Hospital No. 2 – though they could also have come from his hierarchy, the Ninth Service Command, or the SGO. In any case, some people seemed intent on harming and discrediting him in order to block his integration project. Fortunately, the Inspector General refused to make him a scapegoat and completely exonerated him.[29]

Yet, the transfer of medical personnel lamented by Bousfield did bring about a form of de facto integration: Black and white doctors worked side by side at Station Hospital No. 2, a situation that the SGO had been determined to avoid at all costs before the outbreak of the war.[30] When, in June 1945, Colonel Durward Hall, the SGO's Chief of Staff, made a surprise visit to the two hospitals of the virtually empty fort, he noticed, without taking offense, that the vast majority of personnel at Station Hospital No. 2 were black, and that most white officers and civilians wanted to be treated by African-American professionals at the outpatient clinic of Station Hospital No. 1.[31] Although no photographic traces are left of this dual integration of patients and doctors, it was not kept secret at the time – quite the contrary. When the two hospitals were merged at the end of the war, Bousfield, who had not carried out his threat to resign, brought it up several times to persuade the SGO to continue the experiment at Huachuca and elsewhere and to award distinctions to his staff upon sending them back to civilian life. By 1945, virtually all patients, black and white, were seen at Station Hospital No. 1, where they could choose whether to be treated by the black medical team or by the few white doctors who were still at the fort. As Bousfield's correspondence with the SGO indicates, almost all white civilians, even women and even in severe cases, chose to be treated by African-American doctors. In a letter to the Deputy Surgeon General dated August 16, Bousfield insisted that even "poor whites from the South," whom the SGO deemed the most reluctant to accept integrated care, asked to be admitted to Station Hospital No. 1: "Their families come and there is no resentment whatsoever against their being cared for by colored officers, nor does there seem to be any doubt in their minds about their care." Bousfield recounted how a nineteen-year-old white girl, who had been wounded in the abdomen with a rifle, was saved thanks to the operation performed on her by Captain Thomas in the women's ward of Station Hospital No. 1.[32] Writing to the Adjutant General of the War Department to request that the Legion of Merit be awarded to Lieutenant Colonel Thatcher, Bousfield recalled that the chief of medical service at Station Hospital No. 1 had treated the son of Senator "Happy" Chandler of Kentucky, who was studying at a military school about fifty miles from Huachuca, for a serious skin disease, as well as the wife of Grover Land, a former player on the Cubs baseball team, who had taken a civilian job at the fort and had asked to remain there beyond his demobilization so that his wife could complete her treatment.[33] Even celebrities, who had the means and connections to request a transfer to another location, chose to have their loved ones treated by Huachuca's black doctors, whose professional qualities they held in the highest esteem.

For Bousfield, Thatcher's earning of the Legion of Merit "for meritorious service in connection with better race relations in the army" would mean that the SGO officially acknowledged black doctors' ability to treat white patients.[34] Bousfield and his colleagues were adamant that the SGO recognize the credentials and reputation they had earned among the white population. In their eyes, this was a sign that American society was ready for integrated care. They hoped that the Surgeon General would draw conclusions from this experiment that could be applied elsewhere in the Army. Thus, in August 1945, Bousfield wrote to the Deputy Surgeon General:

> At last, as the war closes, we get down to the things I have always said could be done if they were given half a chance. I just presume upon my intuition, when I pay tribute to you, for the opportunity to make these things a matter of record, with the hope that they may forever show the way to a more liberalizing attitude toward the indiscriminate use of colored doctors by the Surgeon General's office.[35]

In May 1944, Leslie Perry, administrative assistant of the NAACP's Washington office, asked the new Surgeon General, Major General Norman Kirk, to draw a picture of the situation of blacks in military hospitals. Kirk pointed to the results of an Army survey that found no evidence of discrimination in medical facilities. Several of the hospitals surveyed were described as treating blacks and whites side by side. While at Camp Maxey in Texas African-American patients were given their own ward (as soon as there were enough of them) on the grounds that both groups "seem to be happier in their own wards," at Camp Stewart Hospital in Georgia they were assigned to specific wards according to their pathology as opposed to their race. Kirk's report also mentioned one case of professional integration, but with no consequences for patient care: At Fort Clark Hospital in Texas, white and black doctors, dentists, and administrators worked together with the assistance of black Wacs and nurses – though white practitioners did not treat black patients.[36] The report made no mention of the unique experiment taking place inside Huachuca's hospitals, even though doing so would have likely eased the pressure exerted by the NAACP on the SGO. This may be a sign that the SGO was not keen to publicize this resolutely innovative form of medical integration: For the first time in the history of the Army, African-American doctors were treating white patients. Nevertheless, the SGO did tolerate the experiment, since it did not stop it despite being fully aware of it.

At Huachuca's two military hospitals, the racial boundaries commonly established between black and white bodies were put to the test and then surpassed without resistance via an unusual form of interracial care: black doctors treating white patients, and no longer just white doctors treating black patients. Within a few weeks, the two hospitals were integrated at the level of both patients and doctors as a result of a dual process: white patients' demand to be treated by black doctors, because of their reputation of excellence, and the transfer of African-American professionals to the white hospital, which was critically short of staff and know-how. Both the separation of bodies and the implicit hierarchy of talents that underpinned the medical segregation officially instituted by the Army were thus circumvented. This de facto integration was not only the result of Bousfield's voluntarist policy, but also the consequence of favorable responses to the demands of the patients themselves and of circumstances that at first sight seemed to work against the interests of black doctors. This decisive stage in the integration of care – the outcome of a challenge to traditional racial boundaries – was made possible by the pragmatism of white patients, who accepted black doctors' offers of care as they wanted to receive the best possible treatment in a context of war and isolation. White patients' indifference to the skin color of their caregivers was especially remarkable, since it concerned the body, both as an object of care and as a site where proximity to black patients could be experienced. The body was nevertheless still seen by a large number of whites, especially Southerners, as a sanctuary that had to be preserved from close contact with African Americans. At Huachuca, physical contact was accepted because health and sometimes even life were at stake. The quest for the best possible care overrode racial apprehensions and prejudices. The elites had shown the path to racial tolerance: The highest-ranking officers and celebrities were the first to choose black medicine, perhaps because the qualifications and bourgeois habitus of African-American doctors created a sense of proximity and justified overcoming the distrust they may have felt toward soldiers from more modest origins – as if the feeling of class proximity could neutralize racial prejudice. Yet, the elites were soon followed by "poor whites from the South," to whom violent racist sentiments were often attributed. Bodily proximity and the momentary ascendancy of blacks over white bodies were also accepted because of the nature of the medical interaction itself: This interaction was short-lived and rarely repeated, and it brought together a person in need of care and another that could provide it. More importantly still, this was a non-ordinary encounter that differed significantly from those entailed in serving, eating, and sleeping side by side every day in the same unit. It is likely because this interracial encounter was non-ordinary and circumscribed within the hospital that it was tolerated by the SGO and even discreetly encouraged by the Ninth Service

Command. Nevertheless, the personal indictment of Bousfield for venality and participation in a narcotics racket suggests that this experiment generated considerable local and regional resistance. The merchants and businessmen of Fry and Bisbee probably saw this challenge to the racial status quo as a threat and Bousfield as a man who refused to stay in the place assigned to him by white society. For the white commanders of the 92nd Division who were new to the camp, the self-confidence of the black medical officers carried the risk that other black officers would challenge the racial rules in place and would demand egalitarian treatment in line with their rank. As a result, the process of spontaneous integration within a formal framework of overt segregation could not extend beyond the medical environment; and indeed, this process did not reshape the racial configuration in other parts of the fort, where segregation was maintained or even accentuated. The contagion effect occurred outside of the military compound – in other medical spaces. The experiment at Huachuca's two hospitals provided evidence that white patients did not object in principle to being treated by blacks, as the SGO had claimed early in the war in order to prevent the integration of care. This demonstration by example allowed the supporters of integration to claim that the Army could function as a social laboratory by embracing interracial care.

9 The First Departure

"Is the 93rd Division merely a token military outfit set up to appease Negroes who were complaining that they were not being given adequate opportunity in the Army?" This question asked by an African-American journalist from the *Cleveland Call & Post* in March 1943 was on the minds of all of the division's soldiers and of many black activists and journalists. It also concerned the other all-black units of the US Army.[1] At the end of 1942, the pilots of the 99th Squadron, Tuskegee's elite black unit, had completed their training and been declared combat-ready by their inspectors, but they continued to fly the skies of Alabama with no prospect of overseas deployment. The 99th Squadron was being closely watched by African-American activists, who saw it as a test of the Army's willingness to reform. Judge Hastie roundly condemned the forced immobility that was imposed on this unit.[2] It was, in fact, the Air Force's decision to segregate officer training that prompted his resignation from his position as Civilian Aide to the Secretary of War. For several months, he had denounced the unequal assignment of white and black combat troops, pointing out that virtually all African-American soldiers, whose qualities and loyalty were constantly called into question, were kept in training in the United States.[3] Out of 504,000 black soldiers in the Army, only 79,000 were sent to combat zones, and several combat units were converted into service units to facilitate their acceptance by white commanders.[4] Given this tug-of-war with black organizations and Judge Hastie, the War Department understood that African-American journalists and activists were keeping a close eye on the 93rd Division and that any assignment less prestigious than the one the unit would have received had it been white risked causing a polemic – something it clearly wanted to avoid. In this context, both the Army and outside observers shifted their gaze from the racial regime that prevailed at the fort to the condition of the soldiers themselves.

In March 1943, shortly before the 93rd Division left for maneuver training in Louisiana, *Life* magazine – the weekly publication with sales of three million copies and twenty million readers – sent the little-known white photographer Charles Steinheimer to report on the situation at Fort

Huachuca. Since its creation in 1936, the magazine had transformed the way Americans engaged with images and the news. In February 1941, Henry Luce, head of the Time Inc. empire that ran the magazine, took a stand in favor of immediate US entry into the war and called on his country to assume global leadership in a famous editorial entitled "The American Century." Once America became involved in the conflict, *Life* celebrated the war and turned troop training and combat into an awe-inspiring visual story. Although critical of Roosevelt's socio-economic programs based on increased federal intervention, Luce transformed his magazine into a champion of patriotism.[5] The editorial team understood the need to portray the 93rd as a valorous black division that enjoyed equal treatment and possessed all the qualities required for combat. Entrusted with this mission, Charles Steinheimer took several hundred snapshots during his stay at Huachuca. These images constitute a unique document of the 93rd Division's final weeks of training and of the state of race relations at the fort.[6] Although Steinheimer was under the authority of the Public Relations Officer, he was free to come and go as he pleased. Indeed, *Life* photographers enjoyed a symbiotic relationship with the Army at that point in the conflict: They were treated like officers, wore uniforms without insignia, and were fully supported by the General Staff. Steinheimer was given a great deal of latitude to carry out his mission at the fort. By 1943, the restrictions laid out in the June 1942 Code of Wartime Practices were not being enforced as strictly as before. Moreover, while the Office of Censorship headed by Byron Pryce checked all the photographs and captions, it was mainly concerned with tracking down information that could be of use to the enemy.[7]

During the few days he spent at Huachuca, Steinheimer mainly focused on the training of the troops, whom he sought to portray in a flattering light. Yet, he also entered the barracks, visited the offices, watched surgeries at the black hospital, and joined the entertainment activities organized for the soldiers. His photographs depict the division both as a unified group of muscular, combat-capable men and as a series of individuals who could act as heroes were they to encounter enemy fire. Aerial shots of the desert in which the soldiers were training give an impression of unity and mass; they also suggest the men's ability to resist in a hostile environment evoking North Africa, where some American troops had already gone to fight.

Pictures of collective training and tactical hikes highlight the muscularity and flexibility of bodies in backlit compositions that accentuate the contrast between the soldiers' agility and physical mastery of exercises and the massive, immobile character of the mountains in the background. With its promise of feats and heroism in battle, this exaltation of martial virility counters the stereotype of the lazy, fearful, and emasculated black soldier then conveyed by the General Staff.

The photographs also show black soldiers ready to take part in modern warfare. The Huachuca infantrymen are depicted wearing their uniforms with pride and easily mastering the technical operations, instruments, and weapons of war. Steinheimer produced a few full-length portraits in which soldiers photographed from the front in a low-angle shot are holding 105-mm shells larger than their torsos. In the absence of any higher authority, they appear as the sole masters of the decision to fire. These photographs illustrating a martial black virility were exceptional for the time, as the Army did not want to awaken the fear of African Americans turning their weapons against whites. Unsurprisingly, they were never published in *Life*.

9.1: A soldier holding a 105-mm shell. © Charles E. Steinheimer/The LIFE Picture Collection/Shutterstock.

Group pictures show soldiers at the service of the collective. Individuality dissolves as the men's eyes are concealed by helmets pulled down over their heads. One can see the concentration and coordination of the soldiers who listen to each other to ensure the success of the unit as a whole: a group of crouching soldiers identifying positions on maps spread out in front of them; three men loading an M2A1 howitzer, the standard American field artillery piece, in preparation for firing at an invisible enemy in the background; infantrymen unfastening in the dust a howitzer from the M2 half-track car that has towed it to the training ground, etc.

A series of photographs taken at ground level, from the perspective of soldiers crawling through the desert, gives a good idea of the type of combat

9.2: A group of soldiers identifying positions on their maps. © Charles E. Steinheimer/The LIFE Picture Collection/Shutterstock.

9.3: Combat training in front of the Huachuca Mountains. © Charles E. Steinheimer/The LIFE Picture Collection/Shutterstock.

the 93rd Division was preparing for. We can only imagine the men who are playing the role of the enemy and toward whom the soldiers are moving with determination. But we can very well see the precision with which these soldiers handle their rifles, their fearlessness as they advance on their stomachs or run under fire. Truly destructive weapons or tanks do not appear in this series – even though they were part of the frontline experience. Nevertheless, Steinheimer depicts soldiers who are virile, aggressive, and ready for battle, as if he were taking a position in the War Department's internal debate on whether or not to deploy black troops to the front.

Steinheimer also followed the company members into their quarters, where his lens captured the barracks, the supply building, the mess hall, and the recreation room. The composition of the photographs does not always reflect the hierarchical superiority of whites over blacks. Thus, in a picture taken in a company administration building, the black first sergeant is elevated above the white captain. Black and white officers are depicted in mess halls relaxing side by side, in a closeness and familiarity that neither the Army nor *Life* wished to convey to people outside the camp.

9.4: The captain of an infantry company (left) and his first sergeant (right) in a company administration building. © Charles E. Steinheimer/ The LIFE Picture Collection/Shutterstock.

In March 1943, as the 93rd Division's forty-one-week training was coming to an end, the Army inspectors published a report that contradicted this image of a black unit ready for battle. Shortly after Steinheimer left the fort, the Inspector General assigned to the headquarters of the 93rd noted that the chain of command did not function satisfactorily during the "D" exercises: NCOs and junior officers seemed indifferent to the tactical situation, and general confusion reigned.[8] Also in March 1943, a confidential memorandum from Colonel Edward S. Greenbaum of the Ordnance Department to the Assistant Secretary of War deplored the poor performance of the black officers of the 93rd Division. He stated that, apart from a few exceptions, they "are disinterested in their work, inefficient, lazy, and unable to learn some of the most elementary things. Most of them do not want to fight and are utterly unable to understand the attitude of those white officers who are eager to get into combat duty."[9] All the reports pointed to the inadequacy of the black officers, though without identifying any other weakness in the rest of the unit. The shortcomings of the 93rd were attributed exclusively to the African-American officers, whom the upper hierarchy continued to distrust and keep at a distance – both physically and hierarchically. The possibility that inadequate supervision or unsuitable equipment might have been at play was completely dismissed. Furthermore, the General Staff refused to consider that the experience of racism in civilian life, and then that of segregation and discrimination in the Army, might have contributed to the officers' lack of motivation. In his report to the Army Ground Forces Chief, the Third Army Commander, General Courtney Hodges, wrote the following: "Experienced officers, who have served for extended periods with colored troops, estimate that it takes from 50 to 100 percent longer time to train colored troops than it does white."[10] And yet, while all analyses converged on the shortcomings of the 93rd Division, Hodges's recommendation to extend the training time was not acted upon.

Brigadier General Benjamin Davis, who had come to Huachuca shortly before the 93rd left for maneuvers, opposed the extension of training. He also rejected the proposal to disband the division into several combat units to be stationed at different bases – a move that could have been interpreted as a sign of mistrust toward the black unit. Instead, he proposed two solutions between which the Army would have to choose at the end of maneuver training, that is, after the reevaluation of the performance of the 93rd Division: sending the division abroad if its performance proved satisfactory, or assigning it to a camp located close to a large black civilian population – for instance, at Fort Dix in New Jersey or at Fort Meade in Maryland – if it did not.[11] The decision was therefore postponed in the hope that the soldiers would catch up during the next phase of training. The Inspector General preferred to delay his verdict in order to avoid having to state publicly that the 93rd Division had not been properly trained, as this would have meant conceding either that the General Staff had not provided sufficient resources for the black soldiers or that it continued to doubt their qualities and loyalty. Yet, there was another, more pragmatic consideration: Fort Huachuca had to be evacuated to make room for the 92nd Division, which was now ready to train as a consolidated unit.

Thus, at the end of March 1943, the 93rd Division prepared to leave for maneuvers in Louisiana. Although none of the newspapers reported this, the men of the 368th Infantry Regiment rebelled just as they were about to leave the camp: Knowing that they would not be returning to Huachuca,

9.5: Black and white officers relaxing in a mess hall. © Charles E. Steinheimer/The LIFE Picture Collection/Shutterstock.

they destroyed some of the sites associated with their humiliating training. A few hours before boarding the train, they ransacked their barracks, smashing over 1,000 windows, removing plumbing from walls, and leaving food to rot. The PX had to be shut down, and the quarters of the 368th were entirely sealed off after its departure to allow time for a complete refurbishment. Outside the camp, the men also destroyed the toilets of the Greentop. The soldiers' anger had been provoked by the order to evacuate at short notice. They had been made to wait long hours in the cold of the night for the morning train, and many of them had forced their way into the barracks to find blankets and a place to sleep.

Soldier revolts on the eve of departure were quite common at the time. However, the men of the 368th had already distinguished themselves by their large presence in the fort's stockade – where they were typically incarcerated for petty theft or brawls – and in the hospital – where they accounted for many of the malingerers. Originating mostly from the northern states, these men rebelled against their humiliating condition far more violently than did the soldiers of the 25th Infantry Regiment, many of whom were southern-born members of the Army Reserve.[12] The revolt of March 1943 may have also reflected their fears about the treatment that awaited them in the Jim Crow South or their irritation with the uncertainty that continued to hang over their future assignment. In addition, they probably suspected that their rebellion would go unpunished because of their transfer to the maneuver grounds. The event was indeed buried and the uprising remained unpublicized. Nevertheless, the men's anger had been aroused, and the fort's commander feared that the soldiers of the 92nd Division, who had been training in the South and whose arrival was now imminent, would likewise rebel against their condition.

On April 3, 1943, the 93rd Division left Huachuca for fourteen weeks of maneuvers in Louisiana. Following the departure of the 14,000 men, all that remained was an empty camp and the military personnel who kept it running: soldiers under the commander's orders, Wacs, and medical staff. Several thousand miles from Arizona, the men of the 93rd fought for three months against white units of the Third Army. It was the first time that they were in contact with white soldiers. It was also the first time that they were operating as members of the Army in a southern environment, where the racial regime in place made their mere presence among whites problematic.[13] Conflicts were common and authority was often defied. Many soldiers deserted or stole Army equipment. Others were confronted with the racism of Louisiana society and, like many other black soldiers training at southern camps, were caught up in clashes with the white community. Yet, at the end of maneuvers, the Third Army Commander, Lieutenant General Walter Krueger, stated that the 93rd Division had behaved well and had provided proof of its ability to fight. The incompetence of the black officers was no longer mentioned, either because it was deemed less problematic than the Huachuca inspections had suggested, or because it had been decided that it should be overlooked so that black troops could be deployed overseas. In April, the Inspector General assigned to the headquarters of the 93rd Division also noted significant progress. After having deplored the poor functioning of the chain of command at Huachuca in March, he was now pleased with the quality of order transmission – from officers to the lowest echelons – in each of the combat units he inspected. There were still a few points to be improved – ammunition supply, assignment of men to vehicles, truck maintenance – but the next phase of maneuver training would take care of this.[14] The Army was now confident and felt that it had nothing left to hide. Thus, at the beginning of May, black journalists and photographers were invited by Truman Gibson and Brigadier General Davis to come and observe, for a period of three days, the men of the 93rd engaged in maneuvers. They were taken to the combat zones to witness the various exercises. Writing in *The Crisis*, the magazine of the NAACP, Roy Wilkins concluded that the

> 93rd was well-trained in all the modern weapons of warfare. [...] The 93rd has every weapon needed by a combat division and the men are very proud of their outfits, especially the tank men. [...] Maj. Gen. Miller is the right man in the right place and in him our men have a leader who is proud of his men, fair to them, and determined that they shall be second to no division in the army.[15]

A series of photographs of the maneuvers followed, all of them designed to leave African-American readers thinking that black soldiers would soon be sent to fight overseas. The General Staff's public relations campaign for blacks had proven successful.

Shortly afterwards, in August 1943, *Life* finally published ten of the hundreds of photographs taken by Steinheimer in March. The images were spread over four pages splashed with advertising.[16] This was the first reportage on the training of the 93rd Division to be published in the white press. The magazine's readers saw the pictures three months after the photo shoot: The men of the 93rd were no longer at Huachuca, but in California's Mojave Desert for the second phase of maneuvers. By that time, any doubts about the division's assignment had been dispelled, and the editorial team was able to assure readers that the soldiers were getting ready to fight in Europe. Steinheimer's photo essay, entitled "Negro Division. It Prepares to Go Overseas," supported the government's goal of pacifying the armed forces in the wake of the July race riots and sought to consolidate the country's confidence in its black troops. The images selected by the editorial team highlighted the unity and determination of the troops as well as the men's consent to being commanded by whites. The photographs were accompanied by the following text: "The 93rd Infantry Division [...] has reached a state of training where it is ready to move out of the country at a moment's notice. [...] Cooperation between the whites and the Negroes throughout the division is usually considered to be excellent."

9.6: "The Negro Division Prepares to Go Overseas." © NLIA, *Life Magazine*, 1943.

The opening photograph, taken during a review, gives pride of place to the commanding officers of the 93rd Division: Behind white Colonel Thomas F. Taylor stand eleven officers, just under half of whom are African-American; further back, we can make out the musicians of the marching band. Another photograph, also taken from an elevated position to accentuate the mass effect, shows columns of soldiers carrying machine guns and returning to camp after a twenty-five-mile hike in the desert. They look exhausted, but order and rhythm have been maintained despite the heat and boredom.

From the parade – a military exercise choreographed by the Army to convey its control and mastery both to itself and to outside observers – *Life*'s editorial team chose to show the ballet of motorized vehicles driven by black infantrymen and armed with heavy machine guns, .50-caliber M2s. The effect of numbers is enhanced by the long line of trucks, the end of which is nowhere in sight. Discipline governs both the bodies of the men – arms folded in front of their chests – and the rhythm of the vehicles. From Steinheimer's photographic essay produced three months earlier, *Life* retained the pictures of virile, disciplined bodies. However, it discarded those of African Americans wielding heavy weapons or handling ammunition or explosive charges in poses that might have been deemed aggressive or threatening.

9.7: "In sweltering desert heat, immediately after a 25-mile hike, Negro soldiers of the 93rd Division march on the parade ground at Fort Huachuca, Ariz." © NLIA, *Life Magazine*, 1943.

Life also distinguished black NCOs and officials of the division by publishing four close-up portraits of men detached from their surroundings: a sergeant who had served in the Army for twenty-four years, one of the two black company captains, First Lieutenant Chaplain Nimrod Cautious Calhoun (the soldiers' spiritual counselor), and a medical officer (the highest-ranking of the four men). The magazine wanted readers to believe that leadership functions were shared equally between blacks and whites at the fort.

However, the magazine remained conservative in its depiction of interactions between whites and blacks. One of Steinheimer's photographs, taken at ground level, features white Major Thomas Simpson lying on his stomach shoulder to shoulder with black Lieutenant Vasco de Gama Hale. Each of the two men is holding a walkie-talkie (or handie-talkie)

9.8: "With arms folded and steel helmets pulled down over their heads, Negro soldiers roll by in their vehicles during the division parade." © NLIA, *Life Magazine*, 1943.

radio, coordinating soldiers invisible on the image and sharing authority in a physical proximity that signifies equality. *Life* cut the photo in half along the line of contact and published the two sections on two facing pages of the magazine, with the effect of merely suggesting the physical contact between the black man and the white man.

9.9: "Top Sergeant Jackson weighs 236 pounds, has been in Army 24 years." © NLIA, *Life Magazine*, 1943.

The image showing white Major Allan Carrell in a position of hierarchical and physical superiority over black Private Leon Smith, sitting at the bottom of a foxhole and calculating lines of fire, was left untouched. These publication choices were made by the editorial team. The Code of Wartime Practices said nothing about relations between blacks and whites; yet, according to the unwritten rules of representation, the latter could never be portrayed in a position of subordination to the former.[17]

The photo essay, designed to convince readers that the 93rd was operating smoothly and was ready for deployment overseas, was published when the men were already in the final stages of maneuvers. Meanwhile, in Washington, Robert Sengstacke and ten other black press editors met with Vice President Henry Wallace, Assistant Secretary of War John McCloy, and Secretary of the Navy William Knox on July 16 and 17. They asked for better access to commanders in order to cover the training, for equal treatment of black troops, and, once again, for the dispatch of African-American soldiers to the front. The Advisory Committee on Negro Troop Policies, headed by McCloy, had been created a year earlier in August 1942; Judge Hastie had neither been informed of its creation nor invited to participate in its working sessions. Members of the committee, which included moderates such as Davis and Gibson, made modest recommendations: increase the number of black soldiers in high-visibility units (such as ambulance companies), create a battalion of African-American paratroopers, and assign black soldiers to combat engineer units.[18] After meeting with the leaders of the black press, the McCloy committee finally demanded that African-American combat troops be dispatched to the front, as this seemed

9.10: Original photograph taken by Charles Steinheimer. © Charles E. Steinheimer/The LIFE Picture Collection/Shutterstock.

9.11: "Using handie-talkie radios, Negro Lieut. Vasco de Gama Hale works [...] with Major Thomas Simpson in directing live-ammunition practice." © NLIA, *Life Magazine*, 1943.

9.12: "In fire direction, Major Allan Carrell supervises the work of Pvt. Leon Smith, in a foxhole, who is computing artillery ranges for the battery and radio operators." © NLIA, *Life Magazine*, 1943.

to be the best way to reduce tensions in the black units.[19] However, the 93rd had to wait a few more months before being given an assignment.

The S-32 survey "Attitude of and toward Negroes," which was conducted in March 1943 by the War Department's Research Branch, which had been created in October 1941, found that 64 percent of black soldiers stationed in the United States did not want to be sent overseas, compared with 41 percent of whites. This was a finding that the Army could use to resist demands from African-American organizations and newspapers. Among the men who were willing to leave, factors such as curiosity, a taste for adventure, a desire to travel, and impatience to escape boredom may have come into play. Moreover, going to Europe was sometimes associated with the possibility of experiencing egalitarian race relations. It may also be that the most educated men, who were also those of highest rank and probably the most sensitive to social recognition by white society, expected combat to bring them benefits in the post-war period or viewed it as an opportunity to denounce the Army's racial prejudice.[20] Nevertheless, most of the men did not want to leave the United States to defend a democracy that did not respect their rights as citizens. They also criticized the elitism of black organizations and newspapers which fought for equal treatment without having to pay the price of its implementation: exposure to fire and perhaps, ultimately, injury, mutilation, or death.[21] As Nelson Peery recalled in his autobiography: "We hated the black newspapers for their constant appeals to the government to send us into action."[22]

In November 1943, Walter White wrote once again to Secretary of War Henry Stimson, urging him to specify what assignment he had in mind for the 93rd Division. The following month, Inspector Davis went to California, where the division was in the last stages of maneuvers, to get an idea of the progress it was making. He was impressed by the performance of the troops and the constructive attitude of the soldiers and officers. He felt that the men were ready for combat.[23] Under the combined pressure of black newspapers and organizations, President Roosevelt finally took the decision to deploy the 93rd overseas. However, he had to wait for a commander to agree to lead African-American soldiers on the front. Ultimately, Lieutenant General Millard Harmon, Commanding General of the US Army Forces, informed the War Department that he needed a division to strengthen his force and that he was indifferent to the race of the men. The 93rd was sent to the Pacific in January 1944, nine months after its departure from Fort Huachuca. Under political pressure, the General Staff gave in and agreed to evaluate on the ground the quality of the men who had been training in a unique segregated configuration. Without waiting for the conclusions of this experiment, it attempted a second instance of all-black training at Huachuca – as had been planned when the 92nd Division was formed at the beginning of the war: same location, same segregated configuration, but with other men and, above all, other white commanders, who implemented a very different racial regime.

10 A Southern Ambiance

In the middle of May 1943, 1,329 railroad cars carrying the soldiers of the 92nd Division – 46 trains from 4 different camps – arrived at Fort Huachuca to fill the space left empty by the departure of the blue helmets, the nickname that had been given to the 93rd Division. The only people still present at the fort were the men and women who kept it running: Colonel Hardy's team, Wacs, doctors, and chaplains. The 92nd Division discovered a camp that was very different from the one, then still under construction, which the 93rd had entered in April 1942. Most of the buildings had been erected, the USO center opened its doors to soldiers during rest periods, and entertainment was provided at the Greentop in the evenings and at weekends. The fort, however, was not only an architectural complex; it was also a racial equilibrium that rested on a unique mode of managing conflict, distractions to ease the frustration, and specific patterns of interaction between men and women on either side of the color line. This equilibrium was unstable, sometimes contested, but it was an equilibrium nonetheless, and one that Hardy and his team had managed to achieve. To avoid altercations, the colonel had limited the presence of black troops to the camp, turning the latter into an enclave with some extensions into civilian territory under Army control. In this vast space, he had encouraged a black togetherness that facilitated the pursuit of leisure and cultural activities, created professional opportunities (for Wacs and medical officers), and made white authority and training conditions more tolerable. He had also fostered a tacit agreement that black troops should be treated with respect. As a result, the soldiers of the 92nd entered a camp that already had a history – an all-black mode of operation unlike anything they had experienced before. Yet, to what extent could this place impose its spirit and equilibrium on the men who had come to occupy it?

When the 92nd Division arrived at Huachuca, Lieutenant Colonel Midian Bousfield took a good look at the officer in command, General Edward Almond, a short man who never went anywhere without his sunglasses and his swagger stick. Some of the soldiers referred to

Almond as "the little midget," while also recognizing that he was a born leader. Shortly after a stone was thrown at the commander's vehicle in Fry, the director of the black hospital wrote to Truman Gibson: "This is the apotheosis of the Virginia method of handling race relations."[1]

Born in Luray in 1892, Almond was a pure product of Virginia's racist society. The only blacks he had come into contact with in his youth were the laborers working on his grandfather's farm.[2] At the age of twenty, he had entered the Virginia Military Institute, a military academy less prestigious than West Point and a white male bastion dominated by statues of Confederate heroes. After graduating third from the top of his class of sixty-five in June 1915 and receiving a commission at the end of November 1916, shortly before the United States entered World War I in April 1917, he had been fortunate enough to be sent to the front and get his first taste of fire. In 1918, he had led a battalion of the 4th Infantry Division alongside French troops into the Second Battle of the Marne, and he had remained in Europe for another year to take part in the occupation of Germany. However, owing to the National Defense Act of 1920, which had reduced the size of the peacetime regular Army and the number of commissioned positions, he had been made to wait for more than ten years before being given the opportunity to command a unit. During the interwar period, he had taught strategy at the Marion Military Institute in Alabama for fourteen years, while continuing to train at the most prestigious military schools, including at the OCS at Fort Benning, where he had caught the attention of the future Army Chief of Staff, Lieutenant Colonel George C. Marshall. In 1930, he had had his first experience of leading segregated troops as the commander of the 3rd Battalion of Philippine Scouts, which had joined the regular US Army in 1921. He had then been appointed to coordinate Latin American military attachés in the Intelligence Division of the General Staff. The Philippines and Latin America were two appointments that had prepared him to command black troops, as had been the case for Colonel Hardy. When war broke out in Europe in September 1939, Almond insisted on being assigned to a command position. In April 1942, the General Staff appointed him Assistant Commander of the 93rd Infantry Division at Fort Huachuca. Three months later, he was sent to Fort McClellan, Alabama, to train the 92nd, the second of the two all-black divisions. Like General Hall, the commander of the blue helmets, he had been chosen not only for his leadership qualities, but also for his southern origins.[3] Some of his contemporaries suspected that his proximity to General Marshall had earned him the post. And yet, Almond had commanded units, both during World War I and during the interwar period, in an Army that had few positions to offer.[4]

In October 1942, Almond took command of a division with a tarnished reputation. Indeed, throughout the interwar years, the white officers who had commanded the 92nd Division during World War I were insistent that it had fought badly and had thus demonstrated black soldiers' unfitness for combat. Yet, the men of the 92nd had so many handicaps that they were never given the chance to show what they could do. Formed as an all-black unit in 1917, the division with the buffalo insignia was dispersed to seven different camps for training. Many of the soldiers had physical disabilities, and 40 percent were illiterate. Their white commanders made no secret of the fact that they would have preferred to lead a white division. Although by the end of training the soldiers had not acquired the technical mastery that was expected of them, the Army refused to transfer better soldiers to the 92nd before it left for France in May 1918. Once in France, the men's experience of the front was limited to a few days of combat. At the start of the Meuse–Argonne offensive, the 368th Regiment acted as liaison between the French and American armies, but was withdrawn from the front after only five days on the grounds that it was disoriented. Following victory, the division underwent rapid demobilization. Black officers later highlighted the lack of proper equipment to explain the alleged failures of the 92nd Division.[5] Yet, no one in the Army considered the possibility that these failings might have also been due to the dispersion and extremely short duration of training.[6]

When the 92nd was reassembled as an all-black division in 1942, the same mistakes were made: dispersal during training, low quality of recruits, and reluctance to command blacks on the part of white officers. At the time, no base other than Huachuca was ready to accommodate 15,000 African-American soldiers, and the fort was already occupied by the men of the 93rd. It was therefore decided to station the 92nd in different camps. The division's headquarters and special units were activated at Fort McClellan in Alabama, one of the southern states with the most restrictive racial laws in the country. The combat teams were distributed among three other bases situated far apart from each other – Camp Atterbury in Indiana, Camp Breckinridge in Kentucky, and Camp Joseph T. Robinson in Arkansas – the latter two being also located in the South. In 1942, all four states (including Indiana) implemented strict segregation in every area of daily life, and they all had laws prohibiting sexual relations and marriage between blacks and whites. William Perry, a twenty-year-old native of Cleveland who had been assigned to the 600th Battalion's medical team at Fort McClellan, recalls having felt "kind of slapped in the face. It began to change my view about the army and what was going on." After a first bus ride to Anniston, he had decided not to ever leave the camp again. Although his Arkansas-born mother had described to him how Jim Crow operated in the South, he had been shocked when refused service in a bar. He was later transferred to Camp Robinson.[7]

In each of the memoranda he sent to the commanders of the 92nd Division's regiments, General Almond repeated that

> The existence of these laws and customs is a fact. [...] It is not our function to attempt to alter the existing order. The problem is social, not military. When we remember that numbers of persons have devoted their entire lifetimes unsuccessfully trying to change these ways of living, we are forced to realize that any effort by this division to that end would be an improper diversion of its time and energy, and contrary to the interests of National Defense. The men of this division will receive fair and just treatment, and they will obey the laws of the state and its communities.[8]

Thus, the racist laws in force in the states where the 92nd Division was training applied to the black soldiers whenever they were on leave from the camps. Coexistence with the surrounding communities was especially difficult, since these military bases were not equipped to accommodate so many black troops: Housing and recreational facilities were still under construction when the African-American soldiers first arrived. Moreover, in segregated black–white camps, specific black facilities had to be built apart from those of white troops; this was the case, for instance, at Fort McClellan, where 26,000 white soldiers had already begun training. At Camp Robinson, a USO center was opened for the soldiers of the 371st Combat Team, and the commander of the fort organized a bus service for African Americans in collaboration with the municipality of Little Rock. In short, up until May 1942, the soldiers and officers of the 92nd Division were subject to the southern regime of race relations.

The vast majority of the men of the 92nd had no experience of military life and had to learn to be soldiers very rapidly. The only ones with military experience were the cadres – 128 officers and 1,200 enlisted men – who had trained with the 93rd Division at Fort Huachuca for a period of 3 months.[9] The team of officers and NCOs was formed out of this particular group. When the division was activated in October 1942, all 550 officers were white and only 1 chaplain was black – despite the fact that some African Americans had commanded the companies of the 92nd during World War I. Most of these white officers were not fully qualified for their positions; as a result, they struggled to make black soldiers obey and deliver the expected results. Nevertheless, Almond did manage to get rid of those deemed "unsuitable for duty with colored troops."[10] The General Staff agreed to replace them. Indeed, since August 1942, it had been widely accepted in the War Department that African-American soldiers had to be commanded with a special kind of firmness.[11]

Yet, at the end of the summer, a directive was issued that the 92nd Division should be considered the second-most-important assignment for African-American officers – of which there were only 817 in the entire Army at the time. From October onwards, black lieutenants arrived in "blocks" (around thirty each month) at the same time as the new classes of OCS graduates, and an equal number of white officers had to leave their posts to free up the positions to which these black officers were entitled. This process, which undermined group cohesion, continued until all lieutenant positions were filled by African Americans. After a few months, Almond asked the regimental commanders to describe the qualities and performance of the black lieutenants: The commanders noted a few weaknesses, particularly in leadership, but were generally positive and confident that the African-American officers would improve with experience and training.[12]

The headquarters and special units at Fort McClellan were made up of men from the Second and Fifth Service Commands in the North, whereas the combat teams were brought in from the Fourth and Eighth Service Commands in the South. As a result, there was some form of social mixing within the division.[13] Yet, the level of education, as measured by the AGCT, was very low in both cases. Almost half of the men were placed in class V (the lowest), a third in class IV, 10 percent in class III, and the rest, a few percent, in classes I and II.[14] In early 1943, Almond asked for the replacement of the weakest soldiers, namely the 7,000 men placed in category V. Scores improved as new men arrived: By January 1943, 21 percent of soldiers were in class V, 41 percent in class IV, 15 percent in class III, 10 percent in class II, and 13 percent were not classified as they were deemed illiterates.[15] Moreover, instructors stepped up their efforts during the first phase of training to ensure that all soldiers had the basic literacy and numeracy skills. Illiterate soldiers were forced to attend evening classes. Each of the four training bases opened a "casual camp," where the least educated men were given a refresher course. Those who managed to reach a sufficiently good level rejoined the rest of the group; those who failed were replaced.[16] At the same time, the General Staff began to realize that scores on the AGCT were not necessarily a reliable indicator of a man's ability to become a good soldier.[17]

Often unenthusiastic about the idea of becoming soldiers and ill-prepared for the demands of this condition, the men were taught to fight by Almond, who as a former captain had been particularly exposed to fire during World War I.[18] Demanding and hot-tempered, Almond's main concern was to prepare the soldiers physically and technically and to fuel their aggression toward Axis enemies. The former captain was acutely aware of the qualities required to fight on the battlefield. On October 15, 1942, during the activation ceremony held at Fort McClellan, Almond, who had a flair for stagecraft and possessed genuine oratorical skills, said the following to the troops who were present:

> Our task of developing this new division is no easy one. But it can and will be accomplished. [...] It demands the transition of these men from peaceful, law-abiding citizens into rugged, determined soldiers who are capable of meeting and defeating a blood-thirsty opponent; an opponent who is certain to be shrewd, crafty, unscrupulous and able! I have fought the Germans and have lived among the Japanese. I thoroughly appreciate and respect the fighting abilities of both. [...] It is not enough to be expert with our weapons, our men must be able to march farther and faster, to suffer greater hardships and to engage in successful, personal combat with this German or Japanese soldier. [...] The disadvantage of the present dispersion of our units in our early training, we must face and overcome. We can and we will.[19]

Almond oversaw the preparation of the troops by rotating between the different camps. He observed the training of soldiers, then left instructions for his deputies to correct any weaknesses or to vary the exercises. He was aided in this task by John E. Wood, a colonel who had just returned from Liberia, where he had led the all-black 41st Engineer Regiment in charge of building an airstrip and monitoring the Firestone rubber plantation. Yet, instead of seeing Wood as an ally, Almond saw him as a rival. He put him in charge of administrative tasks and trained the men himself.[20]

The dispersal of the division, the men's low education level and lack of military experience, and the cadres' poor leadership caused the 92nd to lag behind in training. Lacking confidence in his soldiers, Almond requested that the basic and individual training phases be extended by four weeks. Between January and March 1943, shortly before the troops regrouped at Huachuca, Brigadier General Benjamin Davis inspected the training facilities of the 92nd Division. In three of the four training camps, he found that the troops had superior morale and that relations between white and black officers were without "complications" and sometimes even excellent. He found "no complaints of racial discrimination." Davis gave high marks to Almond and his team, whom he described as "extremely active and efficient." In his report to the Inspector General, he even wrote: "General Almond has shown special aptitude for a command composed of colored and white officers and a colored enlisted personnel. He has secured and maintained the greatest respect and admiration of the colored officers and enlisted personnel by his fairness and sympathy with their problems."[21] And yet, just a few weeks after this report was written, Huachuca was the scene of major unrest. Had Inspector Davis lacked discernment in his judgment of Almond in early 1943? Had he deliberately concealed his doubts so as to avoid challenging the authority of a white general?

When the trains arrived at the fort, the 92nd Division was assembled for the first time. At Huachuca, 15,000 black soldiers, 700 white officers, and 300 African-American officers (almost exclusively first and second lieutenants) were now training side by side, comparing and gauging each other. They had to learn to function as a unit: In other words, they had to transfer, from the separate regiments to the division, the esprit de corps that had been gradually built up over a period of eight months. Once this process had been achieved, unit training was considered complete, and the men could move on to combined training. The M5A1 light tanks that had just been delivered played a key role in this second phase, as would the tank destroyers that would arrive in early 1944.

The men also had to learn to train in the dry, hot Arizona summer, this being a completely new experience for them. Some of them did not have

10.1: Inspection of M10 tank destroyers by soldiers and Wacs. © Fort Huachuca Museum.

the physical stamina; others got discouraged. In July, a twenty-five-mile hike was organized to test their endurance; many cited disabilities as a reason not to go all the way. Six hundred men were identified as not having the physical qualities or energy to fight. They were set apart in a "casual camp" for in-depth training, in the hope that they would be able to catch up with the group. Most of these ailments were feigned: They were the first harbinger of the resistance to training that was to plague the 92nd Division. Almond, who understood too late the importance of racial tensions, subsequently wrote in his notes: "This probably was the first indication of racial instability and for disinclination to enter combat."[22]

White officers from the South were now clearly outnumbered. At the camps where they had earlier trained the men of the 92nd, they had been surrounded by white soldiers and their white commanders, as well as by civilian communities whose racial practices they knew and approved. In other words, they had not felt the sense of isolation that they were experiencing at Huachuca, where they no longer had the advantage of numbers and had not yet mastered the local racial codes. In this context, ignorance and perhaps also fear led them to tighten the racial regime that had been in force in their regiments since October 1942. They forcibly imposed restrictions and ignored the racial status quo that Colonel Hardy had achieved. They sought to restore their power and authority over blacks by introducing new rules and humiliating them.

The white officers acted as if the functioning and rules of the all-black post were identical to those of a segregated camp. In other words, they reinforced the existing segregation. Almond could have decided to put an end to the racial segregation of the officers' clubs, as was now authorized by the Adjutant General's Office directive of March 10, 1943. This directive, adopted following numerous challenges to the segregation of recreational areas at other camps, stated that such areas could not be explicitly assigned to one race or another. However, it did leave open the possibility of permanently or temporarily assigning them to a unit or part of a unit (for instance, through staggered schedules), knowing full well that the units were themselves segregated. Moreover, the directive was formulated in such a general way as to leave it up to the commander to decide whether or not to apply it. Almond did not even bother to ask himself the question. At Huachuca, the two clubs continued to operate in an explicitly segregated manner.[23]

Most importantly, a new form of segregation appeared in places where it had not existed before. In May 1943, Colonel Sterling A. Wood attempted to segregate the officers' mess of the 371st Infantry Regiment: He replaced the African-American mess officer with a white officer, and then reinstated the principle of assigning tables according to officer race. One day, an African-American officer refused to respect the mess hall's new racial configuration and sat down at a table reserved for whites. When the white mess officer tried to move him to another table, the offender injured his hand with a fork. The rest of the black officers boycotted the place and started having their meals at the Mountain View Club, where they were able to meet among themselves without having to suffer the humiliation of segregation. The segregation of the mess hall was ended: The boycott likely paid off on this particular occasion because it targeted a departure from the rule.[24] The newly arrived officers also tried to impose segregation on the owners of private businesses at the fort. General Almond's wife wanted different shopping days to be instituted for blacks and whites in order to prevent them from intermingling. Yet, even southern stores welcomed black and white customers, as long as they complied with the rules of behavior that were tacitly agreed upon by the community.[25] Brigadier General Coburn who, like many white Southerners, was probably convinced that dining next to blacks led to intolerable proximity and intimacy,[26] also tried to segregate the tables at Mar Kim's Chinese Restaurant, which had been an institution at the fort since 1934. One Sunday evening, Chaplain Wactor went with his wife to Mar Kim's as he had always done. As they were about to sit down at a table where three white officers were already seated, they were prevented by Coburn from taking their seats. The general later explained to Inspector Davis that he had wanted to avoid an altercation with the white officers, who had allegedly objected to the presence of the black chaplain: He had preferred to humiliate Wactor instead of reminding his men that they were in a private establishment in Arizona, where a business owner could freely choose who could enter his premises.

The newcomers also tried to regain their ascendancy over blacks by humiliating them: They constantly reminded the soldiers of their supposed inferiority in both rank and race. Almond's wife called a Wac switchboard operator a "nigger" on the phone, and then told her that she did not like black people. At times, the division commander himself publicly addressed the soldiers as "niggers." Moreover, Almond went to see the men training in the desert not by jeep or by truck, but by plane. In this way, he was able to inspect the three regiments in one afternoon, without inflicting on himself the sand and the burning sun; it was the men on the ground who had to swallow the dust as the ultralight Piper Cub pulled away after the inspection. Sergeant William Perry later recalled:

Most of the time we spent out in the field running problems. [...] Then, in the middle of all that, General Almond would come out and do an inspection. There would be about 10,000 of us out there running problems, and we had to stop and get ready for inspection. We would polish up everything and lay it all out in the proper fashion, all displayed properly on the field blanket. And then we'd wait out there in that sun for 4 or 5 hours. Finally he would fly in his little plane and look us over. Zoom, he'd fly over us blowing sand and debris in our faces. That was Almond's kind of inspection.[27]

Some soldiers believed that this humiliation was the price they had to pay for the narcissistic wound that the General Staff had inflicted on the commander by denying him a white division.[28] Away from the control of the Ninth Service Command headquarters in Fort Douglas (840 miles to the north), the white officers developed a sense of impunity, and some of them even resorted to physical violence: First Lieutenant Gerald Hough of the 599th Field Artillery Battalion allegedly hit a drunken soldier over the head with the butt of his pistol; another white officer was said to have kicked two men in the face as they lay belly-down.[29] Such behavior was not punished at first: Almond had temporarily lifted the ban on the use of violence, suggesting to white officers that they were free to mistreat their men.

Even African-American officers were scorned by their white superiors, who denied them equality of training and responsibility lest it should lead to the social equality they desperately wanted to prevent. The symbolic distance between black and white officers felt even worse because of the physical and social proximity between them. The white major who led Company K of the 370th Regiment referred to all the black lieutenants under his command as "boys." Lieutenant Reuben Horner, who was the son of a buffalo soldier and had grown up at Fort Huachuca and then in Tucson, paid the price for protesting: two weeks of garbage duty (the time it took to sort through all the battalion's garbage and ensure that the soldiers had not thrown out any shells or mines), uniform inspection at the cinema entrance, and, finally, enforcement of good behavior in one of the service clubs. This humiliating punishment was meant to discourage any other racially motivated protest.[30] In addition, white officers took over prestigious and visible positions of responsibility which had previously been held by blacks. Thus, one of the post's black chaplains, Major May, was replaced while on leave with a white first lieutenant (i.e., a man of very low rank) instead of the nearest-ranking black officer, Captain Grant Reynolds.[31] Considered excessively contentious by the Army, Reynolds had been bounced from training base to training base before coming to Huachuca, where he also challenged white privilege. Similarly, the black assistant for public relations, Captain Homer Roberts, was replaced with a white officer later that summer.[32]

Black officers were humiliated both in front of their white peers and in front of their men. At Huachuca, Almond created a School of Application and Proficiency for "incompetent officers," which only African Americans were obligated to attend. In so doing, he raised doubts about the qualities and professionalism of black officers, even though they had undergone the same training and passed the same tests as their white counterparts. While the Army had authorized the temporary sidelining of soldiers whose level was deemed inadequate,[33] this practice was not supposed to apply to officers. Nevertheless, at Huachuca, fifty-three African-American officers deemed "difficult" or too "aggressive" were sent to the school without explanation. There, they were treated like ordinary soldiers: They were forced to go on long hikes with bags on their backs under the eyes of their men. The aim was to undermine their authority and to neutralize their power of contestation.[34]

Although black officers did protest their humiliation by (successfully) boycotting the 371st Regiment's mess hall, no other form of collective resistance ever occurred at the fort. The soldiers, for their part, engaged in sporadic violence. One evening in May, Colonel Hardy and a group of white officers from the 92nd set off by car for Fry. They were stopped by a roadblock and a group of men armed with bottles. One of the officers was wounded in the eye and had to be hospitalized at the fort's hospital.[35] White commanders became more vulnerable as soon as they stepped out of the fort, even though the law continued to be on their side. A white officer was hit on the head by a soldier in his sleep and was later treated at the black hospital – which incidentally demonstrated the latter's superiority. After these incidents, a rumor circulated at the fort that the white officers would be massacred as soon as the 92nd was sent to the front.[36] In reality, whites only saw their physical integrity and authority threatened on these three occasions. These incidents were not necessarily the harbingers of a mutiny, especially since no soldier had taken possession of arms or ammunition. Nevertheless, Bousfield did worry about a possible outbreak of violence – as did, no doubt, other high-ranking officers at Huachuca. He sounded the alarm to Truman Gibson, and sought to convince him to come to the fort as soon as possible: "There isn't a Negro, from a buck private up to the lofty rank of 2nd lieutenant, who is not making every possible effort to get out of the 92nd. Better come out here and take a look at this. It gets worse daily."[37] In turn, Gibson warned General Davis of a possible conflagration, writing that "A very serious situation is brewing."[38] In Washington, the inspector was also alerted by Colonel Davison, Chief of Staff at the headquarters of the Ninth Service Command, who was monitoring the arrival of the 92nd at Huachuca from afar. Davison reported the criticism levelled by county and state authorities against Colonel Hardy, who was unfairly held responsible for the deteriorating situation at the fort.[39]

These men would probably not have been so worried if the rest of the country had not been in turmoil at the time. In the North, race riots rocked Detroit, Harlem in New York, and many other cities where public places had become sites of racial tension.[40] Inside the Army, clashes between blacks and whites no longer took place only in garrison towns, but also within the confines of the camps. Thus, fights broke out without any prior civilian interference or police blunder, as had been the case the previous summer. Challenges to the racial regime, which had been individual and limited in scale, were now collective and widespread.[41] At Camp Stewart, an air defense training base located in the middle of the forest near Savannah, black soldiers ambushed white military police convoys on the night of June 6, killing one man and wounding four.[42] The Army feared that the uprisings would spread like wildfire from base to base. At the annual conference of service commands held at the end of July, a representative of the Inspector General's Office warned that "In my opinion the toughest problem confronting service commanders today is the one of preventing disturbances involving colored troops." The Office's assessment had changed considerably since the wave of uprisings of the previous summer. The personal responsibility of commanders was now emphasized: The white officers were insufficiently concerned with the daily lives of their men, insufficiently aware of the extent of the discrimination they faced outside of the camps. Some of them even "permit on their own posts discriminations which are contrary to the War Department policies and instructions" or only "grudgingly accept Negro officers assigned to their unit."[43] Since arriving in Arizona, Almond had been guilty of all these errors.

Hardy had never felt so much tension at the fort, not even during the boycott of the Black Officers' Club in June 1942 or on the day of the 93rd Division's departure. He likely feared that a mutiny would break out, as had happened at Camp Van Dorn and Camp Stewart. He certainly sensed that he was distrusted on the other side of the gates. He wanted to prevent his fort from going up in flames, and believed that the key to racial peace lay in dialogue, in the sharing of moments of conviviality between white and black officers – the latter being uniquely affected by the recent hardening of the racial regime and the expression of racist prejudice. The opening of the black art exhibition at the Mountain View Club was a timely opportunity to bring together the fort's highest-ranking officers from both sides of the color line. To help ease the tensions, Hardy organized a barbecue that suspended military time and created a parenthesis of interracial understanding at a distance from the training grounds. One Saturday in June, he gathered his "brothers officers" in the late afternoon in a quiet clearing at the start of Huachuca

Canyon. He acted as a host both to the officers of the 92nd Division under his command and to the few civilians whom he had invited. Almond, who had had no choice but to attend, acted evasively, making it clear that he feared contact with the black officers and treating them with contempt.

Wooden tables had been set up underneath the tall trees, near the spring closest to the camp. A meal was served by volunteer Wacs to the 600 black and white officers who mingled in the shade. Hardy walked among the men, speaking to them informally and asking for news. He then declared: "The 92nd Division troops have recently come to Fort Huachuca. [...] It is necessary that we know, appreciate and respect each other in a generous and considerate spirit to ably and efficiently work together." Hardy sought to foster a form of mutual esteem and respect across the color line, as had prevailed at times during the training of the 93rd Division.

By comparison, Almond's speech was abrupt and paranoid. "I have every confidence and faith in my officers and men. [...] We have serious work to do. Those who won't or can't keep up will be left behind." Almond also asked those who did not belong to the division to "leave

10.2: The barbecue organized by Col. Hardy (center), surrounded by officers of the 92nd Division. © Fort Huachuca Museum.

[his] men in peace." He was targeting the black officers at the hospital and the camp command – the highest-ranking African Americans, who came from the black intelligentsia and who had been at their posts for over a year, which is to say, the most successful incarnations of racial pride at Huachuca. In his opinion, these men were the instigators and leaders of the protests against the racial regime he had transposed from the training camps in the South. Bousfield summed up Almond's speech to Gibson in these words: "We thank you for your advice but will run the 92nd just as we've been running it."[44] The commander firmly resisted the testing of his racial convictions and practices.

Before long, the master of ceremonies, Lieutenant Colonel Nelson, who had just been appointed as director of the fort's Special Services, restored the relaxed atmosphere.[45] He entrusted the opening of the musical program to Sergeant Lawrence Whisonant, the baritone who had been the understudy for the lead role in *Porgy and Bess* on Broadway. Whisonant performed "Huachuca," a song composed by Captain Joe Jordan, a former ragtime star and now director of the fort's musical section. "Huachuca," a pure tribute to the fort and the Army, was dedicated to Colonel Hardy:

> Hua-chu-ca, Hua-chu-ca, Hua-chu-ca,
> We love your snow top mountains,
> Hua-chu-ca, Hua-chu-ca, Hua-chu-ca,
> We love your springs and mountains
> When soldiers march, with sunken feet
> They blare a rhythm beat
> And brassband
> The sun and the moon don't tighten high
> And they seem to know that you are satisfied
> Skies are bright and pleased
> Heaven seems so near
> Hua-chu-ca, Hua-chu-ca, Hua-chu-ca,
> When the work is done and the day is over,
> Hua-chu-ca, Hua-chu-ca, Hua-chu-ca,
> Skies will still be bright and clear
> And heaven will seem near in Huachuca
> Hua-chu-ca, Hua-chu-ca, Hua-chu-ca ...

Grandiloquent in both lyrics and melody, this sentimental song had only positive things to say about Huachuca. After Whisonant's performance, Sergeant Claude Andrews sang "When Irish Eyes Are Smiling," a well-known classic with no connection to the military experience. Artists on tour with the USO Camp Shows then took over, with singer Rosetta Williams performing Frank Sinatra's "There Are Such Things" and W. C. Handy's "The Saint Louis Blues" and juggler George W. Rowland doing an act with knives, balls, and cigar boxes.

Hardy had thus provided a few hours of entertainment to the black officers, who were the main source of protest at the fort. However, the tension did not subside. Bousfield overheard several conversations in which white officers confided to their peers that they desperately wanted to leave the division.[46]

From July 14 to 19, 1943, Inspector Benjamin Davis finally went to the fort to determine the level of tension for himself and to relay the voice of the military hierarchy. He confided to his wife that he had uncovered a "nasty situation."[47] When he arrived at Huachuca, seven black officers were locked up in the stockade – two for drunken misconduct at the Hook, the others because they had been accused (without proof) of mutiny or insubordination – and one lieutenant had been dismissed for refusing to testify against one of his sergeants.[48] Two captains and twenty-two lieutenants were awaiting punishment from their company commanders – in accordance with Article of War 104, company commanders had the right to impose disciplinary sanctions for minor infractions.[49] As Bousfield later told Gibson, soldiers came to Davis to "spill [...] their guts gladly after being assured that their testimony is for Washington & not for 'the General.'"[50] The inspector began by meeting with the fort's commander. Hardy, who had been the victim of a smear campaign by the local authorities, wanted to clear his name. He tried to persuade Davis that the racial problems that had befallen the fort were the fault of the 92nd Division and its commanders. There had never been such tension between blacks and whites before, and so the problems could only be due to the new officers. Almond's argument that there was "contamination by polluted sources among the post's personnel" did not hold water. Moreover, the commander of the 92nd was at fault for failing to investigate rumors that his white officers had inflicted physical violence on black soldiers. The fort's commander went so far as to question Almond's authority as the head of the 92nd Division.

The next day, Hardy handed Davis a stringent five-page memorandum in which he laid out his conception of the proper method of commanding black troops.[51] No army manual dealt specifically with this question – at least not until the publication, in February 1944, of the War Department's booklet *Command of Negro Troops*, which rejected the thesis of the inferiority of African Americans. In his memorandum, Hardy formalized the five principles he had elaborated on the basis of the mistakes he had made and the successes he had achieved over the previous fifteen months. This rare, pragmatic document, which expressed surprisingly little racial prejudice, reflected a willingness, still uncommon in the Army, to unify the command methods targeting white and black soldiers. Of the five principles laid out by Hardy, equity of treatment came first. Any denunciation of injustice or of abuse of authority by an African-American soldier or officer had to be taken seriously and investigated; the men had to be convinced that those who commanded them wanted justice to prevail, especially when a case had a racial dimension. Hardy was indeed well aware of the racial bias that had underpinned the sanctions imposed on black soldiers and officers since the arrival of the 92nd at Huachuca. The second principle was tolerance of differing points of view, especially in the area of interracial relations. Such tolerance had to prevail in shared moments of relaxation and conviviality between blacks and whites – Hardy cited as examples sports meetings, barbecues, exhibitions, all of which he had organized and found to be effective. The third principle was the obligation to show respect when addressing blacks; here, the colonel could draw on the guidelines adopted the previous year by the War Department on the initiative of Judge Hastie. Screaming, especially by commanding officers, was to be avoided. This principle clearly targeted Almond, as did the fourth principle: the obligation of humility and self-sacrifice. According to Hardy, the men had to be convinced that their commander was concerned with their well-being and not with his own interests, especially when it came to career advancement. These rules of justice and good manners were essential for black soldiers to accept the authority of their white commanders. Hardy concluded with a fifth principle, which was specifically linked to the function of commander: efficiency and skill. These, he wrote, were necessary so as not to give the men the impression of amateurism, which could cause them to doubt the leader's qualifications and could thus give rise to contestation. While there were probably some moral considerations behind this overt concern for efficiency, Hardy did conceal his deep-seated convictions on racial matters in his memorandum to the Army's only black general. The commander had the self-assurance of someone who had been able to maintain relative peace at the fort and had managed to implement many bold initiatives both in the military enclave and in Fry. In the light of the principles whose effectiveness he had himself tested, Hardy felt that the white officers of the 92nd had not been sufficiently aware of the efforts required to command black troops and of the disastrous effects that their refusal to restrain their racist feelings and fear of African Americans might have on the situation at the camp.

Davis, who had not yet met Almond, was invited on July 18 to inaugurate the baseball stadium and to attend the season-opening game that was to follow. In total 10,000 men were seated in the stands. When Almond rose to deliver his speech, he was booed at length by the soldiers. This was an extreme embarrassment, especially in the presence of the Inspector General – a sign that the commander of the 92nd Division was not respected by his men. Davis expressed his alarm in the report he wrote

10.3: Inspector General Benjamin Davis standing in front of the post's HQ. © Fort Huachuca Museum.

on his return to Washington. The men claimed that Almond was tyrannical, racist, and unqualified; rumor had it that he had obtained command of the 92nd through nepotism and string-pulling.

The next day, the inspector met with the commander of the 92nd Division. The meeting, which was supposed to take half an hour, lasted two hours.[52] The general stuck to his guns: All racial tensions between blacks and whites were due to "outside influences," not to the hardening of the racial regime at the camp; African-American officers from the North were subversives who had fueled the animosity of their lower-ranking counterparts in the 92nd Division. He refused to admit that the tensions had been caused by the initiatives he and his white officers had taken. Furthermore, he insisted on the validity of the policy he had implemented at the fort for the promotion of African-American officers. Finally, he assured the inspector that he had taken on board the consequences of the March 1, 1943, abolition of the directive that had hitherto blocked the advancement of black soldiers beyond the rank of lieutenant. He argued that there had been no discrimination in the promotion of the 375 black officers of the 92nd Division; indeed, 55 of them had been promoted on the basis of seniority and performance despite having joined the division after the white officers and despite being less prepared than them. And yet, the division included only one major (the head chaplain), seven captains (five medical officers and two chaplains), and thirty-nine first lieutenants; not a single senior officer had been assigned to command combat troops.[53]

For the first time, Davis spoke out after conducting an inspection at Huachuca, expressing the same concern for appeasement as he had done at the beginning of the year. He clearly highlighted the racial dimension of the tensions at the fort: "The 92nd Division is plagued with widespread discontent. To a considerable extent, black officers and soldiers have lost confidence in their white officers." The context was no doubt exceptional: The level of tension was unprecedented, as was the Army's fear that the uprisings would spread from camp to camp. The Inspector General's Office had already begun to blame the attitude of certain commanders, albeit without naming them. Davis nevertheless hesitated as to the severity of the situation. He wrote at least five drafts before finally settling on a lapidary version, in which he listed the incidents that had occurred at the fort since the arrival of the 92nd, but without qualifying them further. After rewording the passages concerning Almond several times, he chose to minimize the responsibility of the commander. In the third draft of his report, he wrote: "General Almond [...] has overlooked the human element in the training of this Division. Great stress has been placed on the mechanical perfection in the execution of training missions. Apparently not enough consideration has been given to the maintenance of a racial understanding between white and colored officers and men."[54] Later, however, he retracted this statement. In the final version, Almond's personal responsibility was presented as secondary; Davis distinguished the commander's "efforts" from the blunders and faults of the junior white officers, whom he felt lacked the qualities necessary to lead black troops. He blamed the subordinates in order to exonerate the general – "honest, sincere and now aware of the causes of this unrest [...], there is no question as to his professional fitness"[55] – despite the fact that Almond had been the sole initiator of the "inefficient officer school" and had been guilty of extremely offensive remarks against black officers. This very lenient assessment allowed the commander of the 92nd Division to remain in his post – though it may also be that there was no one willing to succeed him. The black inspector – always cautious, timid, complicit some would say – did not go as far in his diagnosis as the War Department was ready to go at the time.

The only serious criticism in Davis's report concerned the treatment of black officers, a point on which the War Department had demonstrated its willingness to act earlier in the spring. Davis, with whom fellow black men had shared their feelings of discouragement and humiliation, recommended that "the special War Department policy as to the promotion of Negro officers [be] rescinded, and colored officers [...] promoted and treated the same as white officers." He included in this treatment the training of troops, the periods of rest, and the attitude of white officers toward their black alter egos. Thus, he advocated an end to the segregation of officers' messes and clubs at Huachuca.[56] Colonel Wood, who had taken the decision to segregate the mess hall of the 371st Regiment, was transferred to another camp, and the dining room was integrated again; however, the two officers' clubs remained segregated. Davis also called for the closing of the Incompetent Officers School. The latter was dismantled in October on the initiative of the commander of the Third Army, who issued a reprimand to Almond.[57] Of the fifty-three officers who had been forced to take the course, twenty-eight were returned to their position, twenty were reclassified, one resigned, and four were court-martialed and dismissed.[58] Disciplinary measures were also taken against white officers who had beaten up soldiers, thus restoring a semblance of justice. The recommendation to unify officer promotion policy – "In all fairness and in the light of the principles on which this country is founded, there should be but one promotion policy to all officers"[59] – extended beyond Huachuca. On the basis of this recommendation, the War Department asked the Army to investigate the promotions of black officers since the beginning of 1943 and to determine how many had not been granted because of the differential treatment. However, while the number of black officers in the Army's ground forces did begin to increase, the promotion policy was not unified.[60]

A point of no return was crossed at Huachuca. Davis's visit and the insufficient measures that followed did not assuage the anger of black officers and soldiers. In the fall, this anger turned to violence, leading to fears of mutiny. The African-American press, which had kept silent on the poisonous atmosphere of the summer because it had wanted to display trust in the Army, began to evoke the tensions, first *sotto voce* and then more explicitly. In the middle of September, New York's *Amsterdam News* ran the headline "Fort Huachuca Is Hell on Earth"; the incriminating article, based on an anonymous letter, was then picked up by other black newspapers. In October, the *Chicago Defender* mentioned the racial tensions that had flared up in May and June. Yet, it also assured readers that these "have been reduced to a minimum and, in fact, seem to be on the verge of disappearing entirely,"[61] which was a complete denial of reality. It was in the columns of other black newspapers, which were less closely monitored by Washington censors, that the deterioration of race relations at Huachuca was denounced. These newspapers' journalists were not accredited to investigate the fort, but they did receive anonymous letters of denunciation from soldiers and officers who came from the states where they were published. The *Louisiana Weekly* ran a piece, based on anonymous information forwarded by the Associated Negro Press, regarding the situation at the fort, which gave every appearance of being in the throes of racial revenge. Several white officers, including a colonel, had been viciously beaten by black soldiers. The officers were said to stay away from the lines during target practice for fear that the men would shoot them. Rumors circulated in Tucson that a conflagration could flare up at any moment. Almond had reportedly ordered the commanders of each unit to lock up ammunition after target practice, lest the men should divert some bullets and stage a mutiny against him and his deputies. There were also reports that night raids had uncovered weapons hidden by soldiers.[62] According to a counter-intelligence report, a grenade was found in a vehicle that several white officers on their way out of the fort were about to enter. The grenade was primed to explode when the vehicle was started, and would have severely injured the car's occupants.[63] A few weeks later, the editor of the *Atlanta Daily World* received a letter written by a Huachuca NCO. The letter, which the author had not signed because he feared reprisals from his commanding officer, claimed that

> conditions are really appalling. This outfit is the most rotten outfit in the World. [...] When General Davis inspects the P.T.U., our cripples are hidden. These are men who are walked "to death" and are physically unfit to carry on. They are really sapping the life out of the fellows. The morale is at as low an ebb as in a whore-house. Nobody gives a d – · about what happens.[64]

In addition, there were rumors that some soldiers had shot Almond, who was described as "rotten" by the author of the letter to the *Atlanta Daily World*. Once again, in November, the commander's presence at a sporting event attended by all the men turned into a personal indictment. In a letter to his wife, James Rucker wrote: "Our general was booed something terrific the other day at a ball game. The booing could be heard all over the Post for a long time. The 92nd song was played and no one sang. The General stepped to the middle of the field insisting that everyone sing ...."[65]

Almond's authority seemed definitively undermined, and he was unable to remedy the situation other than by stepping up the repression. Davis's inspection and report did nothing to alter his behavior. Almond was content to purge the 92nd of its most racist white officers.[66] At the ceremony held on October 15, 1943 to celebrate the 92nd Division's first anniversary (five months after the troops' arrival at Huachuca), he remained as rigid as ever and continued to ignore the human element of training. His entire speech focused on the program for teaching technical skills and toughening up the men. He concluded by speaking of discipline and obedience, principles which he felt had to be reaffirmed even more now that they were being contested.[67]

Fear of mutiny prompted the unit commanders to keep a close eye on weapons and ammunition. After target practice sessions, they kept precise records of the number of bullets to ensure that none had been stolen by the soldiers. They also began to lock away the weapons at night – until then, rifles had been assembled in the middle of the barrack dormitories. From the fall of 1943 onwards, the duty officer was tasked with ensuring that all rifles were stored in the room on the second floor, which now served as the unit's armory. Every night, Sergeant William Perry, from Company K of the 370th Regiment, counted the weapons – "129 M1 rifles, 28 shotguns, 255 pistols, 903 rifles, light machine guns, and bazookas"; he then closed the armory door with three padlocks and handed the duty officer a certificate attesting that all the weapons were present.[68]

In the months that followed the arrival of the 92nd Division, two racial regimes competed with each other at Fort Huachuca. On the one hand, there was the regime that Almond had transposed from the southern camps; in this regime, African Americans were reminded of the inferior position that had been assigned to them by pre-war southern society, and any attempt to get closer to equality was seen as a threat to be countered by the introduction of new regulations and vexatious measures. On the other hand, there was the racial status quo that had emerged from one year of negotiations between Hardy, the black officers permanently based at the fort, and the men of the 93rd Division; in retrospect, this regime seemed more conducive to compromise and understanding, since it allowed for a black togetherness that made strict segregation under white authority more tolerable. In this competition, the southern regime imposed itself with force and with a bang. Racial tensions were exacerbated as soon as black officers became the target of Almond and his deputies. The commander of the 92nd responded by tightening control and increasing surveillance of the men. The move to deepen segregation at Fort Huachuca went against the latest recommendations of the Army, which had chosen to respond to the summer riots with flexibility and greater attentiveness to the demands of black soldiers and officers. These recommendations were as follows: employ more black military police, punish disrespectful white officers, unify officer promotion policy, reduce segregation in recreational areas, gradually deploy black units overseas, and increase the entertainment offer to make the soldiers more tolerant of the Jim Crow regime.[69] This last recommendation, which fell under the responsibility of the fort's commander, was the only one to be implemented at Huachuca.

11 The Mecca of Entertainment?

"The free time I have unless I am writing to you or studying things through is just plain hell, so I work myself into exhaustion. By the end of the week, my nerves are on the edge, no appetite and the threat of a cold hangs around."[1] James Rucker had only just arrived at Huachuca to join the medical battalion of the 92nd Infantry Division when he realized that free time was for him a source of intense suffering, as he wrote in numerous letters to his wife. In his case, the malaise was existential: He wondered about his place and role in this Jim Crow Army, about his reason for being in the world. For the other soldiers, it was precisely in the moments of boredom – when time was no longer filled with mind-numbing drills, weapons handling training, or chores – that doubt and unease crept into the mind. Colonel Hardy was well aware of this. He knew that the psychological impact of monotony and idleness could be highly detrimental to the quality of preparation. And he had certainly noticed that boredom had caused tense situations to flare up at other camps – for instance, in Louisiana in early 1942.[2] The fort's commander therefore strove to fill the empty time as a way of diverting the soldiers' attention from drinking, gambling, and betting.[3] The situation was especially critical in 1943. The camp had been gradually sealed off over the previous year, with soldiers losing access to the many recreational and drinking venues in the surrounding areas. There was an urgent need for quality entertainment that could quell the men's desire to go out of the fort.

Thus, Colonel Hardy turned Huachuca into one of the best-equipped camps in the United States in terms of cultural and sports facilities. He opened theaters, cinemas, an 11,000-seat stadium, a 10,000-seat baseball field, a roller-skating rink, 2 swimming pools, libraries, service clubs, etc. To his superiors and the white press, he justified this deployment of resources – to a level that was unusual for black troops – by invoking the isolation of the camp and the refusal of neighboring communities to provide soldiers with leisure and recreation opportunities.[4] In December 1943, the *Chicago Defender* described Huachuca as a "mecca for troops in training,"[5] which it wanted to believe was a recognition of equality. The facilities made available to black soldiers at the fort were indeed unlike anything they had seen in civilian life.

Before the war, African Americans had fought, both in the South and in the North, to gain access to the entertainment infrastructure that symbolized middle-class status and economic success – sometimes even taking part in bloody riots, as in Chicago in 1919. Yet, all their attempts to open up segregated swimming pools, beaches, ice rinks, or amusement parks were met with intimidation, hostility, and violence. During the war, the African-American struggle for equality likewise involved the desegregation of entertainment facilities. Thus, just as the soldiers of the 93rd Division were arriving at Huachuca, the Congress of Racial Equality was organizing a strong campaign in Chicago against the segregated White City ice rink.[6]

Hardy was at pains to convince the soldiers that the facilities he had opened at the fort were a mark of recognition by the Army. Like the General Staff, he seemed convinced that entertainment and culture could neutralize criticism of the War Department's racial policy or at the very least defuse the anger of the men. This conviction was partly based on the precedent set before the war by the New Deal cultural policy. The federal government had attempted to hide its inability to repeal the Jim Crow regime by hiring unemployed African-American artists and writers and by commissioning from them photographs, paintings, texts, and plays. Although southern Democrats' filibuster in Congress had stopped the Roosevelt administration from initiating civil rights legislation to correct racial inequalities and prevented it from abolishing lynching at the federal level, the Federal Art Project (FAP), run by white liberals, had fostered the production of an autonomous black culture and contributed to breaking some racial stereotypes.[7] After the country entered the conflict, both the War Department and the Office of War Information (OWI) hoped that the promotion of black artists would help put the issue of racial inequality in the Army on the back burner. To mitigate the anger of African-American soldiers, the OWI sought to ensure that the military experience gave them the opportunity to encounter a certain form of black culture, one embodied by respectable figures who did not challenge the racial status quo.[8]

By 1943, Huachuca was equipped to welcome African-American entertainment stars. Several black celebrities from the world of song and film were invited to give concerts to the soldiers. They performed on the large football field in front of crowds delighted by the high-quality shows – or so the Signal Corps photos suggest. Dinah Shore sang for the troops in February 1943. The young woman, one of the only white artists to ever come to Huachuca, had been a radio star since being spotted by

Eddy Cantor in 1939. The men appreciated her southern accent and her "girl next door" image. On leaving the camp, she allegedly said: "The 93rd Division soldiers are one of the grandest audience I have ever sung before. I hope I can come back soon and that I can stay just a little longer than I did this time."[9] In August 1944, in that very same football field, Louis Armstrong gave a concert that was broadcast on short-wave radio to troops stationed overseas.[10]

The fort offered other venues for artists. Eddie Anderson – known to all as Rochester after the servant he played on NBC's *The Jack Benny Program*, the first permanent role given to a black artist on a national radio program – sang in the open-air theater. In March 1943, Lena Horne, accompanied by the Deep River Boys, a male gospel group, performed in service clubs, the gymnasium, and the hospital. She was invited back in August with a busy schedule: She had to attend a baseball game in the giant stadium where the Huachuca team faced the Douglas Air Force Base team, inaugurate the theater that bore her name at the old post, and host the first screening of one of the war's major all-black films, the 20th Century Fox production *Stormy Weather*.[11] In the film, she plays the singer Selena, who partners with the old tap dancer Bill "Bojangles" Robinson. The film recounts Robinson's career, beginning with a flashback to the end of World War I, when he comes home from Europe as a hero. After this triumphant return, the veteran suffers repeated humiliations in the segregated world of show business. This, however, does not make him acquiescent or submissive: At the end of the film, Bill refuses to perform the primitive dance that is expected of him, instead surprising the audience with a virtuoso solo in which he asserts his style and originality. Walter White and the black press found the film to be condescending toward African Americans; they felt that it perpetuated the image of blacks as immature entertainers.[12] Yet, at Huachuca, the reception of *Stormy Weather* was excellent. Lena Horne later claimed that she had felt like she was in the company of brothers, and that she had preferred to perform in this all-black environment rather than in segregated black–white camps. In 1944, she refused to sing at Fort Riley, Kansas, in front of an audience where German POWs were seated in the front rows and black soldiers at the back of the room. She completely stopped singing on tours organized by the USO after this.[13]

The visits of boxer-soldier Joe Louis Barrow, organized by the Army's Special Services Division, generated just as much emotion. Joe Louis came to Huachuca for the first time in May 1943, shortly after the arrival of the 92nd Division. He spent three days at the camp, where he was welcomed like a military hero, with Signal Corps photographers following

The Mecca of Entertainment? 211

11.1: Singer Lena Horne performing at a show organized by the Hollywood Victory Committee. © Fort Huachuca Museum.

him wherever he went. As soon as he got off the plane, Colonel Hardy paid him a tribute worthy of a white celebrity:

> You are worshipped by your people and admired by everybody with whom you have come in contact; by all who have seen you in the ring and out of it, and by everybody who has read about you in the press. All this places upon you a great responsibility and I know that you are not going to let any of us down.[14]

The boxer was then welcomed by the soldiers and General Almond in the football stadium, where he performed two boxing demonstrations against one of his former opponents, who was then serving at the camp; he was cheered by a crowd almost as large as those at Madison Square Garden. Colonel Hardy gave him a full tour of the fort – photographs show him with Lieutenant Colonel Bousfield in the hospital. Yet, in spite of all this, he slept in the barracks with the soldiers.

Six years earlier, Joe Louis had won the heavyweight title against a white man, Jim Braddock – no black man had competed for the title since Jack Johnson's victory twenty-two years earlier. Boxing had the reputation of being a democratic and fair sport and enjoyed immense popularity across all social and ethnic groups. By the end of the 1930s, the number of boxing clubs had skyrocketed in the United States, and the base of boxing fans and amateur boxers was larger than ever before. While Joe Louis was a hero for blacks, he was an ideal figure for the Army. Unlike Johnson, he never questioned the racial divide or the racial codes in place: He was extremely polite, never appeared in the company of white women, and was much less demonstrative when he defeated white boxers.[15] Above all, this was the man who, in 1938, had defeated Germany's Max Schmeling in a fight that was described by all commentators as the triumph of American democracy over the Nazi racial order. For African Americans, this victory was a show of black power against the prejudices that perpetuated notions of racial inferiority. In January 1942, Joe Louis became a patriotic hero for putting his world heavyweight title on the line for the benefit of the Naval Aid Society, where no black man had ever been allowed to serve except in the kitchens. In front of a 17,000-strong crowd at Madison Square Garden, he defeated Buddy Baer for a second time; he donated the $100,000 winnings to the families of the victims of the Pearl Harbor bombings. Two days later, Sergeant Barrow enlisted as a volunteer private, refusing any preferential treatment. For the head of the Morale Branch, F. H. Osborn, "the Army and the government have a tremendous propaganda asset in Joe Louis. To the great majority of the Negroes he appears almost as a god. The possibilities for using him are almost unlimited."[16] Joe Louis's image even appeared on an OWI poster: He was portrayed in a martial pose, brandishing a bayonet against an imaginary enemy and sharing his conviction that: "We're going to do our part ... and we will win because we're on God's side." It was his impeccable reputation that made this image possible – the OWI usually avoided showing black soldiers in aggressive postures.[17] In 1943, the boxer began to tour the camps where black soldiers were being trained, following an itinerary prepared by the Special Services Division: He joined the soldiers' sports training, refereed their matches, and went so far as to offer them a fight. He was acclaimed everywhere he went.[18]

For the Army, sport had obvious benefits: It exhausted the men's bodies while preparing them for combat, channeled their aggression, strengthened their collective spirit, and diverted their attention from vexations and disappointments.[19] In the case of black soldiers, the persistence of preconceived ideas about the "natural" aptitudes of African Americans, all of them based on pseudo-scientific studies of athletes' bodies conducted in the 1930s,[20] played a further role in encouraging regular, intensive practice. Sport was one of the few areas where blacks were allowed to excel and to draw bodily and psychological confidence from their performances. On the Huachuca sports fields, which were as impressive as those of the Ivy League campuses, competitions were regularly organized, especially on holidays, and they offered unifying spectacles. At each of these events, Hardy and the divisional commanders addressed the crowd, reminding them of the rules of discipline and fair play. On July 19, 1943, the baseball field was inaugurated in the name of Rube Foster, the greatest black pitcher at the time. There, 15,000 soldiers gathered to listen to the speech of General Davis, who had come to the fort for an inspection, and to "Rube's" widow, who threw the first pitch before Sergeant Lawrence Whisonant sang "Huachuca" and "America, the Beautiful." In photos of the event, blacks and whites can be seen sitting side by side on the benches.

At Huachuca, the entertainment program was designed by the Special Services. These were responsible for organizing activities in the officers' clubs and the service clubs (reserved for soldiers) and were also in charge of sporting events, evening classes, publications, and programming for all sections: theater, cinema, music, religious services, book clubs, bond-buying campaigns, etc.[21] Each unit had its own Special Services officers. Black actor Spencer Williams, a former sergeant who had always been appreciated by his men, held this position in the 25th Regiment from July 1942 onwards. He had first come to Huachuca in early 1942 to film *Marching On!*, a low-budget production that was both comical and uplifting, and had returned in uniform to take care of the entertainment.[22]

The Bureau of Special Services coordinated the entertainment for the entire fort, with programming in the hands of the 17th Company. For a few months in February 1943, the 17th Company was commanded by Major Charles Blackwood, one of the fort's most senior black officers and a veteran of World War I.[23] However, like many other African-American officers, Blackwood lost his position to a white man, Lieutenant Colonel Caroll F. Nelson, who had previously been adjutant of the post, when the 92nd Division arrived. Nelson had been an infantry captain in World War I, and had then served as a history teacher and as the principal of a Minnesota high school.

While the Special Services team was considered to be all-black, it was in fact racially mixed. The team was composed of soldiers, Wacs, and civilians, and included a number of black artists – conscripts for the men and volunteers for the women – whom the Army felt would be better employed organizing entertainment than serving as soldiers. Among these were the graphic designers Anna Russell and George Everett, singers Joe and Mercedes Jordan, Lawrence Whisonant, playwright Randolph Edmonds (the son of former slaves turned teacher at Dillard College and author of numerous plays, including *The Land of Cotton*), and actor Frederick Douglas O'Neal (one of the founders of the American Negro Theater).[24]

Soldiers and Wacs were enrolled from time to time to act, dance, or sing in the Special Services shows, which toured the other camps of the region. Shirley Graham herself had appropriated the stereotype of the African American as naturally gifted for rhythm and dance. In September 1941, she had written in a letter to Reverend J. Raymond Henderson of the Second Baptist Church in Los Angeles: "Get one thousand Negroes together anywhere and there will be talent enough to man Broadway!"[25]

11.2: Members of the Bureau of Special Services with boxer Joe Louis. Front row, center: Colonel Nelson and Private Joe Louis. Second row, right: Joe Jordan. Third row: Wacs (Army Signal Corps). © Fort Huachuca Museum.

The Special Services were the main producers of the narrative that described – in images, words, and songs – the life of the men of the 92nd Division as a time of fulfillment. The narrative went like this: Nowhere else in the country were black soldiers offered such quality entertainment; this signified that the Army recognized the men's service to the nation; and this offer invalidated the accusations that black soldiers were treated with contempt. By recounting the highlights of training and the complicity established in moments of rest, Special Services publications aimed to convince black soldiers that they were not being wronged, and that the camp where they trained was perhaps indeed the "Mecca" of entertainment described by the *Chicago Defender*. The War Department encouraged each camp and unit to publish its own newspaper, with the Chief of Staff, General Marshall, going so far as to declare: "A soldier's newspaper, in these grave times, is more than a morale venture. It is a symbol of the things we are fighting to preserve and spread in this threatened world. It represents the free thought and free expression of a free people." The content of the entertainment was of course monitored: It could not be critical of army policy, it could not reveal information that might be of use to the enemy, and it had to inspire confidence and pride.[26] At Huachuca, each division had its own newspaper: The 93rd Division began to issue the *Blue Helmet*, and the 92nd followed suit with the *Buffalo*. Likewise, the fort had its own weekly publication, the *Apache Sentinel*, whose first issue appeared in July 1943, and the Bureau of Special Services issued the *Bulletin*.

These newspapers enlisted the help of real professionals. Wac Lucia Pitts, who had arrived at Huachuca in April 1944, wrote regularly for the *Apache Sentinel*. Anna Russell drew illustrations for the fort's newspaper and for almost all issues of the *Bulletin*, for which she also designed the tailpieces of the various columns. To accompany the *Bulletin*'s motto, "Guardian of the Fort Huachuca spirit," she drew what she felt was the identity of the place: the mountain range, an Apache scout, a buffalo soldier.

11.3: *The Apache Sentinel*. © Arizona State Library/Arizona Memory Project.

216   A Black Army

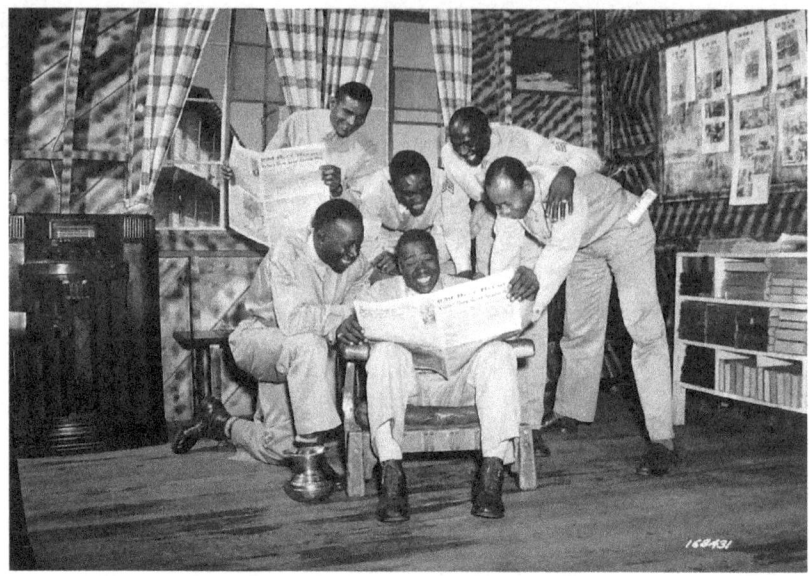

11.4: "Huachuca soldiers reading the first issue of the *Blue Helmet*," September 19, 1942. © Fort Huachuca Museum.

"A singing army is a winning army," insisted Captain Joe Jordan, Post music advisor in Special Services. "A humming soldier is able to walk effortlessly," he also wrote, in an article he penned for the Bulletin. Jordan knew the benefits music could bring to the Army: During training, music gave the soldiers rhythm, force, and courage, and welded them into one group; in moments of relaxation, it made them sing, dance, and forget where they were. The Army employed music advisors in all military camps, published songbooks for the troops, and produced discs ("V-discs" or "Victory discs," compiled from 1943 onwards by the War Department) with music from the Army Hit Kit – patriotic songs, symphonic classics, opera, folk, Broadway hits, jazz, swing, etc.[27] Embracing the stereotype that blacks had innate musical talent, the Army encouraged the formation of jazz bands in African-American units. Swing and jazz, which were still viewed as "black music" despite the existence of racially mixed bands since the 1930s, formed the soundtrack of Huachuca. Their diffusion gave an illusion of tolerance and equality in a place where these values were far from respected.

At the camp, the great ragtime musician Joe Jordan coordinated all musical activities so as to give shape to his vision of a singing army. Jordan had enlisted aged almost sixty and had undergone officer training alongside another great musician, Glenn Miller. Prior to joining the Army, he had composed hundreds of songs and served as musical director in numerous clubs and theaters associated with the development of jazz – including the Pekin Theater, the country's first black-owned and operated theater, which had opened on Chicago's South Side in 1905. In the 1920s and 1930s, he had served as a conductor and composer for several musicals touring the country. Starting in 1933, he had worked for the *Work Projects Administration (WPA) on the* Federal Theater Project (FTP), conducting its black orchestra on such productions as Orson Welles's Macbeth. He had worked at the same time as an arranger for major Broadway musicals, including those of Florenz Ziegfeld.[28] When the war broke out, he decided that music should play a role in mobilizing soldiers. As soon as he was stationed at Huachuca, he was put in charge of directing all-black bands for an all-black audience.

In the music section of the Special Services, Jordan was in good company: first of all, his wife, Mercedes Welcker Jordan, a former celebrity at the Cotton Club who had performed for white audiences under the name "Merceedees." After Pearl Harbor, Mercedes Jordan had enlisted in the WAC and been stationed at Huachuca, where she had worked as a truck driver before serving as a singer and songwriter with the Special Services; it was there that she wrote the song "Do You Know" and the hit "We're the Waacs":

> We're the WAC's, we're the WAC's,
> We're the girls in the khaki,
> And we think the army's grand.
> We're the girls, soldier girls
> Minus frills, minus curls,
> Pretty as a picture in our suits made of tan.
> We answered the call of the man with the beard.
> He's our uncle, we salute him
> With hurray and three cheers!
> We're the WAC's, we're the WAC's
> We're the girls in the khaki
> And all out for UNCLE SAM![29]

Captain Jordan also enrolled the following artists: the baritone Lawrence Whisonant, the understudy of Todd Duncan (Porgy in Gershwin's *Porgy and Bess*), who went by the nickname "Singing Sergeant"; saxophonist and clarinetist Eddie Hughes; singer James Bowder; former Sunset Royal Orchestra soloist Orlando Roberson, who had already recorded several albums with the CBS label; and guitarist Chauncey Lee, among others. The music section coordinated the fort's various bands: the military band, the dance and entertainment orchestras, the Deep River Boys gospel group, etc. Both the 92nd and the 93rd

Figure 11.5: The music section office headed by Captain Joe Jordan. © Fort Huachuca Museum.

Division had its own jazz band, complete with brass and percussion, to accompany parades and light up the dance floor. These were sometimes reconfigured into smaller bands for open-air concerts, dance parties, or music jams in service clubs. The Bouncing Buffaloes and the 368th Swingeroos, who played on Saturday nights at the USO, livened up the evenings while reviving the history of the Harlem Hellfighters. This brass band of the 369th Infantry Regiment, led by James Reese Europe, with the assistance of Noble Sissle as drum major, had introduced jazz to Europe during World War I.

The music section let the soldiers rehearse in its office-studio, organized lectures on classical music (followed by concerts) as part of a series entitled "Music Appreciation Hour," composed songs, and created musical arrangements. It also produced the Huachuca shows, mobilizing the camp's talented Wacs and soldiers. The musical *Bi-Vo-Ac WAAC*, with its all-female cast performing solos and chorus lines, offered a satire of the fort in which the Waacs had completely replaced the soldiers. *GI*

The Mecca of Entertainment?   219

11.6: A jazz concert in one of the service clubs. © NARA, Army Signal Corps.

Rhapsody was also created and rehearsed at Huachuca, before touring the surrounding camps. The tap dancers present at the camp were called upon to participate in many of the in-house productions. Tap dance had enjoyed a renaissance in Harlem in the 1920s and 1930s. Black dancers hitherto confined to the roles of jesters had found stages on which they could revive a dance that continued to revolve around a few step combinations. Bill "Bojangles" Robinson, the Nicholas Brothers, and the Berry Brothers were the first to use syncopation: As they introduced new rhythms and steps, they buried the image of entertainers that had long clung to them, while also asserting themselves as figures of elegance through their "class acts."[30] Maceo Anderson of the Four Step Brothers performed at Huachuca, where he served as a soldier; so did Fayard Nicholas, the eldest of the Nicholas Brothers, who arrived at the fort in August 1943 after completing the first part of his training at Camp Van Dorn. When he entered the camp, Fayard was one of the stars of *Stormy Weather*. He and his brother closed this film with an incredible acrobatic dance number in which they defied the laws of gravity with disconcerting ease. Cab Calloway, whose orchestra accompanied the duo, concluded with the words "Ain't that something to shout about?" – a statement that seemed to apply as much to their dance act as to the shows produced at the camp.

Nelson and Hardy took pride in these shows, as would impresarios extolling the talents of their artists. In December 1943, the head of the Bureau of Special Services told the *Arizona Daily Star*:

> We used to complain that Fort Huachuca received only four traveling army shows in two years. Today we have such an abundance of good talent that we ourselves are traveling to all nearby towns and cities and even to Hollywood to put on shows. We have some of the best talent from the motion pictures, theatre and radio and what is considered one of the best swing bands in the nation.[31]

Furthermore, in 1944, Hardy wrote to the head of the Morale Branch, Major General Osborn: "We have developed here a very excellent Negro Military and Concert Band which also includes one of the best swing bands in this country. In this entertainment group are about 10 high class Negro entertainers which will make anybody, black or white, laugh and feel better. Ask Under-Secretary Patterson about this."[32] Although a critical reader might see in these lines a reformulation of the stereotype of the black man as a public entertainer, the admiration of white officers for these representatives of the "talented tenth" in the arts seemed genuine.

Sports and musical activities in training facilities were frequently encouraged. Far more original was Hardy's use of the fine arts to improve race relations at the camp. It is a mystery how the West Point horseman, who had no known connection to the art world, became convinced that art could have a function other than being decorative. The fact is that after commissioning two paintings from artist Lew Davis for the white officers' club (*The Founding of Fort Huachuca* and *The Surrender of Geronimo*), Hardy came to believe that Davis's murals could mitigate black soldiers' resentment of the Army, which had been growing since the arrival of the 92nd Division.

It was Sidney Curtis, the FAP director for Arizona, who in 1942 had oriented Hardy toward this artist based in Scottsdale (near Phoenix) and known for the two murals he had created for post offices in Los Banos, California, and Marlow, Oklahoma, in response to commissions from the FAP. In 1943, Hardy invited Davis to join the Special Services team as a civilian – with his stipend paid by the WPA. Davis was officially integrated into the Army in 1944 with the rank of sergeant. Once in this position, he convinced Hardy to set up a silk-screening workshop, which would come to employ the stencil specialist George Everett from

The Mecca of Entertainment?

11.7: Anna Russell and Lew Davis working side by side in the painting workshop. © NARA, Army Signal Corps.

Brooklyn, William I. Scales from Baldwin, Mississippi, and Charlie Evans from New Rochelle, New York.

The photographs taken by the Signal Corps in the silk-screening and painting workshops suggest a rare relationship of equality and artistic collaboration across the color line – between Davis and the black artists who worked by his side. In one of the pictures, Anna Russell stands at her easel putting the last touches to a painting of the insignia of one of the units; Lew Davis is sitting to her right, absorbed in his work and showing no sign of authority. Apart from the motifs and inscriptions appearing on the canvas, there is nothing to suggest that this is an army setting.

The press also saw a form of artistic companionship between blacks and whites that was unusual at the time. Davis learned the techniques of stenciling and silk-screening from black soldier artists, and shared with them those of mural painting. In another Signal Corps photograph, we see Ted Shearer and Thurman Dillard putting the finishing touches to *The Surrender of Geronimo* alongside Lew Davis.

To welcome the African-American officers of the 92nd Division and convince them that they would receive full recognition at Huachuca,

Hardy took the initiative – which was rather unusual for a white commander from the South – to hold an exhibition of "37 Negro artists." The selected pieces were hung at the Mountain View Club from May 16 to 22, 1943; they then toured the camp's main entertainment venues, before returning permanently to the black officers' club. The idea of a "black art" with its own objects and aesthetic was born during the Harlem Renaissance, a time when the New Negro became an idealized representation of the African American.[33] There was also a history of white people promoting "black" art – including via the exhibitions and prizes of the Harmon Foundation created by a real estate magnate. Black art was likewise supported by the federal government: The FAP commissioned pieces from African-American artists for a number of public buildings. Thus, in 1934, Aaron Douglas painted the mural *Aspects of Negro Life* for the Schomburg Center, a division of the New York Public Library located in Harlem: The mural recounted the history of blacks on four panels, from Africa to urban emancipation through jazz, in a tension between primitivism and modernism. Perhaps it was through Lew Davis that Hardy came to know this work and became aware of the emancipatory potential of art for African Americans. At the inauguration ceremony, Hardy explained why he had decided to turn the club – a venue belonging to the federal state – into a gallery of black art: "This collection will not only serve as a cause to instill pride in the accomplishments and promise of black artists. It will also serve as an inspiration to us all, for it represents one of the steps towards building a broader and better American citizenship." The fort's commander may have believed that exhibiting black art would prompt African-American officers to take pride in their club, thereby facilitating their acceptance of the segregated venue and mitigating their resentment of the humiliating treatment inflicted on them by General Almond.

Eighty-six works selected from among the most striking pieces commissioned by the FAP were hung at the Mountain View Club. The selection was made by Lew Davis and Holger Cahill, national director of the FAP, former director of exhibitions at the New York Museum of Modern Art, and one of the key actors in the democratization of the arts. The thirty-six artists whose works were exhibited were major figures of African-American art. The most famous were the sculptor Sargent Johnson; painter Archibald Motley Jr., one of the main painters of the New Negro, whose portraits and genre scenes were inspired by the black neighborhoods of Chicago and Washington; printer Dox Thrash, who invented the carborundum print technique, which used silicon carbide grits to enable a very wide palette of grays and blacks; Raymond Steth, a Philadelphia painter who collaborated with Thrash in the FAP graphics division; and muralist Henry Avery, known for decorating the walls of the Masonic Temple and the Regal Theater in his home town of Chicago and one of the founding members of the South Side Community Art Center in Bronzeville. The artists on display at Huachuca may have disagreed on what constitutes black art – would it be the depiction of motifs or models different from those favored by white art? The use of alternative techniques and an embracing of other influences? The production of art for black audiences only? Yet, all of them shared the ambition to instill pride among their people.

The oil painting *Progress of the American Negro* by Charles White was the centerpiece of the exhibition. The mural, measuring five feet by thirteen, was hung in the center of the club, in the middle of the stairs leading to the mezzanine, after having been exhibited in the South Side Community Art Center in Chicago. It was White's first creation as an employee of the mural department of the Illinois Arts Project. One can see in it the young painter's early ambition to give back to African Americans the keys to

11.8: From left to right, Vernon Winslow, Richmond Barthe, Col. E. Hardy, Lieut.-col. Nelson, and Hale Woodruff at the inauguration of the black art exhibition. © Fort Huachuca Museum.

their history so that they might find strength and unity in it. The painting is organized as a triptych whose central panel encapsulates the dialectic of the black experience – an experience torn between the pulpit, where uplifting and sometimes vindictive words are expressed, and the dead tree, the symbol of the lynching and violence to which African Americans were still being subjected at the start of the war. In order to tell this heroic story, White had asked readers of the *Chicago Defender* to name the personalities who had contributed most to the "progress of the race." The five he chose to represent were historical figures who had facilitated the collective uplifting of the group, ones for whom the search for exemplarity and respectability had played a central role in the fight against discrimination and persecution.

On the left of White's mural is the abolitionist Sojourner Truth, recognizable by her Quaker outfit, leading a procession of slaves toward freedom in a time before the Civil War – an allegory of the black force ready to free itself from the chains that continue to hinder it, and perhaps also an echo of black workers' collective actions in the 1930s. Standing to the right of a dead tree is Frederick Douglass, another figure of abolitionism, depicted as the mature man we know him to be, at the end of a life that took him from the plantation in Maryland where he was born a slave to the status of writer, orator, and confirmed activist. Douglass comforts a crying fugitive slave with bare feet and bare torso, embracing him with his strong arms on what appears to be a slave auction platform; the composition makes him both the receptacle of the traumas caused by slavery and the witness of future progress.[34] In the center, the educator Booker T. Washington speaks from the pulpit to three African Americans, symbols of the black bourgeoisie; he is probably seeking to convince them that the most effective response to racism is not the strategy of confrontational struggle but the demonstration of the qualities and morality of the group. To their right, the agricultural scientist and inventor George Washington Carver is observing the results of experiments through his microscope; in Tuskegee, Carver helped to develop alternative crops to cotton, sketching an agricultural future in which southern blacks would finally be free from "King Cotton" and poverty. Standing above him in front of two imposing microphones is the soprano Marian Anderson, the voice of the African-American community, who is finally authorized to tell her story and express her demands. Banned in 1939 from performing at Independence Hall by the Daughters of the American Revolution, Anderson was invited by Eleanor Roosevelt, shortly before the painting was created, to sing the national anthem in front of the Lincoln Memorial on the Mall in Washington. These five founding figures are surrounded by those they have guided toward

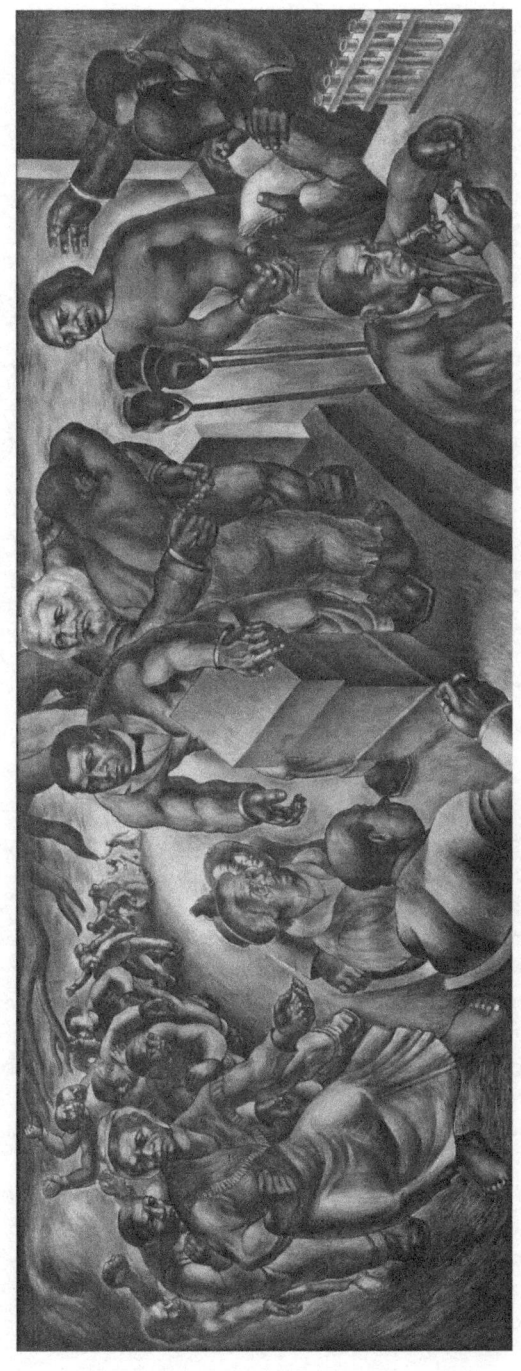

11.9: *Progress of the American Negro*, Charles White, oil on canvas. © NGAA, Howard University.

11.10: The opening of the Black Art Exhibition at the Mountain View Club. © Fort Huachuca Museum.

freedom and uplifted toward science, art, and collective struggle – metaphorical doubles of the viewers of the painting.[35]

Why did Hardy decide to offer these figures of resistance as models by hanging this mural in the officers' club? He likely failed to understand the subversive force of the work. He may have been mainly interested in its uplifting function, or, more insidiously, he may have wanted to assuage the discontent of black officers by making a gesture that demonstrated the Army's recognition of a legitimate racial pride. The exhibition of this painting in an all-black club that had been rejected by African-American officers was also likely aimed at facilitating their acceptance of that club.

Hardy soon realized that a form of art more suited to the military nature of the place should also be exhibited at Mountain View. Given that the Army had demanded that the segregation of all entertainment venues in military camps be ended by March 1943, persuading African-American officers to accept the maintenance of the black officers' club was becoming a pressing issue. Thus, just as he had commissioned two historical murals from Davis for the white officers' club, Hardy asked him in 1944 to create a mural that would illustrate the contribution of black soldiers to the defense of the American nation.[36] In other words, he asked a white man to depict black heroism and sacrifice on the battlefield. To select episodes of black military history which he knew little about, Davis sought advice from the playwright Theodore Browne, one of the founding members of the American Negro Theater and the Negro Playwrights Company and a former director of Seattle's Negro Unit, who was also serving at Huachuca. The five-panel mural, which reads chronologically from left to right, depicts the following events: the Battle of Monmouth, a decisive moment in the War of Independence, in which 700 African-American soldiers fought alongside whites; the campaign led by General Andrew Jackson to drive the British out of New Orleans in 1812; the battle of Fort Wagner during the Civil War, in which the 54th Massachusetts Regiment, the first all-black unit of such size, fought courageously; the charge of San Juan Hill in Cuba during the Spanish–American War, led by volunteers of the 10th Cavalry Regiment; and six infantrymen of the 369th Infantry Regiment holding a trench in France at the cost of their lives in World War I.

The Negro Soldier in America's Wars was unveiled on August 20, 1944, just as the Battle of Normandy was ending victoriously and Paris was being liberated without the participation of black troops. The inauguration ceremony took place at Mountain View, where the mural was to be hung permanently. Colonel Hardy opened the ceremony with a speech in which he justified his decision to make black culture the basis of racial understanding at Huachuca:

It was our purpose to lay a foundation of true and broad culture upon which to build our war effort. [...] It seemed, therefore, entirely fitting that our culture and inspirational program at this Negro post should include some sort of definite representation of the deeds of Negroes in America's wars. It was my belief that this sort of representation would give to our soldiers here, pride in the past, inspiration for the present, and confidence in the future.[37]

Hardy also defended the usefulness of the mural on the grounds that it could raise awareness among white officers about the extent of the patriotism and courage of African-American soldiers. This, he said, was essential to neutralizing the myth of black cowardice.

Then came a ceremony organized by Theodore Browne and accompanied by the fort's black singers and actors. The panels were successively revealed through a series of curtain rises to the sound of fanfare and drum rolls. At each step of the ceremony, a narrator recalled a highlight in the

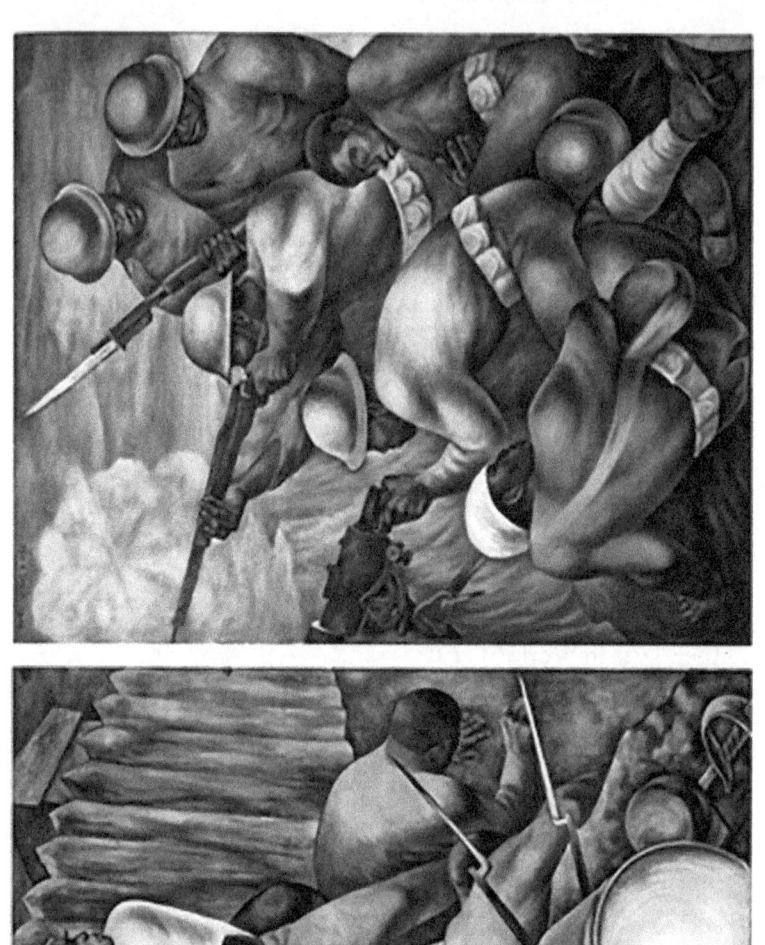

11.11: Two of the five panels of the mural painted by Davis in 1944. © NGAA, Howard University.

history of the contribution of blacks to the war effort. The narrator opened the ceremony with these words: "In each of the great wars he has fought in for the land of his adoption, the Negro has gained a little more freedom than he had ever before enjoyed. Why did he – a slave – volunteer to defend the country that held him in bondage? What was 'independence' to him?" The chorus responded: "EVERYTHING. It spelled 'Freedom.'" For the Civil War episode, Browne gave the floor to Harriet Tubman, the "Moses of her people":

I tell you, my children, they's a-saying that the colored man won't fight, and that he's a-going to run soon as the first shot is fired from yonder Fort Wagner. The eyes of the whole world is on you boy. Let's march on that Fort, let's tear down that flag, and let's put up the Stars and Stripes of the UNION.

The text recalled that each time the nation had rebelled against injustice and tyranny, blacks had volunteered to fight and to defend freedom. Strangely enough, this exaltation of courage took place at the camp of a segregated army which continued to doubt the quality of African-American soldiers. It was nevertheless encouraged by Colonel Hardy, who felt that the patriotism being promoted could serve the interests of the Army as the war was ending, with the 370th Regiment having left Huachuca for Europe and the rest of the 92nd Division preparing to follow in its steps.

The ceremony ended with words in praise of the American troops fighting Nazism and Japan:

Today, Black soldiers are again marching through an enemy land at the summons of duty, face to face with great labors, great dangers in the swamps and jungles of New Guinea, through marshes and among the hedgerows of Normandy, and the mountainous terrain of northern Italy, to fight again, along with freedom-loving men of all races and creeds, the forces of evil.[38]

Yet, with the exception of one experiment on the European front, in which black volunteers were integrated into white companies of the 95th Infantry Division, the US Army remained segregated and the "confidence in the future" to which Hardy referred in his speech was misleading: The War Department did not yet recognize the equality of whites and blacks.

Shortly before leaving the fort in March 1945, Colonel Hardy felt the need to justify the emphasis he had placed on entertainment during his tenure as commander. He had wanted, he claimed, to turn Huachuca into "a seat of Negro culture."[39] By continuing the support given by the New Deal to black culture, he had hoped that a Jim Crow Deluxe in matters of entertainment – a form of segregation that allowed excellence to shine – would render more acceptable the separation imposed by the Army and ease tensions in the absence of progress on racial issues. Yet, in many ways, this encouragement of leisure by the Army echoed the way that masters on plantations in the antebellum South had organized violin concerts and quadrille dances as a form of diversion for slaves.[40] At Huachuca, segregation in the areas of culture and sports was most ambiguous: While all-black quality entertainment helped to instill a feeling of pride among African Americans, it was merely a substitute for recognition of racial equality and black qualities. Culture and sports were areas in which one could make symbolic gestures without calling into question the racial hierarchy that structured all other aspects of life at the camp – with the exception of care in the hospital. Entertainment was the only space where the white command and the black soldiers could find a middle ground. And yet, their motives and expectations were radically different: diversion and channeling of discontent for the former; collective pleasure and racial pride for the latter.

The cultural and sporting activities offered at the fort partly achieved their objectives: To create, within the bounds of military life, moments of collective joy and communion. Photographs taken by the Signal Corps during these events suggest that the military experience was but a succession of shows and distractions. Some female testimonies – Wacs and nurses enjoyed the most lenient conditions of service – fueled this illusion. Nadine Davis Lane, who had worked at Hospital Station No. 1, later recalled:

> I was ecstatic most of the time I served. [...] There were all of the top physical and intellectual people going and coming whom one met and associated with all the time. What more could one ask? I met all of the "elite" personalities from African American society. I had a job I loved, danced, played tennis, bowled, rode horseback, golfed and was entertained by most of the "big name bands" at our officers' club at Fort Huachuca. Stars from Hollywood dropped in anytime. I bumped into people from screen and radio at the officers' club all the time.[41]

By contrast, critics claimed that the entertainment organized by the Special Services was a diversion to mitigate black soldiers' resentment of racial inequality and that it perpetuated the infantilizing stereotype of blacks as needing to sing and dance to be happy. This was the argument advanced by Grant Reynolds – a former Huachuca chaplain who was dishonorably discharged after a psychiatric evaluation diagnosed him with "paranoid tendencies" – in the second article he published in *The Crisis* to denounce the experience of blacks in the military.[42]

Adopting the point of view of producers rather than that of spectators allows us to circumvent the opposition between divergent testimonies and between gendered experiences of life at Huachuca, on the one hand, and to consider the agency involved in this "Mecca of entertainment," on the other. The fort's Special Services team was generally led by a white man, but it was racially mixed and gave pride of place to black artists. Some of the productions were even initiated by black artists – Shirley Graham as representative of the USO in the early years of the camp, Joe Jordan, Anna Russell, George Everett, Theodore Browne, and many others. With the exception of Graham, who was eventually cast aside, none of these personalities used his or her art to challenge the Army's racial policy. None reinterpreted or subverted the cultural forms favored by whites in a way that would call into question the racial order in place at the fort. It would be simplistic, however, to accuse them of having compromised their dignity or having acted in their own personal interest. They seem to have been convinced that Huachuca could serve as a place of culture and education for black soldiers who had not finished school and had never – or rarely – been exposed to culture. The fort offered theaters and cinemas, sports facilities, and a gallery of black art where African Americans could go without restriction. Even in New York and Chicago, few black neighborhoods were as well equipped as Fort Huachuca. In addition, the camp's cultural programs and performances gave a positive image of African Americans – as fighters, as patriots – and made role models out of talented personalities, some of whom were actually capable of surpassing whites. This was real progress compared with the caricatures of black people that had continued to circulate during the interwar period.

12 Ready for Combat

In early 1944, the soldiers of the 92nd Division were ordered to attend a screening of *The Negro Soldier*, a film directed by Frank Capra from a screenplay by the African-American writer Carlton Moss.[1] The men, however, did not see their daily experience of segregation reflected on screen. Commissioned by the federal government to change the image of black soldiers, the film celebrated the heroism, sense of sacrifice, and contribution to nation-building of African-American men. The NAACP and the National Negro Congress praised it as "the best ever made" and called for its widest possible distribution. In February 1944, *The Negro Soldier* became compulsory viewing for all the soldiers training in replacement centers. Although two of the scenes were cut (one where a black officer oversees the command of troops and another where an African-American soldier is massaged by a white nurse), the film suggested that the Army had finally embraced equal opportunity. Segregation was absent from the images, as were tensions between whites and blacks.[2] The scenes showing black soldiers training against a mountainous backdrop, all of them shot in a camp surprisingly similar to Huachuca, felt very familiar to the men of the 92nd Division. However, those featuring blacks and whites exercising side by side in the gymnastics classes dissipated their illusions. The discrepancy between the Hollywood representation of the black experience of war and the reality of training was glaringly apparent to their eyes, especially as racial tensions were flaring up again at the fort.

For General Almond, preparing the 92nd Division consisted essentially of training the men and making them achieve technical mastery. His sole concern was to get the soldiers ready for battle, for the assessment of his leadership qualities and the decision to send the 92nd to the front depended on their ability to fight. And yet, Almond continued to doubt the soldiers' ability to master the exercises and act as a unit. In September 1943, he asked for unit and combined training to be extended by another eight weeks until December 1943. In a letter to the commander of the Third Army, Lieutenant General C. H. Hodges, he justified this demand by invoking the existence of "outstanding deficiencies":

> Outstanding deficiencies which have been particularly manifested are: squad and platoon leadership; slowness in assimilation of technical training; lack of appreciation of team work for crew weapons (mortars and machine guns); communications (wire and radio); carelessness and lack of responsibility in the individual (both for his own and his unit's welfare); lack of initiative, aggressiveness and understanding of a simple order and directives. Although a considerably longer time should improve all units in all particulars, I am confident that the two months extension requested will not greatly affect the division's status in the following respects:
> A. Sense of responsibility in the individual, both platoon officers and squad [enlisted] leaders.
> B. Rate of assimilation of training (individual or group).
> C. Initiative, aggressiveness, and comprehension of military operations.[3]

At a time when the Army was beginning to overcome its prejudices against African-American soldiers, Almond remained convinced of the inferiority of his men and of the impossibility of remedying their weaknesses, which he saw as inextricably linked to black identity. Although he had been granted more than the standard time to bring the 92nd up to standard, he did not consider the possibility that the obstacles faced by the division might explain the men's difficulties. At the event organized to celebrate the first year of training, an occasion on which one would have expected to hear some encouragement, he deplored "weaknesses in combat training. There were cases of negligent command, breaches of basic disciplinary rules and order, and poor maintenance of men and equipment. There have been instances of insufficient energy in the execution of training exercises or individual tasks."[4] The stereotypes of African Americans as lazy and negligent, fueled by the Army's racist military doctrine of the interwar years, were revived without any consideration of the responsibility of white commanders and officers, the social and geographical composition of the group, or the need to adapt the methods of training.

After completing the extended unit and combined training, the 92nd Division began the divisional "D" exercises. In December 1943, the soldiers left the fort to spend time in the sandy hills and windy desert, as those of the 93rd had done the previous year. For three weeks, the men trained in harsh, cold conditions far away from the camp. They learned to maintain and clean their weapons and vehicles, and they were made to take the initiative and deal with the unexpected. Although they encountered supply and logistical difficulties, Almond felt that they managed to overcome them satisfactorily. On December 23, the men of the 92nd returned to Huachuca. For the first time, the commander seemed rather pleased with their performance: The weaknesses observed earlier appeared to have been corrected. Nearly two years into the war, the regional press exaggerated the quality and success of the training in a display of patriotism that was – for once – blind to the color of the soldiers' skin. It insisted on the "realism" of the exercises: an attack against a fictitious enemy under mortar and artillery fire in the foothills of the Huachuca mountains; simulated battles involving coordination between infantry and artillery; assaults by small units; selection of sites for the positioning of weapons to be used by the infantry, etc. According to the *Arizona Daily Star*, "there is no lollypop training being given that Negro division. There are no wasted hours. [...] Their training is identical with other U.S. Army infantry divisions and their equipment is of the finest and latest design."[5] The *Bisbee Daily Review* portrayed Almond as an uncompromising war commander who knew how to galvanize his troops: "You must give your best, you must fight, sweat, and give your blood if necessary, as our men are doing abroad right now. There is no other road to Victory."[6] The articles suggested that the soldiers bravely accepted this draconian training and were eager to go into battle.

However, uncertainty remained as to whether the 92nd would be sent to the front, which weighed heavily on the morale of many soldiers. James Rucker ruled out suicide only because he was opposed to it on principle. In the first letters he wrote from Fort Huachuca to his wife, he confided:

November 13, 1943
As late as 2 years ago I swore that I'd die rather than live in JC [Jim Crow] without fighting. And I find myself in a condition where for 8 months I have accepted JC in its worst forms without raising a finger against it. Instead of fighting JC [...] I am strengthening it with every day's work and don't like this role.

November 16, 1943
It is easy to say that a Negro has every reason to fight. But when they are not allowed to fight what purpose is there in keeping him in a position of utterly uselessness when he could be helping in a war plant on the home front?

African-American officers, whose qualities continued to be questioned, were once again the most vocal in expressing dissatisfaction. They felt that however good and qualified they were, Almond did not believe in their ability to command soldiers for the sole reason that they were black.[7] They were denied equal status, despite the fact that they had undergone the same training and were of the same rank as white officers and now outnumbered them at the camp. According to James Rucker: "The angle of these chauvinists is to prove that Negro officers can't control the soldiers. That Negroes are better soldiers when they have white officers.

[...] All they appoint officers for is to enforce JC, including white and negro officers."[8] African-American officers suffered the consequences of this mistrust by being blocked from promotion. Aware of their anger, the War Department finally took proactive measures to tackle the problem. In January 1944, it issued a directive encouraging the promotion of 25 percent of black officers in the ground forces, air forces, and support forces. Black officers could now be assigned to all units made up of black soldiers, and white officers would be transferred to other positions in order to make room for them.[9] The informal rule that no black officer could be of higher rank than white officers in the same unit was nevertheless maintained; thus, whenever a black officer was promoted within a unit, all white officers of equal or lower rank were automatically transferred to another unit.[10] The January 1944 directive had a considerable impact at Huachuca. Between January 1 and early April 1944, sixty-three officers were promoted within the 92nd Division, namely fifty-five second lieutenants to first lieutenant, six first lieutenants to captain, one captain to major, and one major to lieutenant colonel.[11] However, the highest ranks remained unattainable, and many black officers were left without a promotion.

Several letters denouncing denial of promotion as a manifestation of racial injustice reached Truman Gibson and the NAACP. One of them summed up the situation as follows: "A vacancy seemingly never exists for colored officers."[12] Whereas white officers freshly out of Fort Benning school were made captains in a matter of months, their African-American peers who had graduated from the country's top universities were unable – outside of office settings – to rise above the rank of first lieutenant and found themselves relegated to uninteresting positions that whites did not want. Second Lieutenant Russel H. Dawson of the 600th Infantry Battalion lamented his situation in a letter to Gibson: Despite having a degree in political science from Northwestern University and having been in charge of orientation sessions for new recruits over several weeks, he could no longer rise in rank.[13] First Lieutenant Edward T. Mayfield of the 370th Infantry Regiment presented similar grievances to Gibson: Although aged only thirty-two, he had served for three years as principal of a Julius Rosenwald School in Walterboro, North Carolina, before enlisting in the Army in May 1942. He had first served as a sergeant and had then been selected for the OCS, from which he had graduated as a second lieutenant. In March 1943, he had been promoted to first lieutenant in the Special Services of the 92nd Division. For eleven months, he had coached the division's basketball and cross-country running teams, which he had led to victory. Owing to his excellent grades and evaluations, he had been selected to attend Special Services training in Lexington in August. Although he had completed all the necessary steps to become a captain, he had been retained in the Special Services with the rank of first lieutenant – a dead end with no prospect of advancement. And when he had finally left the Special Services, his position had been given to a white captain. Mayfield implored Gibson to do all he could to get him out of the 92nd Division, where his chances of promotion were nil.[14] As for Lieutenant Castine Davis, he bypassed the 92nd Division command by writing to the Office of the Commanding General of the Ninth Service Command. His letter highlighted all the biographical elements that could help him obtain a promotion. He was born in Liberia to a father who had served as an officer in the country's first army and a mother who had been a tutor to the future first lady. A university graduate in mathematics and science, he had worked for the Chicago Post Office for fifteen years – enclosed with the letter was an article from the Postal Alliance that described him as a model employee. He had then attended Howard University's ROTC program for reserve officers and, in 1926, had trained at Camp Meade, which had allowed him to serve as a reserve officer for thirteen years. He emphasized in his letter that he possessed all the attributes of respectability – diligence, a taste for work, religious observance – and assured the reader of his loyalty to the Army. Despairing at the fact that he could not gain recognition from the institution in which he had placed so much hope, he begged to be granted the promotion that he had been denied at Huachuca.[15]

Between February 6 and April 3, 1944, the entire 92nd Division was assembled for maneuvers in Merryville, Louisiana. There the men learned to cross rivers, go into battle, and confront other divisions. This stage of the training took place under very tense conditions, as had been the case for the 93rd Division in March 1943. Almond was no longer under the control of the fort's commander and the Ninth Service Command. The division was back in the racist South and had to fight other divisions, some of which were white. The men sensed that their training was coming to an end; it would soon be decided whether or not they would be deployed overseas. Resentment toward the white commanders, which had been contained at Huachuca thanks to Hardy's efforts at pacification and dialogue, erupted far from the training bases. Some soldiers threw stones at white officers, and others grew so exasperated that they left the division.[16] The commanders reinforced sanctions for behavior deemed to deviate from the strict segregation rules in force in the South.

One Sunday evening in late January, thirty-four-year-old Second Lieutenant Robert E. Elkins of the 317th Engineer Battalion was allowed to take his fifty soldiers to De Ridder, a small town located nineteen miles from the base, so that they could relax after several weeks of training.

After dropping off his men in the town, Elkins went to a show and then to a restaurant. When he went to find his driver at the Chicago Hotel, he noticed that some of his men were taking part in a fight. His superiors later charged him with drunkenness and disturbing the peace while armed and in uniform, in violation of Articles of War 95 and 96 – the latter prohibiting "Conduct of a nature to bring discredit upon the military service." On his return to Huachuca after the end of maneuvers, Elkins was incarcerated in the stockade before his court-martial, which was unusual for an officer.[17] When he was finally court-martialed in June 1944, he denied that he had been drunk and explained that he had knocked on the men's bedroom doors to let them know it was time to return to the base. However, the court-martial found no mitigating circumstances and dismissed him from the Army.[18] As for twenty-three-year-old Andrew L. Farris, Second Lieutenant of the 559th Infantry Battalion and former member of the Illinois National Guard, he was charged with being AWOL for three days while on maneuvers, failing to return his radio after maneuvers, and driving an army half-track without authorization.[19] The application to black officers of Article of War 96 was a sign that white commanders feared the spread of rebellion within the division.

As pressure from black activists was mounting and the authority of commanders was increasingly being contested, the War Department finally made the decision to deploy the 92nd Division overseas, even as the men were still on maneuvers. Shortly before, a major doctrinal change had taken place with regard to African-American soldiers. In a booklet entitled *Command of Negro Troops*, published in February 1944, the War Department repudiated the racist theories previously espoused by the Army, which Almond had applied with great zeal and conviction.[20] The booklet denied any scientific basis – whether biological, physiological, or genetic – for essentialist judgements about black soldiers, and took into account structural factors to explain differences in quality and performance between black and white soldiers. The War Department now rejected any form of demeaning generalization: "No statement beginning 'All Negroes' is true." Biological explanations were disqualified on the basis of psychological studies, the results of which had actually been known before the war: "In all the vast number of studies by psychologists and other scientists during the past two or three decades, there is not one piece of research which proves that Negroes are, as a group, mentally or emotionally defective by heredity." Thus, the biological considerations that had provided the basis for the differentiated treatment of troops were replaced with socio-economic explanations that focused on the geographical, family, and social origins of soldiers and on the specific difficulties blacks faced during training. The social scientists employed by the War

Department had finally been heard.[21] The booklet stated: "The Negro group has had a history materially different from that of the majority in the Army. Its average schooling has been inferior; its work has been generally less skilled than that of the white man; and its role in the life of the Nation has been limited." The Army was increasingly convinced that specific remedial and upgrade measures would enable black soldiers to acquire the qualities that were expected of them.

The normalization of African Americans' situation in the Army was under way. It entailed a complete revision of the doctrine for the command of black soldiers, according to which a special kind of leadership – a combination of physical strength, aggressiveness, and willpower known only to white officers from the South – was necessary for training to be successful. The new military doctrine recommended applying the same command techniques to black and white troops. If men were not born good soldiers, and if "there is no scientific evidence whatever to support such a view [that there are some mysterious inborn factors – such as courage, fear, or a fighting heart – whose presence or absence is a matter of racial inheritance]," then it was up to the Army to forge these qualities that were essential to success in combat.[22] The accountability of white commanders for the performance and well-being of their men, a principle established by the Inspector General following the racial uprisings of the summer of 1943, was confirmed in the booklet. Since the segregation of units could no longer be based on presumed racial differences, the Army had to find another justification for racial separation. It therefore pointed the finger at the broader society: "The Army accepts no doctrine of racial superiority or inferiority. It may seem inconsistent, therefore, that there is nevertheless a general separation of colored and white troops on duty. It is important to understand that separate organization is a matter of practical military expediency, and not an endorsement of beliefs in racial distinction." By military expediency, the Army probably meant the absence of racial tensions made possible by the maintenance of segregation habits in civilian life. And yet, both in the Huachuca hospital and in some of the newly formed units in the European theater, experiments in racial integration were being successfully carried out. These experiments showed that neither whites nor blacks were bothered by contact with members of the other race, and that this contact did not hamper the smooth running of units.

The revision of the War Department's racial doctrine paved the way for a change in strategy regarding the deployment of black troops. In 1944, the Army continued to retain its African-American combat units on American soil despite being short of forces on the front. Black activists and journalists quickly highlighted this contradiction and stepped up their pressure on the War Department. In March, the McCloy

Committee advised sending African-American units into battle "as soon as possible" in order to reduce racial tensions. It also recommended the reorganization of existing units and the revision of the schedule of troop deployment on the basis of political – not military – considerations. Assistant Secretary of War McCloy wrote to Secretary Stimson: "Selections [of troops to be sent to combat] are made on the basis of efficiency with the result that the colored units are discarded for combat service, but little is done by way of studying new means to put them in shape for combat service."[23] McCloy specifically recommended the overseas deployment of the 92nd and 93rd Divisions, the Army's two largest black units, which were closely followed by the African-American press. Stimson heard this political argument and announced on March 6, 1944 that the two divisions would be sent to the front. The 93rd Division would be deployed in its entirety in the Pacific theater. As regards the 92nd, a combat regiment – the 370th – would be formed from the best elements with a view to immediate overseas deployment. Volunteers would be able to apply to join the regiment, and officers would be selected from the best in the unit without regard to race. The men would be given the best training and the most effective weapons. The rest of the division would join the 370th at a later stage.[24]

Following this announcement, which was made while the 92nd was still on maneuvers in Louisiana, Almond had to prepare the deployment of his men. Ever since the activation of the division, he had been convinced that they were weak and that they lagged behind in acquiring the fundamentals, despite repeated prolongation of training. Accordingly, he stepped up preparations for the confrontation with German troops in Italy. On announcing to his men that they would be deployed overseas, he tried to convince them that they were ready for battle, even though he himself doubted it:

I told this division when it was a cadre of 1400 men and 200 officers a year and a half ago that it had a future, and it has. I have watched it grow, I have watched the reaction of the men and the officers. [...] I see men salute better, perform their duties better, have a better idea of their job. [...] You must take great satisfaction in the fact that you are now about to actually prove your worth.[25]

Up until then, few of the men had believed that training would lead them to the theater of operations. They therefore greeted this announcement with circumspection, as William Perry's testimony indicates: "One day Almond unites us and tells we have been selected for an active theater. It was a surprise! Most of them never thought they would let us fight anybody."[26] Almond and his commanders not only had to persuade the soldiers that they were capable of fighting, they also had to instill in them the desire to fight.

On returning to Huachuca, some of the soldiers claimed that the commitment to deploy the 92nd Division overseas was a lie intended to make them accept more vexation and harder training conditions. These men were reluctant to perform the new exercises. In response, Almond became even more aggressive and authoritarian.[27] Clearly, he had not listened to the Army's recent recommendations. Soldiers deemed unfit for service were reprimanded or sidelined and then replaced by other men. New equipment, particularly shooting equipment, was delivered to the fort. To prepare for the Italian theater, the 370th Infantry Regiment underwent special, fast-track training: mountain climbing, river crossings, patrolling. The deputy commander of the 92nd Division, John E. Wood, was put in charge of the combined infantry, artillery, and tank unit training. The Army wanted to test the regiment's fighting qualities and to ensure that it was ready to win the battle against the German Army.

However, incidents occurred after the 92nd returned to the fort. Readapting to the racial compromise of Huachuca proved difficult, as had been the case in the summer of 1943 for the 93rd Division. During the men's absence, the Army had conceded some demands for equality, as black soldiers in camps across the country had dared to challenge segregation head-on.[28] At Fort Huachuca, black officers suffered the most from the discriminatory regime: Almond and his subordinates continued to impose vexatious separation measures that were not required by Army regulations and that nullified the promise of equality of rank. Starting in the summer of 1943, white officers had implemented de facto segregation in the mess of the 371st Infantry Regiment by systematically reserving tables for their group. In the spring of 1944, a number of black officers sat at their tables with the intention of challenging the status quo, which they considered to be arbitrary and humiliating. The white officers refused to accept this proximity and took their meals elsewhere. This time, it was the whites who left, for army rules were not on their side in the mess. A few days later, the commander of the 371st Regiment, Colonel Notestein, recalled the rule prohibiting segregation in the dining room. However, he also suggested that from now on officers should sit "according to rank and service," thus ensuring that white officers who were at least first lieutenants could stay among their own. The majority of white officers continued to sit at the tables they had reserved for themselves in previous months.[29]

In the white officers' clubs, the principle of racial separation remained sacrosanct, despite the fact that the Army had recently adopted a directive prohibiting exclusion or restriction of access to recreation areas on the basis of race.[30] In July, the white Catholic chaplain, Joseph Griffin, invited two African Americans, Hamilton Martin (the fort's new chaplain) and Miss Matred McKissack (director of the USO center), to have dinner with him at the Lakeside Club. The Mountain View Club was regularly visited by white officers, but this was the first time that the racial status of the white officers' club had been put to the test. The two black personalities were turned away at the door. Hardy approved this decision retroactively, thereby reaffirming the legitimacy of excluding African Americans from Lakeside. Shortly afterwards, Griffin left the fort. According to the newspaper *The Afro-American*, the two events were clearly linked. Yet, a question remained: Had the white chaplain left of his own accord as a sign of protest against segregation, or had he been punished for challenging white exclusivity?[31] At Lakeside more than in any other place at the fort, efforts were made to maintain physical and social separation between individuals who were in fact equal in terms of training and rank.

The soldiers, for their part, responded to the intensification of training with acts of insubordination. Uniform regulations were broken on a massive scale and in an obviously concerted manner. Some soldiers came to training without their helmets, which they claimed gave them headaches. Others showed up with "Harlem hair does" – hair that was too long or resembled the Afro hairstyle – or "zoot uniforms" – custom-tailored outfits of dark shirts and tight bottom trousers.[32] The baggy and eccentric outfits known as zoot suits were worn by black and Latino civilians in major US cities during the war. However, white soldiers and civilians saw their wearers as contesting patriotism and breaking rationing regulations. In June 1943, race riots triggered by the wearing of zoot suits spread to Detroit, New York, and other cities in Texas and Arizona.[33] When the men altered their uniforms at Huachuca, the reference was unambiguous. It was a gesture of defiance, understood as such by those to whom it was addressed. However, the mass scale of the transgression made repression difficult. The commander was worried about the possibility of mutiny. The fort's military police began to search all soldiers who entered or left the camp; it also guarded Almond's residence at the old post twenty-four hours a day.[34]

Given the extreme tensions and the growing challenge to Almond's authority, a series of inspections were conducted at the fort to determine whether the 370th Infantry Regiment and the 92nd Division as a whole were ready to go into battle. The qualification of the soldiers, as assessed by the AGCT, had improved slightly thanks to the refresher and literacy courses that the least educated had been forced to take since the summer of 1943. The replacement of the worst-performing men had also contributed to the rise in AGCT scores. Sergeant Richard Carter of the 597th

Infantry Battalion realized that he had been transferred to the 92nd Division because of his IQ, at a time when all unassigned blacks with high AGCT scores were being relocated to Fort Huachuca.[35] By spring 1944, only 31.6 percent of soldiers remained in the lowest AGCT category. Nevertheless, the level of the men remained low compared with that of soldiers in the white divisions.

When General Davis visited Huachuca again between April 15 and 21, he was the first high-ranking officer to inspect the 92nd Division since the decision had been made to send it into battle. The black inspector, accompanied by Truman Gibson, was sent by Assistant Secretary of War McCloy on a mission to determine whether it was a good idea to deploy the 92nd to Italy. On arriving at the fort, Davis was informed that four black officers were in the stockade, where they awaited trial by court-martial. Two of the men, Second Lieutenants Farris and Elkins, had been incarcerated since early April without being notified of the charges against them. Their mail was censored, their insignia had been taken from them in violation of the Articles of War, and they ate their meals with an escort under the gaze of soldiers.[36] This humiliating treatment undermined any authority they might have over their men if they were to return to service. Second Lieutenant Ballie Wall of the 371st Infantry Regiment, who had been sentenced to life imprisonment for the alleged rape of an African-American civilian working in the laundry, was awaiting his appeal.[37] Another five officers were on parole, including a first lieutenant who had served at the black hospital.[38] Davis did not mention any of this in his inspection report.

Instead, the African-American inspector reported seeing real improvement within the 92nd Division and in general at the fort. He did not doubt Colonel Hardy's word when the latter told him that "the morale of the troops at this station [was] high with very few, if any 'rotten spots.'"[39] He even congratulated Almond on the great progress made by the division, and especially on "the desire [of the men and soldiers] to go and fight, and their confidence in their ability to serve if given the chance."[40] Davis's report to the Inspector General was entirely positive. He recommended deploying the 92nd overseas, preferably to the European theater of operations. In support of this assessment, he highlighted the performance of the division's various units, in particular the results obtained by infantry platoons and battalions in the firing exercises. Davis sensed that this was his last visit to Huachuca and, therefore, his last opportunity to draw the attention of the Inspector General and the General Staff to what he believed to be Hardy's excellent work. In his report to the Inspector General, he wrote that the fort's commander had "by his very sympathetic attitude, developed unusually amicable interracial relations on the post and in near-by towns" by creating multiple entertainment venues, cleaning up the camp's surroundings, significantly reducing the rate of venereal disease, and organizing cultural events that were highly original for a black post. In Davis's view, Hardy clearly deserved to be honored for his service to the Army.[41] In this final report, the African-American inspector made absolutely no mention of the soldiers' acts of insubordination, the excessively harsh repression against black officers, and the lingering doubts about the readiness of the 92nd Division. He failed to report to his superiors any fact that might challenge the decision to deploy the 92nd overseas. Did he believe that the remaining shortcomings would be rapidly corrected? Did he want to avoid casting further doubt on the qualities of the black soldiers? Did his sense of discipline prevent him from questioning the decisions of the General Staff or the command style of Almond (a white superior)?

Higher-ranking white generals who came to inspect the fort in the following weeks did, however, express reservations. The stakes involved in sending the 92nd Division to Italy were considerable, both for military reasons – failure in the field was unthinkable – and for political reasons – black organizations and newspapers would not let the War Department reverse its decision. The Chief of Staff himself came to Huachuca in early May. Even for an anti-militarist like James Rucker, the presence of General Marshall was a sign that army officials finally considered the 92nd to be the equal of other divisions. In a letter dated May 2, 1944, he wrote to his wife:

> Today was an eventful one. The combat team that's alerted was inspected by none other than Gl Marshall. Did we step smartly! The band was in good form and the parade was a honey. [...] It was a big surprise. The transport plane was seen yesterday evening. This morning our platoon was ordered to prepare for a parade at 10 am. There he was. That's a lot more important and morale-building than a lot of discussions and daily newspapers journalism. [...] So we feel pretty important in this man's army. [...] The general inspected three lines at open ranks and stopped occasionally to question or make a remark to a soldier. That's a crack unit's pride and the chief of staff gave us the full measure of what an inspection is supposed to be. So look out Axis! Tremble when you hear of the 92nd being sent against you. You've got an outfit here that has won its pride by the hardest means and will never give it up until its assignment in this people's war is completed.[42]

Whatever General Marshall may have thought about the state of readiness of the 92nd Division, his visit did not bring the army discussion to a close. Several other inspections were conducted at the fort. The Chief of Staff was followed in June by Lieutenant General Lesley J. McNair, the commander of the Army Ground Forces, who expressed the same confidence and satisfaction as General Davis. On his return to Washington, McNair wrote:

12.1: Gen. George C. Marshall inspects a mess hall of the 92nd Division. © Fort Huachuca Museum.

Almond has done a fine job and believes that his division will fight. My own estimate of the value of these troops has risen as they emerge from the painfully slow process of drumming things into them. They are, I believe, a better outfit than the 93rd when it left this country, and their future will be a most interesting contribution as to the value of negro troops.[43]

In his report, written just a few days before the 370th left for the front, McNair focused exclusively on the technical preparation of the men. He neglected the effect that tensions might have on the soldiers' performance in the field, even though he had likely seen the explosiveness of the situation at the fort.

Some of the men who were about to leave for the front were resolutely opposed to the idea of fighting under the authority of whites. In the week of June 4, 1944, around thirty NCOs of the 370th Regiment entered the offices of their commanders and handed over their stripes, saying that they refused to fight overseas under a racist company commander.[44] One court-martial followed another. Before the 370th left for the front, twelve soldiers had been incarcerated for invoking Article of War 121, which entitled service men to lodge a complaint with superiors to redress grievances. They were given only one day's notice to prepare for their court-martial. Black officers who publicly criticized training conditions were imprisoned for minor breaches of regulations. The commander of the 370th, Colonel Sherman, court-martialed more officers than any other commander in the Fourth Army.[45] Visitors to the fort worried about a possible explosion. Carolyn Davenport Moore, executive secretary of the Philadelphia branch of the NAACP, who had spent a few days at the fort at the beginning of June, wrote to the national executive secretary Walter White:

I left Huachuca with the most sinking feeling I think it is possible to experience about Negro men in the Army today. [...] The situation is dynamite and if steps are not taken to correct many of the conditions which exist there, the men may be aggravated to the point where there will really be a minor massacre of white officers.[46]

Fearing an imminent conflagration, several white officers tried by every possible means to leave the 92nd before it was sent to the front.[47]

On June 26, 1944, the 370th Infantry Regiment and the 598th Field Artillery Battalion departed for the front, leaving behind the so-called subversive elements. Tensions were momentarily alleviated. The units of the 92nd that remained at the fort continued their training, which was made more difficult to compensate for the presumed lower level of the men. All in all, these units received one more year of preparation than white units. The following inspections were more critical of the men's technical qualities. In July 1944, Under Secretary Patterson toured the western camps in the company of all of the members of the Congressional Military Affairs Committee and the employees of the Army Public Relations Office. At Huachuca, he was shown all types of training. Patterson congratulated and encouraged the soldiers: "Battles are won by small units. [...] But everywhere we went [on the fort], we saw leadership in squads and platoons pushed to the limit." Yet, on returning to Washington, the Under Secretary expressed his concerns in a letter that failed to question the responsibility of the commander of the 92nd Division: "The standard of performance was not as high as in the other divisions visited. General Almond and his staff have worked hard, however, and deserve a good deal of credit for the way in which they are handling a difficult job. I doubt that anyone could handle the situation to better advantage."[48]

In August 1944, Colonel Morrow of the Ground Forces spent a few days at the fort for a final inspection. The secret memo he sent to Lieutenant General McNair was highly critical. Although the division as a whole was "satisfactory or slightly below average" and the training was "satisfactory," some of the black officers had a barely honorable level and others refused to obey orders or go into battle. Above all, "morale as a whole does not appear to be satisfactory. [...] There is little or no 'will to fight' on the part of the negro personnel either among officers or EM. [...] My impression is that the great majority of [white officers] would prefer to go overseas with some unit other than the 92nd division." Morrow had discovered a "casual camp" in which 950 men were interned and a stockade full of disruptive soldiers – all indications of major malfunctions at the fort.[49]

Following the return of the 92nd from maneuvers, one man in fifteen had been declared unfit for duty for health reasons. The "casual camp" with 950 interned men was full. As far as Morrow was concerned, almost all of them were malingerers: They feigned imaginary pain or pretended to be mad in order to escape training or avoid being sent to the front. The colonel observed the maneuvers and rank training with dismay:

Some of them carried their helmets instead of wearing them, others carried their shoes instead of having them on their feet, wearing low cut shoes instead, others were not wearing their leggings, but were carrying them, and some were carrying chairs, suit-cases, and other impediments. [...] The men did not march in cadence. Many of them limped and some were stooped or bent at the waist.

Psychologists reported cases of hypochondria and neurosis combined with slight physical handicaps that made it impossible for the men to train and perform chores. Morrow himself interviewed around thirty of these "malingerers": One soldier told him that he suffered when walking because one of his testicles was higher than the other; another complained of dizziness and rapid heartbeat; and yet another reported pain against which surgery was powerless. Robert Boyd, a twenty-nine-year-old former farmer from Tifton, Tennessee, who was now a soldier in Company D of the 371st Infantry Regiment, explained his inability to serve in a machine gun unit by invoking a lung condition, calluses that prevented him from walking, and a fear of gunfire. He was declared unfit for service, even though the regimental doctor had not mentioned any contraindication in his medical file. Dave Harper, a twenty-two-year-old native of Alabama who served in a tank company of the 371st Regiment, complained of pain in his shoulder and the arch of his foot and said he had a bad prostate. His medical record mentioned only an old collarbone fracture, but the inspection team suspected infection with a venereal disease. As for Henry Welch, a thirty-seven-year-old gunner who had worked previously in a Mississippi foundry, he said that he suffered from rheumatism and could no longer stand wearing a helmet. The clinical and radiological examination had revealed no pathology, leading to a diagnosis of "100% malingerer."

From these thirty or so cases, Morrow concluded that there was nothing to be done with the men of the "casual camp." Although he did not detect any organized collective resistance, the colonel saw the danger of contagion to the rest of the 92nd Division. Ever since the days of slavery, blacks had been accused of being lazy. A bout of weakness or illness was never seen as a sign of overwork or exhaustion, but always as a subterfuge to get out of chores or work.[50] Morrow believed that this interpretation remained valid for some of the cases observed at the camp. However, given the urgent need to have a division ready for battle, he ruled out repression; instead, he argued that the Army should stop its efforts to reassign these men and should get rid of them as soon as possible. He recommended their immediate transfer to "eliminate the adverse influence on the remainder of the troops at this post," followed by their replacement. However, his recommendation was not acted upon. Indeed, despite Almond's repeated interventions up to the highest echelons of the War Department, the "malingerers" were ultimately sent into battle with the rest of the 92nd Division.[51]

Morrow understood that repression at Huachuca had failed to silence resistance. The number of court-martials convened at the fort was four or five times higher than in comparable divisions. Yet, for the colonel, the proliferation of court-martials was evidence of an extremely high level of insubordination, not of excessive repression. Between October 15, 1942 and June 16, 1944, 2,998 cases were tried by court-martial at the fort (an average of 150 per month), which meant that 4 courts had to sit simultaneously 2 evenings a week.[52] To this must be added all the punishments that were imposed directly, under Article of War 104, by unit commanders. The most common offenses – unauthorized absence due to extended furlough, desertion on a weekend, on pay day, or on the day before a difficult exercise, but also fighting, theft, disrespect toward officers, unauthorized use of an army vehicle, loss or misappropriation of military equipment, and illegal trafficking – were not specific to Huachuca. Nor were the most common punishments – extra chores, suppression of furlough, fines, imprisonment in the stockade, and exclusion on grounds of improper behavior.[53] Unfortunately, the destruction of the fort's court-martial archives makes it impossible to determine whether the offenses were properly classified or whether the punishments were more severe at Huachuca than elsewhere.

For the soldiers of the 92nd Division, the proliferation of court-martials was a sign of arbitrary and excessively harsh repression. After the war,

Sergeant William Perry recalled that during his last year at Huachuca, unit commanders would court-martial soldiers directly, without warning or prior disciplinary action:

> It could be anything, insubordination, talking, minor things. 18 year old kids who had never had this kind of military discipline, it takes a while to get used to it, especially for guys coming from the North East, New York, Chicago, Pennsylvania, who went to school, some had been to college, they had reasoning abilities and they would ask questions.[54]

An anonymous letter sent to George Schuyler, a journalist at the *Pittsburgh Courier*, also denounced the excesses of military justice at Huachuca, particularly with regard to officers:

> For extremely minor offenses, colored officers are court-martialed with alarming frequency. [...] For a colored officer to secure an acquittal is a mathematical impossibility. Here is how it operates. The court is composed of from 6 to 8 bigoted white officers and 2–3 colored officers, but since a 2 thirds vote will secure a conviction, the vote of the 2 colored members is practically nil and the entire process represents nothing more than the simulation of justice by a mixed court.[55]

The racist bias of Huachuca's military justice toward black officers was obvious. While the ratio of black to white officers was 2 to 1 at the beginning of 1944, the ratio of officers court-martialed between the arrival of the 92nd at Huachuca and the first departures for Europe was 17 to 1, with 203 black officers tried compared with 12 white officers. Specifically, fifty-five black officers were court-martialed for being AWOL, forty for neglect of duty, eighteen for insubordination, sixteen for misuse of government vehicles, ten for disrespect, seven for drunkenness, four for drinking on duty, one for rape, and one for "fornication on the highway."[56] At Huachuca, justice specifically targeted black officers as a way of undermining their ability to challenge the racial status quo and to instill subversive ideas in their men. One cannot say whether, for similar offenses, the sentences imposed on blacks were harsher than those imposed on whites at other camps. Yet, consultation of some of the individual files reveals breaches of due process; these were likely intended to punish officers quickly, that is, without giving them a chance to defend themselves. Thus, in June 1944, Second Lieutenant Farris was sentenced to dismissal, total forfeitures, and confinement at hard labor for five years for acts committed in December 1943 at Huachuca and in Louisiana during maneuvers. While confined in a guard house in 1944, he asked for his case to be reviewed by the Office of the Judge Advocate General in Washington. The board of review stated that the defense had been given only two hours' notice of the second hearing and had therefore been unable to read the additional charges against Farris, even though these had been signed two weeks earlier. It also noted that a key witness had been unable to attend the hearing: This witness, the doctor who had operated on Farris in 1943, could have explained why the second lieutenant had failed to arrive on time for the start of "D" exercises on December 3, 1943.[57] The high proportion of appeals reviewed by the Military Justice Division suggests that justice at the fort did not always respect the rights of the defense and tended to be excessively harsh toward black soldiers and officers.

Whether Colonel Morrow's gaze turned toward the "casual camp" or the stockade, the division he inspected was in a worrying state: Nearly 1,000 men were unable to fight and the stockade was full of soldiers who would not bend to the rules of the Army. Morrow's report did not criticize the technical preparations, nor did it question Almond's responsibility or methods, but it did reveal an acute awareness of the tensions and conflicts that risked undermining the performance of the 92nd in combat. The report was kept confidential because it risked jeopardizing the division's departure for Italy and, therefore, the experiment for evaluating the fighting ability of the black troops, who had received the best training and equipment and been commanded by the best officers.[58] The political cost of canceling this experiment was too high, both within the Army and in the eyes of the electorate, the African-American press, and black organizations. However, it is difficult to believe that the Army knowingly sent to the front soldiers in whose abilities it did not entirely trust. Domestic political considerations could not justify taking such a risk against the Germans.

Thus, the Army maintained the departure date for the division's remaining units. Right up to the end, dissenting soldiers expressed their opposition, yet without ever engaging in open mutiny. They destroyed army equipment before leaving the fort, just as the soldiers of the 93rd Division had done a year earlier; like their predecessors, they believed that they would remain unpunished because of their imminent transfer to the front.[59] The ground forces officers who visited the fort a few weeks before the men's departure discovered large quantities of discarded objects and goods – dozens of pairs of shoes, helmet linings, steel helmets, hundreds of bottles of soft drinks and milk, tinned food, cartons of toilet paper, etc. A great many items were burnt. One day, as he was riding his horse, Hardy found the contents of a truck emptied in a canyon 1 mile from the camp: Lying on the ground were 25 ties, 100 socks, around 50 shirts, and huge quantities of trousers, gloves, caps, and bags. As a sign of their rejection of the Army, the soldiers targeted strictly military equipment along with clothing and consumer goods. They did not steal these objects or send them to their families, unlike what had happened at other camps.[60] At Huachuca, the aim was to jam the war machine by artificially creating scarcity and destroying the symbols of military authority. For Hardy, this was just another manifestation of blacks' carelessness in the use and conservation of army property. A white officer of the 92nd Division suggested another explanation: Blacks had never had enough property of their own to learn how to take care of objects.[61] Such prejudices prevented the white officers from seeing the challenge contained in these intentional acts of destruction, all of which were committed before departure to ensure that there would not be time to identify and punish the culprits.

For some of the men, departure for the front had the merit of relieving boredom and provided an opportunity to prove on the ground that prejudices against black soldiers were irrational. For the anti-militarist James Rucker, who was deployed to Italy at the end of July, the departure raised hopes of a radical transformation, as he confided in the last letter he wrote from Arizona to his wife:

July 14 1944

Soon I will be turning my back on the JC United States with not a single regret. It won't be goodbye to JC because the Army seems to have pledged that it will carry JC to the far corners of the Earth, at least I will be away from the main source and frustration of JC. That's a great relief under any circumstances.

For no other reason than JC, I was stationed in the most isolated camp in the country just as distant from you as any of the war theaters. [...] I hope to return to an America that is not JC. I've been hoping that for as long as I can remember. It makes goddam little difference to me if I return at all. [...] Here I have endured and seen as much of fascism as I'd ever expected to see in Germany or Spain. I have seen abuses of an entire people perpetrated in the most cynical fashion that lied and lied to the world. That presumed to improve liberty of peoples all over the world.

Farewell Jim Crow America!

As the 92nd Division was completing training at Huachuca, the gap grew ever wider between the Army's new recommendations in matters of race and the racial regime imposed by General Almond, which was based on a maximalist interpretation of segregation and the systematic use of repression against dissent. The commander's treatment of his men ran counter to the compromises and adjustments now recommended by the Army. Without going so far as to endorse racial integration – which was then being experimented with in the European theatre – the Army revised its doctrine on the use of African-American troops. It condemned essentialist conceptions of race and explained the remaining segregation by invoking the racism of the surrounding society; it put an end to the segregation of recreation areas in mixed camps; and it recognized that commanders were partly responsible for the success or failure of race relations, which were now partly attributed to commanders' ability to entrust black soldiers with responsibilities. At Huachuca, Colonel Hardy had anticipated these recommendations. As for General Almond, he resisted this doctrinal evolution and continued to defend the most conservative racial positions of the interwar period. He saw his men alternately as unfit or rebellious, and at best as difficult soldiers who could be made to obey military rules only via repression. The 92nd Division that left for Italy may have been ready to fight, but it was undermined by racial tensions that none of the arrangements conceived by Hardy and the hospital and Special Services officers had managed to neutralize. The General Staff was only partially aware of this. Those who, like Colonel Morrow, had been willing to open their eyes to the manifestations of racial antagonism hoped that the long-delayed fulfillment of the commitment to deploy the division overseas would lead African-American officers and soldiers to leave their grievances aside and to focus on demonstrating their fighting spirit on the battlefield. As for the commander of the 92nd Division, he was not even sure that his men would be able to stand the test of fire.[62]

Conclusion: The Outcome of an Experiment

Over the course of World War II, Fort Huachuca was the site of an unprecedented and never to be repeated racial experiment: the training of over 14,000 African-American soldiers in a single, isolated location on the US–Mexico border. The historic black post was hastily reactivated in 1941 under the pressure of black newspapers and activist organizations, which had been demanding racial integration and an African-American presence in the military commensurate with black representation in the population. While the General Staff yielded to the second of these demands, it resisted acceding to the first on the grounds that the Army was not a social laboratory. Failing to obtain the integration they ardently desired, African-American activists were forced to settle for a second-best solution: the creation of several black – segregated – military units. Two all-black infantry divisions, the 93rd and then the 92nd, were formed and trained at Fort Huachuca. Out there in the middle of the Arizona desert, the minority group in American society suddenly found itself in the majority. Yet, it was the white commanders who directed the training, set the conditions of relaxation and collective life, determined the racial assignment of space, and controlled the military justice that punished transgressions. In the absence of Army rules specifically designed for an all-black post, it was they who conceived the racial regime for governing interactions at the fort.

Had the Army created a "black ghetto" in confining so many African Americans in this isolated enclave? I refrained from using this term until after I finished recounting Huachuca's racial experiment because I wanted to leave the reader free to consider the black post in all its complexity. This allowed me to recall the metaphor that Huachuca's black soldiers and officers themselves used to refer to the fort, "the plantation," a term evoking the racial form of economic domination that had developed historically in the South. Earlier in the book, I discussed the relevance and limitations of this comparison. Here I propose the metaphor of the ghetto, as it allows one to situate the fort

Conclusion: The Outcome of an Experiment

in its immediate present and in a distinct geography: the large northern cities, where African Americans who had come from the South in the interwar period to sell their labor power to industry were ostracized through organized racial segregation, numerous forms of discrimination, and violence. Such a concentration of black populations in deprived neighborhoods like Chicago's South Side or New York's Harlem could not have taken place without external, coercive intervention reminiscent of the practice of isolating Jews in the medieval cities of Europe.[1] In the United States, the term "ghetto" was first used in 1925 by Louis Wirth in his eponymous thesis, *The Ghetto*, to describe the Jewish neighborhood on Chicago's West Side. The German-born sociologist also applied the term to the "Little Sicilies, Little Polands, Chinatowns, and Black belts," which he claimed were born of ethnic groups' desire to "preserve [their] peculiar cultural forms." Wirth's culturalist approach, however, overlooked the coercive and intentional nature of the segregation of African Americans by white society. Some twenty years later, sociologists Horace Cayton and St. Clair Drake took up the term in their 1944 book *Black Metropolis*, but this time to designate the social and spatial effects of the introduction of the first racially restrictive housing covenants. The ghetto metaphor remained marginal in American social science during the war, as the Nazis were then redefining the spatial and political configuration of the ghetto in Poland with the ultimate aim of destroying the Jews.[2] In this context, it is hardly surprising that Huachuca's black soldiers and officers never resorted to it.

Several of the fort's features nevertheless suggest that the term "black ghetto," as later defined by sociologists,[3] may be aptly applied to the Huachuca experiment. Confinement is, of course, inherent to the military experience. During the war, both black and white soldiers were confined to training bases and restricted in their freedom of movement: To leave and return to the fort, all soldiers and civilians, whether black or white, had to show a pass and to respect exit hours and furlough days. At Huachuca, the rules governing soldiers' activities, interactions, and right to come and go were restrictive largely because of their military nature. Therefore, to speak of the fort as a black ghetto requires showing the specifically racial dimension of the confinement that was imposed in this particular training camp. To determine whether the Huachuca soldiers were treated unfairly relative to others, one must compare Fort Huachuca with a "white fort," namely a camp reserved for the training of white soldiers.

The "all-black post" was as well equipped with facilities as were other training bases, unlike the situation in areas reserved for African-American soldiers at segregated black–white camps; the African-American press even frequently praised the quality and number of hospital facilities and sports and cultural amenities at Huachuca. By contrast, the two black divisions did not have access to the same military equipment as white units: Weapons and the latest tank models were slow to arrive at the fort due to production delays, but also because the General Staff distrusted African-American soldiers and postponed sending them to the front. In this respect, Huachuca's soldiers were unfairly treated relative to whites, just as African Americans living in urban ghettos suffered disproportionally from the retreat of the state.

Another similarity with the black ghetto was the increased and tightened control over the movements of soldiers around the camp, which was aimed at preventing interactions between blacks and whites outside the fort. This reinforced isolation was justified on the grounds that the surrounding white communities distrusted blacks as a result of the racial prejudice that they were deviant (especially in sexual matters). White communities therefore supposedly needed to be protected from the physical proximity of African-American soldiers. Moreover, as in the black ghetto, the numerical imbalance between black and white populations blatantly favored the former, whereas authority remained entirely in the hands of a tiny white minority in charge of implementing the segregation instituted by the Army. In this context, many black soldiers and officers were subjected to humiliating, discriminatory, and excessively harsh treatment. The difference in status between black and white officers was accentuated by the isolation and targeted repression of African Americans. Inside the fort, the most prestigious places were reserved for whites, in particular around the old post, where the residences of the white commanding officers and the white officers' club were located.

In the immediate vicinity of the fort, two enclaves resembling microghettos were created by the fort's commander, who thus extended segregation beyond the camp and into civilian territory. The Hook, an area of regulated prostitution, was delimited by barbed wire, placed under the control of the military police, and subject to regulations regarding opening hours, rights of entry and exit, and behavior. The Greentop, likewise conceived on the initiative of the Army, was a segregated recreation center for black soldiers built and managed by African-American entrepreneurs. It was one of the few Huachuca institutions that presented what Loïc Wacquant calls the protective and integrative face of the ghetto – the other, more immediately perceptible face being exclusion and ostracization.[4] Indeed, in American ghettos, seclusion and the denial of access to white spaces had prompted African Americans to create parallel institutions where members of the community could feel welcome. At Huachuca, the Greentop, the USO club, and the Mountain View Club provided a similar sense of belonging, as did a few other places where black soldiers and Wacs could spend time together beyond the control of white commanders. However, of the two dimensions of the ghetto dialectic – "external hostility" and "internal affinity," the former was far more evident. While a pride-inspiring and unifying togetherness did exist at the fort, it was carved out of white military institutions and only really benefited the black elite.

The experience of confinement within the walls of Huachuca was highly differentiated and therefore variously accepted. There was no single response to military segregation at the fort, but a *continuum* of reactions ranging from the categorical rejection of the place as a "plantation" or "hell on earth" to the embrace – by a small group – of this "Mecca for the black soldier." The diversity of the group – northern educated elites and southern laborers, career soldiers and recent conscripts, men and women – and the range of opportunities offered led to different perceptions of the constraints and limits posed by segregation. Black NCOs of the Army Reserve who were made officers in Arizona during the war remained loyal to a hierarchy that offered them a form of social mobility. Despite earlier opposition, medical officers accepted segregation because it provided them with unprecedented professional opportunities and made it possible to secure Army recognition of their excellence. The artists and sportsmen employed by the Special Services were sensitive to the possibility of placing their talent at the service of blacks, and not just that of whites as they had done in civilian life. Nurses and Wacs, who hailed from the middle and upper classes of the black community, benefited not only from new professional opportunities, but also from an unexpected form of emancipation made possible by the questioning of gender stereotypes at the camp. Yet, for all those who, whether in civilian or military life, did not belong to these privileged groups, the experience of confinement was one of humiliation, restricted possibilities, and very often repression. The men responded to this in different ways – resignation, accommodation, protest, rebellion – depending on their experience of segregation in civilian life, their level of politicization, the personal benefits they were able to draw from military life, the risks they faced within the Army, the support they could expect to receive from black activists and journalists outside the camp, etc.

The use of the term "ghetto" should not obscure the plurality of the modes of segregation that prevailed at Huachuca during the short period of the war. Two racial regimes, associated with two types of command, were successively implemented and came into conflict at the fort. The first, conceived by the pragmatic Colonel Edwin Hardy, was classic segregation, but arranged in such a way as to present advantages for black officers. Worried about the surrounding white communities' hostility and fear of blacks, Hardy gradually isolated the fort and projected military authority into civilian territory in order to accommodate, within confined spaces, the sexual and recreation needs of soldiers. The fort's commander, who remained steeped in cultural prejudices about African Americans, was convinced that the men would accept and even appreciate racial separation if it offered unique cultural and entertainment opportunities. He was also sensitive to class proximity across the color line, and therefore saw the members of the black bourgeoisie – medical officers, Wacs, and commanding officers – as allies with whom he could share the concern for military efficacy and respectability and agree on arrangements that would make segregation beneficial to them. Hardy openly sought appeasement by ensuring that the men of the black divisions were provided with resources of unprecedented quality and quantity in the domains of health and recreation. For some, those with appropriate qualities, there were also professional opportunities. Sincerely convinced of the need to prevent racial tensions from escalating at Huachuca, he insisted on the use of marks of civility in everyday interactions and on the true application of the "separate but equal" principle in all domains of training, including non-strictly military ones. Furthermore, as he himself explained at the end of the war, he sought to make Huachuca the "seat of Negro culture" by encouraging the expression of black pride.[5] To this end, he commissioned works for the fort that celebrated black contributions to the country and organized an exhibition of art by leading African-American artists. At the opening of the exhibition, he declared that the collection would "serve as an inspiration to all of us as representing one of the steps in the development of a broader and better American citizenship." And yet, the colonel maintained the segregation of the officers' clubs until the end of the war, despite the fact that this was one of the main points of contention between black and white officers and that the Army had ended the racial segregation of recreation areas in March 1943.

From April onwards, the arrival of the 92nd Division led to the superimposition of a second racial regime onto the first, undermining the status quo that Hardy had managed – not without opposition – to achieve at the fort. The commander of the 92nd, General Almond, brought with him a strict southern regime of race relations, which he reproduced at the camp through the use of force. Almond extended segregation to new locations, challenged the previously established consensus on the racial assignment of buildings, removed black officers from positions of responsibility and appointed white officers in their place, openly humiliated black soldiers through acts and modes of address that the Army itself condemned, and strengthened the repression and racial bias of military justice at the fort. Continuing a movement that had begun with the establishment of the Jim Crow regime in the South, he reinforced differences in status and treatment between blacks and whites in places and circumstances where proximity might have implied social and racial equality. He targeted black officers first and foremost, thus preventing any form of status equalization or adequation between military hierarchy and racial hierarchy. Entrenched in his views, resistant to the testing of his own prejudices and practices in racial matters, he refused the adjustments and compromises that had been recommended by the Army since mid 1943 as well as those that had been achieved by Hardy and the black officers of the hospital and Special Services. This hardening of racism fueled protests by African-American soldiers and officers; it even prompted condemnation from Colonel Hardy, who worried about the growing tensions at the fort.

In spite of all this, there was no mutiny or rioting at Huachuca – unlike the situation at other camps across the country. The clear demographic advantage of African Americans over whites was a factor of appeasement: If the situation got out of hand, it was not certain that whites would come out on top. Fry was not Tucson, and still less Phoenix, which had large white communities that could easily neutralize the numerical strength of blacks. Nor was Fort Huachuca comparable to Camp Van Dorn in Mississippi or Camp Stewart in Georgia, where white units trained alongside black units no larger than a regiment. Yet, there were other reasons why tensions between blacks and whites failed to erupt into open violence. In many domains, segregation at Fort Huachuca resembled what Karen Kruse Thomas has referred to as "Deluxe Jim Crow":[6] a strict separation that offered African Americans access to rare goods they had never come across before. The fort's black soldiers and officers were provided with medical care and entertainment of a high quality, which even the elite of the group had seldom encountered in civilian life. The post had been so neglected up until 1941 that it had to be rapidly and fully equipped to accommodate the training of 14,000 men, at a time when the Army was convinced of the importance of preventing idleness, which it saw as a threat to morale and discipline.[7] The absence of white soldiers in the newly equipped training camp played to the advantage of African Americans. The lack of racial competition meant that blacks were able to fully enjoy, without spatial or temporal restrictions, the medical and entertainment facilities that the Army had made available at the fort in order to maintain calm. In line with the literary and artistic policies of the New Deal, the Special Services went so far as to give African Americans a form of control over the content of programming and the representation of blacks – though their motives for doing so were not without ambiguity, not least because they were based on racial stereotypes about the supposedly natural talents of African Americans. The absence of white troops also meant that black soldiers were unable to compare their treatment with that of white soldiers, which helped to avoid legitimate resentment. In reality, the lack of competition between blacks and whites may have served as an alibi for the perpetuation of segregation by making it appear as paternalistic benevolence on the part of the Army.

Above all, Fort Huachuca was the site of an unprecedented experiment initiated by members of the northern black elite, who sought to undermine segregation by taking control of non-strictly military domains, namely medicine and culture. Doctors known for their professionalism succeeded in subverting the all-black hospital from within by integrating patients and then doctors, thereby demonstrating the irrationality of the racist prejudice that whites would always refuse to be treated by blacks. Thus, a sequence that had unfolded earlier in civilian life was reproduced at Huachuca during the war: African-American doctors accepted to work in a segregated black medical institution – self-managed but placed under white tutelage – where they planned to demonstrate black excellence and then take full control, with the ultimate aim of integrating care.[8] At Huachuca, the subversion of segregation was facilitated by the obvious superiority of the black hospital over the white one in terms of staff and equipment. The Army opted for pragmatism and acceptance because every man and woman, whether sick or wounded, remained free to make his or her own decisions in a non-strictly military domain. At the fort, medicine, and to a lesser extent culture and entertainment, served as sites of resistance to segregation, and this subversion was all the more effective because it occurred without violence. The Huachuca experiment showed that whites themselves were ready to accept the challenge to the segregationist order, even in Arizona and even where the body and the intimate were concerned.

The experiment in integrated care at Station Hospital No. 1 paved the way for the integration of several field hospitals at the very end of the war. More generally, it demonstrated the excellence of black care and showed that white patients could agree to be treated by black practitioners. In July 1947, Roscoe Giles wrote in the *Journal of the National Medical Association*:

I believe that time will prove to the satisfaction of all that Fort Huachuca served the useful purpose of proving the capacities of our racial group to manage a large hospital under war time conditions. [...] No such further experiments are necessary. [...] The time is now at hand for the complete integration of Negro physicians into the hospitals of this country on the basis of achievement and merit.[9]

However, the SGO's acceptance of integrated care at Hospital No. 1 did not result in the official recognition and institutionalization that Bousfield and his colleagues had so ardently desired. The ambitions of the medical team were indeed thwarted by the departure of the 92nd Division, as the fort – and consequently the hospital – suddenly found itself virtually empty. In the fall of 1944, Bousfield proposed the creation of another black hospital, to which the personnel and equipment of Hospital No. 1 would be reallocated. He envisioned a general hospital this time: The new facility would be larger and would treat a wider range of conditions.[10] When, in March 1945, the Arizona legislature passed a motion asking the Secretary of War to consider the creation of a general hospital at Huachuca, Bousfield thought that his efforts were being rewarded. Disappointingly, the motion was rejected on the grounds that there were now enough military hospitals to accommodate the soldiers returning from the theaters of operations.[11] And yet, at a time when the Army was in vital need of doctors, demobilizing Huachuca's medical officers risked exposing the War Department to strong criticism: On the one hand, whites might complain that African Americans were being released from military duty earlier than they were; on the other, the African-American press saw each demobilization of a Huachuca doctor as proof of the Army's refusal to let black practitioners treat white soldiers who were returning from the front.[12] Unable to decide on the hospital's fate, the War Department let the experiment die: It disbanded the medical team, first by reassigning individual doctors and then by demobilizing the remaining personnel.[13]

Bousfield was keen to preserve the unity of the medical team, which enhanced the visibility of the integration experiment. When he realized that the experiment was coming to an end, he tried to get his best men reassigned to other hospitals of the Ninth Service Command, hoping that they would be "distributed through white hospitals and no more segregated institutions."[14] Some of the team's officers had been reassigned earlier in the war. Thus, in April 1943, a number of Huachuca doctors had been deployed overseas alongside the 93rd Division. Captain Gardner Downing, a dental surgeon at Hospital No. 1, had been transferred to Bougainville Island in Papua New Guinea to treat the division's infantrymen.[15] Several of the team's doctors had been sent as reinforcements to the four black field hospitals set up in overseas: the 25th Station Hospital in Liberia; the 268th in New Guinea, activated in October 1943 and comprising personnel trained at Huachuca; the 335th, activated in August at the fort and then transferred to Tagap in Burma; and the 383rd, formed from the excess personnel of the 335th, also stationed at Tagap.[16] The 268th Station Hospital in New Guinea was headed by Major Arthur

Simmons, one of the old stalwarts of Howard Medical School, who had practiced at Freedmen's Hospital before becoming chief of medical services at Hospital No. 1. While the transfer of Huachuca doctors and nurses was a sign of recognition of their qualities, the new conditions of practice constituted a regression with regard to their racial ambitions.

In 1944, Bousfield began to suspect – rightly so – that medical integration would be easier to achieve overseas, away from the racial prejudices of American society and the control of corporatist organizations. In March 1945, he wrote: "Overseas [...] democratic practices work better."[17] His team was able to play a major role in transforming black field hospitals into integrated ones. In Liberia, the 25th Station Hospital was integrated at both healthcare personnel and patient levels. From 1943 onwards, the 25th was headed by Major John B. West, an African-American doctor who had previously served at Huachuca. The 250-bed unit was administered by 21 medical officers (4 of whom were white) and staffed by 30 nurses and 180 soldiers (all of them black). Susan Freeman, who served as the hospital's head nurse for eight months, had also come from Huachuca.[18] Captain Harsba F. Bouyer, an ENT (ear, nose, and throat) specialist from Chicago, had practiced earlier at Hospital No. 1; he was so highly regarded that in January 1945 the Liberian government awarded him the Order of African Redemption, the country's highest military distinction.[19] The interracial team provided medical care to white soldiers of the US Army and the Royal Air Force in charge of airfield maintenance, as well as to African civilians employed at the base who needed treatment for malaria or venereal disease. Care was likewise integrated in Tagap, Burma, under the leadership of a team from Huachuca. The 335th Station Hospital was directed by Major William H. Strickland, former head of gastroenterology at Mercy Hospital and Douglass Hospital in Philadelphia, who had taken over as head of the general medicine department at Hospital No. 1 in 1942. Strickland's team of highly qualified black doctors and nurses began to practice integrated care in Burma in 1945. Major Robert Wilkinson, the head of surgery, had served earlier at Huachuca, as had the hospital's ten nurses. At the 335th Station Hospital, white (American and British), black, Chinese, Indian, and Burmese patients were treated side by side without incident. One white soldier confided to a journalist of *The Afro-American* that he had never received such good care: "All of us, including myself, my buddies, the Chinese, Indians, and British, get the same treatment and attention." Strickland described the hospital in Tagap as a model of what medical integration should be: "To the majority of our personnel, this hospital represents the fulfillment of an ideal: an ideal that allows free men the opportunity to pursue chosen occupations regardless of race,

Conclusion: The Outcome of an Experiment

creed, or color."[20] Away from the United States and the control of the SGO, any racial arrangement could be implemented to get soldiers back into fighting shape. Huachuca's experiment in medical integration had spread beyond the fort and around the world.

Bousfield hoped for these integrationist practices to be emulated in the United States. He was encouraged in this by the transfer of several Huachuca nurses to non-black hospitals of the Ninth Service Command, following the integration of the Army Nurse Corps. The lieutenant colonel's demand for integration was now fully supported by James Evans, Gibson's new deputy, who repeatedly emphasized the success of the Huachuca experiment to the Army Surgeon General: "The record of station hospital no. 1 has validated the claims that Negro medical men could establish and operate such a facility. The attitude of patients [...] bears further testimony upon the point. [...] It shows the feasibility of proposals for integrated service on this post and by the same token at other installations."[21] In February 1945, the SGO finally agreed to consider reassigning the officers of the Huachuca hospital "to General Hospital staff or on an unsegregated basis to other Medical Department installations, if it is the desire of the War Department General Staff."[22] In the spring, the SGO and the General Staff were ready to transform the Army's policy on the employment of black doctors. Thus, in a letter to the newly elected Democrat Representative of Texas, Tom Pickett, who had expressed surprise that black and white soldiers were being treated in the same hospitals, Adjutant General J. A. Julio wrote the following: "The maintenance of parallel hospital facilities in order to accomplish the segregation of Negro patients is in conflict with existing War Department policies and cannot be justified from a medical standpoint."[23] Julio's response retrospectively called into question the creation of black sections and segregated hospitals at the start of the war.

However, the revision of the SGO's racial stance came too late to have any effect at Huachuca, where the medical team was ultimately disbanded. Conservatism prevailed at the fort: White Colonel Maynard was left at the head of the merged hospital, despite the fact that he was unwell and that the white hospital had virtually disappeared by the summer of 1945.[24] The sad ending of the medical integration experiment, which was unique in the history of the Medical Department and a fortiori of the Army, created a great deal of bitterness among the Huachuca doctors. These men had made financial and political sacrifices by working in a segregated military environment, and they now had to abandon their ambition to extend integration to other hospitals. In May 1944, Roscoe Giles described what his service at Huachuca had cost him: "At the expense of a fortune in money almost, a great sacrifice of my self-respect and long hours of laborious effort. [...] We have accepted all the indignities and humiliations to come to this segregated post to show to the world that Negro physicians can do anything anybody else can do."[25] As for Bousfield, he was denied the promotion that his seniority warranted.[26] As soon as the war was over, the hospital was closed. In 1946, a team of soldiers emptied the facility of its brand-new equipment and handed it over to Cochise County Hospital.[27] The hospital's archives were likely thrown into the dustbin during this clean-up operation. The material traces of the medical integration experiment conducted from 1942 to 1945 disappeared precisely when those who had initiated it returned to civilian life with greater clinical experience and with renewed confidence in their legitimacy to treat white patients.

The Huachuca nurses, who had played an equally important role in the medical integration experiment, contributed significantly to the evolution of the ANC. After having initially been excluded from the corps, black nurses were accepted, under pressure, in a segregated configuration. In July 1944, the entry quota for African-American nurses in the Army was finally removed – though, by the end of the year, only 330 of the 44,000 ANC nurses were black. Nursing had remained segregated until then, but with one exception, also an overseas experiment: the sixty-three African-American nurses assigned in September 1944 to the 168th Station Hospital in England – where they cared for German POWs – as a replacement for white nurses. Among them were Captain Mary Petty and other Huachuca nurses, who had been selected for their excellence and experience in integrated care at the fort's hospital.[28] In early 1945, after the offensives in the Philippines and the Ardennes, there was a shortage of medical personnel to care for the growing number of wounded soldiers. A bill providing for the conscription of nurses was therefore introduced in Congress. Yet, the bill provoked a public outcry: Why would the Army force white nurses to enlist when it refused African-American volunteers? In response, the SGO and the War Department took the decision to integrate the ANC – thereby constituting an exception in the Medical Department, which was still segregated at the time.[29] The Ninth Service Command reassigned Huachuca's best female practitioners to white hospitals. However, most of these hospitals were located in camps for POWs who had been sent to Arizona and neighboring states for the cotton harvest; the General Staff had felt that deploying black nurses would minimize the risk of fraternization between prisoners and caregivers.[30] In addition, twenty-three Huachuca nurses led by Captain Della Raney were assigned to the hospital at Camp Beale, an air base in

Conclusion: The Outcome of an Experiment

California, where they cared mainly for white patients.[31] Once again, the Huachuca nurses played a pioneering role.

Fort Huachuca was also the first training camp where African-American Wacs were given an assignment. Some of the Huachuca Wacs felt that their presence at the fort and their appointment to non-typically feminine positions of responsibility constituted a victory. Yet, overall, the Wacs remained disappointed with the segregation of their corps. A number of them therefore sought a foreign posting. Until then, the only black women in the Army to have been deployed overseas were nurses. In 1945, African-American organizations succeeded in convincing the War Department to pressure commanders in the European theater into accepting black Wacs. At the time, only General Eisenhower was prepared to employ black women: He tasked the Wacs with sorting the mail and parcels that had been held up for months and that had failed to reach the 7 million soldiers to whom they were addressed. In February 1945, 855 women, including 31 officers, were selected for their education and the quality of their service in all-black companies stationed in the United States. Many of these women were Wacs from Huachuca, including Gertrude La Vigne, Mercedes Jordan, Vera Harrison, Lucia Pitts, and Violet Askins. La Vigne later recalled that in mid 1944 "a commission of male officers came to the WAC area, interviewed enlisted women, and selected those of us who would comprise the first all-Negro WAC outfit to go overseas." The all-black 6888th Central Postal Directory Battalion, the only WAC unit to be deployed overseas during the war, was first sent to Scotland, then to Birmingham, and finally to Rouen. The black women of the 6888th encountered an egalitarian social environment in Europe and received a particularly warm welcome from the British and the French.[32] Thus, the Wacs of Huachuca became associated with the belated and limited recognition of the role played by black women near the front lines during the war. Like nurses and medical officers, they extended the challenge to the Army's racial regime beyond US borders. Thanks to these women and men, the Huachuca experiment was emulated in the different theaters of operation.

The Huachuca experiment also had long-lasting effects on the Army's racial policy. The combat performance of the 92nd Division – and to a lesser extent that of the 93rd before it – led to very harsh criticism of the nature of the training offered at Huachuca. Detractors of the black fort had found reason to radically question the creation of this training base. For the white commanders who continued to distrust black soldiers, the disappointment caused by the 92nd was proof of their intrinsic inability to fight. While the Huachuca experiment had largely remained in the shadows until then, the black soldiers who had been sent to the front line were suddenly exposed to the limelight. They found themselves at the center of a controversy over the quality of African-American troops that was to play a key role in defining the Army's post-war racial policy. Yet, was it reasonable to draw general conclusions from this unique experiment?

The 93rd Infantry Division, which had left Huachuca one year before being sent to the Pacific theater, had also proved disappointing. However, this had not led the Army to form a strong opinion about the quality of the men who had trained in a segregated unit of this size. Following an on-the-spot investigation, Walter White, the NAACP executive secretary who had been accredited in 1945 as war correspondent in the Pacific, denied a rumor that the men of the 93rd had dispersed under fire on Bougainville Island, Papua New Guinea. The rumor claimed that despite being given the relatively easy mission of securing the bridgehead, the men had left the front without informing the white division alongside which they were fighting, and that a large number of white soldiers and officers had lost their lives as a result of their cowardice. White showed that the rumor was unfounded and that it had been spread to discredit black soldiers in order to keep them away from combat zones. He pointed out that the men had been assigned support missions and boat-unloading duties, and that African-American officers deemed contentious had been dismissed. He also noted that white divisions that had proved disappointing in the test of fire had been given a second chance.[33] Thanks to the intervention of the NAACP leader with President Roosevelt, the entire division was reassembled in Morotai. The men received new equipment and the best black and white officers were selected to command them.[34] The 93rd then established its reputation for discipline, esprit de corps, and excellence in executing its assigned missions (work in mud and rain at petroleum, oil, and lubricants [POL] dumps, policing areas of which they were in charge, clearing up, and distributing mail), though not for excellence in combat.

Thus, it was not the – honorable – performance of the 93rd Division that was used by the General Staff to make a definitive judgment on the effects of segregated training at Fort Huachuca, but that of the 92nd Division, which had been directly transferred from the camp to the front line in Italy. The 92nd was selected as the test unit for the assessment of the fighting qualities of blacks trained in a segregated configuration, despite the fact that the division had one of the highest illiteracy rates and one of the largest proportions of men classified in the lowest AGCT categories.[35] The 370th Combat Regiment – the elite unit of the 92nd – had taken part, alongside the 1st Armored Division, in the seizure and crossing of the Arno River and in the occupation of the town of Lucca. The operation had been a success. Then, in October 1944, the

370th had been given the mission of taking Massa. However, the mission had failed, and the Germans had gained ground. According to the inspector of the 92nd Division, there had been massive, unordered retreats when the Germans had subjected the unit to bombardment. The soldiers had shown irrational fear, and the officers and NCOs had lacked the authority to calm the men and prevent them from dispersing.[36] General Almond had taken severe action, transferring over 1,300 soldiers and officers and court-martialing and demoting countless others. Yet, many of their replacements had not been given the necessary training to go into battle,[37] which may have explained another underperformance, this time in the February 1945 attack on the Gothic Line: While there had been individual acts of heroism, many soldiers had panicked and fled the battlefield. White commanders later blamed the black officers and their soldiers and tried to get the 92nd withdrawn from the front for good. The report by General Mark Clark, commander of the Fifth Army, was merciless: "Entire organizations have disintegrated under artillery fire." Clark recommended the unit's immediate withdrawal from the front.[38]

Following these events, Truman Gibson was sent to Italy by the War Department to assess the performance of the 92nd and to make recommendations for its future assignment. On March 12, 1945, he submitted a report to Major General Otto L. Nelson, in which he highlighted very low morale on the basis of interviews with 800 soldiers and officers. Gibson explained this state of affairs by invoking the persistence of a differentiated promotion policy for officers, the segregation of recreation areas, and the replacement of black officers with white officers at the head of companies. He also stressed the negative impact of the arrival of huge numbers of ill-prepared replacements for discharged soldiers. He concluded his report by recommending the immediate implementation of merit-based advancement and the introduction of an element of racial pride reinforcement in the training of black troops. The report did not mention Almond's personal responsibility in the situation.[39] On March 15, 1945, Gibson gave a well-attended press conference in Rome. However, the press only picked up his comments about the dispersal of the 92nd Division under enemy fire and the low level of education of the black soldiers.[40] His statements were interpreted as an endorsement of white stereotypes about black soldiers. African-American newspapers accused Gibson of being an "Uncle Tom." In *The Crisis*, Roy Wilkins denounced the report as a "betrayal of the Negro soldier in this war" and the civilian aide as a traitor to the cause.[41] The NAACP Board of Directors asked the War Department to have Gibson replaced.[42]

Gibson maintained that his words had been misrepresented, and he later condemned segregated training with a firmness that had never been heard before.[43] In April, he explained to the McCloy Committee that the underperformance of the 92nd had resulted from inadequate training, which he claimed was symptomatic of poor thinking about the use of black troops. He pointed out that all the General Staff's decisions concerning African-American soldiers, and in particular the two all-black divisions, had been made in haste in order to neutralize pressure from activist organizations. To the men tasked with rethinking the Army's post-war racial policy, he wrote: "The basic Army policy of complete segregation should be critically re-examined in light of the experiences of the 92nd division and the results obtained with the integrated combat units in ETO [European Theater of Operations]."[44] Gibson was referring to the first experiment in troop integration that had taken place in the European theater in March 1945: After major losses in the Battle of the Bulge, 2,000 African-American volunteers had been assembled into 53 black infantry platoons and assigned to the white companies of the 95th Infantry Division stationed along the Rhine.[45] The experiment had been a success. According to a survey conducted by the Army Research Division among seven divisions that had incorporated black platoons, fighting alongside African Americans had positively affected the way white GIs viewed black soldiers: Desegregation was favored by 55 percent of the white officers and 72 percent of the white soldiers surveyed.[46] The experiment had shown that integration, even when limited and voluntary, could lead to military victory and could win the support of those concerned. Gibson could also have mentioned the success of the Tuskegee Airmen in Sicily and in the bombing of Germany. On the basis of the contrast between the combat performance of the segregated 92nd Division and that of the integrated platoons in Germany, he concluded that segregated training of the kind provided at Huachuca should be discontinued. In his November 1945 letter of resignation to Secretary of War Patterson, he wrote: "The Army's rigid policy, decided in 1915, has been pursued for too long. This policy is largely based on the unscientific view that blacks' behaviors and characteristics make them inherently inferior to whites, and that they therefore cannot and should not be used by the Army except in limited numbers."[47] Gibson had finally taken a clear stand in the debate between black activists and the Army over the conclusions to be drawn from the underperformance of the 92nd Division: In his view, the Army should not only discontinue segregated training, but should also use the 92nd and 93rd Infantry Divisions as counter-models. Marcus Ray, lieutenant colonel of the 600th Field Artillery Regiment, who served as civilian aide to the Secretary of War after Gibson's resignation, agreed with this assessment. In a July 1947 letter to New York representative Adam Clayton Powell Jr., Ray

Conclusion: The Outcome of an Experiment

summarized his position as follows: "It is my sincere hope that in the future training of the Negro in the Army, there will never again be a colored post."[48]

A diametrically opposed interpretation of the 92nd Division's test of fire was nevertheless offered. It presented the underperformance of the men not only as definitive proof of the inferiority of black troops, but also as a further argument for the maintenance of segregation. In June 1945, Almond assembled a commission comprising white commanders of the division's main units and tasked it with determining the reasons for the division's failure. The report issued by the commission had racist prejudice against blacks as its central motif. The African-American officer was described as follows: He lacks pride in himself and his accomplishments; he is insufficiently aggressive owing to a history of servility; his ability to command men is hampered by his lack of intelligence; and his authority is undermined by an inherent inferiority complex. The black soldier was portrayed in even more racist terms: He lacks the stamina and determination necessary to withstand physical effort; he does not take care of his equipment; he has no loyalty to his fellow soldiers; and he abandons them on the battlefield to save his own skin.[49] Thus, the report reaffirmed the prejudices against African-American soldiers that the General Staff had formulated in the interwar years, even though these prejudices had been refuted by the most recent fighting. The commission had questioned neither the responsibility of the white commanders nor the validity of the offensive strategy.[50] In 1945, part of the military establishment argued for the maintenance of almost all black soldiers in subordinate positions, citing the performance of the men of the 92nd who had trained at Huachuca. As for Almond, he continued for decades to maintain that black soldiers were lazy by nature. In a 1975 letter to a captain of the Army, which had by then become the symbol of the state's progressivism in racial matters, he wrote without a trace of self-censorship: "The general tendency among [black soldiers] is to avoid effort as much as possible. Those who doubt this need only command black troops to see the results for themselves."[51]

African-American newspapers and organizations argued adamantly that it made no sense to draw Army-wide conclusions from the 92nd Division's unique combat experience. This experience was the central focus of the Gillem report released in October 1945: What should the Army have done with the 700,000 blacks who had enlisted since 1940 and had been assigned only under pressure from activist organizations? What should be done with African-American soldiers in the future? Should the Army continue to duplicate units and training bases (as it had done at Fort Huachuca), or should it put an end to the practice? Relying on feedback from the field, the report, whose conclusions were adopted in April 1946, recommended adjusting segregation in such a way as to offer equality of opportunity to African-American soldiers and officers. To the great disappointment of black activists and journalists, integration was postponed to an unspecified date.[52] The recommended changes included the insertion of small black units into larger white units (on the model of what had been done along the Rhine at the end of the war), the assignment of African-American soldiers to combat and service units, the adoption of uniform procedures for enrolment and assignment, and the gradual and complete replacement of white officers with qualified black officers in black units. Although unit segregation was maintained, the Huachuca experiment had been duly noted. However, the consequences drawn from this experiment were minimal: From now on, there would be no black unit larger than a regiment, which would mechanically limit the advancement of black officers to the rank of captain.[53] According to *The Crisis*, the Army that was to be reorganized along these lines was "still a Jim Crow army." The majority of African-American troops would continue to serve in service and logistical support units, and the maintenance of the racial quota in all army units would remain an insurmountable obstacle to the provision of equal opportunities for blacks and whites.[54]

Despite being unambitious and timid, the reform was met with strong resistance, with Almond and other high-ranking white officers refusing to implement the adjustments recommended by the Gillem Board. Executive intervention was necessary to bring about the desegregation opposed by the Army. In October 1947, President Truman's Committee on Civil Rights issued the report *To Secure These Rights*, in which conclusions were finally drawn from the experiments conducted during the war, including the one at Fort Huachuca: "The war experience brought to our attention a laboratory in which we may prove that the majority and minorities of our population can train and work and fight side by side in cooperation and harmony."[55] Station Hospital No. 1 was one of the "laboratories" in which integration had been successfully achieved. More generally, Huachuca had been the site of a pioneering racial experiment, away from the control of the General Staff and the hostility of large white communities. Shortly after the publication of the report, the Committee against Jim Crow in Military Service and Training, formed by A. Philip Randolph and Grant Reynolds (the former Huachuca chaplain who had accused the War Department of extending Jim Crow to the entire Army in four far-reaching articles published in *The Crisis* in the fall of 1944), threatened to call for mass civil disobedience if the Universal Military Training Bill then under discussion in Congress was passed without an anti-segregation clause.[56] Understanding the urgency of

Conclusion: The Outcome of an Experiment

a presidential gesture, Harry Truman simultaneously adopted two executive orders to bring the federal services and the Army in line with the equality provisions laid out in constitutional texts. Executive Order 9981, adopted on July 26, 1948, abolished discrimination in the armed forces on the basis of "race, color, religion or national origin." While the order explicitly set the goal of "equality of treatment and opportunity," it did not aim to end segregation as such. The officers in charge of personnel policy took advantage of this ambiguity to resist both desegregation and the removal of the racial quota. The tug-of-war between the executive branch and the Army ended only with the fighting in Korea, which forced the Army to implement integration – unit by unit – as wounded white soldiers were replaced by black soldiers. The Army finally announced in September 1953 that 90 percent of African Americans within its ranks were serving in integrated units.[57] It had taken political intervention at the highest level, spurred on by black activist organizations and newspapers, for conclusions to be finally drawn from the racial experiments that had been conducted in the Army during the war.

The Army began to implement, albeit grudgingly, racial integration within its ranks. Fort Huachuca, which could have been the emblematic site of this racial transformation, never saw the effects of the reform. Following the departure of the 92nd Division, the War Department had been unsure what to do with this old and isolated military compound. At the end of the conflict, under the leadership of General Eisenhower, the Army made an inventory of its bases and needs and decided to downsize. Despite the efforts of the Arizona parliamentary delegation to Washington, Congress took the decision to close Fort Huachuca and to hand over ownership to the state government. Several buildings were demolished in order to transform the military enclave into a nature reserve; the army documents that escaped destruction were transferred to Washington. Where black soldiers had trained under white commanders, prairie dogs and coyotes were allowed to roam for years.[58] While decades of struggle and urban policy had failed to break down the invisible walls of urban ghettos, the Huachuca military ghetto disappeared in a matter of weeks following the congressional decision to close the fort. In 1954, a few months after the Korean War ended, the fort was reactivated as a site for the development of electronic technology. Fort Huachuca was now a tabula rasa: Everything had to be built and created anew.

The closure and subsequent reopening of the fort at a time when the Army was forced to implement racial integration explain why the material traces of the attempt to subvert segregation during World War II have all but disappeared. When I visited the fort in the summer of 2018, I could not even find the by-laws that had been applied during the conflict.

Perhaps one day they will reappear in an auction or in the personal archives of a veteran. All that remains in the fort's museum are the photographs taken by the Army Signal Corps during the war, and these are drowned amid a huge number of snapshots from other eras. The documents produced by the command post between 1941 and 1945 are nowhere to be found – even in the form of copies. Only a few random elements have been returned to the fort over the years: donations, bits and pieces of the collections of former medical officers, Wacs, or nurses, etc.

The soldiers' voices have left very few traces at Huachuca. They emerge in an extremely tenuous form, as they are muffled by the testimonies of the members of the African-American elite, who managed to make themselves heard thanks to their external contacts and their ability to record their experiences in writing. Even in the field, many facts and feelings continue to elude investigation. How did the soldiers feel deep down about the experience of segregated training? Did they dread going into battle, or were they desperate to leave this place of boredom and humiliation? What was the true scale of protests at the fort? How repressive was Huachuca's military justice? I am astonished by the fact that despite the bounded nature of Fort Huachuca's history, I am unable to hear all of these voices or to imagine ways of bringing them to life.

The place itself does little to make these voices heard, likely because of its unique history at the end of World War II. The Huachuca buildings remain silent. Although they are identical to what they were in the 1940s, they do not function as repositories of past events. They have become color-blind: They no longer say anything about their racial assignment during the conflict. At the old post, I was able to locate the buildings formerly reserved for white officers: the stone houses on officers' row, the command post, and the swimming pool accessible to blacks only the last day before draining. The size of the buildings and their location close to the parade ground attest to the power of those who lived or worked there at the time. Yet, the white officers' club is nowhere to be seen. Station Hospital No. 2 is no longer standing: It was destroyed, along with the black hospital, in just a few hours in a fire in the 1970s. The bridge that once connected the two hospitals and made materially possible the experiment in racial integration is also gone. The site where the buildings once stood is now overgrown with weeds. All that remains are the stones that marked the entrance to the complex and the – still usable – road that separated the black and white facilities. The best way to picture the once dominant hospitals is to follow these stones.[59] One can also get some idea of the complex's red-roofed wooden buildings by watching David Miller's *Captain Newman, M.D.*, a film starring Gregory Peck and Angie Dickinson and shot in 1963 at the fort. The story of the film is set during the war in the psychiatric hospital of an air force base located in Arizona.

Thanks to the mobilization of local African-American veterans, the old Mountain View Club was saved from destruction. The veterans had hoped to turn the club into a place for the commemoration of the black presence at the fort and the celebration of the patriotism of the soldiers who had served in the 92nd and 93rd Divisions; yet, the fort's administration ultimately decided to house a Range Operations Synchronization Center in the renovated building. Somehow the black veterans forgot that the club had been the object of a boycott by African-American officers as well as a symbol of the Army's refusal to recognize the equality of black and white officers. During the war, Mountain View had been a place of humiliation far more than one of racial pride.

There are other misunderstandings about the history of the fort. The museum's former director was never really interested in learning about Huachuca's situation during the war, which for him amounted to 3 or 4 years in a more glorious history that had lasted nearly 140 years. When I told him about my research and about the segregation that had been practiced at the fort eighty years earlier, he saw me as a troublesome historian who was unnecessarily bringing to light the problematic racial past of an Army that had become one of the key places for the promotion of minorities within the state apparatus. The director feared that the history I was trying to uncover would tarnish the image that Fort Huachuca had chosen for itself: The former post of the Buffalo soldiers – the black soldiers placed at the service of a project to subjugate Indians and to guard newly conquered territories – that was now home to the development of the Army's most advanced surveillance technology. And yet, I am not sure that this narrative is any more flattering than my account of a strict but internally subverted segregation that brought forth the first efforts to integrate the Army – one of the most important showcases of the American state to this day.

Notes

Introduction: An Experiment in Race Relations

1. See Cherstin M. Lyon, *Prisons and Patriots: Japanese American Wartime Citizenship, Civil Disobedience, and Historical Memory* (Philadelphia: Temple University Press, 2012), chapter "The Obligations of Citizenship"; on the assignment of women in the military, see Brenda L. Moore, *Nisei, Serving Our Country: Japanese American Women in the Military during World War II* (New Brunswick: Rutgers University Press, 2003).
2. See Thomas Grillot, *Après la Grande Guerre. Comment les Amérindiens des États-Unis sont devenus patriotes (1917–1947)* (Paris : Éditions de l'EHESS, 2014).
3. Todd J. Moye, *Freedom Flyers: The Tuskegee Airmen of World War II* (Oxford: Oxford University Press, 2010), 71.
4. *The Tuskegee Airmen*, directed by Robert Markowitz (HBO, 1995).
5. Moye, *Freedom Flyers*, 31.
6. Pekka Hämäläinen and Samuel Truett, "On Borderlands," *The Journal of American History* 98, no. 2 (September 2011): 338–61.
7. See Paul Pasquali and Benoît Trépied, "Avant-propos," in Karl Jacoby, *L'Esclave qui devint millionnaire. Les vies extraordinaires de William Ellis*, trans. Frédéric Cotton (Toulouse: Anacharsis, 2018 [2016]), 23–28, and Karl Jacoby "Par les failles de l'histoire," *L'Esclave qui devint millionnaire*, 49–54.
8. Katharine Bjork, *Prairie Imperialists: The Indian Country Origins of American Empire* (Philadelphia: University of Pennsylvania Press, 2019).
9. Karl Jacoby, *The Strange Career of William Ellis: The Texas Slave Who Became a Mexican Millionaire* (New York: Norton, 2016).
10. Julian Lim, *Porous Borders: Multiracial Migrations and the Law in the U.S.–Mexico Borderlands* (Chapel Hill: The University of North Carolina Press, 2017).
11. See in particular Ira Katznelson, *Fear Itself: The New Deal and The Origins of Our Time* (New York: Liveright Publishing Corporation, 2013), and Jefferson Cowie, *The Great Exception: The New Deal and the Limits of American Politics* (Princeton: Princeton University Press, 2016), especially 124–30.
12. David Lucander, *Winning the War for Democracy: The March on Washington Movement, 1941–1946* (Urbana: University of Illinois Press, 2014).

13. See the pioneering work of Harvard Sitkoff, "Racial Militancy and Interracial Violence in the Second World War," *Journal of American History* 58, no. 3 (December 1971): 661–81; see also Daniel Kryder, *Divided Arsenal: Race and the American State during World War II* (Cambridge: Cambridge University Press, 2000), 168–206.
14. Tal Brutmann, Ivan Ermakoff, Nicolas Mariot, and Claire Zalc, "Changer d'échelle pour renouveler l'histoire de la Shoah," in Tal Brutmann, Ivan Ermakoff, Nicolas Mariot, and Claire Zalc, eds., *Pour une microhistoire de la Shoah* (Paris: Éditions du Seuil, 2012), 11–15.
15. On the debate between integrationists and separatists, see in particular Raymond L. Hall, *Black Separatism and Social Reality: Rhetoric and Reason* (Oxford: Pergamon Press, 1977); see also William Van DeBurg, ed., *Modern Black Nationalism from Marcus Garvey to Louis Farrakhan* (New York: New York University Press, 1997).
16. Paul-André Rosental, *Destins de l'eugénisme* (Paris: Éditions du Seuil, 2016), 17 and 30.
17. Omer Bartov, *Anatomy of a Genocide: The Life and Death of a Town Called Buczacz* (New York: Simon and Schuster, 2018).
18. On the contributions of microhistorical experiments, see Romain Bertrand and Guillaume Calafat, "La micro-histoire globale: Affaire(s) à suivre," *Annales. Histoire, sciences sociales* 1 (2018), 1–18.
19. See Jacques Revel, ed., *Jeux d'échelles. La micro-analyse à l'expérience* (Paris: Éditions du Seuil, 1996).
20. Carlo Ginzburg, *Le Fil et les Traces* (Lagrasse: Verdier, 2006), Chapter XIII "Microhistoires."
21. See George Raynor Thompson, ed., *United States Army in World War II, The Technical Services: The Signal Corps: The Test (December 1941 to July 1943)* (Washington, DC: Office of the Chief of Military History, 1957), Chapter XIII "Photo by U.S. Army Signal Corps," 387–426.
22. Gayatri Chakravorty Spivak, "Can the Subaltern Speak?," in Cary Nelson and Lawrence Grossberg, eds., *Marxism and the Interpretation of Culture* (Champaign: University of Illinois Press, 1998), 271–313.
23. Studs Terkel, *"The Good War": An Oral History of World War II* (New York: Pantheon Books, 1984).
24. See, for example, Stephen E. Ambrose, *D-Day, June 6, 1944: The Climactic Battle of World War II* (New York: Simon and Schuster, 1994); Tom Brokaw, *The Greatest Generation* (New York: Random House, 1998).
25. See Richard Polenberg, "The Good War? A Reappraisal of How World War II Affected American Society," *Virginia Magazine of History and Biography* 100, no. 3 (July 1992): 295–322, and John Bodnar, *The "Good War" in American Memory* (Baltimore: Johns Hopkins University Press, 2010).
26. See Lauren Rebecca Sklaroff, *Black Culture and the New Deal: The Quest for Civil Rights in the Roosevelt Era* (Chapel Hill: University of North Carolina Press, 2009), Chapter 6 "Projecting Unity."
27. Gary Gerstle, *American Crucible: Race and Nation in the Twentieth Century* (Princeton: Princeton University Press, 2001), Introduction and Chapter 5 "Good War, Race War, 1941–1945."

28. Ulysses Lee, *The Employment of Negro Troops* (Washington, DC: Center of Military History, 1994 [1963]). See also, in the wake of Lee's pioneering book, Morris J. MacGregor, *The Integration of the Armed Forces, 1940–1965* (Washington, DC: Center of Military History, 1981).
29. Jacquelyn Dowd Hall, "The Long Civil Rights Movement and the Political Uses of the Past," *Journal of American History* 91, no. 4 (March 2005): 1233–63.
30. Richard Dalfiume, "The 'Forgotten Years' of the Negro Revolution," *Journal of American History* 55, no. 1 (June 1968): 90–106.
31. Kathlyn Frydl, *The GI Bill* (Cambridge: Cambridge University Press, 2009).
32. Kevin M. Kruse and Stephen Tuck, eds., *Fog of War: The Second World War and the Civil Rights Movement* (Oxford: Oxford University Press, 2012), 6–7. See "African American Militancy in the World War II South: Another Perspective," in Neil McMillen, ed., *Remaking Dixie: The Impact of WWII on the American South* (Jackson: University of Mississippi Press, 1997), 70–92. Harvard Sitkoff has shown that the war was a period of decline and loss of vehemence in black activism.
33. Thomas Guglielmo, "A Martial Freedom Movement: Black G.I.s' Political Struggles during World War II," *Journal of American History* 104, no. 4 (March 2018): 879–903.
34. The notion of the "talented tenth" was proposed in 1903 by W. E. B. Du Bois, "The Talented Tenth," in Booker T. Washington, ed., *The Negro Problem: A Series of Articles by Representative Negroes of Today* (New York: J. Pott & Company, 2006 [1903]), 31–76.
35. E. Franklin Frazier, *Black Bourgeoisie* (Glencoe: Free Press, 1957).
36. Robert R. Weyeneth, "The Architecture of Racial Segregation: The Challenges of Preserving the Problematical Past," *Public Historian* 27, no. 4 (Fall 2005): 11–44, especially 38.
37. Guillaume Lachenal, *Le médecin qui voulut être roi. Sur les traces d'une utopie coloniale* (Paris: Éditions du Seuil, 2017), 205–06.

1   An All-Black Post in the Middle of the Arizona Desert

1. On the shock experienced by black soldiers on arriving at the fort, see, in particular, Maggi M. Morehouse, *Fighting in a Jim Crow Army: Black Men and Women Remember World War II* (Lanham: Rowman and Littlefield, 2000), 49–50, and Notes from Narrative Reports of U.S.O. Worker in Huachuca Area, October 10, 1941, box 43, folder 10, Shirley Graham Du Bois collection, Schlesinger Library, Radcliffe Institute, Harvard University.
2. Scottsdale Center for the Arts, *Lew Davis: "The Negro in America's Wars" and Other Major Paintings* (Scottsdale: Scottsdale Center for the Arts, 1990); Betsy Fahlman, *New Deal Art in Arizona* (Tucson: University of Arizona Press), 145.
3. This nickname was likely given to the black soldiers because of their frizzy hair, which reminded Native Americans of the curly hair between the horns of buffaloes.

4. Thomas Grillot, "Native Americans: America's Colonial Troops," *Books and Ideas* (September 28, 2011), https://laviedesidees.fr/Native-Americans-Ame rica-s. See also Gerald Horne, *Black and Brown: African Americans and the Mexican Revolution, 1910–1920* (New York: New York University Press, 2005), Chapter 5 "Buffaloed Soldiers," as well as the older works of Arlen L. Fowler, *The Black Infantry in the West, 1869–1891* (Westport: Greenwood, 1971) and Marvin E. Fletcher, *The Black Soldier and Officer in the Army, 1891–1917* (Columbia: University of Missouri Press, 1974).
5. See Horne, *Black and Brown*, Chapter 7 "Negroes Invade Mexico."
6. Richard Dalfiume, *Desegregation of the U.S. Armed Forces: Fighting on Two Fronts, 1939–1953* (Columbia: University of Missouri Press, 1969), 44.
7. Quoted in Robert Jefferson, *Making the Men of the 93rd: Servicemen in the Years of the Great Depression and the Second World War, 1935–1947* (PhD dissertation, University of Michigan, 1995), 186.
8. Thomas Grillot, *Après la Grande Guerre. Comment les Amérindiens des États-Unis sont devenus patriotes (1917–1947)* (Paris: Éditions de l'EHESS, 2014), especially 17–19 and 223–27.
9. Brad Melton and Dean Smith, *Arizona Goes to War: The Home Front and the Front Lines during World War II* (Tucson: University of Arizona Press, 2003), Chapters 1 and 6; Philip VanderMeer, *Phoenix Rising: The Making of a Desert Metropolis* (Dallas: Heritage Media Corporation, 2002), 17–20; Elizabeth Tandy Shermer, *Sunbelt Capitalism: Phoenix and the Transformation of American Politics* (Philadelphia: University of Pennsylvania Press, 2013), Chapter 3 "The Business of War."
10. Richard M. Dalfiume, "Military Segregation and the 1940 Presidential Election," *Phylon* 30, no. 1 (1969): 42–55.
11. Ulysses Lee, *The Employment of Negro Troops* (Washington, DC: Center of Military History, 1994 [1963]), 75–76.
12. Marvin E. Fletcher, *America's First Black General: Benjamin O. Davis, Sr., 1880–1970* (Lawrence: University of Kansas Press, 1989).
13. Richard M. Dalfiume, *Desegregation of the U.S. Armed Forces: Fighting on Two Fronts, 1939–1953* (Columbia: University of Missouri Press, 1969), 116–20.
14. "Workmen at Fort Set Record Pace with 3,100 Payroll," *Bisbee Daily Review*, January 24, 1941, 1.
15. "Huachuca May Garrison 30,000. Army Favors Full Division at U.S. Post," *Bisbee Daily Review*, January 25, 1941, 1.
16. Telegram from Osborn to Hayden, January 27, 1941, folder "Fort Huachuca, 1941–42," box 16, Governors Sidney P. Osborn and Daniel E. Garvey, Arizona State Archives (ASA).
17. Folder "Fort Huachuca, 1941–42," box 16, Governors Sidney P. Osborn and Daniel E. Garvey, ASA.
18. 1940 Census of Population.
19. Mary Melcher Source, "'This Is Not Right': Rural Arizona Women Challenge Segregation and Ethnic Division, 1925–1950," *Frontiers: A Journal of Women Studies* 20, no. 2 (1999): 190–214; Bradford Luckingham, *Minorities in Phoenix: A Profile of Mexican American, Chinese American, and African American Communities, 1860–1992* (Tucson: University of Arizona Press, 1994);

Matthew C. Whitaker, *Race Work: The Rise of Civil Rights in the Urban West* (Lincoln: University of Nebraska Press, 2007).
20. Katherine Benton-Cohen, *Borderline Americans: Racial Division and Labor War in the Arizona Borderlands* (Cambridge, MA: Harvard University Press, 2009).
21. Letter from Gordon Tucker to Paul McNutt, November 17, 1942, Reel 8, frames 437–44, African Americans in the Military, Part 3: Subject Files of Judge William Hastie, Civilian Aide to the Secretary of War "N" through "Z." See Robert F. Jefferson, *Fighting for Hope: African American Troops of the 93rd Infantry Division in World War II and Postwar America* (Baltimore: Johns Hopkins University Press, 2008), 108–09.
22. "Armed Forces Discriminated Against," *Arizona's Negro Journal*, July 10, 1942, 1 and 5.
23. 1940 Census of Population: Volume 2. Characteristics of the Population. Sex, Age, Race, Nativity, Citizenship, Country of Birth of Foreign-Born White, School Attendance, Years of School Completed, Employment Status, Class of Worker, Major Occupation Group, and Industry Group. Part 1: United States Summary and Alabama – District of Columbia, https://www2.census.gov/library/publications/decennial/1940/population-volume-2/33973538v2p1ch5.pdf.
24. *The Negro Motorist Green-Book*, 1940 ed., New York Public Library Digital Collections, https://digitalcollections.nypl.org/items/dc858e50-83d3-0132-2266-58d385a7b928.
25. Kara Dixon Vuic, *The Girls Next Door: Bringing the Home Front to the Front Lines* (Cambridge, MA: Harvard University Press, 2019), 62.
26. Letter from Shirley Graham to Paul McNutt, November 29, 1941, Administrator of the Federal Security Agency, box 43, folder 12, Shirley Graham Papers, Schlesinger Library.
27. Vuic, *The Girls Next Door*, 122.
28. "Condemn 'Pleasure Plan' for Huachuca Troops," *Chicago Defender*, January 24, 1942.
29. Letter from Shirley Graham to Paul McNutt, November 29, 1941, Administrator of the Federal Security Agency, box 43, folder 12, Shirley Graham Papers, Schlesinger Library.
30. Meghan K. Winchell, *Good Girls, Good Food, Good Fun: The Story of USO Hostesses during World War II* (Chapel Hill: University of North Carolina Press, 2012), 16–17.
31. Gerald Horne, *Race Woman: The Lives of Shirley Graham Du Bois* (New York: New York University Press, 2002).
32. Letter from Shirley Graham to W. E. B. Du Bois, October 1, 1941. W. E. B. Du Bois Papers (MS 312). Special Collections and University Archives, University of Massachusetts Amherst Libraries, http://credo.library.umass.edu/view/full/mums312-b094-i531.
33. Letter from Shirley Graham to Helen Wilkins, Secretary for Interracial Relations, National YWCA, December 11, 1941, box 43, folder 13, Shirley Graham Du Bois collection, Schlesinger Library.
34. Letter from Shirley Graham to W. E. B. Du Bois, January 25, 1942. W. E. B. Du Bois Papers (MS 312). Special Collections and University

Archives, University of Massachusetts Amherst Libraries, http://credo.libra
ry.umass.edu/view/full/mums312-b098-i015.
35. Melton and Smith, *Arizona Goes to War*, 21–30.
36. Lee, *The Employment of Negro Troops*, 239.
37. John Modell, Marc Goulden, and Sigurdur Magnusson, "World War II in the Lives of Black Americans: Some Findings and an Interpretation," *Journal of American History* 76, no. 3 (December 1989): 838–48, 841.
38. "Race Army Division Soon Says Marshall," *Norfolk Journal and Guide*, December 13, 1941, and "Plans for Negro Division at Fort Huachuca Revealed," *Atlanta Daily World*, December 10, 1941, 1, quoted in Paul Alkebulan, *The African American Press in World War II: Toward Victory at Home and Abroad* (Lanham: Lexington Books, 2014), 51.
39. Lee, *The Employment of Negro Troops*, 126–27.
40. Of the forty-four army bases identified by the Office of the Chief of Military History, twenty-five were located in nine southern states. See Daniel Kryder, *Divided Arsenal: Race and the American State during World War II* (Cambridge: Cambridge University Press, 2000), 140.
41. Fletcher, *America's First Black General*, 93.
42. Lee, *The Employment of Negro Troops*, 106.
43. Todd J. Moye, *Freedom Flyers: The Tuskegee Airmen of World War II* (New York: Oxford University Press, 2010).
44. G-3 memo of January 18, 1942 on the training grounds of the black troops, quoted in Lee, *The Employment of Negro Troops*, 103.
45. Interview with Robert T. Madison, January 15, 2007, Veterans History Project, Library of Congress, https://memory.loc.gov/diglib/vhp/story/loc.na tlib.afc2001001.48858.
46. "Recreation Major Problem with 93rd," *Pittsburgh Courier*, May 30, 1942.
47. See, in particular, Eric J. Sundquist, "The Japanese-American Internment: A Reappraisal," *American Scholar* 57, no. 4 (Spring 1988): 529–47; on Arizona, see: Thomas Fujita-Rony, "Arizona and Japanese American History: The World War II Colorado River Relocation Center," *Journal of the Southwest* 47, no. 2 (Summer 2005): 209–32.
48. Douglas Walter Bristol, Jr., "Terror, Anger and Patriotism: Understanding the Resistance of Black Soldiers during World War II," in Douglas Walter Bristol, Jr. and Heather Marie Stur, eds., *Integrating the US Military: Race, Gender, and Sexual Orientation since World War II* (Baltimore: Johns Hopkins University Press, 2017), 10–35, 12.

2 Fourteen Thousand Black Infantrymen

1. Blacks represented 17 percent of soldiers in the engineer corps (in charge of road and bridge building, mine detection, etc.) and 24 percent of soldiers in the quartermaster corps (many of whom were also in charge of transporting troops and equipment). See Bryan D. Booker, *African Americans in the United States Army in World War II* (Jefferson: McFarland and Company, 2008), 60; Samuel A. Stouffer, Edward A. Suchman, Leland C. DeVinney, Shirley A. Star, and

Robin M. Williams, Jr., *The American Soldier*, Vol. I: *Adjustment during Army Life* (Princeton: Princeton University Press, 1949), 494.
2. James P. Barnett, Douglas J. Rhodes, and Lisa W. Lewis, *Remembering Historic Camp Claiborne, Louisiana: The Sacrifice* (Asheville: US Department of Agriculture, 2015).
3. Anonymous letter sent to the War Department by a member of the personnel at Fort Huachuca, February 18, 1942, box 207, entry 188, RG 107, NARA.
4. "New 93rd Infantry Division Has Proud Record to Uphold," *Cleveland Call & Post*, June 6, 1942.
5. See Chad L. Williams, *Torchbearers of Democracy: African American Soldiers in the World War I Era* (Chapel Hill: University of North Carolina Press, 2013).
6. See Jeffrey T. Sammons and John H. Morrow, Jr., *Harlem's Rattlers and the Great War: The Undaunted 369th Regiment and the African American Quest for Equality* (Lawrence: University Press of Kansas, 2014).
7. Letter from Shirley Graham to Paul McNutt, November 29, 1941, Administrator of the Federal Security Agency, box 43, folder 12, Shirley Graham Papers, Schlesinger Library.
8. Quoted in Robert F. Jefferson, *Making the Men of the 93rd: African-American Servicemen in the Years of the Great Depression and the Second World War, 1935–1947* (PhD dissertation, University of Michigan, 1995), 233.
9. Letter from Sergeant Percy Roberts to an unnamed soldier, March 29, 1942, box 43, folder 11, Shirley Graham Papers, Schlesinger Library.
10. Jefferson, *Making the Men of the 93rd*, 226. In the early 1990s, Robert Jefferson issued calls for testimonies in the magazines and newsletters of the veterans of the 93rd Infantry Division. Of the 584 men who came forward, 226 responded to his detailed questionnaire. Jefferson also conducted 130 interviews between 1991 and 2002. It is on the basis of these materials that he wrote the history of the 93rd Division before, during, and after it was trained at Huachuca.
11. See the case of Leonard Holmes, who was court-martialed at Fort Huachuca in August 1942 (court-martial record, 38022292 GCM, RG 153, National Archives at Saint Louis).
12. Jefferson, *Making the Men of the 93rd*, 157.
13. Maggi Morehouse interview with Henry Williams, 1987 and 2005, box 6, African American Soldiers in World War II, Maggi Morehouse Collection, Library of Congress.
14. Jefferson, *Making the Men of the 93rd*, 170 and 179.
15. Inspection Data prepared by AC of S, G-2 HQ 93rd for General Davis, July 1942, box 17, folder 8, Benjamin O. Davis Papers, Military History Institute (MHI).
16. See Mark Solomon, *The Cry Was Unity: Communists and African Americans, 1917–1936* (Jackson: University Press of Mississippi, 1998).
17. Solomon, *The Cry Was Unity*, 155.
18. Nelson Peery, *Black Fire: The Making of an American Revolutionary* (New York: The New Press, 1995).
19. Jefferson, *Making the Men of the 93rd*, 228–29.

20. Shirley Graham's speech in Indianapolis, undated, box 43, folder 11, Shirley Graham Papers, Schlesinger Library.
21. Jefferson, *Making the Men of the 93rd*, 229. Figures are from the 1940 Census of Population, https://www2.census.gov/library/publications/decennial/1940/population-volume-3/33973538v3p1ch2.pdf.
22. See Nicholas Lemann, *The Big Test: The Secret History of the American Meritocracy* (New York: Farrar, Straus and Giroux, 2000), 29–40 and 53–54. The test consisted of 150 multiple-choice questions in arithmetic and vocabulary. It was intended to assess the skills of candidates who had graduated from high school without interruption, which was the case for only a small minority of blacks. Stouffer et al., *The American Soldier*, Vol. I, 489.
23. Memorandum from Joseph R. Dorsey to the Commanding General of the 93rd, April 25, 1943, "Notes on the Distribution of AGCT Scores in the 93rd Infantry Division," box "Inspection Tours – United States – Texas – Virginia, Numerical Units," Benjamin O. Davis Papers, Military History Institute, quoted in Jefferson, *Making the Men of the 93rd*, 195–96.
24. Jefferson, *Making the Men of the 93rd*, 223.
25. See James J. Cooke, *Chewing Gum, Candy Bars, and Beer: The Army PX in World War II* (Columbia: University of Missouri Press, 2009).
26. Jefferson, *Making the Men of the 93rd*, 251.
27. Lauren Rebecca Sklaroff, *Black Culture and the New Deal: The Quest for Civil Rights in the Roosevelt Era* (Chapel Hill: University of North Carolina Press, 2009), 183.
28. James Sparrow, *Warfare State: World War II Americans and the Age of Big Government* (Oxford: Oxford University Press, 2013), 84.
29. Scottsdale Center for the Arts, *Lew Davis: "The Negro in America's Wars" and Other Major Paintings* (Scottsdale: Scottsdale Center for the Arts, 1990), 12.
30. See Michael Snape, *God and Uncle Sam: Religion and America's Armed Forces in World War II* (Martlesham: Boydell Press, 2015).
31. Report of August 8, 1942, annex to the health report on venereal diseases, folder "Fort Huachuca," box 239, entry 31, RG 112, NARA.
32. Ulysses Lee, *The Employment of Negro Troops* (Washington, DC: Center of Military History, 1994 [1963]), 285.
33. Letter from Benjamin Davis to Captain John W. Holland, March 22, 1943, folder 10, box 3A, Davis Papers, MHI.
34. This observation was made by Roy Wilkins of the NAACP when he met with Hardy in his office in 1943, see Roy Wilkins, "The West in War Time," *The Crisis*, May 1943, 142.
35. Online notice by Mark Henry, Fort Huachuca Museum, www.flickr.com/photos/cochise100/8083772212.
36. Letter from Midian Bousfield to Truman Gibson, October 12, 1942, Reel 8, frames 407–08, *African Americans in the Military*, Part 3: Subject files of Judge William Hastie, Civilian Aide to the Secretary of War, "N" through "Z."
37. Memorandum of January 26, 1942 on the January 20 conference on segregated prostitution, folder 291.2, box 2, entry 390 decimal correspondence, RG 160, NARA.

38. Edward Almond, Oral History Interview, Part II, 79, Military History Institute, quoted in Michael E. Lynch, *Edward M. Almond and the US Army: From the 92nd Infantry Division to the X Corps* (Lexington: University Press of Kentucky, 2019), 109.
39. In the years 1917–1918, there were only 1,353 African-American officers in the US Army. The vast majority of them were below the rank of major and were assigned to the infantry, medical, and chaplain corps. Under pressure from activist organizations, the Army finally admitted African-American applicants to the segregated Officer Training School at Fort Des Moines in Iowa.
40. Confidential memorandum from Colonel Edward Greenbaum, Ordnance Department, to the Assistant Secretary of War, March 8, 1943, folder "Confidential, Race, Army," box 2, entry 140, RG 107, NARA.
41. Quoted in Mary Motley, ed., *The Invisible Soldier: The Experience of the Black Soldier, World War II* (Detroit: Wayne University Press, 1975), 84.
42. Peery, *Black Fire*, 140.
43. Frank Bolden's testimony in the film The Black Press: Soldiers without Swords by Stanley Nelson, a 1999 PBS production, www.pbs.org/black press/film/transcripts/bolden.html.
44. Note on the inspection report of General Davis, July 14–19, 1942, box 207, entry 188, RG 107, NARA.
45. William Hastie, "Survey and Recommendations Concerning the Integration of the Negro Soldier into the Army," September 22, 1941, quoted in Thomas Guglielmo, "A Martial Freedom Movement: Black G.I.s' Political Struggles during World War II," *Journal of American History* 104, no. 4 (March 2018): 879–903, 885.
46. Letter from William Hastie to the Under Secretary of War, December 30, 1941, quoted in Morris J. MacGregor and Bernard C. Nalty, eds., *Blacks in the United States Armed Forces: Basic Documents*, Vol. V: *Black Soldiers in World War II* (Wilmington: Scholarly Resources, 1977), 56ff.
47. Philip McGuire, *Black Civilian Aides and the Problems of Racism in the United States* (PhD dissertation, Howard University, 1975), 144–45.
48. Note on the inspection report of General Davis, July 14–19, 1942, box 207, entry 188, RG 107, NARA.
49. See, for example, Letter from Benjamin Davis to Midian Bousfield, August 12, 1942, folder 5B, box 3A, Davis Papers, MHI.
50. Marvin E. Fletcher, *America's First Black General: Benjamin O. Davis, Sr., 1880–1970* (Lawrence: University of Kansas Press, 1989), 90–98; Lee, *The Employment of Negro Troops*, 170–71.
51. See, in particular, Louis R. Harlan, "Booker T. Washington and the Politics of Accommodation," in John Hope Franklin and August Meier, eds., *Black Leaders of the Twentieth Century* (Urbana, University of Illinois Press, 1982), 1–18; John T. McCarney, *Black Power Ideologies: An Essay in African American Political Thought* (Philadelphia: Temple University Press, 1992), Chapter 4 "The Politics of Accommodation."

52. File transmitted to the Inspector General by HQ 93rd, notes and report from General Davis to the Inspector General, August 2, 1942, folder 8, box 7, Davis Papers, MHI.
53. Memorandum to General Eisenhower on letterhead of the War Department General Staff, Operations Division, subject "The Colored Troop Problem," April 2, 1942, quoted in MacGregor and Nalty, *Blacks in the United States Armed Forces*.
54. Robert R. Palmer, Bell I. Wiley, and William R. Keast, *United States Army in World War II: The Army Ground Forces – The Procurement and Training of Ground Combat Troops* (Washington, DC: Center of Military History, 1991), "Obstacles to Effective Training," 476.
55. Quoted in Maggi M. Morehouse, *Black Citizen Soldiers* (PhD dissertation, University of California at Berkeley, 2001), 113.
56. "93rd Division Developing Heavy Fire," *Pittsburgh Courier*, October 5, 1943.
57. *Bisbee Daily Review*, February 17, 1943.
58. Palmer, Wiley, and Keast, *United States Army in World War II*, 457.
59. Editorial, *Baltimore Afro-American*, December 13, 1941, quoted in Booker, *African Americans in the United States Army in World War II*, 53.
60. Inspection Data prepared by the Ordnance Officer for the Inspector General, folder 8, box 17, Davis Papers, MHI.
61. See the court-martial record of Leonard Holmes, 38022292, RG 153, National Archives at Saint Louis.
62. Quoted in Motley, *The Invisible Soldier*, 81.
63. The first photographers of the Army Pictorial Service (APS) had been professional photographers in civilian life. Later in the war, the APS had to train new photographers at the Army Public Relations Office and the Signal Corps Photographic Center in Astoria. See George Raynor Thompson, ed., *United States Army in World War II, The Technical Services: The Signal Corps: The Test (December 1941 to July 1943)* (Washington, DC: Office of the Chief of Military History, 1957), Chapter XIII "Photo by U.S. Army Signal Corps."
64. Paul Alkebulan, *The African American Press in World War II: Toward Victory at Home and Abroad* (Lanham: Lexington Books, 2014), Chapter 5.
65. See Mark Whitaker, *Smoketown: The Untold Story of the Other Great Black Renaissance* (New York: Simon & Schuster, 2018), 79–180.
66. Frank Bolden, "93rd Gives Dazzling Display of Military Preparedness," *Pittsburgh Courier*, July 4, 1942.
67. Frank Bolden, "93rd Primes for Regimental," *Pittsburgh Courier*, October 31, 1942.
68. Frank Bolden, "Fort Huachuca's 93rd Near Fighting Peak," *Pittsburgh Courier*, January 30, 1943.
69. Lee, *The Employment of Negro Troops*, 292.
70. Folders 10 and 11, box 2, Frank Bolden Papers, Pittsburgh University, University of Pittsburgh Library System.
71. Ltr, Asst to Dir Mil Pers Div Ninth Service Command to CG NSC, December 28, 1942, copy in Fort Huachuca 333.1 Insps-Post Camps Stations, quoted in Lee, *The Employment of Negro Troops*, 293.

72. Undated handwritten letter from Midian Bousfield to Truman Gibson, Reel 9, frames 88–95, *African Americans in the Military*, Part 3: Subject files of Judge William Hastie, Civilian Aide to the Secretary of War, "N" through "Z."

3 Separated by the Color Line

1. Undated letter by Shirley Graham written in Indianapolis, box 43, folder 11, Shirley Graham Papers, Schlesinger Library.
2. William H. Hastie, "Negro Officers in Two World Wars," *Journal of Negro Education* 12, no. 3 (Summer 1943): 316–23.
3. See A. Salter Krewasky, *The Story of Black Military Officers, 1861–1948* (Abingdon: Routledge, 2015), Chapter 11 "The Gate Opens."
4. Letter from Shirley Graham to W. E. B Du Bois, May 2, 1942, W. E. B. Du Bois Papers, University of Massachusetts Amherst Libraries, http://credo.library.umass.edu/view/full/mums312-b098-i019.
5. With the exception of chaplains and medical officers, black officers had been assigned until then to units of the National Guard, not to black units of the regular army.
6. Memorandum for General Eisenhower, War Department General Staff, subject "The Colored Troop Problem," April 2, 1942, quoted in Morris J. MacGregor and Bernard C. Nalty, eds., *Blacks in the United States Armed Forces: Basic Documents*, Vol. V: *Black Soldiers in World War II* (Wilmington: Scholarly Resources, 1977), 56ff.
7. Richard Dalfiume, *Desegregation of the U.S. Armed Forces: Fighting on Two Fronts, 1939–1953* (Columbia: University of Missouri Press, 1969), 64–66.
8. Memorandum to the attention of the Deputy Chief of Staff, February 4, 1942, quoted in McGregor and Nalty, *Blacks in the United States Armed Forces*.
9. Robert F. Jefferson, *Making the Men of the 93rd: African-American Servicemen in the Years of the Great Depression and the Second World War, 1935–1947* (PhD dissertation, University of Michigan, 1995), 289.
10. Ibid., 290.
11. ANP release "Limit Negro Officers to 1st Lieutenancies," February 1943.
12. On chaplains, see Michael Snape, *God and Uncle Sam: Religion and America's Armed Forces in World War II* (Martlesham: Boydell Press, 2015), 61 ff.
13. Mary Penick Motley, ed., *The Invisible Soldier: The Experience of the Black Soldier, World War II* (Detroit: Wayne University Press, 1975), 79–80.
14. Todd J. Moye, *Freedom Flyers: The Tuskegee Airmen of World War II* (New York: Oxford University Press, 2010), 36.
15. Profiles described in Jefferson, *Making the Men of the 93rd*, 130, 166, and 180.
16. Memorandum, Gen Davis for TIG, August 7, 1943, AGF 210.31/449, AG 210.31 (January 4, 1943), quoted in Ulysses Lee, *The Employment of Negro Troops* (Washington, DC: Center of Military History, 1994 [1963]), 219.
17. "Is the 93rd a Token Outfit?," *The Afro-American*, March 6, 1943.

18. Interview with Roscoe Tyson Spann, Veterans History Project, https://memory.loc.gov/diglib/vhp/bib/loc.natlib.afc2001001.54076.
19. Letter from General Benjamin Davis to Major General Fred W. Miller, March 4, 1943, and letter from General Benjamin Davis to Colonel Hardy, March 26, 1943, box 3A, folder 10, Benjamin O. Davis Papers, MHI.
20. Quoted in Jefferson, *Making the Men of the 93rd*, 253.
21. Ibid., 236.
22. "Major Charles J. Blackwood Special Service Chief at Huachuca," *California Eagle*, February 17, 1943.
23. Memorandum by G. H. McManus, HQ 93rd Infantry Division, Commanding General, June 30, 1943, box 17, folder 8, Davis Papers, MHI.
24. Declaration of Major General R. G. Lehman to AGF Historical Office, October 26, 1944, quoted in Major Bell I. Wiley, *The Training of Negro Troops* (Washington, DC: The Army Ground Forces, Historical Section, 1945), 32.
25. See, in particular, George M. Fredrickson, *The Black Image in the White Mind: The Debate on Afro-American Character and Destiny, 1817–1914* (New York: Harper & Row, 1971).
26. Charles S. Johnson, *Patterns of Negro Segregation* (New York: Harper & Brothers Publishers, 1943), 143–46 and 208.
27. On swimming pools as enclaves of racial purity, see Jeff Wiltse, *Contested Waters: A Social History of Swimming Pools in America* (Chapel Hill: University of North Carolina Press, 2007).
28. Lee, *The Employment of Negro Troops*, 218.
29. Complaints, Colored Officers 93rd Division, box 17, folder 8, Davis Papers, MHI.
30. Frank Bolden, "Soldiers Ordered to Evacuate Homes at Fort Huachuca," *Pittsburgh Courier*, September 19, 1942.
31. Interview with Anna Hairston by Maggie Morehouse, Washington, DC, 2014, www.youtube.com/watch?v=1hUDmInRvMc&t=18s; Letter from Bousfield to Gibson, August 11, 1944, box 207, entry 188, RG 107, NARA.
32. "White Arizona Community Accepts Race Residents," *Pittsburgh Courier*, September 5, 1942.
33. "Armed Forces Discriminated Against," *Arizona's Negro Journal*, July 10, 1942, 1 and 5.
34. Letter from Vincent Browne to Dr. Bunche, July 21, 1942, box 207, entry 188, RG 107, NARA.
35. Note on General Davis's inspection mission, July 14–19, 1942, box 207, entry 188, RG 107, NARA; Marvin E. Fletcher, *America's First Black General: Benjamin O. Davis, Sr., 1880–1970* (Lawrence: University of Kansas Press, 1989), 98.
36. Memorandum from Fort Huachuca Headquarters to the Commander of the Ninth Military Region at Fort Douglas, March 15, 1945, box 87, folder 291.2, "Confidential," entry 26e, RG 159, NARA.
37. Memorandum by Colonel Hardy, June 4, 1942, box 207, entry 188, RG 107, NARA.

38. Adam D. Smith, Susan I. Enscore, and Samuel L. Hunter, *Analysis of the Mountain View Officers' Club: Fort Huachuca, Arizona* (Champaign: US Corps of Engineers, Engineer Research and Development Center, 2012), 66.
39. "Segregation at Fort Huachuca: One Clubhouse for White Army Officers; Another for Colored," *Pittsburgh Courier*, July 4, 1942.
40. Letter from Roscoe Giles to Louis Wright, June 3, 1944, folder "Staff, Walter White, Fort Huachuca trip, 1943–44," Group II box A 606, Papers of the NAACP, Library of Congress (LoC).
41. Letter from William Hastie to the General Staff, July 1, 1942, box 441, folder 291.1, decimal file, RG 165, NARA.
42. Memorandum from John Dean, General Staff, to Judge Hastie, June 14, 1942, quoted in MacGregor and Nalty, *Blacks in the United States Armed Forces*.
43. Memorandum from Inspector General Virgil Peterson to the Chief of Staff, August 6, 1942, box 18, folder 8, Davis Papers, MHI.
44. Memorandum from Fort Huachuca Headquarters to the Commander of the Ninth Military Region at Fort Douglas, March 15, 1945, box 87, folder 291.2, "Confidential," entry 26e, RG 159, NARA.
45. Letter from Bousfield to W. E. B Du Bois, October 12, 1942, Du Bois Papers, Amherst, http://credo.library.umass.edu/view/full/mums312-b098-i022.
46. Interview with Anna Hairston by Maggi Morehouse, *The Oral History Archive of Black World War II Veterans and Their Families*, http://stevensargent.org/BlackSoldiers-Project/items/show/4.
47. Lee, *The Employment of Negro Troops*, 224.

4   A State-of-the-Art All-Black Hospital

1. "Army to Spend 23 Million $ to Build Fort Huachuca Cantonment Buildings," *Bisbee Daily Review*, May 3, 1941.
2. Barbara Brooks Tomblin, *GI Nightingales: The Army Nurse Corps in World War II* (Lexington: University Press of Kentucky, 1996), 186.
3. "Fort Huachuca Medical Wards House 1141 Beds," *Arizona Daily Star*, December 14, 1943.
4. Office of the Surgeon, Station Hospital, Hospital Order no. 24, September 23, 1942, box 207, entry 188, RG 107, NARA.
5. SGO memo, October 25, 1940, "Plan for utilization of Negro officers, nurses and EM in the Medical Department, 1940–41 Military program," folder "Negro personnel, 1940–1941," box 199, entry 31 ZI, RG 112, NARA.
6. Minutes of meeting of March 1941, folder "Negro doctors and nurses," box 199, entry 31 ZI, RG 112, NARA.
7. Charles Herbert Garvin, "The Negro in the Special Services of the U.S. Army: Medical Corps, Dental Corps and Nurses Corps," *Journal of Negro Education* 12, no. 3 (Summer 1943): 335–44, 342.
8. Minutes of the meeting of the NMA representatives with the Surgeon General, March 7, 1941, folder "Negro doctors and nurses," box 199, entry 31 ZI, RG 112.

9. Clarence McKittrick Smith, *The Medical Department: Hospitalization and Evacuation, Zone of Interior* (Washington, DC: Department of Defense, Center for Military History, 1956), 110. The creation of two black wards and two black hospitals by the SGO was insufficient to absorb all African Americans who had to be employed by the Medical Department to meet the 10 percent quota. As a result, the majority of black personnel were assigned to subaltern positions in the medical companies that had been created in October 1940. See Sanders Marble, "'Separate, But Almost Equal': The Army's Negro Medical Field Units in World War II," *Journal of the National Medical Association* 103, no. 11/12 (November–December 2011): 1–8.
10. SGO Plan for the utilization of colored medical department officers, mentioned in January 30, 1942 memorandum for the assistant chief of staff, G-3, folder "Negro personnel, sanitary companies and negro officers, 1940, 1942," box 200, entry 31 ZI, RG 112, NARA.
11. Letter from McAfee, Assistant to the Surgeon General, to the Adjutant General, May 1, 1942, box 108, entry 29, General Subject File, 1943–44, RG 112, NARA; Letter from Bousfield to Thomas Parran, Surgeon General, Public Health Service, March 11, 1943, box 207, entry 188, RG 107, NARA; Letter from Francis Fitts (Medical Corps, Surgeon General Office) to Colonel Lull, March 9, 1942, box 108, entry 9, General Subject File, 1943–44, RG 112, NARA.
12. For a discussion of the "black hospital movement" launched in the late nineteenth century, see Vanessa Northington Gamble, *Making a Place for Ourselves: The Black Hospital Movement, 1920–1945* (Oxford: Oxford University Press, 1995).
13. Darlene Clark Hine, "Black Professionals and Race Consciousness: Origins of the Civil Rights Movement, 1890–1950," *Journal of American History* 89, no. 4 (March 2003): 1279–94.
14. Pete Daniel, "Black Power in the 1920s: The Case of Tuskegee Veterans Hospital," *Journal of Southern History* 36, no. 3 (August 1970): 368–88.
15. See Peter Ascoli, *Julius Rosenwald: The Man Who Built Sears, Roebuck and Advanced Black Education in the American South* (Bloomington: Indiana University Press, 2015).
16. Gamble, *Making a Place for Ourselves*, 36 and 118.
17. Vanessa Gamble, "Black Autonomy versus White Control: Black Hospitals and the Dilemmas of White Philanthropy, 1920–1940," *Minerva* 35, no. 3 (Fall 1997): 247–67, 267.
18. Gamble, *Making a Place for Ourselves*, 59–62.
19. Montague Cobb, "Louis Tompkins Wright, 1891–1952: 'Also the Lord gave Job twice as much as he had before,'" *Journal of the National Medical Association* 45, no. 2 (March 1953): 130–48.
20. Vanessa Gamble, "Midian Othello Bousfield: Advocate for the Medical and Public Health Concerns of Black Americans," *American Journal of Public Health* 99, no. 7 (July 2009): 1185–87.
21. Gamble, *Making a Place for Ourselves*, 131–55.
22. Karen Kruse Thomas, *Deluxe Jim Crow: Civil Rights and American Health Policy, 1935–1954* (Athens, GA: University of Georgia Press, 2011), 36.

23. Gamble, *Making a Place for Ourselves*, 40.
24. Bousfield to the State Organization of the NMA Procurement and Assignment Service, March 12, 1942, folder "291.2 Negro personnel," box 200, entry 31 ZI, RG 112, NARA.
25. Bousfield to W. E. B. Du Bois, October 28, 1942, Series 1A. General Correspondence, W. E. B. Du Bois Papers, http://credo.library.umass.edu/view/full/mums312-b097-i469.
26. Christine Knauer, *Let Us Fight as Free Men: Black Soldiers and Civil Rights* (Philadelphia: University of Pennsylvania Press, 2014), 10 and 24.
27. "War Department to Establish Complete Hospital Unit at Ft. Huachuca, Ariz.," *Chicago Defender*, March 21, 1942.
28. "Fort Huachuca Hospital Compares Favorably with Country's Best," *Pittsburgh Courier*, August 13, 1942.
29. "Dr Kenney Defends Fort Huachuca Hospital," *Pittsburgh Courier*, April 25, 1942.
30. "NMA Censures Dr. Bousfield, April 15, 1942," box 108, entry 29, General Subject File, 1943–44, RG 112, NARA.
31. Reply of the NMA to the purported press release of Hon. Secretary of War, February 20, 1942, folder "291.2 Negro personnel," box 200, entry 31 ZI, RG 112, NARA.
32. "Ft. Huachuca's Separate Hospital Irks Medicos," *Chicago Defender*, April 4, 1942.
33. Thomas A. Guglielmo, "'Red Cross, Double Cross': Race and America's World War II-Era Blood Donor Service," *Journal of American History* 97, no. 1 (June 2010): 63–90, 85.
34. Jean-Paul Lallemand-Stempak, *Peaux noires, blouses blanches: Les Afro-Américains et le Mouvement pour les droits civiques en médecine (1940-1975)* [*Black Skins, White Coats: African Americans and the Medical Civil Rights Movement, 1940-1975*] (PhD dissertation, École des hautes études en sciences sociales, 2015), 138.
35. Guglielmo, "Red Cross, Double Cross," 65.
36. Frank Bolden, "Sees Bright Future for Race Medical Men at Huachuca," *Pittsburgh Courier*, August 29, 1942.
37. McKittrick Smith, *The Medical Department*, 14–38.
38. Bolden, "Sees Bright Future for Race Medical Men at Huachuca."
39. Karen Kruse Thomas referred to this movement as "Deluxe Jim Crow" in her eponymous book *Deluxe Jim Crow*.
40. This section relies significantly on the analysis of the hospital conducted by Mathilde Estève as part of her Master's thesis defended at the University of Nantes in 2016.
41. "*Who's Who* of Negro Medicine Makes Fort Huachuca Hospital 'Best Anywhere,'" *Chicago Defender*, December 5, 1942.
42. Langston Hughes, "Ft. Huachuca Hospital One of Nation's Finest," *Pittsburgh Courier*, May 20, 1944.
43. Gamble, *Making a Place for Ourselves*, 7–12 and 42.
44. As E. Franklin Frazier explained in his seminal book on the black bourgeoisie, people of mixed race had a privileged position in the African-American

community; this position was perpetuated from one generation to the next through endogamous marriage strategies. See E. Franklin Frazier, *Black Bourgeoisie* (New York: The Free Press, 1957).

45. Handwritten letter from Midian Bousfield to Truman Gibson, December 9, 1942, box 207, entry 188, RG 107, NARA.
46. Letter from Colonel Hugh J. Morgan, SGO, to Brigadier General C. C. Hillman, SGO, September 8, 1942, box 239, entry 31, RG 112, NARA.
47. Letter from Bousfield to Davis, August 19, 1942, folder 5B, box 3A, Davis Papers, MHI.
48. Moye, Todd J., *Freedom Flyers: The Tuskegee Airmen of World War II* (New York: Oxford University Press, 2010), 81.
49. Letter from Captain Allen to Mr. Morchand, correspondence section, *Journal of the National Medical Association* (July 1942).
50. "Meet the Hinksons," *Ladies' Home Journal*, August 1942.
51. Letter from Hinkson to Mrs. Mary Cookman, Executive Editor of the *Ladies' Home Journal*, December 1, 1942, folder "Correspondence, medical career 1940s–1950s," box 9, DeHaven Hinkson Collection, African-American Museum in Philadelphia (AAMP).
52. Letters between DeHaven Hinkson and General Benjamin Davis, August 1942, folder 5A, box 3A, Davis Papers, MHI.
53. Not everyone in the black community shared the patriotic enthusiasm of the black press. This was true even among the bourgeoisie – as shown by the examples of sociologist Horace Cayton and historian John Hope Franklin, both of whom refused to serve in a segregated Army. See Heather Marie Stur, *Integrating the US Military: Race, Gender, and Sexual Orientation since World War II* (Baltimore: Johns Hopkins University Press, 2017), 12.
54. Letter from Colonel Hugh J. Morgan, medical corps, SGO, to Brigadier General C. C. Hillman, SGO, September 8, 1942, box 239, entry 31, RG 112, NARA.
55. Montague Cobb, "Roscoe Conkling Giles, 1890–1970," *Journal of the National Medical Association* 62, no. 3 (May 1970): 254–56.
56. "Dr. Julian Owen Blache," *Journal of the National Medical Association* 56, no. 3 (May 1964): 297.
57. Prudence Burns Burrell, *Hathaway* (Grandville: Harlo, 1997), 56–61.
58. Charissa Threat, *Nursing Civil Rights: Gender and Race in the Army Nurse Corps* (Champaign: University of Illinois Press, 2015), Chapter 2.
59. Interview with Madine Davis Lane by Maggi Morehouse, 1998, box 3, African American Soldiers in World War II Collection, LoC.
60. These men were much more representative of blacks who served in the Medical Department: Of the 25,976 African Americans employed by the Medical Department in October 1943, 25,296 were NCOs or privates.
61. "Ex-Cabbies and College Profs Join Hands to Run First-Rate Hospital at Huachuca," *Chicago Defender*, December 12, 1942, 13.
62. Roy Brown's memoirs, folders 9–11, box 5, Jesse Johnson Military Collection, Schomburg Center, New York Public Library.
63. Letter from Bousfield to Truman K. Gibson Jr., October 13, 1942, box 207, entry 188, RG 107.

64. See Gladys L. Hobby, *Penicillin: Meeting the Challenge* (New Haven: Yale University Press, 1985); Roswell Quinn, "Rethinking Antibiotic Research and Development: World War II and the Penicillin Collaborative," *American Journal of Public Health* 103, no. 3 (March 2013): 426–34.
65. "Miracle Drug Is Given Hospital for Experiment," *Apache Sentinel*, January 21, 1944.
66. Letter from Bousfield to Truman K. Gibson Jr., January 3, 1944, box 207, entry 188, RG 107, NARA.
67. "A Report of 271 Venereal Disease Cases Treated with Penicillin," *Journal of the National Medical Association* 40, no. 5 (September 1948): 219–20.
68. Letter from Bousfield to Dr. John W. Lawlah, March 8, 1943, box 207, entry 188, RG 107, NARA.
69. See the many letters between Bousfield and Gibson in box 207, entry 188, RG 107, NARA.
70. Draft of a note from Bousfield to the Army Surgeon General, June 1943, folder "330–339 Fort Huachuca, 1943–1944," box 239, entry 31, RG 112, NARA; Letter from Bousfield to Hall, March 6, 1944, folder "291.2 Negro personnel," box 200, entry 31, RG 112, NARA; Letter from Bousfield to Major General Lull, February 17, 1945, box 207, entry 188, RG 107, NARA.
71. Letter from Bousfield to General Hines, June 7, 1943, box 207, entry 188, RG 107, NARA.

5 Fry: City of "Vice"

1. Letter from Shirley Graham to Paul McNutt, November 29, 1941, folder "Fort Huachuca," box 239, entry 31, RG 112, NARA.
2. See F. James Davis, *Who Is Black? One Nation's Definition* (Philadelphia: The Pennsylvania State University Press, 1991), 60–61; Martha Hodes, *White Women, Black Men: Illicit Sex in the Nineteenth-Century South* (New Haven: Yale University Press, 1997).
3. Frank Bolden, "Censored – Four Persons Held in Tucson Riot," *Pittsburgh Courier*, July 4, 1942, 11.
4. Data from the 1940 Census.
5. Matthew C. Whitaker, "The Rise of Black Phoenix: African-American Migration, Settlement and Community Development in Maricopa County, Arizona 1868–1930," *Journal of Negro History* 85, no. 3 (Summer 2000): 197–209; Bradford Luckingham, *Minorities in Phoenix: A Profile of Mexican American, Chinese American, and African American Communities, 1860–1992* (Tucson: University of Arizona Press, 1994), 149–56.
6. Statement from Ollie North to his sister Edith North Johnson, April 19, 1943, and letter from Leslie Perry (NAACP) to Charles Browning (*Chicago Defender*), folder "Soldier trouble, Fort Huachuca," box B159, NAACP Papers, Library of Congress.
7. "2 Killed, 12 Shot in Negro-Troop Riot at Phoenix," *New York Herald Tribune*, November 28, 1942; "Army Probes Phoenix Riots," *Arizona Republic*, November 28, 1942; "General Believes All Riot Inciters Are Held

in Jail," *Arizona Republic*, December 1, 1942; "Gen. Davis Probes Phoenix Riots," *Pittsburgh Courier*, December 5, 1942; Enoch Waters Jr., "Inside Story of Arizona Riot! Blame Girls for Fatal Battle: 3 Dead, 11 Shot," *Chicago Defender*, December 5, 1942, 1.
8. Anonymous letter sent to Walter White from Huachuca, April 13, 1943, box II B 159, folder "Soldier trouble, Fort Huachuca," NAACP Papers, Library of Congress.
9. Thomas J. Ward Jr., "Competent Counsel: Thurgood Marshall, the Black Press, and the Alexandria Soldiers' Rape Trials," *Louisiana History: The Journal of the Louisiana Historical Association* 61, no. 3 (Summer 2020): 229–66, 236–38.
10. Elizabeth Tandy Shermer, *Sunbelt Capitalism: Phoenix and the Transformation of American Politics* (Philadelphia: University of Pennsylvania Press, 2013), 123.
11. Bill Perry, quoted in Maggi Morehouse, *Fighting in a Jim Crow Army: Black Men and Women Remember World War II* (Lanham: Rowman & Littlefield, 2000), 82.
12. See Alice Baumgartner, *South to Freedom: Runaway Slaves to Mexico and the Road to the Civil War* (New York: Basic Books, 2020); Karl Jacoby, *The Strange Career of William Ellis: The Texas Slave Who Became a Mexican Millionaire* (New York: Norton, 2016), Chapter 4 "The Land of God and Liberty"; Karl Jacoby, "Racial Borders and Historical Borderlands: African Americans in Latin America," *Diplomatic History* 31, no. 3 (June 2007): 571–74.
13. James R. Curtis and Daniel D. Arreola, "Zonas de Tolerancia on the Northern Mexican Border," *Geographical Review* 81, no. 3 (1991): 333–46; Valentin Edward, Jr., "Off Duty: Black Soldiers and Mobility in the U.S.–Mexico Borderlands 1866–1890," *Western Historical Quarterly* 54, no. 2 (Summer 2023): 103–16.
14. Ulysses Lee, *The Employment of Negro Troops* (Washington, DC: Center of Military History, 1994 [1963]), 282.
15. James A. Sandos, "Prostitution and Drugs: The United States Army on the Mexican–American Border, 1916–1917," *Pacific Historical Review* 49, no. 4 (1980): 621–45.
16. Undated letter from Lt. Col. Bousfield to Truman Gibson, box 207, entry 188, RG 107, NARA.
17. Letter from Col. Hugh Morgan to Brigadier General Hillman, SGO, September 8, 1942, folder "Fort Huachuca," box 239, entry 31, RG 112, NARA.
18. Letter from commander McGee to Governor Osborn, February 25, 1942, box 16, Governors Sidney P. Osborn and Daniel E. Garvey, RG 1, SG 14–15, Arizona State Archives.
19. Letter from Col. Hugh Morgan to Brigadier General Hillman, September 8, 1942, folder "Fort Huachuca," box 239, entry 31, RG 112, NARA.
20. Memorandum of January 26, 1943 regarding the conference on segregated prostitution held on 20 January, folder 291.2, box 2, entry 390 decimal correspondence, RG 160, NARA.

21. On the stereotype of "the Negro as beast" or "brute," see George M. Fredrickson, *The Black Image in the White Mind: The Debate on Afro-American Character and Destiny, 1817–1914* (New York: Harper & Row, 1971), 273–82 and 287–88; Tommy L. Lott, *The Invention of Race: Black Culture and the Politics of Representation* (Hoboken, NJ: Wiley-Blackwell, 1999), Chapter "Racist Discourse and the Negro–Ape Metaphor," 7–13.
22. Annual report of Medical Department activities at Fort Huachuca to the commanding general, services of supply, War Department, February 10, 1943, attention Surgeon General, signed by E. B. Maynard, post surgeon, folder "Fort Huachuca," box 239, entry 31, RG 112, NARA.
23. See Marilyn E. Hegarty, *Victory Girls, Khaki-Wackies, and Patriotutes: The Regulation of Female Sexuality during World War II* (New York: New York University Press, 2008), Chapter 3 "Reservoirs of Infections."
24. On the prohibition of interracial sex since the Reconstruction period, see Charles Frank Robinson II, *Dangerous Liaisons: Sex and Love in the Segregated South* (Fayetteville: University of Arkansas Press, 2003).
25. Hegarty, *Victory Girls, Khaki-Wackies, and Patriotutes*, 78–79.
26. Allan M. Brandt, *No Magic Bullet: A Social History of Venereal Disease in the United States since 1880* (Oxford: Oxford University Press, 1987), 122–60; Karen Kruse Thomas, *Deluxe Jim Crow: Civil Rights and American Health Policy, 1935–1954* (Athens, GA: University of Georgia Press, 2011), 62–68.
27. See James H. Jones, *Bad Blood: The Tuskegee Syphilis Experiment* (Cambridge, MA: The Free Press, 1993); Susan M. Reverby, ed., *Tuskegee's Truths: Rethinking the Tuskegee Syphilis Study* (Chapel Hill: The University of North Carolina Press, 2000).
28. These are the very principles of what Karen Kruse Thomas refers to as "Deluxe Jim Crow" in medicine. See Karen Kruse Thomas, *Deluxe Jim Crow*, 129ff.
29. Thomas H. Sternberg, Ernest B. Howard, Leonard A. Dewey, and Paul Padget, *Preventive Medicine in World War II*, Vol. V: *Communicable Diseases Transmitted through Contact or by Unknown Means* (Washington, DC: Office of the Surgeon General, 1961), Chapter X "Venereal Diseases," 188 and 195.
30. Inspection data prepared by division surgeon HQ 93rd Division for Inspector General Davis, folder 8, box 17, Davis Papers, MHI.
31. See Margot Canaday, *The Straight State: Sexuality and Citizenship in Twentieth-Century America* (Princeton: Princeton University Press, 2009), 87–90.
32. Leisa D. Meyer, *Creating GI Jane: Sexuality and Power in the Women's Army Corps during World War II* (New York: Columbia University Press, 1996), Chapter 5; Mary Louise Robert, *What Soldiers Do: Sex and the American GI in World War II France* (Chicago, Chicago University Press, 2013), Part II "Prostitution."
33. 1st Ind, HQ Ft. Huachuca, to CG Ninth Service Command, August 4, 1942, papers in CSOIG 333.9 Ft. Huachuca, Arizona (18), quoted in Lee, *The Employment of Negro Troops*, 283.
34. According to Christina S. Jarvis, relationships with "bad women" (understood in the moral, social, racial, and medical sense) held responsible for the

contagion were seen by the military hierarchy as more problematic than the sexual act itself. See Christina S. Jarvis, *The Male Body at War: American Masculinity during World War II* (DeKalb: Northern Illinois University Press, 2004), 79–81.

35. Letter from the Adjutant General to all generals on improving moral conditions in the vicinity of camps, March 22, 1941, quoted in Sternberg, Howard, Dewey, and Padget, *Medical Department, U.S. Army, Preventive Medicine in World War II*, Vol. V, Chapter X "Venereal Diseases," 141–42.
36. Notes of Col. E. Hardy, July 9, 1942, box 207, entry 188, RG 107, NARA.
37. Memorandum of Col. Hardy, August 1942, quoted in memorandum from Col. Quigley to the Inspector General, March 2, 1943, folder 291.2, box 2, entry 390 decimal correspondence file, Records of the Director of Administration, RG 160, NARA; Confidential letter to Col. Hardy, March 31, 1943, folder "Fort Huachuca, town of Fry," 1943, box 23, Governor Osborn Archives, Arizona State Archives.
38. Lee, *The Employment of Negro Troops*, 284.
39. Office VDC Ft Huachuca to Post Surgeon, May 10, 1943, Ft Huachuca 726.1 (VD control), quoted in Lee, *The Employment of Negro Troops*, 284.
40. Letter from Hardy to McNair, March 17, 1943, folder 10, box 3A, Davis Papers; Venereal Report, December 1943, folder 721.5-1 "Fort Huachuca, 1943–...," box 239, entry 31, RG 112, NARA.
41. Memorandum from Col. Quigley to the Inspector General, March 2, 1943; Memorandum from Major General George Grunert, Chief Administrative Officer, to the Director, Control Division and Service Forces, April 2, 1943, folder 291.2, box 2, entry 390 decimal correspondence file, Records of the Director of Administration, RG 160, NARA.
42. Letters from Brigadier General Benjamin Davis to Col. Hardy, March 5, 1943 and March 26, 1943, folder 10, box 3A, Davis Papers, MHI.
43. Letter from Col. Hardy to Governor Osborn, July 1943, folder "Fort Huachuca, town of Fry," 1943, box 23, Governor Osborn Archives, Arizona State Archives.
44. Venereal Report, December 1943, folder 721.5-1 "Fort Huachuca, 1943–...," box 239, entry 31, RG 112, NARA.
45. Memorandum from Lt. Col. Thomas B. Turner (SGO) to Dr. J. R. Heller Jr., Deputy Surgeon, General Public Health Service, December 29, 1943, box 751, entry (NM30) 31 geographic series 1938–44, RG 112, NARA.
46. Memorandum, Lt. Col. Thomas B. Turner, MC, for Director, Preventive Medicine Division, October 13, 1943, Report of Conference on Venereal Disease Control Problems among Colored Troops, quoted in Sternberg, Howard, Dewey, and Padget, *Medical Department, U.S. Army, Preventive Medicine in World War II*, Vol. V, Chapter X "Venereal Diseases," 189ff.
47. Letter from James Rucker to his wife, October 24, 1943, Correspondence of James Bernard Rucker, Tamiment Library and Robert F. Wagner Labor Archive, New York University.
48. Elvyn V. Davidson Collection (AFC/2001/001/30014), Veterans History Project, American Folklife Center, Library of Congress.
49. "No Vice Den for Huachuca," *Pittsburgh Courier*, October 3, 1942.

50. "Soldiers Are Accused of Fry Man's Murder," *Arizona Republic*, January 13, 1942; "Death Penalty Imposed upon Three Negroes," *Tucson Daily Citizen*, July 21, 1942.
51. See Kara Dixon Vuic, *The Girls Next Door: Bringing the Home Front to the Front Lines* (Cambridge: Harvard University Press, 2019), 61ff.
52. Letter from Shirley Graham to Reverend J. Raymond Henderson, September 7, 1941, folder 14, box 43, Shirley Graham Du Bois collection, Schlesinger Library.
53. See Kevin K. Gaines, *Uplifting the Race: Black Leadership, Politics, and Culture in the Twentieth Century* (Chapel Hill: University of North Carolina Press, 1996).
54. Cheryl Mullenbach, *Double Victory: How African American Women Broke Race and Gender Barriers to Help Win World War II* (Chicago: Chicago Review Press, 2013), 105–06.
55. Sam Lebovic, "'A Breath from Home': Soldier Entertainment and the Nationalist Politics of Pop Culture during World War II," *Journal of Social History* 47, no. 2 (Winter 2013): 263–96.
56. Mullenbach, *Double Victory*, 198–200.
57. See Barbara Dianne Savage, *Broadcasting Freedom: Radio, War, and the Politics of Race, 1938–1948* (Chapel Hill: The University of North Carolina Press, 1999).
58. Davis, *Who Is Black?*, 150–56. Davis discusses Lena Horne's "struggle for her racial identity" and notes that she considered "passing" as white for a while.
59. Lauren Rebecca Sklaroff, *Black Culture and the New Deal: The Quest for Civil Rights in the Roosevelt Era* (Chapel Hill: The University of North Carolina Press, 2009), 211–14.
60. "'Cabin' Cast Entertains for Ft. Huachuca Soldiers," *New Journal and Guide*, October 3, 1942.
61. Letter from Hardy to Gibson, July 20, 1942; Letter from Brigadier General John Coulter to Mr. Duncan, Superintendent, Arizona Liquor License and Control, February 16, 1942; Letter from commander McGee to Arizona Liquor License and Control, February 24, 1942, box 16, Governors Osborn and Garvey Papers, Arizona State Archives.
62. Letter from Hardy to Governor Osborn, December 18, 1943, folder "Fort Huachuca, town of Fry," box 23, Governor Osborn Papers, Arizona State Archives.
63. Letter from Hardy to Governor Osborn, August 11, 1942, box 16, Governors Osborn and Garvey Papers, Arizona State Archives.
64. Truman Gibson Jr., *Knocking Down Barriers: My Fight for Black America* (Evanston: Northwestern University Press, 2005), 155.
65. See Adam Green, *Selling the Race: Culture, Community and Black Chicago, 1940–1955* (Chicago: University of Chicago Press, 2009).
66. See, in particular, Douglas S. Massey and Nancy A. Denton, *American Apartheid: Segregation and the Making of the Underclass* (Cambridge, MA: Harvard University Press, 1993), 40.
67. Green, *Selling the Race*, 21.

68. Notes of Col. Hardy, "Development of Fry, Arizona, with Negro capital," July 9, 1942, box 207, entry 188, RG 107, NARA.
69. Report from Lt. Col. John Harlan to the Inspector General, October 26, 1944, folder "Fort Huachuca," box 44, entry 26f General correspondence 1939–1947, RG 159, NARA; Memorandum from Deputy Inspector General, Brigadier Philip E. Brown to the Assistant Secretary of War, November 1, 1944, box 237, entry 183, RG 107, NARA.
70. "Paul Revere Williams," in Jessie Carney Smith, ed., *Encyclopedia of African American Business*, Vol. II (Westport: Greenwood, 2018), 825–29; Karen E. Hudson, *The Will and the Way: Paul R. Williams, Architect* (New York: Rizzoli, 1994).
71. Sara A. Butler "Ground Breaking in New Deal Washington, DC: Art, Patronage, and Race at the Recorder of Deeds Building," *Winterthur Portfolio* 45, no. 4 (Winter 2011): 277–320; Edmund Barry Gaither, "The Mural Tradition," in William E. Taylor and Harriet G. Warkel, eds., *A Shared Heritage: Art by Four African Americans* (Indianapolis: Indianapolis Museum of Art, 1996). According to Gaither, Scott "remained conservative in his treatment of race" (131).
72. "Eight Murals Decorate Fort Huachuca USO Center," *Chicago Bee*, March 28, 1943, 6.
73. Letter from Col. Davison, Ninth Service Command, to Benjamin Davis, March 17, 1943, folder 10, box 3A, Davis Papers, MHI.
74. *Pittsburgh Courier*, March 24, 1943.
75. Report from Lt. Col. John Harlan to the Inspector General, October 26, 1944, folder "Fort Huachuca," box 44, entry 26f, General correspondence 1939–47, RG 159, NARA.

6 A "Plantation"?

1. Letter from Shirley Graham to Percival Prattis, May 29, 1942, folder 14, box 43, Shirley Graham Du Bois collection, Schlesinger Library.
2. Letter from Shirley Graham to W. E. B Du Bois, October 30, 1942, Du Bois Papers, University of Massachusetts Amherst Libraries, http://credo.library.umass.edu/view/full/mums312-b098-i022.
3. Letter from Shirley Graham to W. E. B. Du Bois, November 9, 1942, Du Bois Papers, http://credo.library.umass.edu/view/full/mums312-b098-i025.
4. Shirley Graham, "Negroes Are Fighting for Freedom," *Common Sense*, February 1943, quoted in Gerald Horne, *Race Woman: The Lives of Shirley Graham Du Bois* (New York: New York University Press, 2002), 94.
5. Frank Bolden, "Censored – Four Persons Held in Tucson Riot," *Pittsburgh Courier*, July 4, 1942, 11.
6. Frank Bolden, "Censored – Three Soldiers Wounded in Huachuca Gun Battle," *Pittsburgh Courier*, July 11, 1942.
7. Ethan Michaeli, *The Defender: How the Legendary Black Newspaper Changed America* (New York: Houghton Mifflin, Harcourt, 2016), Chapter 13 "Victory through Unity."

8. Mark Whitaker, *Smoketown: The Untold Story of the Other Great Black Renaissance* (New York, Simon & Schuster, 2018), 180.
9. Letter from Governor Osborn to Senator Berkeley Bunker, June 16, 1942, folder "Labor 1941–42," box 17, Governors Osborn and Garvey Collection, ASA.
10. Letter from Glendale District of Commerce to Governor Osborn, October 27, 1942, folder "Labor 1941–42," box 17, Osborn and Garvey Collection, ASA.
11. Letter from Governor Osborn to the Regional Director of War Manpower Commission, September 3, 1942, folder "Labor 1941–1942," box 17, Osborn and Garvey Collection, ASA.
12. Letter from Governor Osborn to William Smith (Phoenix), November 24, 1942, folder "Labor 1941–42," box 17, Osborn and Garvey Collection, ASA.
13. See Neil Foley, *The White Scourge: Mexicans, Blacks, and Poor Whites in Texas Cotton Culture* (Berkeley: University of California Press, 1999), Conclusion.
14. Robert F. Jefferson, *Making the Men of the 93rd: African-American Servicemen in the Years of the Great Depression and the Second World War, 1935–1947* (PhD dissertation, University of Michigan, 1995), 259.
15. Letter from Midian Bousfield to Truman Gibson, March 7, 1943, box 207, entry 188, RG 107, NARA.
16. Letter from Walter White to Governor Osborn, November 5, 1942, folder "Soldier complaints, 1942–43, 'H,'" box II B148, NAACP Papers, Library of Congress.
17. "Army Orders Troops to Aid in Picking AZ Cotton," *Bisbee Daily Review*, February 24, 1943.
18. "Order for Soldiers to Pick Cotton in AZ Recalled," *Bisbee Daily Review*, February 26, 1943; "Cotton Picking Assignment for Men in Army Is Frowned upon. Fear Huachuca Would Be Chief Victims," *Atlanta Daily World*, March 3, 1943, 1; "No Cotton Picking for 93rd. 93rd Division Won't Pick Arizona Cotton," *Chicago Defender*, March 6, 1943.
19. "The Army and Cotton Picking," *New York Amsterdam Star-News*, March 6, 1943, 10.
20. See Kenneth M. Stampp, *The Peculiar Institution: Slavery in the Ante-Bellum South* (New York: Vintage Books, 1956).
21. Jefferson, *Making the Men of the 93rd*, 224.
22. Folder 3, box 1, Papers of James Bernard Rucker, Tamiment Library and Robert F. Wagner Labor Archive, New York University.
23. Letter from an anonymous officer to Lieut.-Col. Marshall S. Carter, War Department, February 2, 1943, quoted in Bell I. Wiley, *The Training of Negro Troops* (Washington, DC: The Army Ground Forces, Historical Section, 1945),16.
24. *Military Justice Procedure, War Department Technical Manual TM 27–255* (Washington, DC: United States Government Printing Office, 1945), www.ibiblio.org/hyperwar/USA/ref/TM/TM27-255/TM27-255-3.html.
25. Anonymous letter sent from Huachuca to Walter White, April 13, 1943, folder "Soldier trouble, Fort Huachuca," box II B159, NAACP Papers, LOC.

26. Court-martial record of Leonard Holmes, 38022292, RG 153, National Archives at Saint Louis.
27. "Young Florida Soldier Is Hanged for Murder," *Pittsburgh Courier*, November 14, 1942.
28. "Fort Huachuca Matron Slain," *Arizona's Negro Journal*, June 26, 1942, 1; "Fort Huachuca Man Is Hanged," *Arizona Republic*, January 20, 1943.
29. On the racist bias of American court-martials in Europe, see Robert Lilly and J. Michael Thomson, "Executing U.S. Soldiers in England World War II: Command Influence and Sexual Racism," *The British Journal of Criminology* 37, no. 2 (Spring 1997): 262–88; Alice Kaplan, *The Interpreter* (Chicago: Chicago University Press, 2005), Chapter 7 "The Court-Martial."
30. See Peter Kolchin, *American Slavery, 1619–1877* (London: Penguin, 1995); Raymond A. and Alice H. Bauer, "Day to Day Resistance to Slavery," *Journal of Negro History* 27, no. 4 (1942): 388–419.
31. See, for instance, the undated letter Midian Bousfield wrote to Truman Gibson before the 93rd left for maneuvers, box 207, entry 188, RG 107, NARA. For Robin Kelley, these acts of resistance constitute a form of "*infra politics.*" See Robin Kelley, "'We Are Not What We Seem': Rethinking Black Working-Class Opposition in the Jim Crow South," *Journal of American History* 80, no. 1 (June 1993): 75–112.
32. Confidential memorandum from Colonel Edward Greenbaum, Ordinance Department, to Assistant Secretary of War, March 8, 1943, folder "Confidential, race, army," box 2, entry 140, RG 107, NARA.
33. On the civilian allies of black soldiers, see Thomas Guglielmo, "A Martial Freedom Movement: Black G.I.s' Political Struggles during World War II," *Journal of American History* 104, no. 4 (March 2018): 895–900.
34. On Ollie North, see folder "Soldier trouble, Fort Huachuca," box II B 159, NAACP Papers, LOC.
35. On the notion of an "afterlife of slavery," see Saidiya Hartman, *Lose Your Mother: A Journey along the Atlantic Slave Route* (New York; Farrar, Straus and Giroux, 2007).
36. Grant Reynolds, "What the Negro Soldier Thinks about the War Department," *The Crisis*, October 1944, 316–18 and 328.
37. Irma Cayton, "A First WAC," folder 4, box 1, Irma Cayton Wertz Papers, Harsch Collection, Chicago Public Library.
38. See Guglielmo, "A Martial Freedom Movement."

7 Respectable Women

1. Lucia Mae Pitts, "A Wac Speaks to a Soldier," *Negro Story*, December 1944–January 1945.
2. Frank E. Bolden, "Sight of Women Soldiers Is Inspirational for Enlisted Men," *Pittsburgh Courier*, December 12, 1942.
3. Welcoming speech of Commander Hardy, December 7, 1942, box 207, entry 188, RG 107, NARA.
4. See Leisa D. Meyer, "Creating a Women's Corps: Public Response to the WAAC/WAC and Questions of Citizenship," in Paula Nassen Poulos, ed.,

A Woman's War Too: U.S. Women in the Military in World War II (Collingdale: Diane Publishing Co., 1997), 26–46, 28.
5. Leisa D. Meyer, *Creating GI Jane: Sexuality and Power in the Women's Army Corps during World War II* (New York: Columbia University Press, 1996), 90–91.
6. Enoc P. Waters "Segregation Rules WAAC Training Camp: Race Volunteers Lag Far Behind Quota," *Chicago Defender*, January 16, 1943.
7. Confidential memorandum from Lieutenant Parker to Commander Hobby, April 13, 1943, box 49, entry 54, RG 165, NARA.
8. Brenda L. Moore, *To Serve My Country, to Serve My Race: The Story of the Only African-American WACS Stationed Overseas during World War II* (New York: New York University Press, 1997), 7–8.
9. Dovey Roundtree, quoted in Janet Sims-Wood, "Service Life in the Women's Army Corps and Afro-American Wacs," in Paula Nassen Poulos, ed., *A Woman's War Too: U.S. Women in the Military in World War II* (Collingdale: Diane Publishing Co., 1997), 128–41, 130.
10. Meyer, *Creating GI Jane*, 66–67.
11. Judy C. McKinnon, February 9, 2001, Women Veterans Historical Project, Oral History Collection.
12. WAAC release "Women's Auxiliary Corps School Enrolls 40 Negro Officer Candidates," July 20, 1942, reproduced in Morris J. MacGregor and Bernard C. Nalty, eds., *Blacks in the United States Armed Forces: Basic Documents*, Vol. V: *Black Soldiers in World War II* (Wilmington: Scholarly Resources, 1977).
13. Charity Adams Earley Oral History, quoted in Sims-Wood, "Service Life in the Women's Army Corps and Afro-American Wacs," 131.
14. See for instance "Rumored Discrimination at Ft. Des Moines," *Chicago Defender*, August 25, 1942.
15. Irma Cayton Wertz, "A First Wac," folder 4, box 1, Irma Cayton Wertz Papers, Harsch Collection, Chicago Public Library. This is the source of all the quotations below.
16. See the definition of "race men" in Horace R. Cayton and St. Clair Drake, *Black Metropolis: A Study of Negro Life in a Northern City* (Chicago: Chicago University Press, 2015 [1945]), 394–96.
17. Memorandum from Charles P. Howard to Mary McLeod Bethune, "Handling of Negro Officer Candidates," August 26, 1942, folder 291.2, box 50, entry 54, RG 165, NARA.
18. See for instance "Army's Jim Crow Policies Hurt WAACs," *PM*, December 10, 1942; Letter from Gloster B. Current to Leslie Perry, NAACP, September 29, 1943, "Reports of Discrimination at Fort Des Moines," folder 291.2, box 49, entry 54, RG 165, NARA.
19. Eileen Boris, "'You Wouldn't Want One of 'Em Dancing with Your Wife': Racialized Bodies on the Job in World War II," *American Quarterly* 50, no. 1 (March 1998): 77–108.
20. Meyer, "Creating a Women's Corps," 38.
21. "Officer Cayton, Typical Patriot, Loves Army Life," *Pittsburgh Courier*, January 2, 1943, 11.
22. Horace Cayton, *Long Old Road* (New York: Trident Press, 1965), 234–52.

23. Cayton, "A First Wac."
24. Judy C. McKinnon Oral History, Women Veterans Historical Project, The University of North Carolina at Greensboro.
25. *Pittsburgh Courier*, January 21, 1943.
26. "WAAC Chauffeur Was Beautician," *The Afro-American*, April 17, 1943; Cheryl Mullenbach, *Double Victory: How African American Women Broke Race and Gender Barriers to Help Win World War II* (Chicago: Chicago Review Press, 2013), 107.
27. Lucia M. Pitts, *The Small Fire and How It Grew: Manuscript for a Proposed Book* (University of Wisconsin-Madison Library, unpublished); Lucia M. Pitts, *One Negro WAC's Story* (Los Angeles: privately published, 1968).
28. Letter from Eleanor Roosevelt to Mrs Hobby, May 4, 1944, box 49, entry 54, RG 165, NARA.
29. Pitts, *The Small Fire and How it Grew*.
30. "3 Chicago Waacs Now 2nd Officers," *Chicago Defender*, January 10, 1943.
31. Ruth Gaddy Oral History, Women Veterans History Project, The University of North Carolina at Greensboro.
32. See Alvia J. Wardlaw, *Charles Alston* (Portland: Pomegranate, 2007), especially 40.
33. The allocation of functions in the WAC reflected the racial, class, and gender structure of the pre-war labor market far more than it did the changes taking place in the civilian sector during the war. See Meyer, *Creating GI Jane*, Introduction.
34. Paula Giddings, *When and Where I Enter . . .: The Impact of Black Women on Race and Sex in America* (New York: William Morrow and Company, 1984), 232; Census of 1940.
35. Judy C. McKinnon Oral History.
36. Karen Tucker Anderson, "Last Hired, First Fired: Black Women Workers during World War II," *Journal of American History* 69, no. 1 (June 1982): 82–97.
37. Langston Hughes, "Fort Huachuca's Wacs among Nation's Finest," *Chicago Defender*, June 3, 1944.
38. On the notion of respectability, see Evelyn Brooks Higginbotham, *Righteous Discontent: The Women's Movement in the Black Baptist Church (1880–1920)* (Cambridge, MA: Harvard University Press, 1993); Victoria W. Wolcott, *Remaking Respectability: African American Women in Interwar Detroit* (Chapel Hill: The University of North Carolina Press, 2001).
39. Cayton, "A First Wac."
40. Judy C. McKinnon Oral History.
41. This is the thesis defended by Leisa Meyer in *Creating GI Jane*.
42. Leisa D. Meyer, "Creating G.I. Jane: The Regulation of Sexuality and Sexual Behavior in the Women's Army Corps during World War II," *Feminist Studies* 18, no. 3 (Fall 1992): 581–601, 587.
43. Cayton, "A First Wac."
44. Meyer, *Creating GI Jane*, Chapter 7; Allan Bérubé, *Coming Out under Fire: The History of Gay Men and Women in World War II* (New York: Free Press, 1991), 28–35 and 58–60. On the Army's difficulty in defining lesbian acts, see

Margot Canaday, *The Straight State: Sexuality and Citizenship in Twentieth-Century America* (Princeton: Princeton University Press, 2011), 190.
45. Violet Hill Askins Gordon Collection (AFC/2001/001/00146), Veterans History Project, American Folklife Center, Library of Congress, https://memory.loc.gov/diglib/vhp/bib/loc.natlib.afc2001001.00146.
46. Henrietta Stevenson Ingram Oral History, February 3, 1999, Women Veterans Historical Project, Oral History Collection.
47. Court-martial record of Ballie Wall, 01289513, RG 153, National Archives at Saint Louis.

8 An Experiment in Integration

1. Letter from Bousfield to Gibson, June 1942, box 207, entry 188, RG 107, NARA.
2. Letter from Bousfield to Colonel Durward Hall, SGO, September 19, 1942, box 207, entry 188, RG 107, NARA.
3. Vanessa Northington Gamble, *Making a Place for Ourselves: The Black Hospital Movement (1920–1945)* (Oxford: Oxford University Press, 1995), 45; Karen Kruse Thomas, *Deluxe Jim Crow: Civil Rights and American Health Policy (1935–1954)* (Athens, GA: University of Georgia Press, 2011), 31–35. See also Edward H. Beardsley, *History of Neglect: Health Care for Southern Blacks and Mill Workers in the 20th Century South* (Knoxville: University of Tennessee Press, 1987). On the high rate of rejection of blacks by draft boards, see George Q. Flynn, "American Medicine and Selective Service in World War II," *Journal of the History of Medicine and Allied Sciences* 42, no. 3 (July 1987): 305–26, 314–15.
4. Inspection data prepared by Division Surgeon HQ for Inspector General, July 1942, folder 8, box 17, Davis Papers, MHI.
5. Letter from Earl Renfroe to Truman K. Gibson, January 9, 1944, box 207, entry 188, RG 107, NARA.
6. Interview with Madine Davis Lane by Maggi Morehouse, 1998, box 3, African American Soldiers in World War II Collection, LoC.
7. Confidential memorandum of Bousfield, undated (probably from early 1943), box 207, entry 188, RG 107, NARA.
8. "List of Patients with Severe and Serious Illnesses," Registrar's Office (Station Hospital No. 1), March 31, 1943, box 207, entry 188, RG 107, NARA.
9. Court-martial record of Andrew L. Farris, RG 153, National Archives at Saint Louis.
10. Letter from Bousfield to W. E. B. Du Bois, October 28, 1942, Du Bois Papers, Amherst, http://credo.library.umass.edu/view/full/mums312-b097-i469.
11. Letter from Bousfield to Colonel Durward Hall, SGO, September 19, 1942, box 207, entry 188, RG 107, NARA.
12. Letter from Bousfield to Gibson, October 13, 1942, box 207, entry 188, RG 107, NARA; Letter from Bousfield to Brigadier General B. O. Davis, August 7, 1942, folder 5B, box 3A, Davis Papers, MHI.

13. Enoc Waters, "*Who's Who* of Negro Medicine Makes Fort Huachuca Hospital 'Best Anywhere,'" *Chicago Defender*, December 5, 1942.
14. "Statement of Patient Strength," Registrar's Office (Station Hospital No. 1), March 6, 1945, box 207, entry 188, RG 107, NARA.
15. Letter from Bousfield to Colonel Hall, September 19, 1942, box 207, entry 188, RG 107, NARA.
16. Charles S. Johnson, *Patterns of Negro Segregation* (New York: Harper & Brothers, 1943), 51–55.
17. Letter from Roscoe Giles to Louis T. Wright, May 16, 1944; Letter from "Bob" to Doctor Louis T. Wright, May 21, 1944, folder "Staff, W. White, Fort Huachuca Trip," box A 606, Group II, NAACP Papers, LOC.
18. Unsigned letter from Roscoe Giles to Louis T. Wright, May 16, 1944, folder "Staff, W. White, Fort Huachuca Trip," box A 606, Group II, NAACP Papers, LoC.
19. Letter from Bousfield to Gibson, November 1944, box 207, entry 188, RG 107, NARA.
20. Letter from Bousfield to Gibson, July 20, 1942, box 207, entry 188, RG 107, NARA.
21. See, for instance, Letter from Bousfield to Gibson, November 4, 1942; Letter from Bousfield to Colonel Hall, March 15, 1943; Letter from Bousfield to Gibson, March 31, 1943, box 207, entry 188, RG 107, NARA.
22. Letter from Roscoe Giles to Louie (Louis Wright), June 3, 1944, folder "Staff, W. White, Fort Huachuca Trip," box A 606, Group II, NAACP Papers, LoC.
23. Letter from Robert Patterson to Mabel Staupers, August 7, 1944, folder "Negroes," box 447, entry 144, RG 207, NARA.
24. Letter from Mabel Staupers to Robert Patterson, July 19, 1944, folder "Nurses," box 225, entry 188, RG 107, NARA.
25. Letter from Bousfield to Truman K. Gibson, July 20, 1944, box 207, entry 188, RG 107, NARA.
26. Alexis Clark, *Enemies in Love: A German POW, a Black Nurse, and an Unlikely Romance* (New York: New Press, 2018).
27. Richard R. Taylor, ed., *Medical Training in World War II* (Washington, DC: Office of the Surgeon General, 1974), 132; Report of the Deputy Chief of Staff "Basic Training School for Negro Trained Nurses," August 11, 1944, box 443, decimal file 291.2, War Department General Staff G-1, entry 13, RG 165, NARA.
28. Letter from Bousfield to Col. Franklin McLean, November 6, 1944, box 207, entry 188, RG 107, NARA.
29. Report from Lt.-Col. John Harlan to the Inspector General, October 26, 1944, folder "Fort Huachuca," box 44, entry 26f General correspondence 1939–47, RG 159; Memorandum from the Deputy Inspector General, Brigadier Philip E. Brown, to the Assistant Secretary of War, November 1, 1944, box 237, entry 183, RG 107, NARA.
30. Letter from Bousfield to Col. Franklin McLean, November 6, 1944, box 207, entry 188, RG 107, NARA.
31. Memorandum from Colonel Durward Hall, June 6, 1945, folder 330–39 "Fort Huachuca, 1943–1944," box 239, entry 31, RG 112, NARA.

32. Letter from Bousfield to General Lull, Deputy Surgeon General, August 16, 1945, box 207, entry 188, RG 107, NARA.
33. Letter from Bousfield to Adjutant General, August 9, 1945; Letter from Bousfield to Truman Gibson, August 14, 1945, box 207, entry 188, RG 107, NARA.
34. Letter from Bousfield to the Deputy Surgeon General, August 9, 1945; Letter from Bousfield to Gibson, August 14, 1945, box 207, entry 188, RG 107, NARA.
35. Letter from Bousfield to General Lull, Deputy Surgeon General, August 16, 1945, folder 323–29, box 1469, entry 31, RG 107, NARA.
36. Letter from Norman Kirk to Leslie Perry, May 26, 1944, folder "US Army General 1944," box A645, NAACP Papers, LoC.

9   The First Departure

1. "Claim 93rd Division a Token Outfit," *Cleveland Call & Post*, March 20, 1943.
2. Todd J. Moye, *Freedom Flyers: The Tuskegee Airmen of World War II* (New York: Oxford University Press, 2010), 91 and 97.
3. Memorandum from William Hastie to Assistant Secretary of War McCloy, January 30, 1943, quoted in Richard Dalfiume, *Desegregation of the U.S. Armed Forces: Fighting on Two Fronts (1939–1953)* (Columbia: University of Missouri Press, 1969), 85.
4. Dalfiume, *Desegregation of the U.S. Armed Forces*, 92.
5. On Henry Luce, see, in particular, Alan Brinkley, *The Publisher: Henry Luce and His American Century* (New York: Knopf, 2010), Chapters IX and X.
6. All of these photographs, now in the possession of the Getty Foundation, are available online at Google Arts Life, https://artsandculture.google.com/search?q=huachuca. None of the photographs is captioned.
7. Andrew Mendelson and C. Zoe Smith, "Part of the Team: *Life* Photographers and Their Symbiotic Relationship with the Military during World War II," *American Journalism* 12, no. 3 (Summer 1995): 276–89.
8. Memorandum from Lieutenant Colonel Erwin Jones to Brigadier General Davis, April 24, 1943, box 3A, folder 11, Davis Papers, MHI.
9. Confidential memorandum from Colonel Edward Greenbaum to Assistant Secretary of War, March 8, 1943, folder "Confidential, Race, Army," box 2, entry 140, RG 107, NARA.
10. Letter from Lieutenant General Courtney Hodges to Lesley J. McNair, April 8, 1943, file 322, AGF, RG 337, NARA, quoted in Robert Franklin Jefferson, *Making the Men of the 93rd: African-American Servicemen in the Years of the Great Depression and the Second World War (1935–1947)* (PhD dissertation, University of Michigan, 1995), 196.
11. Memorandum from Virgil Peterson to the Deputy Chief of Staff, March 2, 1943, quoted in Memorandum from Major General George Grunert, Chief of Administrative Service, to the Director, April 21, 1943, box 2, entry 390, RG 160, NARA.

12. Undated handwritten letter from Midian Bousfield to Truman Gibson, box 207, entry 188, RG 107, NARA.
13. On segregation in Louisiana, see Jerry Purvis Sanson, *Louisiana during World War II: Politics and Society, 1939–1945* (Baton Rouge: Louisiana State University Press, 1999), Chapter 10.
14. Memorandum from Lieutenant Colonel Erwin Jones to Brigadier General Davis, April 24, 1943, box 3A, folder 11, Davis Papers, MHI.
15. RW, "Maneuvers Show 93rd Is Ready," *The Crisis*, June 1943, 170–71.
16. "Negro Division. It Prepares to Go Overseas," *Life Magazine*, August 9, 1943, 37–40.
17. Office of Censorship, *Code of Wartime Practices for the American Press* (Washington, DC: Government Printing Office, 1942); George H. Roeder, *The Censored War: American Visual Experience during World War II* (New Haven: Yale University Press, 1993), 46.
18. Marvin E. Fletcher, *America's First Black General: Benjamin O. Davis, Sr. (1880–1970)* (Lawrence: University of Kansas Press, 1989), 101.
19. Dalfiume, *Desegregation of the U.S. Armed Forces*, 93.
20. Samuel A. Stouffer, Edward A. Suchman, Leland C. DeVinney, Shirley A. Star, and Robin M. Williams, Jr., *The American Soldier: Adjustment during Army Life* (Princeton: Princeton University Press, 1949), 507–09, 521, 524–25.
21. Douglas Walter Bristol, Jr., "Terror, Anger, and Patriotism: Understanding the Resistance of Black Soldiers during World War II," in Douglas Walter Bristol, Jr., and Heather Marie Stur, eds., *Integrating the US Military: Race, Gender, and Sexual Orientation since World War II* (Baltimore: Johns Hopkins University Press, 2017), 10–35, 12.
22. Nelson Peery, *Black Fire: The Making of an American Revolutionary* (New York: The New Press, 1995), 152.
23. Letter from Benjamin Davis to Lieutenant Colonel Midian Bousfield, January 28, 1944, folder 4, box 4, Davis Papers, MHI.

10 A Southern Ambiance

1. Letter from Midian Bousfield to Truman Gibson, May 22, 1943, box 207, entry 188, RG 107, NARA.
2. On Almond, see Michael E. Lynch, *Edward M. Almond and the US Army: From the 92nd Infantry Division to the X Corps* (Lexington: University Press of Kentucky, 2019).
3. Edward Almond, Oral History Interview, Part II, 79, MHI, quoted in Lynch, *Edward M. Almond and the US Army*, 109.
4. Lynch, *Edward M. Almond and the US Army*, 111.
5. Ulysses Lee, *The Employment of Negro Troops* (Washington, DC: Center of Military History, 1994 [1963]), 5, 8–13.
6. Robert W. Kesting, "Conspiracy to Discredit the Black Buffaloes: The 92nd Infantry Division in World War II," *The Journal of Negro History* 72, no. 1–2 (Winter–Spring 1987): 1–19, 2–3.

7. A. William Perry Collection (AFC/2001/001/51117), Veterans History Project, American Folklife Center, Library of Congress.
8. HQ, 92nd ID Staff Memorandum, Subject: Resume of Racial Laws of Alabama, October 30, 1942, box 13695A, RG 407, NARA, quoted in Lynch, *Edward M. Almond and the US Army*, 128.
9. Lee, *The Employment of Negro Troops*, 489.
10. Ibid., 186.
11. Memorandum from General Joseph T. McNarney, Deputy Chief of Staff, to Commanding General, Services of Supply, Subject: Professional qualities of officers assigned to Negro units, August 10, 1942, entry 94, RG 407, NARA, quoted in Dale E. Wilson, "Recipe for Failure: Major General Edward M. Almond and Preparation of the U.S. 92d Infantry Division for Combat in World War II," *Journal of Military History* 56, no. 3 (July 1992): 473–88, 477.
12. Lynch, *Edward M. Almond and the US Army*, 130–33; Oral History Interview – Part III (1943–1945), March 27, 1975, p. 1, box 1, folder 4, Edward M. Almond Papers, MHI.
13. Lee, *The Employment of Negro Troops*, 249.
14. Ibid., 242–45.
15. G-1 Operations report, box 11288, entry 427, RG 407, NARA.
16. Lynch, *Edward M. Almond and the US Army*, 138.
17. Ibid., 253–55.
18. On soldiers' reluctance to serve, see Douglas Walter Bristol, Jr., "Terror, Anger, and Patriotism: Understanding the Resistance of Black Soldiers during World War II," in Douglas Walter Bristol, Jr., and Heather Marie Stur, eds., *Integrating the U.S. Military: Race, Gender, and Sexual Orientation since World War II* (Baltimore: Johns Hopkins University Press, 2017), 10–35, 12ff.
19. Folder "Press Clippings – 92nd Div," box 24A, Almond Papers, MHI.
20. Lynch, *Edward M. Almond and the US Army*, 68.
21. Memorandum from Brigadier General Benjamin Davis to the attention of the Inspector General, Subject: Special Inspection of Colored Troops at Fort McClellan, February 23, 1943, box 17, Davis Papers, MHI, quoted in Lynch, *Edward M. Almond and the US Army*, 146.
22. Almond training notes, 5, box 41, Almond Papers, MHI, quoted in Lynch, *Edward M. Almond and the US Army*, 144.
23. Lee, *The Employment of Negro Troops*, 308–09.
24. Handwritten letter from Bousfield to Gibson, May 9, 1943, and letter from Chaplain Nelson to Truman Gibson, May 22, 1943, box 207, entry 188, RG 107, NARA. All the incidents mentioned in the rest of this paragraph are cited by General Davis in his report to the Inspector General, "Survey Relative to Conditions Affecting Racial Attitudes at Fort Huachuca," August 5, 1943, folder 8, box 18, Davis Papers, MHI.
25. Charles S. Johnson, *Patterns of Negro Segregation* (New York: Harper & Brothers, 1943), 63–65.
26. Ibid., 209.
27. Testimony of William Perry, quoted in Maggi Morehouse, *Black Citizen Soldiers* (Berkeley: University of California Press, 2001), 135.

28. *Louisiana Weekly*, September 11, 1943, 1.
29. Letter from Chaplain Nelson to Truman Gibson, May 22, 1943, box 207, entry 188, RG 107, NARA; Memorandum from Col. Edwin Hardy to Brigadier General Benjamin Davis, July 15, 1943, folder 7, box 18, Davis Papers, MHI.
30. Colonel Reuben L. Horner, III Oral History by C. Strickland, 1991, http://parentseyes.arizona.edu/esteban/bios_military_horner.html.
31. Letter from Midian Bousfield to Truman Gibson, May 22, 1943, box 207, entry 188, RG 107, NARA.
32. Letter from Grant Reynolds to Truman Gibson, August 23, 1943, box 207, entry 188, RG 107, NARA; Christine Knauer, *Let Us Fight as Free Men: Black Soldiers and Civil Rights* (Philadelphia: University of Pennsylvania Press, 2014), 2–3.
33. Major Bell I. Wiley, *The Training of Negro Troops* (Washington, DC: The Army Ground Forces, Historical Section, 1945), 9.
34. Letter from Midian Bousfield to Truman Gibson, May 27, 1943, box 207, entry 188, RG 107, NARA.
35. Letter from Chaplain Nelson to Truman Gibson, May 22, 1943, box 207, entry 188, RG 107, NARA.
36. Letter from Midian Bousfield to Truman Gibson, May 22, 1943, box 207, entry 188, RG 107, NARA.
37. Letters from Midian Bousfield to Truman Gibson, May 22, 1943 and May 1, 1943, box 207, entry 188, RG 107, NARA.
38. Letter from Gibson to Davis, June 3, 1943, box 207, entry 188, RG 107, NARA.
39. Letters from Colonel Davison, Chief of Staff, HQ Ninth Service Command, Fort Douglas, to General Benjamin Davis, May 23, 1943 and June 9, 1943, folder 11A, box 3, Davis Papers, MHI.
40. See Harvard Sitkoff, "The Detroit Race Riots of 1943," *Michigan History* 53 (Fall 1969): 183–206; Howard W. Odum, *Race and Rumors of Race: Challenge to Urban Crisis* (Chapel Hill: University of North Carolina Press, 1943).
41. Lee, *The Employment of Negro Troops*, 366; Bristol, "Terror, Anger, and Patriotism," 19ff.
42. Daniel Kryder, *Divided Arsenal: Race and the American State during World War II* (Cambridge: Cambridge University Press, 2000), 168–207.
43. Address, Col. Pierre V. Kieffer, IGD, Annual Inspection of Service Commands, Proceedings, ASF Conference of Commanding Generals, Service Commands, July 22, 1943 to July 24, 1943, Chicago, Illinois, 17–18, quoted in Lee, *The Employment of Negro Troops*, 377.
44. Handwritten letter from Bousfield to Gibson, June 1, 1943, box 207, entry 188, RG 107, NARA.
45. See "Over 600 Huachuca Officers Attend Barbecue at Post," *Bisbee Daily Review*, June 1, 1943.
46. For Bousfield's account of the afternoon, see his letter to Truman Gibson, June 1, 1943, box 207, entry 188, RG 107, NARA.
47. Letter from Benjamin Davis to Sadie Davis, July 16, 1943, folder 20, box 8, Davis Papers, MHI.

48. Handwritten letter from Bousfield to Gibson, July 19, 1943, box 207, entry 188, RG 107, NARA.
49. "Survey Relative to Conditions Affecting Racial Attitudes at Fort Huachuca," August 5, 1943, decimal file 291.1, box 37, entry 183, General Correspondence of John McCloy, RG 107, NARA.
50. Handwritten letter from Bousfield to Gibson, July 19, 1943, box 207, entry 188, RG 107, NARA.
51. Memorandum from Col. Edwin Hardy to Brigadier General Benjamin Davis, July 15, 1943, folder 7, box 18, Davis Papers, MHI.
52. Letter from Benjamin Davis to Sadie Davis, July 20, 1943, folder 20, box 8, Davis Papers, MHI, quoted in Wilson, "Recipe for Failure," 484.
53. Memorandum from Major General Almond, "Study of Promotion of Colored Officers of 92nd Div," July 8, 1943, folder 7, box 18, Davis Papers, MHI.
54. Third draft of the report to the Inspector General, August 5, 1943, folder 8B, box 18, Davis Papers, MHI.
55. Ibid.
56. IG 333.1-Ft. Huachuca, Draft report from the Inspector General, re: special inspection of colored troops at Fort Huachuca, August 2, 1943, box 207, entry 188, RG 107, NARA.
57. "Morale at Low Ebb in 92nd Division," box 207, entry 188, RG 107, NARA.
58. Letter from Major General J. A. Julio to Hon. Louis E. Miller, September 9, 1943, box 207, entry 188, RG 107, NARA.
59. "Survey Relative to Conditions Affecting Racial Attitudes at Fort Huachuca," August 5, 1943, folder 8, box 18, Davis Papers, MHI.
60. Wiley, *The Training of Negro Troops*, 26.
61. Sam Lacy, "Huachuca Get House Cleanings, Now Model Camp, Scribe Finds," *Chicago Defender*, October 30, 1943.
62. Article in the *Louisiana Weekly*, September 11, 1943, 1, cited by Jack Leckhart in his letter to Col. F. V. Fitzgerald, Chief of the War Intelligence Division, Bureau of Public Relations, September 25, 1943, box 553, RG 216, NARA.
63. "Counter-intelligence Summary," November 1943, Eleventh Naval District, Van Deman Collection, Senate Internal Security Subcommittee Papers, box 32, RG 46, NARA, quoted in Gerald Horne, *Race Woman: The Lives of Shirley Graham Du Bois* (New York: New York University Press, 2002), 93.
64. Letter from anonymous NCO to the editor of the *Atlanta Daily World*, November 23, 1943, reproduced in Philipp McGuire, *Taps for a Jim Crow Army: Letters from Black Soldiers in World War II* (Santa Barbara: Clio Books, 1983), 45–46.
65. Letter from James Rucker to Helen Mulnik, November 18, 1943, folder 3, box 1, James Bernard Rucker Papers, Tamiment Library, New York University.
66. Sam Lacy, "Huachuca Get House Cleanings, Now Model Camp, Scribe Finds," *Chicago Defender*, October 30, 1943.
67. Folder "The Black Soldier," box 132, Almond Papers, MHI.

68. A. William Perry Collection (AFC/2001/001/51117), Veterans History Project, American Folklife Center, Library of Congress.
69. Lee, *The Employment of Negro Troops*, 378.

11 The Mecca of Entertainment?

1. Letter from James Rucker to his wife, November 6, 1943, folder 3, box 1, James Bernard Rucker Papers, Tamiment Library, New York University.
2. "Soldiers Are Treated Like Bad Boys," *Chicago Defender*, February 21, 1942, 5; Ollie Stewart "Here's Stewart's Riot Prediction," *Baltimore Afro-American*, January 21, 1942, 5, cited in Paul Alkebulan, *The African American Press in World War II: Toward Victory at Home and Abroad* (Lanham: Lexington Books, 2014), 57.
3. On boredom in the Army and the opposition between empty time and full time, see Thomas A. Bruscino, *A Nation Forged in War: How World War II Taught Americans to Get Along* (Knoxville: University of Tennessee Press, 2010), Chapter 4 "Hours of Boredom," 95–125; Bård Maeland and Paul Otto Brunstad, *Enduring Military Boredom: From 1750 to the Present* (London: Palgrave Macmillan, 2009), 24–31 and 175–80.
4. B. Cosulich, "Recreation Is Training Aid at Fort Huachuca," *Arizona Daily Star*, December 16, 1943, 1 and 12.
5. "In the Camps," *Chicago Defender*, December 8, 1943.
6. See, in particular, Victoria W. Wolcott, *Race, Riots, and Roller-Coasters: The Struggle over Segregated Recreation in America* (Philadelphia: University of Pennsylvania Press, 2012).
7. On the negative impact of New Deal legislation on African Americans, see Ira Katznelson, *When Affirmative Action Was White: An Untold History of Racial Inequality in Twentieth-Century America* (New York: Norton, 2005). On New Deal cultural policy, see Lauren Rebecca Sklaroff, *Black Culture and the New Deal: The Quest for Civil Rights in the Roosevelt Era* (Chapel Hill: University of North Carolina Press, 2009), Introduction.
8. Sklaroff, *Black Culture and the New Deal*, 159.
9. "Dinah Shore Likes Huachuca Soldiers," *Pittsburgh Courier*, February 13, 1943.
10. Adam D. Smith, Susan I. Enscore, and Samuel L. Hunter, *Analysis of the Mountain View Officers' Club: Fort Huachuca, Arizona* (Champaign: US Corps of Engineers, Engineer Research and Development Center, 2012), 44–48.
11. "Lovely Lena Horne Is Guest at Fort Huachuca Baseball Game," *Apache Sentinel*, August 21, 1943.
12. Sklaroff, *Black Culture and the New Deal*, 220–21.
13. Cheryl Mullenbach, *Double Victory: How African American Women Broke Race and Gender Barriers to Help Win World War II* (Chicago: Chicago Review Press, 2013), 102–03.
14. "Sgt. Barrow (Joe Louis) Makes Tour of Huachuca," *Chicago Defender*, June 5, 1943.

15. Gerald Early, "Joe Louis, l'homme de l'entre-deux," in Daniel Soutif, ed., *"The Color Line." Les Artistes africains-américains et la ségrégation (1865–2016)* (Paris: Flammarion, 2016), 134–41.
16. Quoted in Lauren Rebecca Sklaroff, "Constructing G.I. Joe Louis: Cultural Solutions to the 'Negro Problem' during World War II," *Journal of American History* 89, no. 3 (2002): 958–83, 973.
17. George H. Roeder, *The Censored War: American Visual Experience during World War II* (New Haven: Yale University Press, 1993), 46.
18. Sklaroff, "Constructing G.I. Joe Louis."
19. See Donald J. Mrozek, "The Habit of Victory: The American Military and the Culture of Manliness," in J. A. Mangan, ed., *Manliness and Morality: Middle-Class Masculinity in Britain and America, 1800–1940* (Manchester: Manchester University Press, 1987), 220ff.
20. See Patrick B. Miller, "The Anatomy of Scientific Racism: Racialist Responses to Black Athletic Achievement," in Patrick B. Miller and David K. Wiggins, eds., *Sports and the Color Line: Black Athletes and Race in Twentieth-Century America* (New York: Routledge, 2004), 353–404; Nicolas Martin-Breteau, *Frontline Bodies: Sports and Black Struggles for Justice since the Late Nineteenth Century* (Baltimore: Johns Hopkins University Press, 2024).
21. On the growing role of the Special Services in the Army, see James J. Cooke, *American Girls, Beer, and Glenn Miller: GI Morale in World War II* (Columbia: University of Missouri Press, 2012).
22. Letter from Col. E. M. Yon, commander of the 25th Regiment, to General Osborn, July 29, 1942, folder 5B, box 3A, Davis Papers, MHI.
23. "Major Charles J. Blackwood Special Service Chief at Huachuca," *California Eagle*, February 17, 1943.
24. "Theatrical Personalities Abound at Fort Huachuca," *New Journal and Guide*, August 7, 1943; Henry Louis Gates Jr. and Evelyn Brooks Higginbotham, eds., *Harlem Renaissance Lives from the African American National Biography* (Oxford: Oxford University Press, 2016), 179–80.
25. Letter from Shirley Graham to Reverend J. Raymond Henderson, September 7, 1941, folder 14, box 43, Shirley Graham Du Bois collection, Schlesinger Library, Harvard University.
26. Alfred E. Cornebise, "American Armed Forces Newspapers in World War II," *American Journalism* 12, no. 3 (Summer 1995), 213–24, 214.
27. Annegret Fauser, *Sounds of War: Music in the United States during World War II* (Oxford: Oxford University Press, 2013), 106.
28. Rudi Blesh, *They All Played Ragtime: The True Story of an American Music* (Oakhurst: Nelson Press, 2008), 155–59.
29. *The Afro-American*, October 23, 1943.
30. Pauline Peretz, "Harlem, capitale du 'tap dance' dans l'entre-deux-guerres," *Africultures* 28 (November 2007): 236–39.
31. Bernice Cosulich, "Recreation Is Training Aid at Fort Huachuca," *Arizona Daily Star*, December 16, 1943.
32. Letter from Col. Hardy to Major General Osborn, September 1, 1944, box 207, entry 188, RG 107, NARA.

33. On the Harlem Renaissance, see, in particular, Ann Douglas, *Terrible Honesty: Mongrel Manhattan in the 1920s* (New York: Farrar, Straus, and Giroux, 1996); Nathan Irvin Huggins, *Harlem Renaissance* (Oxford: Oxford University Press, 2007).
34. Celeste-Marie Bernier, *Characters of Blood: Black Heroism in the Transatlantic Imagination* (Charlottesville: University of Virginia Press, 2012), Chapter 5 "'A Work of Art': Frederick Douglass's 'Living Parchments' and 'Chattel Records,'" 251–98.
35. Robert Bone and Richard A. Courage, *The Muse in Bronzeville: African American Creative Expression in Chicago, 1932–1950* (New Brunswick: Rutgers University Press, 2011), Chapter 7 "The Documentary Eye," 139–60, 149–51.
36. *Apache Sentinel*, August 25, 1944.
37. Quoted in *Apache Sentinel*, August 25, 1944.
38. Scottsdale Center for the Arts, *Lew Davis: The Negro in America's Wars and Other Major Paintings* (Scottsdale: Scottsdale Center for the Arts, 1990), 5–9.
39. Confidential letter from Colonel Hardy to the General Commander of the Ninth Service Command, March 15, 1945, decimal file 291.2, box 87, entry 26e, RG 159, NARA.
40. Saidiya V. Hartman, *Scenes of Subjection: Terror, Slavery, and Self-Making in Nineteenth-Century America* (Oxford: Oxford University Press, 1997), 42–47.
41. Barbara Brooks Tomblin, *GI Nightingales: The Army Nurse Corps in World War II* (Lexington: University Press of Kentucky, 1996), 194.
42. Grant Reynolds, "What the Negro Soldier Thinks about the War Department," *The Crisis*, October 1944, 316–18 and 328; Christine Knauer, *Let Us Fight as Free Men: Black Soldiers and Civil Rights* (Philadelphia: University of Pennsylvania Press, 2014), 2–3.

12 Ready for Combat

1. Experimental Film Study, "Negro in World War II" S-75, Research Division, Surveys on Troop Attitudes 1942–June 1945, box 992, entry 93, RG 330, NARA.
2. Thomas Cripps and David Culbert, "*The Negro Soldier* (1944): Film Propaganda in Black and White," *American Quarterly* 31, no. 5 (Winter 1979): 616–40; Lauren Rebecca Sklaroff, *Black Culture and the New Deal: The Quest for Civil Rights in the Roosevelt Era* (Chapel Hill: University of North Carolina Press, 2009), Chapter 6 "Projecting Unity."
3. Letter from General Almond to Lieutenant General C. H. Hodges, September 7, 1943, Rcds AGO, 40–48, RG 407, NARA, cited in Robert W. Kesting, "Conspiracy to Discredit the Black Buffaloes: The 92nd Infantry Division in World War II," *Journal of Negro History* 72, no. 1/2 (Winter–Spring 1987): 1–19, 6.
4. Folder "The Black Soldier," box 132, Almond Papers, MHI.
5. "Heavy Training Program for Huachuca Troops Is Outlined," *Arizona Daily Star*, December 5, 1943.
6. *Bisbee Daily Review*, November 21, 1943.

7. See, for example, the testimony of Captain Hondon B. Hargrove, quoted in Mary Penick Motley, ed., *The Invisible Soldier: The Experience of the Black Soldier, World War II* (Detroit: Wayne University Press, 1975), 322.
8. Letter from James Rucker to his wife, November 13, 1943, folder 3, box 1, Rucker Papers, Tamiment Library and Robert F. Wagner Labor Archive, NYU.
9. War Department Policy Letter, AG 210.31, "Policy on Promotion and Assignment of Negro Officer Personnel," January 17, 1944, box 13695A, RG 407, NARA, cited in Michael E. Lynch, *Edward M. Almond and the US Army: From the 92nd Infantry Division to the X Corps* (Lexington: University Press of Kentucky, 2019), 157.
10. Testimony of Lieutenant Wade McCress Jr, 365th Infantry Regiment, quoted in Motley, *The Invisible Soldier*, 294.
11. Memorandum from Lieut.-Gen. Osborn to Brig.-Gen. Benjamin Davis relative to the promotion of black officers, April 18, 1944, folder 7, box 18, Davis Papers, MHI.
12. Anonymous letter to Walter White, January 3, 1944, folder "Soldier Complaints 1943–45, A," box II B148, NAACP Papers, LoC.
13. Letter from Russel H. Dawson to Truman Gibson, June 1, 1944, box 207, entry 188, RG 107, NARA.
14. Letter from Edward Mayfield to Truman Gibson, October 21, 1943, box 207, entry 188, RG 107, NARA.
15. Letter from Lieutenant Castine Davis to Office of the Commanding General, Ninth Service Command, March 23, 1944, box 207, entry 188, RG 107, NARA.
16. Report from Carolyn Davenport Moore to Walter White, June 23, 1944, folder "Staff. W. White Fort Huachuca Trip," Group II, box A 606, NAACP Papers, LoC.
17. Letter from Robert Elkins to the Inspector General, May 1, 1944, "Complaint of Wrong AW 121," folder "Staff. W. White Fort Huachuca Trip," group II, box A 606, NAACP Papers, LoC.
18. Court-martial record of Robert Elkins, 01107403, RG 153, NARA Saint Louis.
19. Court-martial record of Andrew L. Farris, 01171997, RG 153, NARA, Saint Louis. See *A Manual for Courts-Martial, 1928, Corrected to April 20, 1943*, Chapter XXVI "Punitive Articles": www.ibiblio.org/hyperwar/USA/ref/MCM/MCM-26.html.
20. "Command of Negro Troops," War Department Pamphlet 20-6, February 29, 1944.
21. See Hélène Solot, *La rencontre. Les social scientists et les soldats américains, 1941–1953* (PhD dissertation, École des hautes études en sciences sociales, 2022).
22. For an example of analysis of the weaknesses of black soldiers and of the qualities required to command them, see confidential EJM G-1 memorandum "Removal of Unqualified Commissioned Personnel," folder "History, 92nd Inf Div," box 11281, entry 427, RG 407, NARA.

23. Memorandum from Assistant Secretary McCloy to the Secretary of War, March 2, 1944, cited in Richard Dalfiume, *Desegregation of the U.S. Armed Forces: Fighting on Two Fronts, 1939–1953* (Columbia: University of Missouri Press, 1969), 95–96.
24. Ulysses Lee, *The Employment of Negro Troops* (Washington, DC: Center of Military History, 1994 [1963]), 484; Truman Gibson, *Knocking Down Barriers: My Fight for Black America* (Evanston: Northwestern University Press, 2005), 163.
25. Quoted in Lee, *The Employment of Negro Troops*, 494.
26. A. William Perry Collection (AFC/2001/001/51117), Veterans History Project, American Folklife Center, Library of Congress.
27. Lee, *The Employment of Negro Troops*, 341–42.
28. On the "campaign for non segregation," see Thomas Guglielmo, "A Martial Freedom Movement: Black G.I.s' Political Struggles during World War II," *Journal of American History* 104, no. 4 (March 2018): 879–903, 890–91.
29. "Mess Hall Jim Crow Stirs Huachuca," *The Afro-American*, July 8, 1944.
30. Guglielmo, "A Martial Freedom Movement," 890.
31. "Why Did Chaplain Leave Huachuca?," *The Afro-American*, July 22, 1944.
32. Report from Carolyn Davenport Moore to Walter White, June 23, 1944, folder "Staff. W. White Fort Huachuca Trip," group II, box A 606, NAACP Papers, LoC; Bell I. Wiley, *The Training of Negro Troops* (Washington, DC: The Army Ground Forces, Historical Section, 1945), 15.
33. Mauricio Mazon, *The Zoot-Suit Riots: The Psychology of Symbolic Annihilation* (Austin: University of Texas Press, 1984); Stuart Cosgrove, "The Zoot-Suit and Style Warfare," *History Workshop* 18, no. 1 (Fall 1984): 77–91, 78.
34. Report from Carolyn Davenport Moore to Walter White, June 23, 1944, folder "Staff. W. White Fort Huachuca Trip," group II, box A 606, NAACP Papers, LoC.
35. Testimony of Sergeant Richard Carter, quoted in Motley, *The Invisible Soldier*, 294.
36. "Situation at Fort Huachuca as Reported to NAACP," May 27, 1944; Letters from Robert Elkins and Andrew Harris to the Inspector General, written from the Fort Huachuca stockade, May 1, 1944, "Complaint of Wrong AW 121," folder "Staff W. White Fort Huachuca Trip," group II, box A 606, NAACP Papers, Library of Congress.
37. Court-martial record of Ballie Wall Holmes, 1289513, RG 153, National Archives at Saint Louis.
38. Memorandum from the Provost-Marshal's Office to General Davis, April 18, 1944, folder 7, box 18, Davis Papers, MHI.
39. General Benjamin Davis's notes on his inspection at Fort Huachuca, April 15–21, 1944, folder 7, box 18, Davis Papers, MHI.
40. Letter from Benjamin Davis to General Almond, April 24, 1944, folder 3B, box 4, Davis Papers, MHI.
41. Memorandum from Benjamin Davis to the Inspector General on the inspection of black troops at Fort Huachuca, May 13, 1944; Note from Benjamin Davis to the Inspector General, May 20, 1944, folder 7, box 18, Davis Papers, MHI.

42. Letter from James Rucker to his wife, May 2, 1944, folder 4, box 1, Rucker Papers, Tamiment Library and Robert F. Wagner Labor Archive, NYU.
43. Memorandum of July 6, 1944 dictated by General McNair before his departure for the European theater, cited in Lee, *The Employment of Negro Troops*, 496.
44. Report from Carolyn Davenport Moore to Walter White, June 23, 1944, folder "Staff. W. White Fort Huachuca Trip," group II, box A 606, NAACP Papers, LoC.
45. Charge sheet, Fort Huachuca, June 5, 1944, folder "Soldier Trouble, Fort Huachuca, June 1944," box B159, NAACP Papers, LoC.
46. Report from Carolyn Davenport Moore to Walter White, June 23, 1944, folder "Staff. W. White Fort Huachuca Trip," group II, box A 606, NAACP Papers, LoC.
47. Testimony of Lieutenant Wade McCress Jr, 365th Infantry Regiment, quoted in Motley, *The Invisible Soldier*, 294.
48. Memorandum from Under Secretary of War Patterson to the Chief of Staff, July 4, 1944, re inspection trip to four divisions in the West, OPD Exec Files, cited in Lee, *The Employment of Negro Troops*, 496.
49. Secret memorandum from Colonel N. P. Morrow to the Commander General of the Army Ground Forces, August 14, 1944, "Report on a Visit to Fort Huachuca," folder "Inspection Reports to the Chief of Staff, August 1944," box 509, entry 55 (NM55), RG 337, NARA.
50. George M. Fredrickson, *The Black Image in the White Mind: The Debate on Afro-American Character and Destiny, 1817–1914* (New York: Harper & Row, 1971), 251–52, 273–75, 287–88.
51. Oral History Interview – Part III (1943–1945), March 27, 1975, 6, box 1, folder 4, Almond Papers, MHI.
52. Information furnished by Lieut.-Col. Gebhart, Justice Advocate, 92nd Div, June 17, 1944, cited in Wiley, *The Training of Negro Troops*, 16.
53. *Military Justice Procedure, War Department Technical Manual TM 27-255* (Washington, DC: United States Government Printing Office, 1945), www.ibiblio.org/hyperwar/USA/ref/TM/TM27-255/TM27-255-3.html.
54. A. William Perry Collection (AFC/2001/001/51117), Veterans History Project, American Folklife Center, Library of Congress.
55. George S. Schuyler, "View and Reviews," *Pittsburgh Courier*, May 6, 1944. On the conditions of sentencing by court-martial, see Alice Kaplan, *The Interpreter* (Chicago: Chicago University Press, 2007).
56. Information furnished by AGE Hist Off by G-1 92nd Div, June 19, 44, cited in Wiley, *The Training of Negro Troops*, 33.
57. Court-martial record of Andrew L. Farris, O1171997, RG 153, NARA at Saint Louis.
58. Lee, *The Employment of Negro Troops*, 496.
59. On the destruction of property as rebellion, see Guglielmo, "A Martial Freedom Movement," 886.
60. Wiley, *The Training of Negro Troops*, 11–12.
61. Statement of G-2 92nd Div to AGF Hist Off, July 16, 1944, cited in Wiley, *The Training of Negro Troops*, 12.
62. Oral History Interview – Part III (1943–1945), March 27, 1975, 8, box 1, folder 4, Almond Papers, MHI.

Conclusion: The Outcome of an Experiment

1. See Robert Weaver, *The Negro Ghetto* (New York, Harcourt, Brace and Co., 1948), 6.
2. Daniel B. Schwartz, *Ghetto: The History of a Word* (Cambridge, MA: Harvard University Press, 2019), Chapter 3 "The Ghetto Comes to America."
3. On the defining characteristics of the ghetto in American social science, see Mitchell Duneier, *Ghetto: The Invention of a Place, the History of an Idea* (New York: Farrar, Straus and Giroux, 2017), 222ff.
4. Loïc Wacquant, "A Janus-Faced Institution of Ethnoracial Enclosure: A Sociological Specification of the Ghetto," in Ray Hutchinson and Bruce D. Haynes, eds., *The Ghetto: Contemporary Global Issues and Controversies* (Boulder: Westview Press, 2011), 1–32.
5. Confidential letter from Colonel Hardy to Commanding General, Ninth Service Command, March 15, 1945, Decimal file 291.2, box 87, entry 26e, RG 159, NARA.
6. See Karen Kruse Thomas, *Deluxe Jim Crow: Civil Rights and American Health Policy, 1935–1954* (Athens, GA: University of Georgia Press, 2011).
7. See James J. Cooke, *American Girls, Beer, and Glenn Miller: GI Morale in World War II* (Columbia: University of Missouri Press, 2012).
8. Vanessa Northington Gamble, *Making a Place for Ourselves: The Black Hospital Movement* (Oxford: Oxford University Press, 1995).
9. Roscoe C. Giles, "Post-war Adjustments in Medicine," *Journal of the National Medical Association* 38, no. 4 (July 1946): 124–27.
10. Memorandum from Bousfield "Disposition of Section I Huachuca ASF Regional Hospital," September 14, 1944; Letter from Bousfield to Evans, March 8, 1945, box 207, entry 188, RG 107, NARA.
11. Letter from Norman Kirk to Governor Osborn, March 12, 1945, folder 323–29 "Fort Huachuca, 1945–...," box 1469, entry 31, RG 112, NARA.
12. See, for instance, "Huachuca Medics Face Army Ouster," *Chicago Defender*, March 17, 1945.
13. Letter from Truman Gibson to Assistant Secretary of War McCloy, September 21,1944, box 207, entry 188, RG 107, NARA.
14. Letter from Bousfield to Major General Lull, February 17, 1945; letter from Bousfield to James Evans, March 8, 1945, box 207, entry 88, RG 107, NARA.
15. *The Afro-American*, September 2, 1944.
16. Clarence McKittrick Smith, *The Medical Department: Hospitalization and Evacuation, Zone of Interior* (Washington, DC: Office of the Surgeon General, 1956), 223.
17. Letter from Midian Bousfield to General Hall, March 23, 1945, box 207, entry 188, RG 107, NARA.
18. Report of Medical Department activities in North Africa, by Susan Freeman, Chief Nurse of 25th Station Hospital, December 24, 1943, box 218, entry 302, RG 112, NARA.
19. "Liberia Honors Fort Huachuca Officer," *The Afro-American*, January 13, 1945.
20. "2nd All-Colored Hospital Unit Overseas Minister to Men of All Races in Burma," *The Afro-American*, June 30, 1945.

21. Memorandum from James Evans to the Army Surgeon General, March 29, 1945, box 207, entry 188, RG 107, NARA; Confidential memorandum from James Evans for files, June 7, 1945, box 89, entry (NM20) 32, geographic series 1945–46, RG 112, NARA.
22. Memorandum from James Evans for files, March 13, 1945, box 207, entry 88, RG 107, NARA.
23. Letter from J. A. Julio, Adjutant General, to representative Tom Pickett, March 1, 1945, folder 319.2, box 171, entry 54A, RG 112, NARA.
24. Report on a visit to Fort Huachuca by Colonel Hall, June 6, 1945, box 89, entry (NM20) 32, geographic series, 1945–46, RG 112, NARA.
25. Letter from Roscoe Giles to Louis T. Wright, June 16, 1944, folder "Staff, W. White, Fort Huachuca Trip," group II, box A606, NAACP Papers, LoC.
26. See, for instance, letter from Bousfield to Gibson, March 31, 1943, box 207, entry 188, RG 107, NARA.
27. Memoirs of Roy Brown, folders 9–11, box 5, Jesse Johnson Military Collection, Schomburg Center for Research in Black Culture, New York Public Library.
28. "First Nurses Reach European War Theater," *Baltimore Afro-American*, August 26, 1944, 1.
29. Charissa Threat, *Nursing Civil Rights: Gender and Race in the Army Nurse Corps* (Champaign: University of Illinois Press, 2015), Chapter 2.
30. Barbara Brooks Tomblin, *GI Nightingales: The Army Nurse Corps in World War II* (Lexington: University Press of Kentucky, 1996), 196.
31. "Captain Della Raney, 23 Nurses to Staff Camp Beale Hospital," *The Afro-American*, March 17, 1945.
32. Janet Sims-Wood, "Service Life in the Women's Army Corps and Afro-American Wacs," in Paula Nassen Poulos, ed., *A Woman's War Too: U.S. Women in the Military in World War II* (Collingdale: Diane Publishing Co., 1997), 128–41, 135; Gertrude La Vigne cited by Brenda L. Moore, *To Serve My Country, to Serve My Race: The Story of the Only African-American Wacs Stationed Overseas during World War II* (New York: New York University Press, 1997), 82.
33. Report by Walter White to President Roosevelt, February 12, 1945, folder "Ninety-Third Division, 1943–1946," group II, box A648, NAACP Papers, LoC.
34. Ulysses Lee, *The Employment of Negro Troops* (Washington, DC: Center of Military History, 1994 [1963]), 531.
35. Letter from Roy Wilkins to the editor of the *New York Times*, March 20, 1945, folder "Ninety-Second Division, 1945," group II, box A648, NAACP Papers, LoC.
36. Excerpt from a letter to 92nd Division headquarters on combat effectiveness, November 27, 1944, folder 1, box 42, Almond Papers, MHI.
37. Robert W. Kesting, "Conspiracy to Discredit the Black Buffaloes: The 92nd Infantry Division in World War II," *The Journal of Negro History* 72, no. 1/2 (Winter–Spring 1987): 1–19, 8–11.
38. Report of General Clark, box 3, Truman Gibson Collection, LoC.
39. Report from Truman Gibson to Major General O. L. Nelson based on the inspection of the 92nd Division, March 12, 1945, box 3, Truman Gibson Collection, LoC.

40. "Army Studying More Effective Negro Fighting," *New York Times*, March 15, 1945.
41. Roy Wilkins, "The Negro Soldier Betrayed," *The Crisis*, April 1945, 97.
42. Press release, "NAACP Votes against Leadership of Gibson," May 24, 1945, folder "Ninety-Second Division, 1945," Group II, box A648, NAACP Papers, LoC.
43. Truman Gibson, *Knocking Down Barriers: My Fight for Black America* (Evanston: Northwestern University Press, 2005), 174–75.
44. Confidential memorandum from Truman Gibson to John McCloy, April 23, 1945, box 3, Truman Gibson Collection, LoC.
45. Morris J. MacGregor, *Integration of the Armed Forces, 1940–1965* (Washington, DC: Government Printing Office, 1985), 51–56; David P. Colley, *Blood for Dignity: The Story of the First Integrated Combat Unit in the US Army* (New York: St Martin's Press, 2003).
46. Samuel Stouffer, Edward A. Suchman, Leland C. DeVinney, Shirley A. Star, and Robin M. Williams, Jr., *The American Soldier: Adjustment during Army Life* (Princeton: Princeton University Press, 1949), 588 and 591.
47. Press release from the War Department, "Truman Gibson Jr. Resigns Post as Civilian Aide to the Secretary of War," November 19, 1945, "92nd Division, 1945," Group II, box A648, NAACP Papers, LoC.
48. Letter from Marcus Ray to Adam Clayton Powell, July 3, 1947, box 207, entry 188, RG 107, NARA.
49. "Proceedings of a Board Review Appointed by Almond on the Subject of Combat Effectiveness of Negro Officers and Enlisted Men," June 24–25, 1945, folder 1, box 42, Almond Papers, MHI.
50. Roi Ottley, "The Troops' Own Story on 92nd Division's Record," *PM*, June 1, 1945.
51. Oral History Interview – Part III (1943–1945), March 27, 1975, p. 40, box 1, folder 4, Almond Papers, MHI.
52. Richard Dalfiume, *Desegregation of the U.S. Armed Forces: Fighting on Two Fronts, 1939–1953* (Columbia: University of Missouri Press, 1969), 149–51; Christine Knauer, *Let Us Fight as Free Men: Black Soldiers and Civil Rights* (Philadelphia: University of Pennsylvania Press, 2014), 51–54; Desmond King, "'The Longest Road to Equality': The Politics of Institutional Desegregation under Truman," *Journal of Historical Sociology* 6, no. 2 (June, 2006): 119–63.
53. Recommendations mentioned in Stouffer, Suchman, DeVinney, Star, and Williams, *The American Soldier*, 597–99.
54. Dalfiume, *Desegregation of the U.S. Armed Forces*, 166–202.
55. *To Secure These Rights: The Report of the President's Committee on Civil Rights* (Washington, DC: Government Printing Office, 1947), 47.
56. See Knauer, *Let Us Fight as Free Men*, Chapters 3–5.
57. Dalfiume, *Desegregation of the U.S. Armed Forces*, 101ff.
58. Box 31, Governors Sidney P. Osborn and Daniel E. Garvey Papers, ASA.
59. Lauret E. Savoy, *Trace: Memory, History, Race, and the American Landscape* (Berkeley: Counterpoint Press, 2015), Chapter "Madeline Traces."

Sources and Select Bibliography

Sources

Archives

National Archives and Records Administration (NARA), College Park
RG 112 Records of the Office of the Surgeon General, entry 31, 31 ZI, 54A (ZI), 29, (NM20)32, (NM30)29, (NM30)31.
RG 107 Records of the Office of the Assistant Secretary of War, entry 188, 140, 143.
RG 159 Records of the Inspector General, entry 26e, 26f.
RG 160 Records of the Headquarters Army Service Forces, entry 196A.
RG 165 Records of the Office of Director of Personnel and Administration, entry 54, 55.
RG 77 Records of the Office of the Chief of Engineers, entry 391, 393.
RG 337 Records of the Headquarters Army Ground Forces, entry 55.

Library of Congress, Washington, DC
NAACP Papers: group II, box A 641–648, box B 148–159, 166, 170.
Truman K. Gibson Papers.
US 92nd Infantry Division Collection.
African American Soldiers in World War II – Maggi Morehouse Collection.

US Army Military History Institute, Carlisle Barracks
Benjamin O. Davis Papers.
Edward M. Almond Papers.

Other Collections
African American Museum of Philadelphia, Anna Russell Jones Papers.
Arizona State Archives (Phoenix), Governors Sidney P. Osborn and Daniel E. Garvey Collection.
Chicago Public Library, Harsh Research Collection, Irma Cayton Wertz Papers.
Howard University, Moorland-Spingarn Research Center, Dr. William Allen Papers.

New York Public Library, Schomburg Center for Research in Black Culture, Jesse J. Johnson Military Collection.
New York University, Tamiment Library and Robert F. Wagner Labor Archive, James Bernard Rucker Papers.
Schlesinger Library, Radcliffe Institute, Harvard University, Shirley Graham Du Bois Papers.
University of Massachusetts Amherst Libraries, Special Collections and University Archives, W. E. B. Du Bois Papers (MS 312).

Photographs (Main Collections)

NARA, Army Signal Corps, Still Pictures Branch, RG 111, series SC.
African American Museum of Philadelphia, Anna Russell Jones Collection.
Arizona Memory Project website.
Chicago Public Library, Harsh Research Collection, Irma Cayton Collection.
Pittsburgh University, Frank Bolden Papers.
Photographic essay by Charles Steinheimer for *Life Magazine*, April 1943: https://artsandculture.google.com/entity/fort-huachuca/m05slrg?categoryId=place.
US Army Military History Institute, Carlisle Barracks, Benjamin O. Davis Papers.

Oral Histories

Veterans History Project, collection World War, 1939–1945, Library of Congress, Washington.
Women Veterans History Project, Betty H. Carter Women Veterans Historical Project (WVHP), The University of North Carolina at Greensboro.

Press

Regional press:
Arizona Daily Star.
Bisbee Daily Review.
Regional African American press:
Arizona's Negro Journal.
The Arizona Sun.
The Arizona Tribune.
The Phoenix Index.
National African American press:
Cleveland Call & Post.
The Afro-American.
The Chicago Defender.
The Crisis.
The Pittsburgh Courier.
Army newspapers:
The Apache Sentinel, newspaper published by Service Command Unit 1922, July 1943–1945, followed by *Postscript*.

The Blue Helmet, 93rd Infantry Division newspaper.
The Buffalo, 92nd Infantry Division weekly newspaper, May 1943–1945.

Select Bibliography

On Race during the New Deal and World War II

Alkebulan, Paul. *The African American Press in World War II: Toward Victory at Home and Abroad*. Lanham: Lexington Books, 2016.
Bristol, Douglas, and Heather Stur, eds. *Integrating the US Military: African Americans, Women, and Gays since World War II*. Baltimore: Johns Hopkins University Press, 2017.
Davis, F. James. *Who Is Black? One Nation's Definition*. University Park: Pennsylvania State University Press, 1991.
Frazier, Edward F. *Black Bourgeoisie*. Glencoe: Free Press, 1957.
Fredrickson, George M. *The Black Image in the White Mind: The Debate on Afro-American Character and Destiny, 1817–1914*. New York: Harper & Row, 1971.
Gaines, Kevin. *Uplifting the Race: Black Leadership, Politics, and Culture in the Twentieth Century*. Chapel Hill: University of North Carolina Press, 1996.
Gerstle, Gary. *American Crucible: Race and Nation in the Twentieth Century*. Princeton: Princeton University Press, 2001.
Giddings, Paula. *When and Where I Enter: The Impact of Black Women on Race and Sex in America*. New York: William Morrow and Company, 1984.
Green, Adam. *Selling the Race: Culture, Community, and Black Chicago, 1940–1955*. Chicago: University of Chicago Press, 2009.
Hale, Grace E. *Making Whiteness: The Culture of Segregation in the South, 1890–1940*. New York: Vintage Books, 1998.
Johnson, Charles S. *Patterns of Negro Segregation*. New York: Harper & Brothers Publishers, 1943.
Jung, Moon-Kie. *Beneath the Surface of White Supremacy: Denaturalizing U.S. Racisms Past and Present*. Stanford: Stanford University Press, 2015.
Katznelson, Ira. *Fear Itself: The New Deal and the Origins of Our Time*. New York: Liveright Publishing Corporation, 2013.
Kelley, Robert D. G. *Race Rebels: Culture, Politics, and the Black Working Class*. New York: Free Press, 1994.
Lucander, David. *Winning the War for Democracy: The March on Washington Movement, 1941–1946*. Urbana: University of Illinois Press, 2014.
Mazon, Mauricio. *The Zoot-Suit Riots: The Psychology of Symbolic Annihilation*. Austin: University of Texas Press, 1984.
McMillen, Neil, ed. *Remaking Dixie: The Impact of World War II on the American South*. Jackson: University of Mississippi Press, 1997.
Michaeli, Ethan. *The* Defender: *How the Legendary Black Newspaper Changed America*. New York: Houghton Mifflin, Harcourt, 2016.
Ndiaye, Pap. *La Condition noire. Essai sur une minorité française (The Black Condition: Essay on a French Minority)*. Paris: Calmann-Lévy, 2008.

Odum, Howard W. *Race and Rumors of Race: Challenge to American Crisis.* New York: Negro University Presses, 1969 [1943].

Savoy, Lauret. *Trace: Memory, History, Race, and the American Landscape.* Berkeley: Counterpoint, 2015.

Sitkoff, Harvard. *A New Deal for Blacks: The Emergence of Civil Rights as a National Issue: The Depression Decade.* New York: Oxford University Press, 1978.

Sklaroff, Lauren R. *Black Culture and the New Deal: The Quest for Civil Rights in the Roosevelt Era.* Chapel Hill: University of North Carolina Press, 2009.

Sullivan, Patricia. *Days of Hope: Race and Democracy in the New Deal Era.* Chapel Hill: University of North Carolina Press, 2006.

Summers, Martin A. *Manliness and Its Discontents: The Black Middle Class and the Transformation of Masculinity, 1900–1930.* Chapel Hill: University of North Carolina Press, 2005.

Willis, Deborah, ed. *Picturing Us: African American Identity in Photography.* New York: New Press, 1994.

Wolcott, Victoria W. *Race, Riots, and Roller Coasters: The Struggle over Segregated Recreation in America.* Philadelphia: University of Pennsylvania Press, 2012.

On the US Army during World War II

Anderson, Karen. *Wartime Women: Sex Roles, Family Relations, and the Status of Women during World War II.* Westport: Greenwood Press, 1981.

Bailey, Beth, and David Farber. *The First Strange Place: The Alchemy of Race and Sex in World War II Hawaii.* New York: The Free Press, 1992.

Bérubé, Allan. *Coming Out under Fire: The History of Gay Men and Women in World War II.* New York: Free Press, 1991.

Blum, John M. *V Was for Victory: Politics and American Culture during World War II.* New York: Harcourt Brace, 1976.

Canaday, Margot. *The Straight State: Sexuality and Citizenship in Twentieth-Century America.* Princeton: Princeton University Press, 2009.

Cooke, James J. *Chewing Gum, Candy Bars, and Beer: The Army PX in World War II.* Columbia: University of Missouri Press, 2009.

American Girls, Beer, and Glenn Miller: GI Morale in World War II. Columbia: University of Missouri Press, 2012.

Jarvis, Christina. *The Male Body at War: American Masculinity during World War II.* DeKalb: Northern Illinois University Press, 2004.

Kaplan, Alice. *The Interpreter.* Chicago: Chicago University Press, 2007.

Kennett, Lee. *GI: The American Soldier in World War II.* Norman: University of Oklahoma Press, 1997.

Koppes, Clayton R. *Hollywood Goes to War: How Politics, Profits, and Propaganda Shaped World War II Movies*: New York: Free Press, 1987.

Kruse, Kevin M., and Stephen Tuck, eds. *Fog of War: The Second World War and the Civil Rights Movement.* New York: Oxford University Press, 2012.

Kryder, Daniel. *Divided Arsenal: Race and the American State during World War II.* Cambridge: Cambridge University Press, 2000.

Litoff, Judy B., and David C. Smith. *We're in This War, Too: World War II Letters from American Women in Uniform.* New York: Oxford University Press, 1994.

Lutz, Catherine. *Homefront: A Military City and the American Twentieth Century.* Boston: Beacon Press, 2001.

Meyer, Leisa D. *Creating GI Jane: Sexuality and Power in the Women's Army Corps during World War II.* New York: Columbia University Press, 1996.

Palmer, Robert R., Bell I. Wiley, and William R. Keast, *United States Army in World War II, The Army Ground Forces: The Procurement and Training of Ground Combat Troops.* Washington, DC: Center of Military History, 1991.

Roeder, George H. *The Censored War: American Visual Experience during World War II.* New Haven: Yale University Press, 1993.

Sparrow, James. *Warfare State: World War II Americans and the Age of Big Government.* New York: Oxford University Press, 2013.

Stouffer, Samuel A., Edward A. Suchman, Leland C. DeVinney, Shirley A. Star, and Robin M. Williams Jr. *The American Soldier: Adjustment during Army Life.* Princeton: Princeton University Press, 1949.

Treadwell, Mattie E. *The Women's Army Corps.* Washington, DC: Office of Chief of Military History, 1954.

Vuic, Kara D. *The Girls Next Door: Bringing the Home Front to the Front Lines.* Cambridge, MA: Harvard University Press, 2019.

Winchell, Meghan K. *Good Girls, Good Food, Good Fun: The Story of USO Hostesses during World War II.* Chapel Hill: University of North Carolina Press, 2012.

Winkler, Allan. *The Politics of Propaganda: The Office of War Information, 1942–1945.* New Haven: Yale University Press, 1978.

On African Americans in the US Army

Astor, Gerald. *The Right to Fight: A History of African Americans in the Military.* Novato: Presidio, 1998.

Booker, Bryan D. *African Americans in the United States Army in World War II.* Jefferson: McFarland and Company, 2008.

Dalfiume, Richard. *Desegregation of the U.S. Armed Forces: Fighting on Two Fronts, 1939–1953.* Columbia: University of Missouri Press, 1969.

Fletcher, Marvin E. *America's First Black General: Benjamin O. Davis, Sr., 1880–1970.* Lawrence: University of Kansas, 1989.

Hargrove, Hondon B. *Buffalo Soldiers in Italy: Black Americans in World War II.* Jefferson: McFarland & Co, 1985.

Jefferson, Robert J. *Fighting for Hope: African American Troops of the 93rd Infantry Division in World War II and Post-war America.* Baltimore: Johns Hopkins University Press, 2008.

Johnston, Carolyn. *My Father's War: Fighting with the Buffalo Soldiers in World War II.* Tuscaloosa: University of Alabama Press, 2012.

Knauer, Christine. *Let Us Fight as Free Men: Black Soldiers and Civil Rights.* Philadelphia: University of Pennsylvania Press, 2014.

Kryder, Daniel. *Divided Arsenal: Race and the American State during World War II.* New York: Cambridge University Press, 2000.

Lee, Ulysses. *The Employment of Negro Troops.* Washington, DC: Center of Military History, 1994 [1963].

Lentz-Smith, Adriane. *Freedom Struggles: African Americans and World War I.* Cambridge: Harvard University Press, 2009.
Lynch, Michael E. *Edward M. Almond and the US Army: From the 92nd Infantry Division to the X Corps.* Lexington: University Press of Kentucky, 2019.
MacGregor, Morris J. *Integration of the Armed Forces, 1940–1965.* Washington, DC: Government Printing Office, 1985.
MacGregor, Morris J., and Bernard C. Nalty, eds. *Blacks in the United States Armed Forces: Basic Documents,* Vol. V: *Black Soldiers in World War II.* Wilmington: Scholarly Resources, 1977.
McGuire, Philipp, ed. *Taps for a Jim Crow Army: Letters from Black Soldiers in World War II.* Santa Barbara: Clio Books, 1983.
McGuire, Philipp. *He, Too, Spoke for Democracy: Judge Hastie, World War II, and the Black Soldier.* New York: Greenwood Press, 1988.
Mershon, Sherie, and Steven Schlossman. *Foxholes and Color Lines: Desegregating the U.S. Armed Forces.* Baltimore: Johns Hopkins University Press, 1998.
Moore, Brenda L. *To Serve My Country, to Serve My Race: The Story of the Only African-American WACS Stationed Overseas during World War II.* New York: New York University Press, 1997.
Morehouse, Maggi M. *Black Citizen Soldiers.* Lanham: Rowman & Littlefield, 2007.
 Fighting in a Jim Crow Army: Black Men and Women Remember World War II. Lanham: Rowman & Littlefield, 2000.
Motley, Mary P., ed. *The Invisible Soldier: The Experience of Black Soldier, World War II.* Detroit: Wayne University Press, 1975.
Moye, Todd J. *Freedom Flyers: The Tuskegee Airmen of World War II.* New York: Oxford University Press, 2010.
Salter, Krewasky A. *The Story of Black Military Officers, 1861–1948.* Abingdon: Routledge, 2015.
Williams, Chad L. *Torchbearers of Democracy: African American Soldiers in the World War I Era.* Chapel Hill: University of North Carolina Press, 2010.
Wynn, Neil. *The African American Experience during World War II.* Lanham: Rowman & Littlefield, 2010.

On Race and the Healthcare System

Gamble, Vanessa N. *Making a Place for Ourselves: The Black Hospital Movement:* Oxford: Oxford University Press, 1995.
Hine, Darlene C. *Black Women in White: Racial Conflict and Cooperation in the Nursing Profession, 1890–1950.* Bloomington: Indiana University Press, 1989.
Lallemand-Stempak, Jean-Paul. *Peaux noires, blouses blanches: Les Afro-Américains et le mouvement pour les droits civiques en médecine (1940–1975)* (*Black Skins, White Coats: African Americans and the Medical Civil Rights Movement, 1940–1975*). PhD dissertation, École des Hautes Études en Sciences Sociales, Paris, 2015.
Thomas, Karen K. *Deluxe Jim Crow: Civil Rights and American Health Policy, 1935–1954.* Athens, GA: University of Georgia Press, 2011.

Smith, Clarence McK. *The Medical Department: Hospitalization and Evacuation, Zone of Interior.* Washington, DC: Office of the Surgeon General, 1956.
Threat, Charissa. *Nursing Civil Rights: Gender and Race in the Army Nurse Corps.* Champaign: University of Illinois Press, 2015.
Tomblin, Barbara B. *GI Nightingales: The Army Nurse Corps in World War II.* Lexington: University Press of Kentucky, 1996.

On Arizona and the American West

Horne, Gerald. *Black and Brown: African Americans and the Mexican Revolution, 1910–1920.* New York: New York University Press, 2005.
Jacoby, Karl. *Shadows at Dawn: A Borderlands Massacre and the Violence of History.* New York: Penguin, 2008.
——. *The Strange Career of William Ellis: The Texas Slave Who Became a Mexican Millionaire.* New York: W. W. Norton, 2016.
Luckingham, Bradford. *Phoenix: The History of a Southwestern Metropolis.* Tucson: University of Arizona Press, 1989.
——. *Minorities in Phoenix: A Profile of Mexican American, Chinese American, and African American Communities, 1860–1992.* Tucson: University of Arizona Press, 1994.
Melton, Brad, and Dean Smith. *Arizona Goes to War: The Home Front and the Front Lines during World War II.* Tucson: University of Arizona Press, 2003.
Shermer, Elizabeth T. *Sunbelt Capitalism: Phoenix and the Transformation of American Politics.* Philadelphia: University of Pennsylvania Press, 2013.
Smith, Cornelius C., Jr. *Fort Huachuca: The Story of a Frontier Post.* Honolulu: University Press of the Pacific, 2000.
Whitaker, Matthew C. *Race Work: The Rise of Civil Rights in the Urban West.* Lincoln: University of Nebraska Press, 2007.

Index

Page numbers in *italics* refer to content in figures.

10th Cavalry Regiment, 19, 29, 227
24th Infantry Regiment, 19, 34
25th Infantry Regiment, 19, 25, 31, 34, 177
   assignments, 20, 33
   band, 15, 58
   black officers, 55, 66, 68, 70
   malingering, 126
   veterans of, 39–40
25th Station Hospital, 260
32nd and 33rd WAAC Companies, 136–37, 141
318th Engineer Battalion, 131
318th Medical Battalion, 66, 70
320th Barrage Balloon Battalion, 10
335th Station Hospital, 260–61
364th Infantry Regiment, 101–3, 123
365th Infantry Regiment, 68
368th Infantry Regiment, 25, 34, 39, 41, 65
   assignments, 33
   black officers, 70–71
   insubordination and punishment, 126, 130–31
   rebellion, 175–77
   support groups, 43–44
   training, 55
   World War I (1914–18), 188
369th Infantry Regiment, 39, 64, 68–69, 218
   insubordination and punishment, 126
   training, 55
   World War I (1914–18), 39, 227
370th Infantry Regiment, 35, 195
   combat performance, 264–65
   deployment preparations, 239, 240, 241, 244–45
371st Infantry Regiment, 193–94, 240
372nd Infantry Regiment, 34, 39
569th Field Artillery Battalion, 44, 128
593rd Field Artillery Battalion, 39, 59
598th Field Artillery Battalion, 245
6th Cavalry Regiment, 17, 19

69th Infantry Regiment, 31
6888th Central Postal Directory Battalion, 263
733rd Military Police Battalion, 101–2
761st Tank Battalion, 10, 38
92nd Infantry Division, 2–3, 13, 20, 177
   arrival at Fort Huachuca of, 186, 192–93
   background and reputation of, 188–89
   combat performance, 10, 263–68
   deployment preparations, 237, 238–40, 241–44, 249–51
   easing of tensions, 197–200, *198*
   entertainment, 215, 218
   formation of, 34–35
   leadership of, 186–88, 189–90, 234–36
   resistance and tensions, 194, 196–97, 200–6, 241, 244–50
   segregation and humiliation, 193–96, 240–41
   training, 190–93, *192*, 232–34, 236–37, 240
93rd Infantry Division, 2–3, 13, 33–35
   arrival of, 15–16
   black hospital treatment, 79, 82
   black officers, 65, 67–69, 71
   combat performance, 10, 264
   cotton-picking plan, 125–26
   deployment preparations, 169, 185, 239
   entertainment, 103, 112–15, 218
   leadership of, 48, 49–53
   maneuvers in Louisiana, 175–78
   plantation metaphor, 127
   recruitment, 39–43
   resistance, 132
   training, 54–63, *61*, 169–75, *171*, *179*
   venereal disease prevention, 47–48
   and Women's Army (Auxiliary) Corps (WAAC/WAC), 134–35
95th Infantry Division, 229
99th Pursuit Squadron, 169

Index

Abraham Lincoln Brigade, 128
activists, 4, 22–25, 64, 132, 266
  deployment of black soldiers, 237, 238
  Shirley Graham, 123, 124
  Women's Army (Auxiliary) Corps (WAAC/WAC), 137–38
administrative work, 145–47, *146*
Advisory Committee on Negro Troop Policies (McCloy Committee), 164, 182–84, 238–39, 266
The Afro-American, 57, 115, 132, 241, 260
alcohol, 114–15, 120–21
Alexander, Frances, 134, 137, 143, 152
Alexandria, LA, 103
Allen, William E., 77, 90
Almond, Edward, 189–93, 198–99
  background of, 186–88
  combat performance outcomes, 265, 267
  deployment preparations, 239–40, 242, 245
  racial prejudice, 52–53, 234, 256–57
  racial tensions, 200, 201–4, 205–6
  training, 194–95, 232–34
Alston, Charles H., 148
Aluminum Company of America (Alcoa), 22
American College of Surgeons, 89
American Indians, 1, 18–19, 21
American Medical Association (AMA), 80, 93
American Negro Exposition (1940), 115, 117
Anderson, Eddie, 210
Anderson, Ernest, 96
Anderson, Maceo, 219
Anderson, Marian, 224
Andrews, Claude, 199
Apache scouts, 17, 19, 21
Apache Sentinel (army newspaper), *215*, 215
Arizona Daily Star, 220, 234
Arizona Liquor Licenses and Control department, 115
Arizona's Negro Journal, 30
Armstrong, Louis, 210
Army General Classification Test (AGCT), 43, 44, 65–66, 190, 241–42
Army Nurse Corps (ANC), 93, 94, 138, 163–64, 261, 262
Army Public Relations Office, 57–58, 245
Army Reserve, 66, 177, 255
Army Signal Corps photographs
  Apache scouts, 21
  Arthur Bates, *58*
  black hospital, 87, 89–90, *97*, *159*
  entertainment, 113, *114*, *218*, *219*
  Mountain View Club, 75

O. P. Hall, *50*
painting workshop, *221*, 221
post exchange, *45*
Special Services team, *214*
training, 8, *56*, 57, 59–61, *60*
Women's Army (Auxiliary) Corps (WAAC/WAC), 134, *135*, 141, *144*, 147, *149*, 150, *151*
art, 16–19, *18*, 220–27, *225*, *228*, 256
Articles of War, 129–30, *131*, 132, 155, 200, 237, 244–45
Askins, Violet, 141, 143, 154, 155, 263
Associated Negro Press, 205
Atlanta Daily World, 205
Avery, Henry, 223
AWOL, 132, 237, 248

Baker, Vernon, 10
Ballou, Charles, 20
Barnes, Charles, 91
Barthe, Richmond, *223*
Bartov, Omer, 6
Bates, Arthur, *58*
Beaumont General Hospital, 160
Benson, AZ, 70
Berry Brothers, 219
Bethune, Mary McLeod, 132, 137–38, 139, 140
Biddle, Francis, 124
Bisbee Daily Review, 25, 234
Bisbee, AZ, 18, 20, 25–30, *30*, 99, 152
Bishop, Olive, 77
Blache, Julian O., 90, 93
black art exhibition, 222–27, *223*, *226*, 256
black bourgeoisie, 115–17, 119, 142–43, 224, 256
Blackwood, Charles, 68–69, 213
Blair, Omar D., 2
blood segregation, 86, 132
Blue Helmet (army newspaper), 215, *216*
Bolden, Frank, 52, 57–59, 86, 87, 99, 123–24
borderlands, 3–4, 17
Bousfield, Midian, 8, 49, 87, 89–90, 104, 262
  and 92nd Infantry Division, 186, 199, 200
  appointment of, 77–78, 82, 83–86
  attempts to discredit, 164–65, 168
  fear of violent outbreaks, 196
  and malingering, 62
  medical integration, 81, 92, 156–57, 159–60, 162, 165–66, 259–60, 261
  Mountain View Club, 73–74, 75, *88*
  nurses' training center, 163

Index

recruitment of doctors, 88–89, 162–63
successes of Station Hospital No.1, 96–98
Bouyer, Harsba F., 260
Bowder, James, 217
Bowen, Paul, 68
boycotts, 52, 70–71, 73–74, 132, 194
Boyd, Robert, 246
Branch, Phyllis, 147
Brotherhood of Sleeping Car Porters (BSCP), 23
Brown, Roy, 96
Browne, Theodore, 227–29
Browne, Vincent, 70–71
Bryant, James, 132
Buffalo (army newspaper), 215
Buffalo soldiers, 14, 19, 20, 271
Bulletin (army newspaper), 215–16
Bunche, Ralph, 71, 132
Burma, 260–61
Burrel, Prudence Burns, 93–94
Bushnell General Military Hospital, 87, 97

Cahill, Holger, 222
Calhoun, Nimrod Cautious, 180
Calloway, Cab, 117, 220
Camp Atterbury, IA, 188
Camp Beale, CA, 262–63
Camp Breckinridge, KY, 188
Camp Claiborne, LA, 38, 103
Camp Custer, 158
Camp Joseph T. Robinson, AR, 188
Camp Lee, VA, 53
Camp Livingston, LA, 81, 90, 94
Camp Maxey, TX, 166
Camp Robinson, NE, 48, 189
Camp Shows Inc., 112, 199
Camp Stewart, GA, 5, 166, 197, 257
Camp Van Dorn, MS, 5, 197, 257
Campbell, Everett W., 90
capital punishment, 131
Captain Newman M.D. (1963), 270–71
Carlisle Barracks, 66
Carmichael family, 20, 32, 111
Carnegie Foundation, 71
Carrell, Allan, 182, *184*
Carter, Richard, 241–42
Carver, George Washington, 224
Cayton, Horace, 132, 140, 141–43
  Black Metropolis (1944), 142, 253
Cayton, Irma, 9, 151–52, 154
  background and enlistment, 141–43
  insubordination, 139
  plantation metaphor, 133
  segregation, 155

celebrities, 113, 209–13, *211*
Celestine, Joseph, 102
censorship, of newspapers, 123–24, 170
Chandler, Albert Benjamin "Happy," 165
chaplains, 47–48, 64, 189, 194
Charleston, AZ, *56*, 56
Chicago, 84, 116–17, 209, 253
Chicago Bee, 119
Chicago Defender, 124, 132, 142
  black art, 224
  black hospital, 85, 88, 96, 161
  entertainment for soldiers, 209
  racial tensions, 205
  Women's Army (Auxiliary) Corps (WAAC/WAC), 150
Chinese immigrants, 253
chores, 44, 128, 130, 246
Citizens' Military Training Corps, 42
civil rights, 10–11, 12, 86, 209
Civilian Conservation Corps (CCC), 40, 128
Clark, Mark, 265
Cleveland Call & Post, 39, 43–44, 169
clubs, officers'
  Lakeside, 71, 241
  Mountain View, 71–75, *72*, *73*, *88*, 194, 222–27, 271
clubs, service, 32, 44, 64
Cochise County, 4, 21, 25–26, 33, 74, 105, 109–10
Code of Conduct, 153
Code of Wartime Practices, 182
Colbern, William Henry, 148
combat performance reports, 263–68
Command of Negro Troops (1944), 200, 238
Committee against Jim Crow in Military Service and Training, 268
Committee on Appropriations, 22, 25
Committee on the Participation of Negroes in the National Defense, 22, 24
Common Sense magazine, 123
Communist Party, 41–42, 127, 129
Congressional Military Affairs Committee, 245
conscription, 22–23, 41–42, 142
construction work, 25–26, 78, 117
copper mining, 28–30
cotton picking, 42, 124–27
court-martials, 100, 102, 130–31, 155, 237, 244–45, 247–49, 265
Craigh, Hazel, 131
The Crisis, 37, 133, 178, 230, 265, 268
Cuban–American War (1898), 19

culture, black, 209, 229–31. *See also* entertainment
  fine arts, 16–19, *18*, 220–27, *225*, *228*, 256
  musical activities, 216–20, *218*, *219*
Curry, William, 100
Curtis, Sidney, 220

Daily Worker, 42
Dalfiume, Richard, 10
Davidson, Elvyn, 111
Davis, Benjamin O., 57, 102, *202*
  appointment of, 24
  and black officers, 52–54, 67, 70, 71, 74–75
  and doctors, 90, 92
  inspection of 92nd Division, 191–92, 242–43
  racial tensions, 196, 200, 201–4
  support for Edwin N. Hardy, 49, 109
  training, 175, 178, 185
Davis, Castine, 236
Davis, Frank, 130
Davis, Lew, 45, 220–22, *221*
  The Founding of Fort Huachuca (1943), 16–17, *18*
  The Negro Soldier in America's Wars (1944), 227, *228*
  The Surrender of Geronimo (1943), 18–19, 221
Davis, Troye, 96
Davis-Monthan Air Force Base, 22, 100
Dawson, Russel H., 235
Defreeze, Hulda, 152
Del E. Webb Construction Company, 25
dental care, 157
deployment preparations
  92nd Infantry Division, 237, 238–40, 241–44, 249–51
  93rd Infantry Division, 169, 182–85
derogatory language, 52–53, 62, 194
desertion, 132, 177
DeVeaux, John A., 64
DeWitt, John J., 36
Diggs, Willie, 29–30
Dillard, Thurman, 221
discharge, 59, 131, 154, 230
discipline, 55, 61, 179. *See also* insubordination
discrimination, 10–11, 53, 197. *See also* prejudice; segregation
  cotton-picking plan, 125–27
  measures to reduce, 4, 12, 22–23, 24–25, 140, 269
  housing arrangements, 70
  in medical facilities, 166

doctors, 79–85, 87–93, 258. *See also* hospital (black or No. 1)
"double victory" campaign, 36–37, 59, 122, 141
Douglas Air Field, 22, 157–58
Douglas, Aaron, *Aspects of Negro Life* (1934), 222
Douglass, Frederick, 224
Downing, Gardner, 259
Drake, St. Clair, *Black Metropolis* (1944), 142, 253
drill exercises, 143
Du Bois, W. E. B., 11, 37, 53
  letters to, 32–33, 75, 85, 122–23, 132, 159

eating spaces, 69, 70–71, 193–94, 240
Edmonds, Randolph, 214
educational programs, 47–48, 65, 110, 190
Eisenhower, Dwight D., 54, 65, 263, 269
Elkins, Robert E., 236–37, 242
Ellington, Duke, 117
Ellis, William, 3
enlistment, 22–23, 33, 40–41, 138–39
entertainment, 31–32, 43–44, 229–31. *See also* culture, black; leisure
  barbecue of June 1943, 197–200, *198*
  black art exhibition, 222–27, *223*, *226*, 256
  celebrity appearances, 113, 209–13, *211*
  Greentop recreation center, 115–21, *118*, *120*, 254–55
  Lakeside Club, 71, 241
  medical staff, 90
  Mountain View Club, 71–75, *72*, *73*, *88*, 254–55
  musical activities, 216–20, *218*, *219*
  service clubs, 32, 44, 64
  Special Services team, 65, 213–18, *214*, 231
  sports training, 212–13, 220
  USO recreation center, 111–13, *114*, 254–55
equipment supply, 56–57, 58–59, 240, 254
Europe, James Reese, 218
European Theater of Operations (ETO), 266
Evans, Charlie, 221
Evans, James, 261
Everett, George, 214, 220
Executive Order 8802 (1941), 24–25, 140
Executive Order 9981 (1948), 12, 269

Fair Employment Practices Committee, 24–25
Faith, Don, 140

Index

Farm Security Administration (FSA), 125, 126
Farris, Andrew L., 237, 242, 248–49
Federal Art Project (FAP), 209, 220, 222–23
Federal Bureau of Investigation (FBI), 58, 121, 123–24
Federal Security Agency (FSA), 31, 99, 109, 112, 115
Federal Theater Project (FTP), 32, 217
feigned ailments, 126, 128, 193, 246–47
Ferguson, Geneva, 139
Fisk University, 118, 142
flirting, 152–53
Fort Apache, AZ, 21
Fort Benning, GA, 64, 65–66, 67, 187, 235
Fort Bragg, NC, 34, 53, 81, 94
Fort Clark, TX, 166
Fort Des Moines, IA, 138–40, 145
Fort Dix, NJ, 35, 103, 175
Fort Douglas, AZ, 98, 154
Fort Jackson, SC, 112
Fort Leavenworth, KS, 20, 131
Fort McClellan, AL, 53, 187–89, 190–91
Fort Meade, MD, 35, 175
Fort Riley, KS, 20, 210
Foster, Rube, 213
Francis E. Warren Air Force Base, WY, 52–53
Fraser, Reuben, 65
Frazier, E. Franklin, 11
Freedmen's Hospital, 89, 94, 260
Freeman, Susan, 94, 260
Fry, AZ, 14, 20, 26, 49, 152
   Greentop recreation center, 115–21, *118, 120*, 164, 176
   housing for officers, 70
   prostitution, 104–5, 107–9, *108*
   USO recreation center, 111–13, 122–23
Fry, Oliver, 107
furlough, 99–100, 103–4, 110–11

Gaddy, Ruth, 147
Gaines, Clarence, 43–44
Galley, Robert, 44
Garrett AiResearch, 22
Gatewood, C. B., 19
Geronimo, 18–19
Gerstle, Gary, 9
ghetto metaphor, 252–55
GI Bill (1944), 10–11
Gibson, Sr., Truman, 116, 164
Gibson, Truman, 126, 178, 242
   fear of violent uprisings, 196
   Greentop recreation center, 115–16

   letters to, 38, 98, 132, 156, 159, 162, 187, 235–36
   report on combat performance, 265–66
Giles, Roscoe, 77, 89, 90, 92–93, 158, 261–62
   medical integration, 161, 258–59
Gillem Board, 267–68
Ginzburg, Carlo, 7
Good Shepherd Community Center, 142
Goodyear Tire and Rubber Company, 22, 124
Gothic Line (Italy), 10, 265
Graham, Shirley, 9, 40, 42, 99
   entertainment planning, 31–33, 48–49, 111–12, 214–15, 231
   forced departure of, 122–23, 124
Grayson, Wilnet C., 144–45
Great Depression, 9, 11, 40, 41, 100
Great Migration, 145, 150
Greenbaum, Edward S., 174–75
Greentop recreation center, 115–21, *118, 120*, 164, 176, 254–55
Greer, Allan J., 20
Gregory, Stephen, 13
Griffey, Durward P., 66
Griffin, Joseph, 241
Guglielmo, Thomas, 11
gynecology, 162

Hale, Vasco de Gama, 180–81, *183*
Hall, Durward, 156, 160, 165
Hall, Jacquelyn Dowd, 10
Hall, O. P., 49–51, *50*, 69, 159
Hansberry v. Lee (1940), 115
Hardy, Edwin N., 16–17, 98, 186, *223*, 242–43, 255–57
   and control of sexual behavior, 47–49, 104, 105, 107, 109
   efforts to ease racial tensions, 197–201, *198*
   entertainment provision, 208–9, 211–12, 220–22, 226–27
   officers' clubs, 71, 75, 241
   and racial tensions, 196, 249–50
   recreation centers, 111, 113–15, 116–17, 119–21, *120*
   and Women's Army (Auxiliary) Corps (WAAC/WAC), 136–37, 140
Harlem Hellfighters. *See* 369th Infantry Regiment
Harlem Renaissance, 118, 222
Harlem riots, 197
Harmon, Millard, 185
Harmon Foundation, 222
Harper, Dave, 246

Harris, Andrew L., 158
Harrison, Vera, 134, 263
Hastie, William, 29, 81, 132, 182, 201
  appointment of, 24
  attempts to tackle prejudice, 52–53, 74
  and deployment of black troops, 169
  and Midian Bousfield, 82, 84
  and Truman Gibson, 115–16
Hayden, Carl, 21–22, 25, 125
Headman, Ferguson & Carollo, 26
health, soldiers', 157–58
Henderson, J. Raymond, 214–15
Hill, Arnold, 23
Hinkson, DeHaven, 77, 90–92
Hobby, Oveta Culp, 137, 138–39, 148, 152, 153
Hodges, Courtney, 175, 233
Hollywood Victory Committee, 112–13, *114*
Holmes, Leonard, 130–31
homosexuality, 154
Hook, the, 107–10, *108*, 115, 200, 254
Horne, Lena, 113, 210, *211*
Horner, Reuben, 195
hospital (black or No. 1), 77–80, *78*, *80*, *159*
  collaboration with white hospital, 162–68
  construction and facilities, 86–87
  integration aims, 258–59, 261–62
  non-commissioned staff, 94–96, 147
  patients with psychogenic symptoms, 62
  recruitment of doctors, 87–93
  recruitment of nurses, 93–94, *95*
  ruins of, 270–71
  successes and qualities of, 96–98, 157–58
  support for and criticism of, 84–86
  treatment of white patients, 158–62
hospital (white or No. 2), 78–79, *80*, 86, 162–63
  medical integration, 165, 166–67
  ruins of, 270–71
hospitals (general), 81–84, 259–61, 262–63
Hough, Gerald, 195
House, Russell, 100
housing, 69–71
Howard University, 66, 70, 89, 93, 236
Howard, John, 68
Hoyt, Ross, 103
Huachucans group, 43–44
Hughes, Eddie, 217
Hughes, Langston, 41, 88, 142, 149–50
humiliation, 10, 68, 75, 193–96
  daily chores, 44, 128
  in training, 55, 61

Ickes, Anne Wilmarth, 145
Ickes, Harold, 145
income, 40–41, 66, 148–49
Indian Wars, 18–19
Industrial Workers of the World (IWW), 29
Ingram, Henrietta Stevenson, 154–55
insubordination, 62, 139, 241, 247–48. *See also* resistance
  punishment for, 126, 129–31
  warnings against, 44–45
insurance companies, 84, 116–17, 164
integration, medical, 80–81, 83, 156, 258–63
  collaboration and merger between the two hospitals, 162–68
  pre-war movement for, 92–93
  white patients and black doctors, 5, 158–62
integration, post-war, 9–10, 269
internment, 9, 36
interracial relations, 6
interracial relationships, 105, 111

Janison, C. E., *159*
Japanese Americans, 9, 36
Jefferson, Frederic, 42
Jefferson, Robert, 40, 42–43
Jefferson, Ronald F., 90
Jenkins, Floyd, 132
Jenkins, Ray, 41
Jim Crow, 2, 3, 4, 83, 268
Johnson, Campbell C., 24
Johnson, Charles C., 161
Johnson, Phillip T., 89
Johnson, Sargent, 222
Johnson, Thelma R., *97*
Jones, Anne, 152
Jones, Lazarus, 130–31
Jordan, Joe, 199, *214*, 214, 216–17, *218*
Jordan, Mercedes, 150, 214, 217, 263
Journal of the National Medical Association, 93, 258–59
Julio, J. A., 261
Julius Rosenwald Fund, 81, 83–84, 92, 97, 105–6, 118, 142

K Company, 195, 206
Kamer, Harry, 162
Kenney, John A., 85
Kirk, Norman, 166
kitchen patrol (KP) duty, 44, 130
Knapp, Cleon, 31
Knox, William, 182
Krueger, Walter, 177

Index

Kruse, Kevin, 11
Ku Klux Klan (KKK), 82

La Vigne, Gertrude, 263
labor unions, 24, 29
Lachenal, Guillaume, 12
Ladies' Home Journal, 91
Lakeside Club, 71, 241
Land, Grover, 165–66
Lane, Madine Davis, 94, 157, 230
leadership qualities, 65, 68–69, 189–90, 238
League of Struggle for Negro Rights, 41
learning abilities, 43
Lee, Chauncey, 217
Lee, Ulysses, *The Employment of Negro Troops* (1966), 10
Lehman, Raymond G., 68, 69
Leighton, George N., 66
leisure, 31–32, 43–44, 69–70, 229–31.
  See also culture, black
  barbecue of June 1943, 197–200, *198*
  black art exhibition, 222–27, *223, 226*, 256
  celebrity appearances, 113, 209–13, *211*
  Greentop recreation center, 115–21, *118, 120*, 254–55
  Lakeside Club, 71, 241
  medical staff, 90
  in Mexico, 103–4
  Mountain View Club, 71–75, *72, 73, 88*, 254–55
  musical activities, 216–20, *218, 219*
  riots during furlough, 99–103
  service clubs, 32, 44, 64
  Special Services team, 65, 213–18, *214*, 231
  sports training, 212–13, 220
  USO recreation center, 111–13, *114*, 254–55
  Women's Army (Auxiliary) Corps (WAAC/WAC), 151–52
lesbianism, 154
Liberia, 260
Library of Congress, 8
Life magazine, 117, 158, 169–71, *171*, 178–82,
Little Rock, AR, 103
living conditions, 69–71
Logan, Leo, 68
The Longest Day (1952), 9
Looney, George, 51, 65–66
Louis, Joe, 87, 210–13, *214*
Louisiana, 103, 236–37
Louisiana Weekly, 205

Luce, Henry, 170
Luke Air Force Base, 22

M Company, 43–44
Madison, Robert T., 35
Magee, James, 80–82, 85
malingering, 126, 128, 193, 246–47
maneuvers, 175–78, 182, 185, 236, 246
Manhattan Central Medical Society, 83, 85–86
Mansfield, Monte, 31
marriage, 153, 188
Marshall, George C., 24, 34, 49, 74, 187, 215
  inspection of 92nd Division, 243, *244*
Martin, Hamilton, 241
May Act (1941), 106–7, 109
Mayfield, Edward T., 235–36
Maynard, E. B., 78–79, 98, 105, 162, 163, 164, 261
Mayo, Lucille, *144*
McCloy, John, 164, 182–84, 238–39, 242
McCormick, Ada, 31–32
McDaniel, Hattie, 112
McFarland, Ernest, 25
McGee, Colonel, 32, 47, 104–5, 114–15
McKinley Thomas, William, 66
McKinnon, Judy, 138, 143, 148–49, 152
McKissack, Matred, 241
McNair, Lesley J., 243–44, 245
McNarney, Joseph T., 125, 126
McNutt, Paul, 99
medical integration. *See* integration, medical
medical separatism, 82–83, 86, 156–57
medical units, 84
Meharry Medical College, 66, 89
Mexican workers, 3, 29, 70, 124–25
Mexico, 3–4, 19, 33
  leisure time in, 103–4, 152
Miles, Nelson, 18
military justice, 100, 102, 103, 130–31, 155, 237, 244–45, 247–49
military police, 34, 99–100, 101–2, 107, 120, 123, 130–31
Miller, Fred W., *61*, 61, 67, 178
Miller, Glenn, 217
mining, 28–30
Mojave Desert, 178
Moore, Carolyn Davenport, 245
Moore, Clay H., 29–30
morale, 51–52, 205, 242, 246, 265
Morehouse, Maggi, 41
Morgan, Hugh J., 90, 92, 105
Morris, Spurgeon J., 116

328   Index

Morrow, F. P., 245–47, 249
Moten, Etta, 113
Motley Jr., Archibald, 222
Moton, Robert, 82
Mountain View Club, 71–75, *72*, *73*, *88*, 194, 254–55, 271
  black art exhibition, 197, 222–27, *226*
Mulnik, Helen, 129
Murdock, John, 26
Murray, Peter Marshall, 83
musical activities, 216–20, *218*, *219*
mutiny, 200, 257
  fear of, 52, 197, 206, 241
  Phoenix riots (1942), 100–3
Myrdal, Gunnar, 71

Nation, The, 142
National Association for the Advancement of Colored People (NAACP), 2, 29, 101, 132–33, 245
  combat performance reports, 264, 265
  cotton-picking plan, 125–26
  employment of Shirley Graham, 123
  hospitals, 83, 86, 166
  integration aims, 22–23
  segregation at Fort Des Moines, 139–40
National Association of Colored Graduate Nurses (NACGN), 81
National Hospital Association (NHA), 82–83
National Medical Association (NMA), 80–83, 84–86, 88, 93
National Museum of African American History and Culture, 10
National Negro Insurance Association, 84
National Urban League, 93, 101
National Youth Administration, 23, 137
Nazism, 42
Negro Motorist Green Book, 30–31, 101
The Negro Soldier (1944), 232
Nelson, Caroll F., 199, 213, *214*, *223*
Nelson, Otto L., 265
New Deal, 4, 21, 105, 125, 209
New Masses, 42
New York Amsterdam News/Star-News, 127, 204–5
newspapers, 22, 33–34, 35, 115
  army publications, *215*, 215–16
  black art, 224
  calls for black officer training, 64
  censorship of, 123–24
  combat performance reports, 265, 267–68
  communist publications, 42
  cotton-picking plan, 127
  daily life accounts, 43–44
  deployment of black soldiers, 182–85
  "double victory" campaign, 36
  equipment for black soldiers, 57
  Horace and Irma Cayton, 142
  hospitals, 85, 86, 87, 88, 96, 158–61, 260
  letters to, 74, 122, 132
  military justice, 248
  portrayal of 93rd Infantry Division, 169–73, 178–82
  prejudice and segregation, 30, 52, 241
  pride and patriotism, 8, 39, 59, 234
  profile of DeHaven Hinkson, 91
  recreation, 111, 119, 120, 209, 220
  tensions and violence, 99, 204–5
  training reports, 57–61, 234
  Women's Army (Auxiliary) Corps (WAAC/WAC), 134, 136, 139–40, 141–42, 143–44, 150
Nicholas Brothers, 219–20
Ninth Service Command, 48, 111, 119, 196–97
  hospitals, 62, 163, 168, 259, 262–63
  prostitution and disease prevention, 104, 109, 154
  violent incidents, 102
  and Women's Army (Auxiliary) Corps (WAAC/WAC), 150, 154
Nisei soldiers, 1
non-commissioned officers (NCOs), 94–96, 180, 189, 244, 265
North, Ollie, 102, 132
Notestein, James, 240
nurses, 8, 11, 77–78, 93–94, *95*, *160*
  discrimination against, 138
  integrated care, 260–61, 262–63
  Midian Bousfield's support for, 84
  positive experiences of, 230
  training, 163–64

Office of War Information (OWI), 45, 148, 209, 212
office work, 145–47, *146*
Officer Candidate School (OCS), 64, 65–66, 190
officers, black, 64–67, *176*, 180. *See also individual officer entries*
  clubs, 64, 71–75, *72*, *73*, *88*
  criticisms of performance, 174–75, 177–78
  leadership experiment, 68–69
  living conditions, 69–71
  prejudicial treatment of, 193–96, 202–4, 234–36, 240–41
  promotion policies, 67, 203, 204, 235–36

Index

punishment of, 200, 245, 248–49
resistance, 132–33, 194
officers, white, *176*, 189–90, 200, 201–4, 245. *See also individual officer entries*
reinforcement of segregation, 39, 193–97, 240–41
O'Neal, Frederick Douglas, 214
Osborn, F. H., 212
Osborn, Sidney P., 26, 105, 119, 124–26

Parran, Thomas, 106, 157
patriotism, 59, 77, 85, 149–50, 227–29, 234
Patterson, Robert, 23, 163, 245, 266
Pearl Harbor attack (1942), 33
Peery, Nelson, 42, 51–52, 185
  Black Fire (1995), 133
penicillin, 96–97
Perry, Leslie, 166
Perry, William, 188–89, 194–95, 206, 239, 248
Pershing, John, 19
Peterson, Virgil, 24, 53
Petty, Mary L., 77, 94, 163, 262
Phelps Dodge mining company, 29–30
Philadelphia, 90–91
philanthropy, white, 83
Phoenix, AZ, 100–3
photographs, 8
  army publications, *215*
  art, *18, 225, 228*
  Arthur Bates, *58*
  Benjamin O. Davis, *202*
  Bisbee, AZ, *30*
  black art exhibition, *223, 226*
  black hospital, *78, 80,* 87, *89–90, 97, 159*
  entertainment, 113, *114, 198, 211, 218, 219*
  Fort Huachuca views, *13, 16, 17*
  Fry, AZ, *108*
  George C. Marshall, *244*
  Greentop recreation center, *118, 120*
  Mountain View Club, *72, 73,* 75, *88*
  nurses, *95, 160*
  O. P. Hall, *50*
  painting workshop, *221,* 221
  post exchange, *45*
  posters, *46, 47*
  Special Services team, *214*
  training, 56, 57, 59–61, *60,* 170–73, *171,* 178–79, *179, 192,*
  Women's Army (Auxiliary) Corps (WAAC/WAC), 134, *135,* 141, 143–44, *144, 146,* 149, 150, *151*
physicians. *See* doctors
Pickett, Tom, 261

Pitts, Lucia, 134–35, 145–46, 215, 263
Pittsburgh Courier
  black hospital, 85, 86, 87
  censorship of, 123–24
  "double victory" campaign, 36
  immensity of Fort Huachuca, 35
  letters to, 122, 132
  military justice, 248
  prejudice and segregation, 52
  recreation, 111, 120
  tensions and violence, 99
  training reports, 57–61
  Women's Army (Auxiliary) Corps (WAAC/WAC), 134, 136, 141–42, 143–44
plantation metaphor, 127–29, 133, 252
Plessy v. Ferguson (1896), 1, 23
Plummer, John O., 82
Poindexter, Hildrus A., 96
police, military, 34, 99–100, 101–2, 107, 120, 123, 130–31
post exchange, 45, 150
posters, 44–47, *46, 47*
Powell, Elinor, 163–64
Powell, Jr., Adam Clayton, 129
prejudice, 233, 250, 267. *See also* discrimination; segregation
  black officers, 66, 69, 267
  cotton-picking plan, 125–27
press. *See* newspapers
prisoners of war (POWs), 262
promotions, 67, 148, 162, 203, 204, 235–36
propaganda, 147–48, 212
prophylactic stations, 46–47, 104, 106, 108, 110–11, 157
prostitution, 48, 49, 104–5, 106–10, *108,* 120–21, 154
protests, 64, 75, 125–26, 195. *See also* resistance
  boycotts, 52, 70–71, 73–74, 132, 194
Provident Hospital, 89, 92
Pryce, Byron, 170
Public Health Service (PHS), 105–6, 108, 110
Public Housing Administration (PHA), 145
public relations, 57–61, 178
Public Works Administration (PWA), 145
punishment, 129–31, 195, 200, 247.
  See also military justice

Rabb, Charlie, 43
race riots, 7, 197, 241
racial nationalism, 9

racial regime, 3, 6–7, 38–39, 62, 255–57.
  See also segregation
  92nd Infantry Division, 188–89, 193–96
  93rd Infantry Division, 177
  plantation motif, 127–29
racist language, 52–53, 194
Randolph, A. Philip, 23, 24, 268
Raney, Della, 262–63
rape, 105, 154–55
Ray, Marcus, 266–67
rebellion, 132, 175–77, 237. *See also* resistance
recreation. *See* entertainment; leisure
recruitment. *See* enlistment
Red Ball Express, 10
Red Cross, 86, 91, 93, 142, 158
Renfroe, Earl W., 90, 157
Reserve Officers' Training Corps (ROTC), 34, 50
resistance, 4–5, 11, 75, 132–33
  boycotts, 52, 70–71, 73–74, 132, 194
  cotton-picking plan, 125–27
  passive, 61–62, 128
  rebellion, 132, 175–77, 237
  tension and violence, 99–103, 196–97, 204–6, 241, 244–50
Reynolds, Grant, 133, 195, 230, 268
riots, 99–103, 197, 241
Roberson, Orlando, 217
Roberts, Homer, 195
Roberts, Percy, 40
Robinson, Bill, 219
Rogers, Timmie, 44
Roosevelt, Eleanor, 2, 94, 137, 224
Roosevelt, Franklin D., 4, 7, 131, 170, 264
  censorship of black newspapers, 124
  concessions to black organizations, 23–25, 185
  cultural policy, 209
Rosental, André, 6
Roundtree, Dovey, 138
Rowe, James, 131
Rowland, George W., 199
Rucker, James, 110, 128–29, 205–6, 208, 234–35, 243, 250
Russell, Anna, 9, 147–48, 152–53, 214, 215, *221*

S-32 survey, "Attitudes of and toward Negroes" (1943), 184
Scales, William I., 221
School of Application and Proficiency, 195–96, 204
Schuyler, George, 248
Scott, William E., 117–19

Scottsboro trial, 41
segregation, 1, 4–7, 35, 38–39, 253–58.
  See also hospital (black or No. 1); integration, medical
  activist demands for integration, 23–25
  in Arizona, 28, 29–31, 100–1
  Benjamin Davis' tolerance of, 53
  black officers, 69–76, 240–41
  impact of combat performance on, 264–68
  recreation centers, 111–13, 115–21
  and sexuality, 99
  white officers' reinforcement of, 39, 193–94
  Women's Army (Auxiliary) Corps (WAAC/WAC), 137–38, 139–40, 155
Selective Training and Service Act (1940), 22–23
Sengstacke, John, 124
Sengstacke, Robert, 182
"separate but equal" doctrine, 48, 140
  clubs, 71
  hospitals, 81, 98
separatism, medical, 82–83, 86
Service Command Unit 1922, 40, 79
sexual violence, 154–55
sexuality, 99
  prostitution, 104–5, 106–10, *108*
  racist stereotypes, 105–6
  Women's Army (Auxiliary) Corps (WAAC/WAC), 152–55
sexually transmitted diseases, 46–48, *47*, 96–97, 104–6, 109–11, 153, 157
Shearer, Ted, 221
Shedd, William, 98
Sherard, Corrie, 134
Sherman, Raymond G., 245
Shields, Joseph, 131
Shore, Dinah, 209–10
Shuffer, George, 40–41
Simmons, Arthur, 259–60
Simpson, Thomas, 180–81, *182*
Sipp, Joseph, 101–2
Sissle, Noble, 218
slavery, afterlife of, 127–29, 133
Smith, Leon, 182
social life. *See* leisure
Social Security Act (1935), 106
Solomon Islands, 10
Spann, Roscoe Tyson, 67
Special Services, 199, 213–18, 231, 257–58
  publications, 147–48, 153
  recruitment and training, 65, 235–36
  visit of Joe Louis, 210, *214*
  sports training, 212–13, 220

Index

Station Hospitals. *See* hospital (black or No. 1); hospital (white or No. 2)
Staupers, Mabel, 81, 94, 132, 138, 163–64
Steinheimer, Charles, 158, 169–73, 178–82
stereotypes, 105, 125–26, 214–15, 220, 233. *See also* prejudice
Steth, Raymond, 222–23
Stimson, Henry, 64, 125, 126, 137, 185, 239
Stormy Weather (1943), 210, 219–20
Strickland, William H., 260–61
support groups, 43–44
Supreme Life Insurance Company, 84, 116–17, 164
Surgeon General's Office (SGO), 77, 78, 85, 90, 121
   blood segregation, 86
   medical integration, 156, 165–66, 168, 261
   opening of Station Hospital No.1, 79–82
   recruitment of hospital staff, 94, 162–63
   venereal disease, 47, 96–98, 109–11, 153
swimming, 69–70
Sykes, Jerry, 131

tanks, 3–4, 57, 192
Taylor, Thomas Fenton, 68, 179
technology, military, 3–4, 12–13
tensions, racial, 196–97, 200–6, 241, 244–45
Terkel, Studs, 9
Thatcher, Harold, 89, 90, 96–97, 155, 159–60, 165–66
Thomas, Karen Kruse, 257
Thrash, Dox, 222
To Secure These Rights (1947), 268
Tombstone, AZ, 17–18, 26, 65
training
   92nd Infantry Division, 190–93, *192*, 232–34, 236–37, 240
   93rd Infantry Division, 54–63, *56*, *60*, 169–75, *171*, *179*,
   humiliation of, 129–30
   nurses, 163–64
   officers, 64
   Women's Army (Auxiliary) Corps (WAAC/WAC), 138–40
Truman, Harry S., 268–69
Truth, Sojourner, 224
Tubman, Harriet, 229
Tuck, Stephen, 11
Tucson, AZ, 22, 30–32, 99–100, 123
Turner, Thomas, 110
Tuskegee airmen, 2, 10, 169, 266
Tuskegee experiment (1932), 105–6

Tuskegee Institute, 1–2, 53, 81, 82, 90, 91–92
Tuskegee Veterans Hospital, 2, 82

United Service Organizations (USO), 31–32, 49, 64, 199
   recreation center, 111–13, *114*, 122–23, 254–55
University of Illinois Medical School, 89
Uris, Leon, *Battle Cry* (1953), 9
US Employment Service, 125
USS Arizona, 33

Vanguard League, 129
Vaughn, Arthur, 81, 85
venereal diseases, 46–48, *47*, 96–97, 104–6, 109–11, 153, 157
Veterans History Project, 8
Victory Farm Volunteers program, 125
violence, 5, 34, 123, 196–97, 204–5
   riots, 99–103, 197, 241
   sexual, 154–55
   by white officers, 195, 200
Virginia Military Institute, 187
Voluntary War Farm Corps of Youths and Women, 127
volunteers, 40–41, 239

Wacquant, Loïc, 254
Wactor, James W., 194
Wade, Ruth, *144*
Wall, Ballie, 155, 242
Wallace, Henry, 182
War Department, 7, 29, 103, 109
   assignments for 93rd Infantry Division, 169
   black hospital, 82, 87, 163–64, 259
   and black officers, 50, 53, 70, 71, 74–75, 132, 204
   combat performance assessment, 265
   cotton-picking plan, 124, 126–27
   development of Fort Huachuca, 2, 26
   and Edwin N. Hardy, 119
   entertainment and culture, 209
   integration of Army Nurse Corps, 262
   promotion policies, 235
   race policy of 1940, 23–24
   reactivation of black divisions, 33–34
   S-32 survey (1943), 184
   and treatment of black soldiers, 190, 200–1, 238
   and Women's Army (Auxiliary) Corps (WAAC/WAC), 263
War Manpower Commission (WPC), 125
Warner, W. Lloyd, 142

Washington, Booker T., 1, 53, 82, 224
Waterhouse–Friderichsen syndrome, 158
Waters, Enoch, 88, 160–61
Welch, Henry, 246–47
Wells, A. J., 40
Wesly, Charles, 55
West Point Academy, 48, 50
West, John B., 260
Westray, Rosalyn, 155
Whisonant, Lawrence, 199, 213, 214, 217
white philanthropy, 83
White, Charles, *Progress of the American Negro* (1939), 72, 223–24, *225*
White, Thomas, 41
White, Walter, 139, 185, 210
   combat performance reports, 264
   cotton-picking plan, 126
   integration demands, 23
   letters to, 102, 132, 245
Whitside, Samuel, 17, 21
Wilkins, Roy, 178, 265
Wilkinson, Robert, 260
Williams, Bismarck, 128
Williams, Curtis, 130–31
Williams, Henry, 40, 41, 43
Williams, Paul Revere, 117
Williams, Rosetta, 199
Williams, Spencer, 213
Winslow, Vernon, *223*
Wirth, Louis, *The Ghetto* (1925), 253
Women's Army (Auxiliary) Corps (WAAC/WAC), 8–9, 11, 79, 263
   arrival of, 134–37, *135*
   duties and job allocations, 143–49, *144*, *146*, *149*
   enlistment and training, 138–41
   Irma Cayton's experience, 133, 139, 141–43
   leisure and entertainment, *151*, 151–52, 217, 218, 230
   public opinion of, 137–38
   reputation and respectability of, 149–50
   sexuality, 152–55
Women's Defense Corps of America, 143
Wood, John E., 191, 240
Wood, Sterling A., 193–94, 204
Woodruff, Hale, *223*
Works Progress Administration (WPA), 21, 119, 142, 217, 220
World War I (1914–18), 50, 68, 90–91
   92nd Infantry Division, 19–20, 188
   93rd Infantry Division, 39
   black doctors, 80–81
Wormley, Lowell C., 158
Wright, Louis T., 83, 132, 161
Wright, Richard, 142

Young Men's Christian Association (YMCA), 29
Young Women's Christian Association (YWCA), 122–23
Young, Charles, 21

zoot suit riots (1943), 241